THE FUTURE OF THE WORLD

The Future of the World

Futurology, Futurists, and the Struggle for the Post-Cold War Imagination

JENNY ANDERSSON

OXFORD
UNIVERSITY PRESS

OXFORD
UNIVERSITY PRESS

Great Clarendon Street, Oxford, OX2 6DP,
United Kingdom

Oxford University Press is a department of the University of Oxford.
It furthers the University's objective of excellence in research, scholarship,
and education by publishing worldwide. Oxford is a registered trade mark of
Oxford University Press in the UK and in certain other countries

First Edition published in 2018

Impression: 1

Published in the United States of America by Oxford University Press
198 Madison Avenue, New York, NY 10016, United States of America

British Library Cataloguing in Publication Data
Data available

Library of Congress Control Number: 2018933809

ISBN 978–0–19–881433–7

Printed and bound by
CPI Group (UK) Ltd, Croydon, CR0 4YY

For Liv

Maman, tu travailles vraiment sur le futur? Mais c'est quoi, en fait?

Acknowledgments

This book came not only out of my personal research but also out of the collective efforts of the Futurepol project in Paris. I acknowledge funding from the European Research Council through grant 283706. The ERC grant allowed for extensive archival and documentary work. Egle Rindzeviciute, Viteszlav Sommer, Sybille Duhautois, Pauline Prat, and Adam Freeman were a truly outstanding group of scholars and I thank all of them for their input to this book. I hope that I have done justice to their work in the coming pages. I particularly want to acknowledge the invaluable help from Vita Sommer as well as from Malgorzata Mazurek, Lukas Becht, and David Priestland on what became Chapter 7. I also want to thank two research assistants, Kecia Fong who helped me access Lewis Mumford's materials at UPenn when I could not travel, and Grayson Fuller in Paris.

The book as a whole has benefited from many colleagues in different disciplines: Erik Westholm, Marie-Laure Djelic, Michael Gordin, Dominique Pestre, Nicolas Guilhot, Sonja Amadae, Martin Giraudeau, Benoit Pelopidas, Daniel Steinmetz Jenkins, Mathieu Leimgruber, Mathias Schmelzer, Jennifer Light, John Hall, Paul Edwards, Gabrielle Hecht, Stephane van Damme, Barbara Adam, Sandra Kemp, Jakob Vogel, Paul Warde, Marc Lazar, Nicolas Delalandes, Ariane Leendertz, Patricia Clavin, Caspar Sylvest, Or Rosenboim, Wolfgang Streeck, Robert Fishman, Marion Fourcade, Desmond King, and Jens Beckert. Particular thanks go to Nils Gilman and Duncan Bell for their comments on the first draft manuscript, as well as to the Oxford editors for their enthusiasm and reactivity.

I have relied extensively on the work of librarians and archivists in many fine institutions. Ngram views can take you a bit of the way but, thankfully, we still have libraries and archives. I am particularly indebted to the people that I interviewed and talked to during the research for the book. As these conversations ranged from proper interviews to more informal talks, I list them here: Lars Ingelstam and Göran Bäckstrand in Sweden, Bart van Steenbergen in the Netherlands, Theodore Gordon in upstate New York, Anthony Judge in Brussels, Wendell Bell in New Haven, James Dator in Paris and Honolulu, Jennifer Gidley in Melbourne, Hugues de Jouvenel in Paris, and Jerome Glenn in Washington. Particular thanks to Eleonora Masini, whose living room I invaded for a week while her grandchildren carried boxes of old documents up and down the stairs, and to Ted Gordon for the use of personal photos.

About halfway through this book, I fell very ill. As I was diagnosed, many of my friends and colleagues became the pillars of a monumental support network. Thanks to everyone at Sciences Po, MaxPo, and CEE and particularly Florence Faucher, Linda Amrani, Renaud Dehousse and Laurie Boussaguet, Sarah Gensberger, Imola Streho, Sandrine Perrot, Olivier Godechot, Allison Rovny, and Patrick Legales. Thanks to my friends, Ann Gallagher and Frank Roselli in Somerville, who let me use my old postdoc room while working in Cambridge archives, and thanks to Paul Edwards and Gabrielle Hecht for an edifying dinner conversation as I finished my archival research at Ann Arbor. Thanks also to Nina Larriaga and Jenny Bastide and their families, and to Rana and Lars Wedin. My sister Lina Cronebäck, Henrik, Lovisa, and Estelle and my parents have been by my side. So has my husband Olivier Borraz, with whom I have shared some very difficult moments but also the very happiest ones. Liv Andersson Borraz is the light of my life, my lovely, courageous, curious, clever daughter. *Vous êtes mes amours. Merci* also to Rouzbeh Parsi.

The cover image of the book shows the Future Boardgame, invented by Ted Gordon, Olaf Helmer, and Hans Goldschmidt in 1969 for the American company Kaiser Aluminum. The game is in Ted Gordon's possession.

Contents

List of Figures

List of Abbreviations

BNF	Bibliothèque nationale de France
CdP	Centre de Prospective
CFF	Congress for Cultural Freedom
CRC	Centre d'études et de recherches des chefs de l'entreprise
CY2000	Commission for the Year 2000
FFA	Ford Foundation Archives
FFEPH	Fondation française de l'étude des problèmes humains
IIASA	International Institute for Applied Systems Analysis
ISA	International Sociological Association
MPS	Mont Pelerin Society
MSH	Maison des sciences de l'homme
RAC	Rockefeller Archives Center
RAND	Research and Development Corporation
SEDEIS	Société d'études et de documentation économiques industrielles
WFSF	World Futures Studies Federation

1

Introduction

THE PROBLEM OF THE FUTURE

In a number of essays published in a book with the title *Between Past and Future* in 1961, Hannah Arendt wrote that Mankind had severed its links to the past, thereby losing all hope of a human future.[1] The future, cut loose from all past experiences, was adrift in a sea of meaningless time. History was no more. Time was but a simple prolongation of a deeply anguished present. As the realm of dreams of human improvement, the future had no sense. This empty future was the starkest sign, to Arendt, of a pervasive crisis of Man. In its magnanimous belief in science and technology, humanity had replaced all eschatological and moral notions with the totalizing idea of constant progress. In such a futuristic world, no future was possible.[2]

Hannah Arendt was not alone in understanding, after World War 2, the future as a fundamental political problem. Walter Benjamin's famous essays on history identified progress as a totalitarian force and the future as a mechanistic and oppressive dystopia personified in the terrifying vision of an angel blowing backwards on a storm called progress.[3] Before his suicide on the Spanish border in November 1940, Benjamin handed the German manuscript of *Theses on the Philosophy of History* to Arendt, and Arendt carried it in her suitcase to New York, where she published it.[4] Benjamin's conception of the future as a totalitarian sphere would, in her own work, translate into a set of arguments about the future as a fundamental problem for the "human condition." After 1945, freedom was threatened by a set of earth changing factors. The futurism born in an interwar romance with machines, science, and technology had developed into the ideology of totalitarianism, the totalizing nature of which lay precisely in its grasp on the human future. Through the negation of the plural nature of the future, totalitarianism projected *one future* that was also a *non-future* as the open character of the future was by definition a threat to totalitarian power. A fundamentally hollowed out category, the future was up for grabs, empty to be filled with new forms of meaning.[5]

[1] Hannah Arendt, *Between Past and Future. Eight Exercises in Political Thought* (New York: Penguin classics, 1961).

[2] Hannah Arendt, *The Human Condition* (Chicago: The University of Chicago Press, 1958, 1998), 1–6, and sections 34, 35.

[3] Walter Benjamin, *Illuminations* (New York: Houghton Mifflin Harcourt, 1968).

[4] Elisabeth Young-Bruehl, *Hannah Arendt: For Love of the World* (New Haven: Yale University Press, 2004), 166–7.

[5] Hannah Arendt, "Tradition and the Modern Age", in *Between Past and Future*.

Arendt's conception of a threatened future was central for her understanding of the shifting nature of political power in the post-war world. Arendt was not a futurist. But her apprehensions of the consequences of a closing down of the future for any kind of philosophical optimism or political agency were shared in the post-war period by an unexpected mix of intellectuals and thinkers, such as the urban theorist Lewis Mumford and the journalist Robert Jungk, the German Marxist Ossip Flechtheim, the Quaker couple Elise and Kenneth Boulding, and the American economist John McHale. These thinkers would be central in the laying of the foundations of the eclectic field of futurism.[6] Futurists argued that humanity needed new forms of knowledge, new instruments and tools with which to shape, alter, and ultimately salvage, future developments, and through those, the world itself. They were deeply troubled by the spread of new forms of prediction as part of the Cold War struggle, and with the rise of a new scientific expertise over what was in the 1950s and 1960s referred to as the "long term." The coming chapters explain this category, a product of ballistic engineering and space research.[7]

This book lays out the history of the complex activity called *futurism*, *futurology*, *futures studies*, *prognostics*, or, quite simply, *future research*. It explains that these strands were composed of profoundly different claims about how to know and change the future, and through that future, the world. The future that emerged after 1945 was, I propose, a field of struggle between different conceptions of how to control, or, radically transform, the Cold War world. An idea of the future as a fundamentally moral category stood against the "long term" as a category of control and management. The post-war future was a terrain of both imagination and scientist reasoning. This reflects a fundamental dividing line in the contemporary notion of the future between conceptions of the future as coming physical reality and as the product of law bound developments, or, as a quintessential social construct, beginning in the minds and hearts of people and reachable only through a transcendental act of love and imagination.[8] These different categories ascribed very different conceptions not only of the scope of human influence on the world, but also to the place of human beings within that world.

There were specific reasons why the future emerged as a core problem of human action after 1945. The post-war world was, more than any previous historical world, marked by the idea of human influence, and with the idea of unprecedented influence came new conceptions of consequence, reach, and responsibility. The "long term," post-1945, was understood not as a distant and free floating continent of time, but as a set of direct and aggregate consequences of the present, an outcome of myriads of forms of decision and multiple forms of action, some of which led to good futures, and some of which seemed profoundly undesirable. In addition, predictive experimentation after 1945 turned the future into a manageable and

[6] I use futurism here to denote a set of approaches to the future that came out of post-war social science and that have no relation to the interwar revolutionary art movement.

[7] Jenny Andersson, "The Great Future Debate and the Struggle for the World," in *American Historical Review*, 2012, 117 (5): 1411–31.

[8] See Kenneth Boulding, *The Image. Knowledge in Life and Society* (Ann Arbor: University of Michigan Press, 1956).

rationalized entity. In the social sciences, prediction had been confined to the dustbins since the grand schemas of Condorcet and Comte, with the exception of economics.[9] But after 1945, a range of predictive experiments appeared, including attempts to foresee the evolution of technology, the international system, human values, and political decision making. The effect of this was that the future, which had been discussed as a moral and philosophical category since the seventeenth century, became an object of social science. That the future lacked physical presence and could therefore not be the object of direct observation was a problem long discussed in the history of probabilistic reasoning.[10] But after 1945, the progress in quantitative surveys and multivariate analysis, in computer led simulation and modeling in a range of fields seemed to give long-term developments empirical and observable shape. Forms of probabilism could therefore be complemented with empirical and manipulable observations of changes both in human behavior and the surrounding world order. The future could take on a form of presence.

This presence was highly ambiguous. In many ways, the idea that the future could be rendered visible and hence inherently governable can be thought of, in the historian James Scott's terms, as part of a high modernist attempt of rationalization of uncharted territory.[11] Futurology, from this perspective, would seem to mark the high point of planning rationalities and attempts at active steering and problem solving in the post-war era. The book does not contradict this, but it argues that futurology was a highly complex project, one that in fact included not only important attempts to control the Cold War world, but also central forms of protest and dissent. Futurology contained both reassured notions of the stable structures of the present, and anxious notions of unforeseen and radical changes. As such, futurology seems to stand on the verge between high modernity and its postulated crisis, and I put forward the argument that futurology enacted a central debate in intellectual history on the malleability of coming time. The years between 1964 and 1973, the high point of future research, were marked by a not unique but nevertheless historically specific understanding that the present was a far from stable structure. Social, economic, and technological developments of modern industrial societies posed challenges to particular conceptions of stability and continuity, as industrial societies turned into post-industrial ones. New versions of positivism in modernization theory and behavioralism in the 1950s were attempts to capture the nature of this present. As the belief in positivism and technocracy faded toward the latter half of the 1960s, the question remained of how, absent such forms of reassurance of relative predictability, the future could be addressed. Futurology played out pervasive discourses of those decades on post-industrialism,

9 Phillip Mirowski, *More Heat than Light: Economics as Social Physics, Physics as Nature's Economics* (New York: Cambridge University Press, 1991); Phillip Mirowski, *Machine Dreams. How Economics Became a Cyborg Science* (Cambridge: Cambridge University Press, 2002).

10 Ian Hacking, *The Emergence of Probability: A Philosophical Study of Early Ideas about Probability, Induction and Statistical Inference* (New York: Cambridge University Press, 2006); Ian Hacking, *The Taming of Chance* (New York: Cambridge University Press, 1990).

11 James C. Scott, *Seeing Like a State. How Certain Schemes to Improve the Human Condition Failed* (New Haven: Yale University Press, 1998); see also Timothy Mitchell, *The Rule of Experts. Egypt, Technopolitics, Modernity* (Berkeley: University of California Press, 2002).

value shocks, and social trends, importantly not only for the Western world but also for the socialist economies, as well as for global temporalities.[12] As the product of this concern of stability and instability, continuity and change, the post-war period saw the production of massive amounts of future facts and data, and future research developed into a myriad of forms of knowledge, technologies, and expertise.

REPERTOIRES OF FUTURE MAKING: ORIGINS OF FUTURE EXPERTISE

The mathematicians and engineers who rediscovered prediction after 1945 and who went searching for what they called a "general theory of the future" were no ordinary scientists. They were not, they argued, interested in predicting grand schemas of development (although one can argue that this is exactly what they did) and they were certainly not, they argued, utopians attempting to dream up other worlds. They claimed rather, to be detached rational engineers, attacking what they saw as a problem of logistics: how to choose, between a myriad of possible developments, the optimal future? Convinced that they knew the answer to this question, these scientists invented a purposeful new tool of social engineering for the Cold War era in modern prediction.

The next chapter argues that for much of intellectual history, future research has been misunderstood as mainly a carrier of discursive, ideological, or cultural representations of the future. It makes more sense to think of it as an intervention into the present and as an attempt to shape coming times through the creation of manifold technologies, devices, and forms of future expertise.[13] Future research reflected the rapidly shifting future visions of the post-war era, including not only post-industrialism but also both profoundly optimistic notions of world development, and catastrophist discourses of nuclear war and ecocide. Future research also gave rise to artifacts: technologies and methods intended to have an active bearing on the future. Most of these artifacts were based on expertise, and it can be argued that future research gave rise over time to the emergence of a very particular form of expertise, a kind of meta expertise in world futures, equipped with forecasts and scenarios of world development. It is important for this argument that prediction turned out to be a highly specific form of knowledge production. Predictive techniques rarely sought to produce objective representations of a probable future, they tried, rather, to find potential levers with which to influence human action. As such they were "decision tools," or triggers of the imagination, designed to push

[12] Daniel Rodgers, *Age of Fracture* (Cambridge MA: Harvard University Press, 2013), 107–9.

[13] This is closer to how fields such as sociology or anthropology have dealt with the problem of prediction, devices, and performativity: see Donald MacKenzie, *An Engine, Not a Camera. How Financial Models Shape Markets* (Cambridge MA: MIT Press, 2002); Gregoire Mallard and Andrew Lakoff, "How claims to know the future are used to understand the present," in Michele Lamont et al. eds, *Social Knowledge in the Making* (Cambridge MA: Harvard University Press, 2012), 339–79; Harro Van Lente, "Navigating Foresight in a Sea of Expectations, Lessons from the Sociology of Expectations," in *Technology Analysis and Strategic Management*, 2012, 24 (8): 789–802.

human beings to act for the future in various ways. Predictors took what historians of science have referred to as a post-positivist stance: they embraced the performativity of the self-fulfilling prophecy, and in so doing they performed a crucial step from the claim to know the future to a claim of influence on that future.[14]

It is in many ways this claim of influence that explains the variety of future research as both science and politics. As explained, the post-war period saw not one, but several rivaling forms of engagement with the future, as the future was, to some, a logical problem of science, rationality, and optimal preference, and to others a sacred moral ground or radical sphere of protest.[15] Methods and technologies of prediction mirrored this variety. For this reason, it makes little sense to understand the logic or coherence of future research as *one* form of expertise, or indeed, see prediction as one particular kind of rationalistic future making. The many forms of knowledge production mobilized by future research came from fields as different as the social sciences, technoscience in think tanks, planning, and Cold War corporations such as Xerox, Bell Laboratories, or Royal Dutch Shell, and from alternative forms of knowledge in science fiction, journalism, and religion.[16] This variety is important, because the many collisions and controversies between these different forms of future knowledge is what leads to the argument that the post-war future was a field of struggle made up of a multitude of conflicting claims over how the world could be shaped and reshaped. The variety of future research is also indicative of the complex genealogies of not only the notion of future, but also the notion of expertise in the post-war era. Future research moved between fields. Over time, we find a blending of technological utopianism with social and political critique, a kind of hippie language with new notions of management and rationalization.[17] Future research also resembles what Thomas Medvetz referred to in his important study of American think tanks as hybridity, of a kind of knowledge production in between academia, public debate, and the market. Hybridity is meanwhile an awkward term for an historian because it is retrospective, and what Medvetz describes as hybridity has been described by historians as a particular knowledge culture produced by a time specific constellation of social science, technical knowledge, and new forms of advice or consultancy in the 1970s and

[14] Frank Fischer, "Beyond Empiricism: Policy Inquiry in Post Positivist Perspective," in *Policy Studies Journal*, 1998, 26 (1): 129–146; Bruno Latour, *Reassembling the Social* (Oxford: Oxford University Press, 2005).

[15] Recent works have begun to account for this variety, see R. J. Williams, "World Futures," in *Critical Inquiry*, 2016, 42: 473–546; and Jamie L. Pietruska, *Looking Forward. Prediction and Uncertainty in Modern America* (Chicago: The University of Chicago Press, 2017).

[16] There was a strong corporate dimension to Cold War technoscience, which was directly involved in a geopolitical struggle for resources such as steel or uranium. Telecom industries were key actors in the rise of systems analysis and predictive methods, and companies dependent on key raw materials such as aluminum and oil were central clients of future research, for instance Kaiser Aluminum (see Chapter 5) and Shell. See M. Sheller, *Aluminum Dreams: The Making of Light Modernity* (Cambridge MA: MIT Press, 2014); Gabrielle Hecht, *Being Nuclear: Africans and the Global Uranium Trade* (Cambridge MA: MIT Press, 2012).

[17] See Patrick McCray, *The Visioneers: How a Group of Elite Scientists Pursued Space Colonies, Nanotechnologies, and a Limitless Future* (Princeton NJ: Princeton University Press, 2012); Fred Turner, *From Counterculture to Cyberculture: Stewart Brand, the Whole Earth Network, and the Rise of Digital Utopianism* (Chicago: The University of Chicago Press, 2006).

1980s.[18] The boundaries of the social sciences in the post-war period were much less fixed than they are today, and the Cold War gave rise to notions of expertise derived from particular constellations between social science, corporations, and planning system, not only in the US but in Europe as well.[19]

As I began my research for the book, it seemed important to view the variety in future research as significant, because it interested me that future research seemed to play out a central struggle over how the future could be influenced, and by and for whom. The confrontation between the claims to influence of different strands within future research seemed to me a more interesting problem than the question of whether future research actually impacted on the world and whether it was right or wrong in its predictions of what would come. The question of impact and influence, meanwhile, is complicated. It is not clear that futurists left much of a mark on the world, indeed those futurists who thought in the 1960s and 1970s that they could save the world from environmental disaster and nuclear war were disappointed. The book proposes that the history of future research is important for two reasons. First, future research in its different strands performed a critical reflection on what I want to call the malleability of the world, and the multiple ways of knowing the future developments of that world. That future research moved in and out of social science is indicative of the fact that it stands through the post-war period as a reflection on the limits of human rationality and the borders of the knowable. This is fascinating in its own right. But secondly, I want to propose that while not all futurists were influential or memorable people, they gave rise to forms of expertise, methods, and technologies that have become part of governmentalities of the contemporary.[20] It was, the book proposes, more than anything through the production of these technologies and artifacts of expertise that futurists gained influence. The history of these devices is part of a powered history of the present, and the book makes the argument that it is highly important for intellectual historians of the last decades to pay attention not only to discourses and ideas of new universalizing projects, such as neoliberalism, in the decades from the 1970s onwards, but also to the way that these become embedded in artifacts and technologies of intervention. Prediction, I argue, should be understood as a technology of future making and world crafting, a social and political technology in the Foucauldian sense.

The enduring significance of some of the predictive technologies developed by futurists, for instance the so called Delphi technology or the scenario tool, stands in an interesting contrast here to how futurists themselves can seem an eclectic and somehow curious group of actors in intellectual history. The unconventional

[18] Thomas Medvetz, *Thinktanks in America* (Chicago: The University of Chicago Press, 2012).

[19] Gil Eyal and Lisa Buchholz, "From the Sociology of Intellectuals to the Sociology of Interventions," in *Annual Review of Sociology* 2010, 36: 117–37; Joy Rohde, *Armed with Expertise. The Militarization of American Social Research During the Cold War* (Ithaca: Cornell University Press, 2013); Antoine Vauchez and Stephanie Lee Mudge, "Building Europe on a Weak Field. Law, Economics and Scholarly Avatars in Transnational Politics," *American Journal of Sociology*, 2012, 118 (2): 449–92.

[20] Graham Burchell et al., *The Foucault Effect. Studies in Governmentality* (Chicago: University of Chicago Press, 1991).

appearance of some of the futurists led one of the reviewers for this book to speak of hucksters. But huckstering is arguably part of the contemporary history of prediction. In the Cold War era, prediction is based on eclectic repertoires and fuzzy boundaries between rationality and speculation, science and art, and as the chapters of the book show, future research could use all of these different repertoires. The American historian Daniel Rodgers has used the term "psychoscience" to denote some successes of future research in the 1960s that were particularly apt at making a kind of highly time specific bombastic speculation of coming world transformations.[21] Figures such as Alvin Toffler, the journalist and writer who figures fleetingly in this book, stand out here, and both Toffler's *Future Shock* and John Naisbitt's *Megatrends* (1979) popularized concepts such as "weak trends" and "unforeseens" that have since become staples of a kind of future research with strong links to the consultancy community in business and management studies.[22]

Toffler's own contributions to future research were unoriginal. The importance of *Future Shock* and *The Futurists* lay mainly in the way they popularized future research and helped establish Toffler himself as a new breed of public intellectual, specialized in the making of very large claims. Meanwhile, Toffler wrote several papers on future research that were read and discussed by futurists, and many futurists, even while less well known, were a bit like Toffler. They projected a carefully constructed image of themselves as thinking outside of the box, and they pursued careers as jack-of-all-trades (journalism, academia, business advice) somehow developing into a position of future expert or professional conjurer. Toffler was himself not unlike the Babson character in Walter Friedman's *Fortunetellers*. Friedman tells a fascinating story of how, in the aftermath of the Wall Street crash, financial forecasters took over the lucrative business of fortunetelling from the actual oracles who walked Wall Street in the early twentieth century, selling investment advice to businessmen. Financial forecasters—Babson, Dow, Fisher, Moody—emerged after 1929 as a new breed of social engineers for an era obsessed with understanding discontinuities and movements in financial markets (and applying models and metaphors derived from electricity and weather). Through the collection of statistical data and the production of artifacts such as the Babson Barometer, forecasters attempted to stabilize this turbulence and allow for financial actors to make wiser decisions in light of possible market moves.[23] Toffler's version of futurology was of course different as it did not seek to stabilize a set of expectations or calm what Keynes called the "animal spirits," rather, it was obsessed with painting gaudy images of new technological revolutions, with the underlying

[21] Rodgers, *Age of Fracture*, 79–80, 107–9, 111, 295–6. In the closing years of the 1960s and early years of the 1970s, a number of television documentaries, popularized science mags and publications also documented the "new science," see *New York Times Magazine,* April 19, 1964.

[22] Correspondence for *The Futurists,* in Toffler papers, Butler Library, Columbia, Alvin Toffler, *Future Shock* (New York: Bantham book, 1971); Alvin Toffler, *The Futurists* (New York: Random House, 1972); Manjoo, F., "The future Toffler saw is already upon us," *New York Times*, July 6, 2016; Matthew Connelly, "Future shock. The end of the world as they knew it", in Niall Fergusson et al. eds, *Shock of the Global*, 337–51.

[23] Walter Friedman, *Fortune Tellers: The Story of America's first Economic Forecasters* (New Haven: Princeton University Press, 2013) 8–9.

message that these had to be popularly embraced.[24] It can well be argued that this too was a form of stabilization of the present, and that the purpose of forms of prediction after 1945 was exactly to establish a measure of control by shaping forms of action toward foreseeable and desirable goals. The question is who set out these visions of desirable goals. Toffler is also a good example of the links between future research and consultancy: in the 1970s Toffler set up a think tank for the future which had fleeting connections with the neoconservative movement in the US; and, as a consultant in the 1980s, Toffler also advised the Chinese government on post-industrial economics and management tools of the "Third wave."[25]

UNDERSTANDING THE SPACES OF FUTURISM: A NOTE ON METHOD

When Toffler published his book on the futurists in 1972, he drew public attention to an activity that dated back to at least the early 1940s, and had during the Cold War decades been an important field of transnational activity. I suggest that this transnational activity was constitutive of a form of expertise in world futures, which drew on the circulation of specific methods and technologies of prediction. This expertise resembles what Paul Warde and Sverker Sörlin have referred to as meta expertise, a very particular form of expertise that was not based on the grasping of a particular subject matter, but rather, on the capacity to conjure synthetic and encompassing images of dramatic and threatening developments. In future research, this expertise on world futures could encompass forms of world utopianism as well as new versions of global technocracy.[26]

The research for the book has been guided by the attempt to understand the constitution of this expertise by tracing the circulation of actors, ideas, and technologies of futurism in a transnational field. As such, the argument that I present is different from existing accounts of future research, which classify it along lines of planning versus normative futures studies, or American vs. European forms of futurism.[27] My interest has been, rather, to understand the emergence, in a global

[24] See Jens Beckert, *Imagined Futures. Fictional Expectations and Capitalist Dynamics* (Cambridge MA: Harvard University Press, 2016) in particular, Chapters 1 and 6.

[25] Julian P. Gerwirtz, "The Futurists of Beijing. Alvin Toffler, Zhao Ziyang, and China's new technological revolution, 1979–91." Unpublished.

[26] Paul Warde and Sverker Sörlin, "Expertise for the Future. The Environment and the Emergence of Modern Prediction, 1920–1970," in Jenny Andersson and Egle Rindzeviciute, eds, *The Struggle for the Long Term in Transnational Science and Politics: Forging the Future* (London: Routledge, 2015), 38–63. Compare Nicolas Guilhot, *The Democracy Makers: Human Rights and the Politics of Global Order* (New York: Columbia University Press, 2008); Marie Laure Djelic and Sigrid Quack, *Transnational Communities. Shaping Global Economic Governance* (New York: Cambridge University Press, 2010); Egle Rindzeviciute, *Power of System: How Policy Sciences Opened up the Cold War World* (Ithaca: Cornell University Press, 2016).

[27] See Wendell Bell, *Foundations of Futures Studies. Human Science for a New Era* (Transaction Publishers, New Brunswick, 1998); Kaya Tolon, "Futures Studies: A New Science Rooted in Cold War Strategic Thinking" in Mark Solovey and Hunter Heyck, eds, *Cold War Social Science, Knowledge Production, Liberal Democracy and Human Nature* (London and New York: Palgrave, 2012) 45–63;

space, of a set of rivaling claims to know the future. I have understood these rivaling claims as central to the making of a field of futurism. The sociological literature makes use of the notion of field in order to describe the communities of experts or movements that transnational historians have identified as connected, supra national, or global.[28] This is a useful notion in order to understand future research as emanating from many different spaces that, while they are interconnected, are also different in kind. Most transnational history has tended to focus on international organizations that are in themselves global hubs, and that have deposited archival materials in organized and relatively accessible sites. Future research was not in this way an established global site. That made it not only difficult to understand but it also created a practical problem as there are few convenient archives of future research. Making links between different positions of futurism can seem counter intuitive, as future research was composed of sometimes directly colliding claims as to how the future could be approached and known. The networks of futurists also cut across the established political history of the post-war period, from the networks and exchanges of German and East European Jews discussed in Chapter 3, the liberals and neoliberals of the Congress for Cultural Freedom discussed in Chapter 4, mathematicians and nuclear strategists in Chapter 5, budding neoconservatives in Chapter 6, revisionist Marxists in Chapter 7, peace activists in Chapter 8, and American hippies, libertarians, counter culturalists, "visioneers", and proto neoliberals in Chapter 9. Some of these networks were direct products of the Cold War; others were created in opposition to the Cold War world order and involved new forms of activism and militancy. Tracing this history can seem like an odyssey in the post-war history of ideas, and the reader might well ask why all these incarnations of future thinking should be considered as part of the same history?

There are two answers to this question. First, the controversies and arguments between different strands of future research tell a crucial story about competing ideas of the future in the post-war period, and about the claims to influence and control over this future. Second, futurists were involved in what the sociologist Lisa Stampnitzky, in her study of terrorism experts, calls disciplining of an unruly field. Futurists organized conferences, wrote books, and corresponded, sometimes very extensively, about their particular concepts, methods and techniques. They not only invented methods and branded these as belonging to a particular strand

Elke Seefried, *Zukunfte. Aufstieg und Krise der Zukunftsforschung 1945–1980* (Berlin: Walter de Gruyter, 2015) 75–154.

[28] Patricia Clavin, "Defining Transnationalism," in *Contemporary European History*, 2005, 14(4): 421–39; Patricia Clavin, "Time, Manner, Place: Writing Modern European History in Global, Transnational and International Contexts," in *European History Quarterly*, 2010, 40(4): 624–40; Christopher Bayly, Sven Beckert, Matthew Connelly, et al. "AHR Conversation: On Transnational History," in *The American Historical Review*, 2006, 111 (5): 1441–64; Akira Iriye, ed. *The Palgrave Dictionnary of Transnational History* (Basingstoke: Palgrave, 2009); Pierre Yves Saunier, "Circulations, connexions et espaces transnationaux," *Genèses*, 2004, 4: 110–26. I am not referring to field in Bourdieu's sense of an organized field here, but rather to Stampnitzky's idea of an unruly field, Lisa Stampnitzky, *How Experts Invented Terrorism* (New York: Cambridge University Press, 2013) see also Neil Fligstein and Douglas MacAdam, *A Theory of Fields* (New York: Oxford University Press, 2012).

of future research, they also created repertoires and bibliographies of future relevant literature, directories of futurists, and lists of relevant research institutes. It is clear from the coming pages that some actors played a key role in structuring this field, for instance Bertrand de Jouvenel, Daniel Bell, or Ossip Flechtheim. At a certain moment in time futurists venture far into social science. There were several conferences on forecasting and prediction in the early to mid 1960s, at Yale Law School in 1962, the International Political Science Association in 1964, at the French Institut d'etudes politiques in 1966, and the American Political Science Association in 1967. In particular the Ford Foundation and the National Science Foundation funded and assisted future research, motivated by the hope that it might represent a new behavioral science in the making. Several disciplines also developed conferences and subcommittees on the themes of prediction, future research, or futures studies. The American Anthropological Association created, in 1972, a subcommittee for future anthropology under the benediction of Margaret Mead. The International Sociology Association, ISA, created a research committee for the sociology of futurology in 1970. Some sciences—psychology, economics, political science, international relations—saw future research as a way of putting their rationality postulates to the test of predictive capacity. Other disciplines, such as anthropology and sociology, emerging from their earlier focus on strict categories of class or race, took an interest in future research as an interrogation into culture, values, and human diversity.[29]

Certain institutes and organizations functioned as specific spaces of future research, such as the Institute for Applied Systems Analysis (IIASA), or the Club of Rome. A number of study groups, conferences, and organizations with varying institutional solidity figure in the coming pages. Futurists created a number of rival power houses for the future: the Paris based *Futuribles* venture: Fred Polak's HiFI of democratic superplanning: Ossip Flechtheim's Zentrum fur Zukunftsfragen: Robert Jungk's Zukunftsbibliothek in Salzburg: Olaf Helmer's and Daniel Bell's Institute for the Future in the US. By 1970 the competition for the world future was fierce. From the late 1960s on, futurists also came together in not one, but two, world organizations, the World Futures Studies Federation in 1973 and the Washington World Future Society created in the year before. They gave rise to key publications such as the Mankind 2000 volume published in 1969, the World Future Society Newsletter, Ossip Flechtheim's journal *Futurum*, the UNESCO Social Science Journal, and Toffler's book *The Futurists*. In 1969 and 1970 futurists created the scientific journals *Futures* and *Technological Forecasting and Social Change*. All of these activities were, I propose, constitutive of futurism as a kind of expertise, and it was important therefore to pay attention not only to the ideas of futurists, but also to what they in fact did.

From the 1970s on, future research was marked by a process of professionalization that led futurists of very different orientation to come together around a notion of expertise with strong links to an emerging consultancy market. Shifts

[29] See Margaret Mead, "A note on the contribution of anthropology to the science of the future", to the American Anthropological Association Symposium on Cultural Futurology, 1971.

over time in the organization of futurism from networks with diametrically different positions *on* the world's future, to networks of consultants carried by the idea that they possessed a specific kind of knowledge *about* the world's future is a highly significant process. Through this process, in the end, future expertise somehow became more important than the future itself. In many ways this process was carried through the technologies and methods of prediction.

Stampnitzky's idea of a field has been useful in order to understand this phenomenon and process and link an intellectual history understanding of the idea of the future to a more social analysis of the future as a problem of knowledge and power.[30] Futurists are not that different from Stampnitzky's terrorism experts. In Stampnitzky's description, terrorism experts are largely self-appointed experts equipped with a number of non-conventional tools through which they make predictive claims about unknowable events. These tools include artifacts such as scenarios and simulations that function as forms of role play or enactments of the future, but also bibliographical canons and attempts to gather and systematize terrorism knowledge through indexes, indicators, and abstract services. As Stampnitzky points out, these function as devices of expertise, and can be understood as crucial elements in the constitution of forms of scientific authority in an area of vague standing in the established social sciences.[31] Futurists, quite like terrorism experts, failed many times in their attempts to turn future research into an academic discipline. The many organizations, think tanks, and institutes that futurists created also often had a fragile existence.[32] Meanwhile, as argued, the artifacts and devices that futurists created endured, and many lived on to become staples of global governance. The Delphi tool, discussed in Chapter 5, is used both by ratings agencies in financial markets and by the UN climate panels. Scenarios are used in security politics and processes of risk management on levels ranging from US diplomacy to Davos.[33]

Reconstructing the field of future research was possible through the crossing of many different archival and personal materials, visual materials, and sometimes interviews. Much of this archival work had not been done before. It required, in fact, a documentary effort, through which I gathered much of the material from the World Futures Studies Federation (WFSF) and its futurists. The WFSF has now itself made such a documentary effort and published many of its central documents online. The closest thing to a future studies archive is Jim Dator's collection at the

[30] See Sheila Jasanoff, "Future imperfect. Science, technology and the imaginaries of modernity," in Sheila Jasanoff and S.Y. Kim, *Dreamscapes of Modernity. Sociotechnical Imaginaries and the Fabrication of Power* (Cambridge MA: Harvard University Press, 2016).

[31] Liza Stampnitzky, *Disciplining Terror: How Experts Invented Terrorism* (New York: Cambridge University Press, 2013).

[32] Stampnitzky, *Disciplining Terror*, 3–15, 25, 84. This is not to say that there are not elements of an academic future research: there are university departments and courses in future studies in many places, usually in fields such as management and innovation or risk studies.

[33] See Mallard and Lakoff, "How claims to know the future influence the present," and Christina Garsten and Adrienne Sorbom, "Risk, resilience and alternative future. Scenario building at the World Economic Forum." Unpublished.

University of Manoa, Honolulu, and Ossip Flechtheim's very extensive collection of the materials of East European futurists in Frankfurt. It should be added, in part as caveat, that the use of these archives was what allowed me to work on forms of future research that would otherwise not have been available to me, in particular the Chinese and Japanese materials and the East European and Russian material in both Flechtheim's and Dator's correspondence. I also accessed email lists and web-based materials of futurists and attended several world conferences. In the end, I conducted nine interviews and gathered email correspondence and chats with many more. At one point during the research, futurists discovered that they were the object of an historian's attention and that allowed me to make a number of anthropological observations. A minor stir on the member list led to me being invited in 2013 for the thirty-year anniversary of the WFSF's formal first conference in Bucharest, to give a keynote of what became Chapter 9. I did this, no one spoke to me, and I went quietly back home, but I was able to make field notes from a four day conference. Throughout, I have made an attempt to work with visual materials, graphic illustrations, and images.

THE STRUCTURE OF THE BOOK

The next chapter presents a historiographic argument about the way that historians have dealt with the future, and proposes that historians need to reengage with the future. I argue that in the decades following the cultural turn, historians lost sight of the future and turned to constructions of a past dominated by memory, nostalgia and loss, and I propose instead a transnational history of the future, which engages with a recent historiography of world temporalities, modernization, and planning. Chapter 3 traces the emergence of futurism to a range of writings on the human destruction of the nuclear age by intellectuals such as Hannah Arendt, Ossip Flechtheim, and Lewis Mumford immediately after the Second World War. Chapter 4 visits the Congress for Cultural Freedom (CCF) and proposes that the spread of futurology by the CCF, the Ford Foundation, and the so called *Futuribles* project in Paris was a conscious attempt to create a liberal alternative to the theory of history of Marxism. Chapter 5 examines the invention of the idea of the future as the "long term" through experimentations with contemporary forms of prediction at American RAND. It shows that prediction was understood at RAND in a highly specific way, as a social technology for shaping desirable developments. Chapter 6 follows the social technologies developed at RAND into a reflection on the American future which took place within the so called Commission for the Year 2000 (CY2000), created in 1964 in the American Academy of Arts and Science under the chairmanship of Daniel Bell. In Chapter 7, the argument turns to the rediscovery of the future in revisionist debates in the socialist bloc before 1968, and examines the role of East European futurists in the transnational networks of future research. It shows that East European futurists were important in reintroducing the idea that futures were human constructs and central to forms of protest and resistance. Chapter 8 explores the creation of so called futures studies as a rejection of prediction and protest against the Cold War world order. Taking as its focus the World Futures Studies Federation, the chapter suggests that futures studies were an example of a kind of neo-utopianism for the Cold War era, which not only claimed that alternative worlds were possible but also tried to construct new ways of envisioning and realizing such worlds. In Chapter 9, I explain how futurism changed in the 1980s and 1990s. Paradoxically, in their desire to create new images of the future capable of providing exits from the status quo of the Cold War world, futurists reinvented the technologies of prediction that they had initially rejected, and made them the basis of a new activity of paid futures advice and consultancy.

2

A New History of the Future? From Conceptual History to Intellectual World History

WHY DID HISTORIANS LOSE SIGHT OF THE FUTURE?

This book proposes to view the future as a field of struggle over time, constituted by a variety of future claims relying on different forms of futuristic expertise, predictive technologies, and future artifacts. With this understanding in mind, it lays out a different history of the future from the one that has preoccupied historians in the past.

The core of an earlier future history was the German historian Reinhart Koselleck's futures past argument, based on a conceptual history approach (*Begriffsgeschichte*) that placed the modern concept of the future as the key stone in a history of Western modernity. It is interesting to note that Koselleck's concept of future history came out of a larger interest in the future in sociology and history in the 1960s and 1970s, an interest that somehow paralleled the contemporary interest in futurology but without any clear dialogue between the two fields. Koselleck's key work, *Vergangene Zukunft*, was written as part of a transdisciplinary research project in Bielefeld, devoted to the role of utopia in modernity.[1] For some reason, the future entered the horizon of the humanities and social sciences at the very point in time that later historians have seen as the breaking point between modernity and post-modernity.[2]

At the core of German *Begriffsgeschichte* stood the notion of a horizon of expectation. The concept of a horizon of expectation was central to the argument that the future had been invented in the German so called *Sattel Zeit*, the shift from *ancien regime* to Enlightenment or modernity, and been vested there with an unprecedented political power. Koselleck argued that it was the modern idea of progress, the idea of acceleration, and the idea of the linearity of time that marked

[1] Koselleck and Norbert Elias worked in the same research project in Bielefeld, see Elias, *Uber die Zeit* (Merkur: Stuttgart, 1982).

[2] Reinhart Koselleck, "The Temporalization of Utopia." *The Practice of Conceptual History: Timing History, Spacing Concepts* (2002), 84–99; Reinhart Koselleck, *Futures Past. On the Semantics of Historical Time*, (Cambridge MA: MIT Press 1985 (published in German in 1979 under the title *Vergangene Zunkuft*)).

the invention of the future as a category of coming time, embodied in the German concept *Zukunft,* literally time-to-come.[3] For Koselleck, in striking contrast to Hannah Arendt cited at the beginning of this book, it was the separating out of a secular and manmade future from the grip of Christianity that gave the future its political relevance. Koselleck had not lived through the experience of destruction that Arendt, Benjamin, and a range of other post-war thinkers on the future had—thinkers who aligned themselves with the critique of modernity of the first and second Frankfurt schools.[4] For Koselleck, firmly rooted in a German hermeneutic tradition, there was a direct link between the idea of the future and the idea of modernity, through the process of secularization and democratization. This process had transformed the future from a problem of divine destiny, to a problem of scientific and political rationality. To Arendt this rationalization was a process of destruction, but to Koselleck, it was a great opening, indeed the beginning of history, as the future became a problem of human agency.[5]

This resituation of the future within the realm of scientific rationality and political will was to Koselleck the great prerequisite of modern political life. As the "ends of time" that had been projected by the apocalyptic and messianic visions of Christianity fell by the wayside, the future appeared as open for prognostication, planning, and control.[6] To Koselleck, this was a freeing up of the horizons of humanity. In his footsteps, Koselleck's followers, in particular the German historian Lucien Holscher, similarly argued that what distinguished the modern notion of the future from the seventeenth century onwards was an "end to the end," a demise of all theological notions of human finality.[7] Chapter 3 in this book takes issue with this position by arguing that the idea of an immanent end, created by nuclear apocalypse or environmental destruction, is on the contrary central to the post-war concept of the future.

Meanwhile, Koselleck's argument that history could be written as a series of "vergangene Zukünfte" became central to cultural history, which in the coming decades misunderstood, I argue, profoundly the importance of the idea of the future to the Cold War era and beyond. Drawing on Koselleck's notion of an horizon of expectation, and taking Hannah Arendts' observations in her *Past and Future* essays as his steppingstone, the French cultural historian Francois Hartog argued that in the decades after 1945, the future was no more an horizon of expectation

[3] Koselleck, "The Temporalization of Utopia."

[4] Aaron Rabinbach, *In the Shadow of the Catastrophe. German Intellectuals between Apocalypse and Enlightenment* (Berkeley: California University Press, 2001).

[5] As in the quote by Robespierre that informs his future past argument: "The time has come to call upon each and everyone to realize his own destiny. The progress of human reason has laid the basis for this great Revolution, and the particular duty of hastening it has fallen to you." Reinhart Koselleck, "Modernity and the Planes of Historicity," in *Economy and Society* 1981, 10 (2): 166–83.

[6] Koselleck, "Modernity and the Planes of Historicity," 173. Koselleck makes no mention either of Arendt's essays on *Past and Future,* nor of Walter Benjamin's *Notes on History*. Koselleck was a member of Hitlerjugend and a volunteer in the Wehrmacht before being taken prisoner of war by the Russians. He studied after the war with Heidegger and Carl Schmitt. See Niklas Olsen, *History in the Plural. An Introduction to the Work of Reinhart Koselleck* (New York: Berghahn) 2012, 13–16, 29.

[7] Lucien Holscher, "The History of the Future. The Emergence and Decline of a Temporal Concept In European History," in *Conceptual History Newsletter*, 2002, (5): 10–15.

of any importance.[8] In doing so, Hartog missed that in fact Arendt did not only lament or observe the loss of future, but she also argued for the absolute necessity of the future as a category and imperative of action, as did many of her fellow intellectuals. The following chapter begins with this observation. But Hartog's argument sat at the center of a revision of the notion of the future in cultural history, which from the 1990s on began to see the future as a problem of historicity and temporality and as a site of loss and nostalgia.[9] The core concept in Hartog's work was *presentism,* an argument according to which contemporary societies, following an acceleration of time (noted by Koselleck and Hartmut Rosa) and a perpetuation of symptoms of crisis since the 1970s oil crises, had turned their backs on the future and made the present the only relevant horizon.[10] Squeezed between the rise of the category of historical memory and a perpetual present, the future was a shrinking horizon.

In stipulating that the future had lost its relevance, historians joined a large choir from the social sciences that preached, in the wake of 1989, that the future was no more. This went far beyond Francis Fukuyama's gloating concept of the end of history and into critical theory. David Harvey, the Marxist geographer, argued in an important book in 1989 that globalization could be understood as a form of time space compression, systematically squeezing out the future by suffocating all forms of alternative from the process of global capitalist development.[11] The post-modern theorist Fredric Jameson proposed that in that strange condition that he called postmodernism, all utopias were dead, and there could be nothing else than a kind of ongoing and outstretching version of futurism in the shape of neoliberalism, itself perhaps the strongest utopia of all.[12] In the coming decades, the social sciences put forward pervasive concepts of risk societies and reflexive modernities, which projected a fundamental dividing line between a predictable and stable set of future horizons and futures marked by unpredictability, uncertainty, and decline. In historiography, and in particular in German *Zeitgeschichte*, this was matched by pervasive notions that the post-war period could be neatly divided in two, an era of faith in progress, science, and politics, and an ensuing era of gloom and crisis.[13]

[8] Francois Hartog, *Régimes d'historicité. Présentisme et expériences du temps* (Paris: Seuil, 2014), 14.

[9] Peter Fritzsche, *Stranded in the Present. Modern Time and the Melancholy of History* (Palo Alto: Stanford University Press, 2004); Stephen Kern, *The Culture of Time and Space 1880–1918*, (Cambridge MA: Harvard University Press, 2003); Lynn A. Hunt, *Measuring Time, Making History* (Budapest: Central European University Press, 2008); Roxana Panchasi, *Future Tense: The Culture of Anticipation in France Between the Wars* (Ithaca: Cornell University Press, 2009); Peter Osbourne, *The Politics of Time. Modernity and Avant Garde* (London: Verso, 1995).

[10] Hartog, *Régimes d'historicité*, 107, 120, 143; Hartmut Rosa, *Alienation and Acceleration. Toward a Critical Theory of Late Modern Temporality* (London: Verso, 2010).

[11] David Harvey, *The Condition of Postmodernity. An Inquiry into the Origins of Cultural Change* (London: Verso, 1989).

[12] Frederic Jameson, *Postmodernism, or, the Cultural Logic of Late Capitalism* (Durham: Duke University Press, 1991).

[13] See Anselm Doering-Manteuffel and Lutz Raphael, *Nach dem Boom. Perspektiven auf die Zeitgeschichte seit 1970* (Bonn: Vandenhoeck and Ruprecht, 2012) and Elke Seefried, "Reconfiguring the Future. Politics and Time from the 1960s to the 1980s," in *Journal of Modern European History*, 2015, 13 (3): 306–316; and, for an, in my view, more productive perspective, Rudiger Graf and

Through its focus on transnational circulation of future expertise over the long post-war period from 1945 to the early 1990s (and some arguments go back even further in time) this book challenges this dichotomous representation of the post-war period. It also challenges the core idea of *Begriffsgeschichte*, that a pervasive shift occurred in the post-war concept of the future from notions of progress to notions of crisis. Instead we should view ideas of crisis and progress as integral to the contemporary notion of the future, and what defines the post-war idea of the future is not a pervasive shift in horizons of expectation from progress to decline, but rather, the way that the future is caught between fundamental processes of liberation and control. The book also argues that the future returned in the post-war period as a category with direct links to notions of human fate and end. One of the key arguments set out in the coming pages is that there are strong links after 1945 between the idea of the future and the idea of humanity or "Mankind" as joined together by a common destiny. Both concepts of long term and future were also directly linked to the idea of a world, which by the mid to late 1960s was understood as a systemic aggregate of human action and product of human intervention. As the world became a space made by human beings, the future became the space of hopes and fears of what this world would become. In this capacity of the aggregate consequences of the global present, the future reiterated historic notions of the world as a human cosmos, with the great difference that after 1945, human beings held, as Arendt put it, "cosmic powers," the power to unmake cosmos and destroy the universe.[14] In order to understand this, it is crucial to see that the post-war intellectual history is full of ends, and that the idea that the end stemmed not from the Gods but from human action had implications on intellectual history as important as the "discovery of the future" posited by Koselleck and Holscher.[15] Indeed science in the contemporary era is not only a source of rationalization, it also enabled the return of fundamentally morally charged notions of human fate, apocalypse, and salvation. The publication of Herman Kahn's *Thermonuclear War* in 1960 or the Club of Rome's 1972 report *Limits to Growth* both projected clear ends to human civilization, and for both, this raised the stakes of humanity by pointing to the necessity of action.[16]

The book also argues that instead of thinking of futurology as a somehow last whisper of a high modernist attempt at social control, we should understand it as a set of reiterations of forms of technocracy and claims to social control that have

Benjamin Herzog, "Von der Geschichte der Zukunftsvorstellungen zur Geschichte ihrer Generierung. Probleme und Herausforderungen der Zukunftsbezugs im 20ten Jahrhundert." *Geschichte und Gesellschaft* 42 (3): 497–515.

[14] Jenny Andersson and Sibylle Duhautois, "Futures of Mankind. The emergence of the global future" in Caspar Sylvester and Rens van Munster, *Politics of Globality since 1945. Assembling the Planet* (New York: Routledge, 2016), 106–126; Sebastian Conrad, & Dietrich Sachsenmaier, *Competing Visions of World Order. Global Moments and Movements, 1880s–1930s* (London: Palgrave Macmillan 2007); Jens Bartelson, *Visions of World Community* (New York: Cambridge University Press, 2009).

[15] See John R. Hall, *Apocalypse: From Antiquity to the Empire of Modernity* (New York: John Wiley & Sons, 2013).

[16] Herman Kahn, *On Thermonuclear War*, 1960; Donatella Meadows et al., eds *The Limits to Growth*, 1972.

marked the entire twentieth century. It is not difficult to demonstrate that future research peaked in the years between 1964 and 1973 (between the publication of the first long range forecasting study at RAND, and Opec I), but doing so does not say much about origins or consequences. While the book situates future research in the Cold War, as a quintessential reflection on the Cold-War world, it shows that the genealogy of future research goes back at least to the interwar period, and that against all assumptions, future research is also very far from dead. The end of the high modernist era was not the end of futurology, but rather its beginning. The American historian Daniel Rodgers has most recently suggested that the oil crisis opened an age of fracture, as national economies became unpredictable and ungovernable, at least when using the same instruments and forms of power as previously.[17] The same era marks the peak of futurology. This is not in actual fact a paradox, but explainable through the way in which forms of prediction and anticipation would substitute, from the 1960s onwards, technologies of planning as the core political technologies of the present.[18] The artifacts of future research blossomed after 1973 as part of an extension, at least initially, of claims to control that now included the pretension to govern complexity, feedback mechanisms, and unintended consequences over both time and space. Over time, the future became, like so many other things, caught up in processes of management, expertise, and consultancy, and this changed what future research meant, but in no way did futurological reasoning come to an end. I want to insert futurology, therefore, in a very different context from that of Holscher and Hartog, and argue that it is not primarily an example of changing regimes of historicity but rather an example of attempts to influence and actively shape social temporalities after 1945. From this perspective futurism traces important continuities across the post-war era, and the call to a rationalization of the future links interwar technocracy to emergent forms of neoliberalism.[19]

REVISITING SOCIAL TIME

As cultural historians redefined Koselleck's notion of a horizon of expectations in the 1980s and 1990s as the idea of historicity, or *régime d'historicité*, they lost sight of some of the relevance in Koselleck's admittedly complex and often underdefined work. Koselleck, while emphasizing the future as a question of progress and modernity, saw the links between prediction and power. In an article in *Economy and Society* in 1981, the first translation into English of the essays of *Zeitschichten*, Koselleck wrote of prediction that it "produces the time within which and out of

[17] Rodgers, *Age of Fracture*, 256f.

[18] See Matthias Schmelzer, "The Crisis Before the Crisis: The Problems of Modern Society and the OECD 1968–1974" in *European Review of History* 2012, 19(6): 999–1020; Peter Wagner, *A Theory and History of the Social Sciences. Not All That is Solid Melts into Air* (London: Sage, 2001), 63–89; Ariane Leendertz, "Losing control. Complexity theory, public policy, and the exhaustion of solutionism", unpublished paper to Losing Social Control Conference, Max Planck Institute for the Study of Market Societies, June 1016.

[19] Fischer, *Technocracy and the Politics of Expertise.*

which it weaves." Scientific prediction, emanating from the modern social sciences, replaced religious conceptions of *telos* with new, secular understandings of the order of events. Through processes of rational foresight, futures were, once again, made probable and knowable, and forms of order restored, only this time in the hands of the absolute state. For Koselleck, then, the scientification of the future that followed from the great relocation was profoundly about replacing one form of power with another, and importantly, he describes this as a closing of a dangerously open future.[20]

These insights into the powered aspects of prediction as a secular political technology disappeared from the work of Koselleck's followers, in particular Lucien Holscher, whose 1997 book *Die Entdeckung der Zukunft* discussed the many kinds of futurology and futures research that, at the time of Koselleck's writing, were booming in Germany (and on which Koselleck never commented). But Hölscher reduced this complexity to one single claim of scientification of the future, rather than seeking to understand what the different nature of the many strands of futurology expressed. The result of this was that Hölscher underlined the idea of the future as the quintessential modernist category, but at the same time he undid Koselleck's attempt at an analysis of the future as a source of power also for a secular age.[21]

Cultural historians also backed away from some of Koselleck's key arguments. Koselleck's central contribution to historiography was the notion of historical time, as distinct from the natural process of time. Historical time, to Koselleck, was caught in a dialectics of sorts, a hermeneutic process between experience and expectation. This opened up, in Koselleck's original thinking, to a dynamic theory of time as a question of multiple social temporalities. Cultural historians, however, chose to retain the universalistic and metahistorical claims underlying *Begriffsgeschichte*.[22] From such a monolithic vantage point, the variety of forms of future making across the post-war period was not considered important. The idea of presentism also arguably stopped cultural historians from scrutinizing to any closer degree the futuristic content in the globalistic and universalizing discourses of the 1970s and 1980s. Cultural history took little interest in the magnificent return of grand schemas of world development after 1973, and they disregarded the role played by futurological techniques such as the scenario tool or global forecasts within these projects (they left this to anthropology and sociology). Michael Gordin and Gyan Prakash have argued that utopian projects ended neither with 1973 nor with 1989, and one needs only to look at the universalizing ambitions of the stewards of globalization such as the OECD or the World Bank in the 1990s and 2000s to realize that modernization theory is far from dead.[23] In my view,

[20] Koselleck, "The Planes of Historicity," 176–9.

[21] Lucien Hölscher, *Die Entdeckung der Zukunft* (Frankfurt: Fischer Verlag 1999).

[22] Reinhart Koselleck, *Zeitschichten: Studien zur Historik* (Frankfurt: Suhrkamp, 2000); Helge Jordheim, "Against periodisation. Koselleck's theory of multiple temporalities", in *History and Theory*, 51, May: 151–171; Alexandre Escudier, "Temporalisation et modernité politique: penser avec Reinhart Koselleck." *Annales*, 2009, (6): 1269–301.

[23] Michael Gordin, Helen Tilley, and Gyan Prakash, "Introduction. Utopia and Dystopia beyond Space and Time," in Gordin, Tilley, and Prakash, eds, *Utopia, Dystopia. Conditions of Historical*

therefore, the idea of presentism is a false lead, because it takes us away from understanding the way that the future after 1945 became a space for conflicts over global time.[24] The remainder of this chapter proposes that if we want to understand the future as a field of struggle, we need to move from the cultural history perspectives to a much more situated perspective borrowing from intellectual history, the history of science, environmental and social history as well as anthropology and sociology, and investigate the future as a constitutive category and repertoire of world making. The first step in this process is to consider the future as a global category.

THE FUTURE AS GLOBAL CATEGORY

Let us begin first with what a history that takes the future as a global category is not. Future history made a comeback, perhaps with limited success, in David Armitage's and Jo Guldi's *The History Manifesto*. Armitage and Guldi argued that historians need to develop a new history of the future, an "annalistics" devoted to long time.[25] Annalistics, in their account, is a new global history, based on big data and focused on investigating the whole "deep time" of human and pre-human existence.[26] Despite important work in the history of science, Armitage and Guldi disregarded entirely that categories of time are categories of action and constituted in complex processes of interaction between science and politics (as demonstrated indeed by the contested time frames and concepts such as future generations in the context of climate change or financial crisis).[27] They never explored the complex meanings of the term "long term," which they borrowed from the French historian Fernand Braudel's article on la *longue durée*. Braudel argued that historians needed to understand the long-term structures of capitalist society and the multiple social temporalities of history. There were real historical links between Braudel's *longue durée* and the rise of futurology as discussed in this book. Braudel's interest in the *longue durée* was a historiographic reflection of the interest in conjectures and

Possibility (Princeton: Princeton University Press, 2010) 1–21; Ravi Abdelal, *Capital Rules. The Construction of Global Finance* (Cambridge, MA: Harvard University Press, 2007).

[24] Compare Sebastian Conrad, "What Time is Japan? Problems of Comparative (Intercultural) Historiography," in *History and Theory*, 1999, 38(1), 67–83; Vanessa Ogle, *The Global Transformation of Time: 1870–1950* (Cambridge MA: Harvard University Press, 2015).

[25] Joe Guldi and David Armitage, *The History Manifesto* (Cambridge MA: Harvard University Press, 2014).

[26] Armitage and Guldi, *The History Manifesto*, 51, 63; David Armitage and Joe Guldi, "The Return of the Longue Duree. An Anglosaxon Perspective," in *Annales*, 2015, 70 (2), in which futurology stands as an example of "dirty longue duree" and of the evacuation of long time from the field of serious history; David Armitage and Joe Guldi, "For an Ambitious History': A Reply to Our Critics", *Annales*, 2015, 70 (2): 293–303, David Armitage, "What's the Big Idea? Intellectual History and the Longue Durée" in *History of European Ideas*, 2012, 38 (4): 493–507.

[27] See Jean Baptiste Fressoz, *L'apocalypse joyeuse* (Paris: Seuil, 2013); Amy Dahan Dalmedico et al. *Les modeles du futur* (Paris: La Decouverte, 2006); Henrich Hartmann and Jacob Vogel, eds, *Zukunftswissen. Prognosen in Wirtschaft, Politik und Gesellschaft seit 1900* (Frankfurt: Campus Verlag, 2011).

business cycles in economics.[28] The *longue durée* was Braudel's encouragement to historians to develop a metadiscipline or synthetic history by which such representations of time in the social sciences would be complemented by an understanding of the historical process. It was not a big epistemological step, in the 1950s, to apply the idea of the *longue durée* to coming, instead of past, time. Indeed, Braudel entrusted his friend Gaston Berger with this intellectual project in the ongoing construction of the so called *Sixième Section* of the French Maison des Sciences de l'Homme (see Chapter 4). It is important that the first response to Braudel's 1956 article in the pages of *Annales* came from the American economist and modernization theorist par excellence, Walt Rostow. Possibly Braudel himself was not familiar with the contemporaneous experimentations with the long term at RAND, but Walt Rostow certainly was. In his reaction to Braudel's article, Rostow urged Braudel to develop a theory of the future that took into account not only the long-term cycles of price movements but also an understanding of the mechanisms which shaped the images of the future that guided political leaders. If this mechanism could be identified, then the process by which countries of the communist and developing world chose certain social and economic models could be understood and influenced.[29] In other words, the long term was not an innocent notion of the future but a geopolitical category of action. Braudel, who thought that social temporalities were complex and plural, did not take this idea on. It was not his concern to influence decision making by producing desirable images of the future. Braudel was never part of the group of French prospectivistes who took these American cues to heart; he left this first to Berger and then to the philosopher Bertrand de Jouvenel (see Chapter 4).

The *Annales* school had enormous influence on the new economic and social history of the 1960s and 1970s, but fell out of historical grace in the subsequent decades. Recently historians have, like Armitage and Guldi, lamented the cultural turn as the beginning of a crisis for the history discipline and the sign of an historical profession turning inwards and losing sight of the world beyond discourse, ideas, and meaning.[30] But the cultural turn was an historiographical attempt to contribute to core processes of soul searching that affected Western societies, afflicted with multiple forms of crises since the 1970s. In the same way that important elements of critical theory were produced by the social sciences in these decades, the cultural turn contributed to a crucial introspection of the historical discipline and to the systematic investigation of a set of metaclaims embedded in Western historiography. In particular, it contributed to dethroning the notion of modernity that had underpinned so much of the writings of conceptual history, and the kind of universalizing claims that arguably still inform Armitage's global history. It is important to

[28] Fernand Braudel, "Histoire et sciences sociales: La longue duree," *Annales*, 1958, 4: 725–53; Giuiliana Gemelli, *Fernand Braudel* (Paris: Odile Jacob, 1995).

[29] Walt Rostow, "Histoire et sciences sociales, la longue duree," in *Annales* 1959, 4: 710–18.

[30] See Darrin McMahon and Samuel Moyn, "Introduction: Interim Intellectual History", in *Rethinking European Intellectual History* (Oxford: Oxford University Press, 2014), 3–13; Isobel Gilcher-Holtey and Willibald Steinmetz, *Writing Political History Today* (Frankfurt: Campus Verlag, 2013).

retain these insights if we return to the future as a historical category in Koselleck's sense, a problem of the ordering of multiple temporalities.

The conceptual history perspective on the future as a site of nostalgia and loss was not only a gloomy one, but also ended up reiterating the idea that the European nation state was the carrier of the great visions of modernity. In later essays, both Hartog and Hölscher have argued that the future ended with the great European projects of modernity, and that it lost its meaning with the end of colonization and the subsequent demise of European empire.[31] This idea that somehow beyond the nation state and after colonialism there could be no more future needs of course to be challenged. The future is not a universal element of a given history. Rather, the idea of the future is an element of construction in post-war history, a category of competing universalizing ambitions and of attempts to constitute specific versions of modernity. As proposed by postcolonial scholars such as Deepesh Chakraborty or Arjun Appadurai, the future is directly wound up with geopolitical notions of world and world order.[32] It stands in close relationship to notions such as progress, development, or globalization.[33] As such, the future is a product of the historical contingencies and power structures of the present that make certain conjectures possible and others not in distinct historical universes.[34] Perhaps one of the reasons why cultural historians lost sight of the future was precisely that as an object of historical study the future is a challenge for a framework of historical interrogation set by purely ideational perspectives, by the national space, and by a chronology defined by notions of Western modernity. The post-war concept of the future is profoundly marked by material processes of scientific circulation.[35] It is also directly connected, after 1945, with emerging notions of globality and interdependence; with notions of world, planet, and humanity.[36] It is of the essence

[31] Francois Hartog, "The Modern Regime of Historicity in the Face of Two World Wars" in B. Bevernage and Chris Lorenz, eds, *Breaking up Time: Negotiating the Borders Between Present, Past and Future* (Amsterdam: Vandenhoeck and Ruprect, 2013), 124–33; Lucien Hölscher, "Mysteries of Historical Order: Ruptures, Simultaneity and the Relationship of the Past, the Present," in B. Bevernage and Chris Lorenz, eds, *Breaking up Time: Negotiating the Borders Between Present, Past and Future* (Amsterdam: Vandenhoeck and Ruprect, 2013), 134–52.

[32] Deepesh Chakraborty, *Provincialising Europe. Post-colonial Thought and Historical Difference* (Princeton: Princeton University Press, 2004).

[33] Appadurai refers to this as the "future as cultural fact," Arjun Appadurai, *The Future as Cultural Fact* (London: Verso, 2013) 286, 287, 299. See also Johannes Fabian, *Time and the Other: How Anthropology Makes its Object* (New York: Columbia University Press, 2014 (1983)).

[34] Gordin et al., *Conditions of Possibility*.

[35] See the social history of time: Ogle, *Global Time*; Peter Galison (2004). *Einstein's Clocks and Poincaré's Maps: Empires of Time* (New York: WW Norton & Company, 2004); Daniel Rosenberg and Anthony Grafton, *Cartographies of Time: A History of the Timeline* (Princeton: Princeton Architectural Press, 2013).

[36] Sylvest and Van Munster, *Politics of Globality*; Akira Iriye, *Cultural Internationalism and World Order* (Baltimore: John Hopkins Press, 1997); Matthew Evangelista, *Unarmed Forces: The Transnational Movement to End the Cold War* (Ithaca, Cornell University Press, 2002); Bruce Mazlish, *The New Global History* (New York: Routledge, 2006); Samuel Moyn and Andrew Sartori, eds, *Global Intellectual History* (New York: Columbia University Press, 2013); Niall Ferguson, Charles Maier, Eres Manela, and Daniel J. Sargent, eds, *The Shock of the Global: The 1970s in Perspective* (Cambridge MA: Harvard University Press, 2011); Duncan Bell, "Writing the World: Disciplinary History and Beyond," in *International Affairs*, 2009, 85(1): 3–22; Jens Bartelson, "The Social Construction of Globality," in *International Political Sociology*, 2010, 4(3): 219–35.

therefore to understand the future as, in Sebastian Conrad's term, a project of world making.[37]

As argued in the introduction, forms of prediction played a key role in not only constructing visions of the future of world order, but also in designing technologies and forms of knowledge that could shape or change such world order. Future research gave rise to specific spaces that were key sites for the production of globality, for instance the UNESCO or the International Institute for Applied Systems Analysis.[38] In such spaces, predictive technologies served what historians of science would call a performative role as scenarios, models, and forecasts producing not only visions of world interdependence but also core arguments about how to manage problems of world order. In this capacity, prediction was a form of world making. Environmental historians have shown how ideas of the planet were constituted by assemblages of planetary data in meteorology and climatology from the late nineteenth century on.[39] In the post-war period, prediction plays a key role in establishing, in fields such as political science or international relations, the idea not of a planet with biophysical boundaries, but of a world as a social and political system (see Chapters 4 and 7). This system was understood as being made up of complex and antagonistic relationships, and caught in fragile forms of balance.[40] Importantly, this world system needed new forms of knowledge on a meta or systems level. Similar to the ecologists discussed by Warde and Sorlin, the futurists from the 1950s on began constituting a form of world expertise built on the capacity to depict complex relationships between man and nature, values and technologies, nation states, and global order.[41]

The statement that prediction was a source of globality relies on a causality or historical sequence that is clearly traceable in the development of predictive technologies after 1945. Forms of prediction began in the interwar period in many different fields, but within the national space. With the onset of the Cold War, prediction became a core technology with which to think bipolarity and the balance between the systems. Such depictions, however, ended up producing representations of commonalities between the two systems, of shared issues and common problems for the two systems, and eventually, for the world. Egle Rindzeviciute

[37] Sebastian Conrad, *What is Global History?* (Princeton: Princeton University Press, 2016), 7. I want to retain a distinction between transnational history, which explores connections and spaces of transnational activity and circulation, and which is still quite dominated by Western historians who rely on predominantly English speaking archives and fall back on chronological and spatial categories rooted in American and European history, and global history as represented by non-European histories, chronologies and materials. The world history proposed here is not representative of such global future histories, it is rather the history of the universalizing ambitions embodied in prediction and a transnational history of the spaces of future research.

[38] See Sibylle Duhautois, "Etudes sur le futur et conscience globale," PhD. diss., Centre d'histoire, Sciences Po, 2017; and Rindzeviciute, *Power of System*.

[39] Sverker Sorlin and Paul Warde, *Nature's End* (Princeton: Princeton University Press, 2012); Craig Miller and Paul Edwards, *Changing the Atmosphere: Expert Knowledge and Environmental Governance* (Cambridge MA: MIT Press, 2001); Paul Edwards, *A Vast Machine: Computer Models, Climate Data, and the Politics of Global Warming* (Cambridge MA: MIT Press, 2010).

[40] T. Robertson, "Total War and the Total Environment: Fairfield Osborn, William Vogt and the Birth of Global Ecology," in *Environmental History* 2012, 17: 336–64.

[41] Andersson and Duhautois, "Futures of Mankind."

has shown how prediction in transnational spaces produced by the Cold War, in her case the IIASA, ended up projecting future issues that transcended the bipolar divide and necessitated understandings of common and global challenges that also permitted new forms of collaboration. Prediction thus shifted from describing antagonistic power relations to producing visions of world interconnectedness in a systemic whole.[42] There were several attempts at using the future as a bridge across bipolarity, see Chapters 7 and 8. Sibylle Duhautois has demonstrated that post-war projections of the future were directly linked to the projection of human problems at the world level. Systems analysis allowed for depicting problems—armaments, development, environment—as shared world problems confronting humanity as a whole.[43] Prediction witnessed, in the post-war decades, a snowballing effect in sophistication. This process can be traced in a succession of graphs and models, from an immediate post-war concern with a limited number of variables and correlations generally concerning the national level or the relationship between national currencies or trade relationships in a world economy dominated by two systems, to the development of world models and ensuing depictions of global issues such as population, environment, and hunger that could be given visibility only through forms of multivariable and computer assisted systems analysis.[44] The Futures boardgame, seen on the cover of the book and displayed in Figure 2.1, is another example of predictive artifacts that allowed for the visualization and experimentation of complex global issues.

The category of the future thus grew remarkably from 1945 to the peak of modeling in the mid 1970s. This process, if studied through the workings of simulations and forecasts, is a fascinating attempt at capturing both forms of world chaos and ambitions of control over a world of ever growing complexity, as each variable that forecasters tried to rein in seemed to produce an additional set of correlations. By the early 1970s, the future of, what was by then referred to as, "advanced industrial societies" was modeled as a question of complicated interactions between technology and human value change, social trends, and world relationships including both natural resources, trade, and interdependence with the developing world.

The predicted world was by the 1970s a tremendously complex place, producing vertiginous problems of steering and management. This leads us to a second aspect of future research as a form of world making, having to do with the role of prediction as not only constituting a global category of the future, but as a political technology for the world in Foucault's sense.[45] A core argument of this book is that future research emerged as part of a reflection on the dangerously open nature of the future, and that modern prediction was a technological reflection on how a potentially infinite plurality of good and bad futures could be managed. From this

[42] Egle Rindzeviciute, "Toward a Joint Future beyond the Iron Curtain: East–West Politics of Global Modelling," in Jenny Andersson and Egle Rindzeviciute, eds, *The Struggle for the Long Term in Transnational Science and Politics: Forging the Future* (London and New York: Routledge, 2015), 115–43; Egle Rindzeviciute, "Purification and Hybridisation of Soviet Cybernetics: The Politics of Scientific Governance in an Authoritarian Regime," in *Archiv für Sozialgeschichte*, 2010, 50: 289–309.

[43] Duhautois, "Etudes sur le futur et conscience globale."

[44] Mahrane, Y., Fenzi, M., Pessis, C., Vieille Blanchard, E., Korczak, A., and Bonneuil, C., "De la nature à la biosphère: la construction de l'environnement comme problème politique mondial," 1945–1972, in *Vingtième siècle-Revue d'histoire*, 2012, (113): 127–141.

[45] Burchell et al., *The Foucault Effect.*

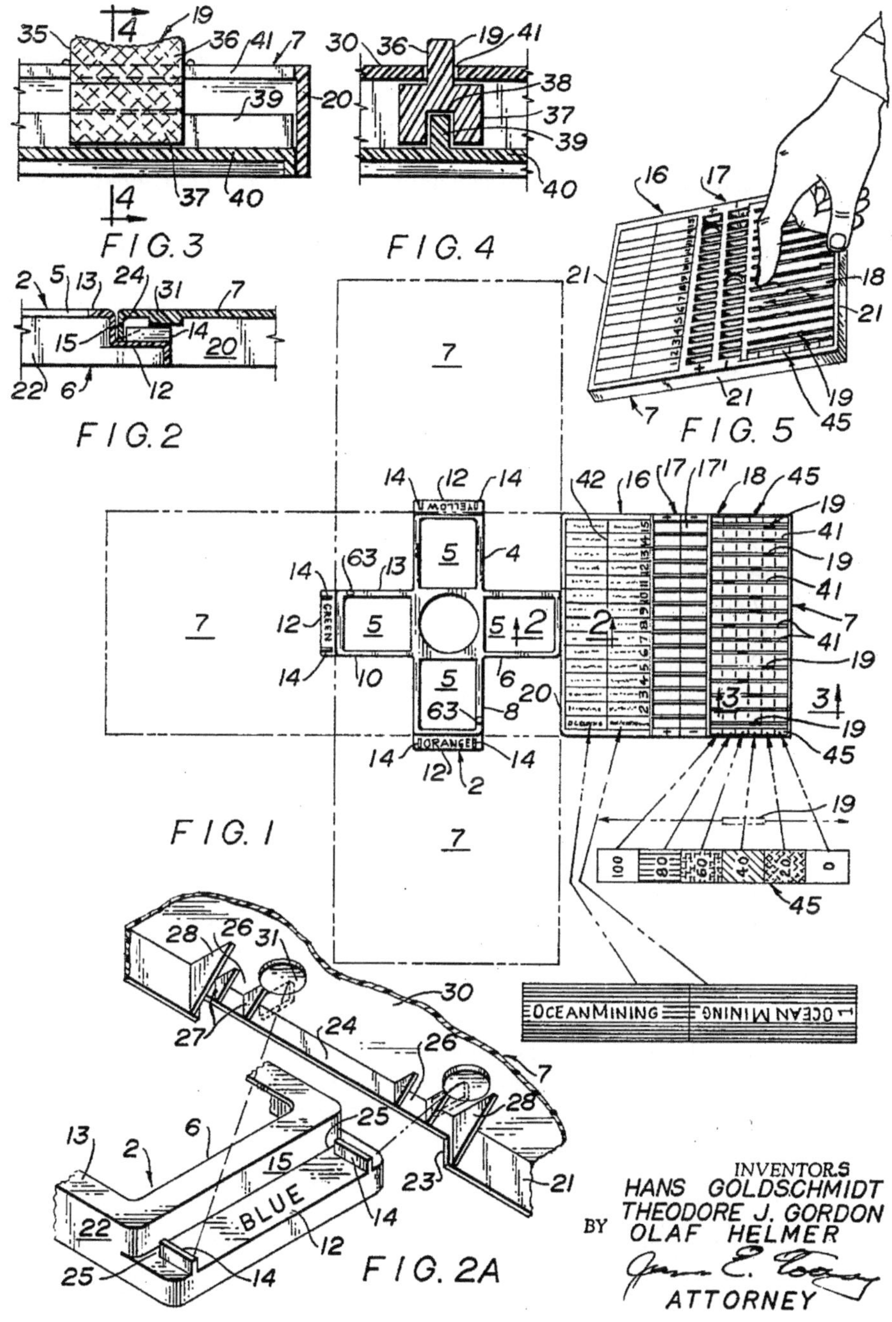

Figure 2.1. Apparatus for Playing a Game Involving Forecasting of Future Events, 1969.

The Future Board Game was patented by Olaf Helmer, Theodore Gordon, and Hans Goldscmidt in 1969. The game comprised a set of event cards, a card receiving and orienting device, and game boards indicating a series of different future events, a percentage of proability scale, and a marker for each event that could be moved along the probability scale. The positions of the markers were determined by rolling a dice with one blank face and other faces indicating different probability values. Points won by correct forecasting were noted on a score sheet for each player, and play money could be used to invest in events and thus influence the position of the markers (US Patent Office, 3473802, October 21, 1969).

perspective, the core problem of the future for the post-war era was not a sudden turn from progress to crisis, but rather the problem of knowing whether the world had one or many different futures, whether futures could be narrowed down to a range of identifiable outcomes in a grand theory of modernization, and whether the world future was in fact a potentially limitless array of social horizons and open ended forms of change. In the post-war decades, both liberal and authoritarian regimes invested heavily in forms of forecasting and prediction as ways of monitoring the social trends of industrial and post-industrial society. The Cold War transposed this problem of the social "trends" of mass society to the level of world, and future research became a quintessential reflection on modernization and its possible outcomes.

IMAGINING A POST-COLD WAR WORLD

The variety of future research can only really be understood if we see it as a struggle for the temporalities of the Cold and post-Cold War world, and as a both scientist and utopian attempt to shape and reshape world order.[46] A core argument set out in the coming pages is that future research embodied both key attempts at control of the Cold War world, and important attempts at dissent and resistance. The book makes the argument therefore that future research was not merely a product of the Cold War era, but also a result of the dream of escaping the very same Cold War. Certain strands of future research emerged in this context as metaphorical bridges or "third ways" out of bipolarity, by opening up alternative world temporalities and unimagined horizons. Future research fits therefore with how recent scholarship has begun understanding the Cold War less as an East–West military conflict, and more as a global struggle over processes of world development.[47] Both liberalism and Marxism were aggressive and imperialist theories of time, imposing certain visions of the future but also entrenching these visions into planning systems and technologies in their respective spheres of influence. Both liberalism and Marxism gave birth to planning technologies and predictive artifacts that ventured far into the territories and bodies of the global South.[48]

Futurology developed, as I argue in Chapters 4, 5, and 6, as a liberal mirror image of the Marxist theory of history, as a tool of persuasion meant to encapsulate

[46] See Or Rosenboim *The Emergence of Globalism. Visions of World Order in Britain and the United States, 1939–1950,* (Princeton: Princeton University Press, 2017), 5–13.

[47] Arne Odd Westad, *The Global Cold War: Third World Interventions and the Making of Our Times* (Cambridge MA: Harvard University Press, 2005); David Engerman and Corinna Unger, "Introduction: Towards a Global History of Modernization", in *Diplomatic History*, 2009, 33(3), 375–85; Corinna Unger, "Histories of Development and Modernization: Findings, Reflections, Future Research," *H-Soz-u-Kult*, 2010, 9; Corinna Ungar, "Towards global equilibrium: American foundations and Indian modernization, 1950s to 1970s", in *Journal of Global History*, 2011, 6(1): 121–42.

[48] Westad, *The Global Cold War*; David Engerman, Nils Gilman, Mark Haefele, and Michael Latham, *Staging Growth. Modernisation, Development and the Global Cold War* (Amherst and Boston, 2003). Matthew Connelly, *Fatal Misconception. The Attempt to Control World Population* (Cambridge MA: Harvard University Press, 2009).

particular notions of a liberal future, but also as a set of concrete technologies with which to inscribe that future into concrete forms of expertise and social knowledge. The decolonization process shook assumptions not only of a stable bipolar system, but also of a foreseeable modernization process on the global level. As such it introduced the idea that world temporalities were complex, and that there could be other sources of the future than Western social science or Marxist five-year plans. Attempts to influence planning systems and visions of change in different parts of the world, on behalf of both blocs, also encountered resistance and protest. American modernization theory clashed, on the "ground," in countries such as India, Iran, or Japan, with indigenous visions of modernity, including nationalism, post-industrialism, and postcolonialism. Soviet exported plans for modernization met with pan Africanism and national versions of communism. From the late 1960s on, postcolonialism, nationalism, and traditionalism all enter into the future imagination.[49]

Here, my argument complicates the historiographical debate on so-called Cold War science. An emerging literature, partly in history and partly in other disciplines such as security studies, anthropology or sociology, has emphasized the Cold War origins of prediction and future research and sought to trace a line of continuity between particular forms of expertise produced by military concerns in the Cold War and later forms of neoliberalism and neoconservatism.[50] The term Cold War science denotes what historians have understood as a particular American approach to social science as an inherently rationalist and applied enterprise, and as the spread of such conceptions of social science from the American to the global context.[51] Several chapters in this book point out connections between future research and emergent forms of neoliberalism, but the history of future research also shows the many contradictions in Cold War science. Future research not only reiterated much earlier forms of social science thinking, but also played out important forms of dissent against Cold War world order. This came from the fact that prediction was a far more heterogeneous field than has been accounted for by primarily American historians, and prediction, as argued in the Introduction, did

[49] Westad, *The Global Cold War*, 73f; Kevin Baker, "Virtually Nigeria," in Andersson and Rindzeviciute 2015; Eden Medina, *Cybernetic Revolutionaries: Technology and Politics in Allende's Chile* (Cambridge MA: MIT Press, 2011); Raphael Popp, "An Application of Modernisation Theory During the Cold War. The Case of Pahlavi Iran," in *The International History Review*, 2008, 30 (1): 76–98.

[50] Stephen Collier, and Andrew Lakoff, "Distributed Preparedness: The Spatial Logic of Domestic Security in the United States," in *Environment and Planning D: Society and Space*, 2008, 26(1), 7–28; Claudia Aradau and Rens van Munster, *Politics of Catastrophe. Geneaologies of the Unknown* (New York: Routledge, 2011).

[51] The notion of Cold War science is most clearly traced in Solovey et al., *Cold War Social Science, Knowledge Production, Liberal Democracy and Human Nature* (London and New York: Palgrave, 2012). For important critiques, see David Engerman, "American Knowledge and Global Power," in *Diplomatic History*, 2007, 31: 4; David Engerman, "Social Science in the Cold War," in *Isis*, 2010, (2): 393–400; Joel Isaac, "The Human Sciences in Cold War America," in *Historical Journal*, 2007, 50 (3): 725–46; Paul Erickson, Jenifer Klein, Lauren Daston, Rebecca Lemov, T. Sturm, and Michael Gordin, *How Reason Almost Lost its Mind: The Strange Career of Cold War Rationality* (Chicago: University of Chicago Press, 2013); Jenny Andersson, "Midwives of the Future. Futurism, Futures Studies and the Shaping of the Global Imagination," in Jenny Andersson and Egle Rindzeviciute, eds, *The Struggle for the Long Term in Transnational Science and Politics, Forging the Future* (Abingdon: Routledge, 2015), 16–38.

not only encompass scientist and rationalist notions of the future, but also ideas of the future as a fundamental moral category and as a problem of human intuition and imagination. This emphasis on the profound heterogeneity of prediction is also what finally helps us to distinguish between the terms futurology, future research, or futures studies as used in the chapters of this book, as these were based on profoundly different assumptions of what constituted human rationality.[52] Chapters 5 and 6 returns to the question of Cold War science.

Futurology, as distinct from futurism or futures studies, was an avatar of Cold War science. It was a child of the peculiar alliance created by the Cold War between applied social science and military operations research in fields such as behaviorism, international relations, psychology, and political science. As such it was an expression of the rise to prominence in the 1950s and early 1960s of mechanistic notions of social development and modernization theory, and the centrality of claims to prediction and foreseeable laws of social development and human behavior of these intellectual projects. Meanwhile, futurology was also the product of the insecurities produced by modernization theory, and has to be understood in the context of its crisis from the 1960s onwards.[53] If the future did not conform to assumptions of an ordered and essentially liberal process of modernization, then it required new techniques of control. Moreover, the origins of futurology and future research were far from strictly American. Chapter 4 shows that a French version of technocratic thinking, *prospective,* was a key influence on American futurology. *Prospective*, in turn, grew out of an interwar eugenicist and fascist concern with the future of race and population, carried over after the Second World War into modern social science.

What is discussed in Chapter 8 as futures studies was a counter project to futurology, a form of counter expertise based on the rejection of key forms of Cold War science. Futures studies drew on a much earlier strand of futurism in the immediate post-war period that emphasized the imagination and the need to conjure peaceful and loving images of the future (Chapter 3). By the mid 1960s, futurism gave rise to specific forms of action and mobilization that illustrate what historians such as Akira Iriye and Pierre Yves Saunier have understood as emergent forms of global consciousness and world militancy from the 1960s onwards. Conrad reminds us that forms of globality and global consciousness have existed at different points in time, and accompany both medieval cosmologies and the modern history of empire. Iriye and Saunier pinpoint however the specific context of forms of world consciousness in relation to new patterns of transnational agency and mobilization from the 1960s onwards.[54] Chapter 9 of this book discusses the role of new technologies of global activism such as the world conference, the stenographed newsletter, and email discussion lists.

[52] Gordin et al. *When Reason Almost Lost Its Mind.*

[53] See Joel Isaac, and Duncan Bell, *Uncertain Empire. American History and the Idea of the Cold War* (Oxford, Oxford University Press, 2012).

[54] Akira Iriye, *Global Community: The Role of International Organizations in the Making of the Contemporary World* (Berkeley: University of California Press, 2002).

As such, futures studies contained a certain radical potential for the Cold War era in a utopian projection of a united world.[55] Both futurology and futures studies remained on the margins of the social sciences. In this capacity of marginality, they performed what I suggest is an important reflection on the role and limits of social science in the world, the limits of knowability and influence discussed in the beginning of this chapter. Both futurology and futures studies were also products of complicated and sometimes unlikely forms of transnational circulation of social scientists, planners and technocrats, journalists and activists. It is precisely in this capacity that they complicate the picture of Cold War science with its hard core rationality assumptions. Cold War science was not the closed world enterprise that it has been portrayed. In some ways it was much more open than contemporary social science, and in order to understand it we need to take it out of reified closed worlds of modeling and experts and insert it into a much wider intellectual and political history of the post-war era.[56]

[55] Compare Samuel Moyn, *The Last Utopia: Human Rights in History* (Cambridge MA: Harvard University Press, 2010).

[56] Paul Edwards, *The Closed World: Computers and the Politics of Discourse in Cold War America* (Cambridge MA: MIT Press, 1997).

3

The Future as Moral Imperative. Foundations of Futurism

If the story of utopia throws any light upon the story of Mankind it is this: our utopias have been pitifully weak and inadequate...[1]

THE END

Hannah Arendt was one of many scholars and intellectuals in the immediate post-war period for whom the future had become a pressing concern. The very notion of the human condition, which appeared not only in Arendt's works but in a range of other titles of the post-war years, included the idea that humanity had lost its connection to the future, and that this loss had transformed the conditions for human existence.[2] The idea of pervasive future crisis was widely shared among intellectuals who were, like Arendt, troubled by the destructive uses of science and technology. In their writings, they—coming from fields as different as political philosophy, international relations, architecture, history, and journalism—began to draw up the philosophical interpretation of the nuclear age, with arguments that would dominate post-war discussions and later echo from the Frankfurt school.[3] A common element to these thinkers, ranging in this chapter from Arendt and her lifelong friend, the philosopher Hans Jonas, and the architect and urban theorist Lewis Mumford, to the German Marxist sociologist Ossip Flechtheim and the journalist Robert Jungk, was the idea of the lost future. According to their arguments, humanity existed in a void. This void was a gulf created by two opposed forces: on the one hand, the extension of the reach of instrumentalist human rationality, and on the other, the diminishing moral capacities of human beings to control their actions over time.

In 1927, Martin Heidegger had argued that *being* meant to be situated in time, and that the groundedness that came from *being-in-time* was what being human

[1] Lewis Mumford, *The Story of Utopias* (London: Boni and Liveright, 1922), 25.

[2] Hannah Arendt, *The Human Condition* (Chicago: The University of Chicago Press, 1958); Lewis Mumford, *The Condition of Man* (London, Harcourt Brace, 1944); Karl Jaspers, *The Future of Mankind* (Chicago, The University of Chicago Press, 1961); Gunther Anders, *Die Antiquiertheit des Menschen* (Munchen: CH Beck, 1956); Mark Greif, *The Age of the Crisis of Man. Thought and Fiction in America, 1933–1973* (Princeton, NJ: Princeton, 2015).

[3] See Casper Sylvest and Rens van Munster, *Nuclear Realism. Global Political Thought during the Thermo-Nuclear Revolution* (Abingdon: Routledge, 2016).

was all about.[4] If this sense of being-in-time collapsed because of such opposed forces in the human collective psyche, then what did it mean to be human? In a now well known and partly mythologized story, Heidegger's futurism ended up in a Nazi salute, while his former master, the founder of continental philosophy's grand project of phenomenology, Edmond Husserl, was forced to leave the University of Heidelberg in 1933. These events changed the course of history, and certainly, the understanding of what history was. To Husserl, to be human held a transcendental component, and Husserl's idea of being included a notion of future consciousness that was both romantic and idealistic. But in Heideggerian philosophy, the notion of being-in-time became aggressively futuristic, as human beings made the future through their mastering of time. The marriage between Heidegger's political thought and national socialism was a shock to his disciples, and it put the notion of being into acute crisis. Arendt and Jonas were the former disciples of Heidegger, and exiles, therefore, also from the philosophical project of phenomenology—literally thrown out of *being*.[5]

To Heidegger, science, technology, and progress were all forces for *being*. But to the thinkers of concern in this chapter, human rationality had gone astray, and the Atomic bomb itself was the product of a technological genie let out of the bottle. What was left was a fundamentally schizophrenic condition. The "infernal machine," as Lewis Mumford put it, was the very metaphor for this situation. The infernal machine undid the foundations for being, and it transformed forever what it meant to be human.[6]

For the thinkers in focus in this chapter, the post-war world was not a new world of peace. It was rather a world in which wartime had become the new normal. 1945 was not a break for them, not a "zero hour"—on the contrary.[7] In their understanding, 1945 had ushered in forces of destruction in a vicious cycle of perpetual threats to human survival. The paradox of this situation was that threats came from the failings of human rationality, resulting in what many scholars referred to as the promise of organized suicide or planetary genocide.[8]

Recent Cold War scholarship has seen the distinction between applied forms of rationality and situated reason as the fundamental dividing line of the Cold War era.[9] This chapter proposes that the notion of the future, as it appears between 1945 and 1955, was precisely an attempt to overcome this divide and thereby cure the schizophrenia in the human condition. The future appears in the writings cited

[4] Heidegger, *Sein und Zeit*; Richard Wolin, *The Politics of Being. The Political Thought of Martin Heidegger* (New York: Columbia University Press, 1982).

[5] Richard Wolin, *Heidegger's Children. Hannah Arendt, Hans Jonas, Hans Kollwitz, Herbert Marcuse* (Princeton: Princeton University Press, 2007); Richard Wolin, *The Frankfurt School Revisited* (Routledge: New York, 2006). Ossip Flechtheim, the father of the notion of futurology, had had his doctoral dissertation rejected by Carl Schmitt in Heidelberg.

[6] Lewis Mumford, *Values for Survival*, 3. Thomas Hughes and Agatha Hughes, *Lewis Mumford, Public Intellectual* (Oxford: Oxford University Press, 1990).

[7] Compare Hagen Schulz-Forberg, ed., *Zero Hours. Conceptual Insecurities and New Beginnings in the Interwar Period* (Brussels: Peter Lang, 2016).

[8] See Lewis Mumford, *Values for Survival* (Oxford, Abingdon Press, 1946).

[9] Ericson et al. *When Reason Almost Lost its Mind. The Strange Career of Cold War Rationality*, (Chicago: University of Chicago Press, 2013).

here in a highly paradoxical state. On the one hand, Apocalypse had moved from the sphere of heavenly threat to something that human beings could bring onto themselves; and their idea of the future would seem to epitomize, therefore, Koselleck's and Holscher's argument about the desacralization of the future. But on the other hand, if human beings held the keys to the impending destruction of the universe, the only possible hope of salvation was to change humanity itself, and somehow restore a sense of the future in human beings.[10] The future, to the thinkers discussed in the chapter, was therefore a kind of moral and political imperative, a new kind of utopia that was not in the domain of dreams and fantasies of a fulfilled humanity, but a matter of incredible urgency and responsibility for survival. Other scholars have argued that Arendt opened the door to the rejection of utopia that would come in the coming decades, as utopia became associated with totalitarian projects.[11] I want to argue however that the shift from utopia to "future" is crucial to understanding these decades. As an imperative, the future to these thinkers was a new domain of action, regulation, and necessary constraints on the human capacity to do evil, including a fundamental process of reform of Man. The utopia was the necessity of a new human engagement with the future. To Ernst Bloch's "I am. We are. Now we can start," Lewis Mumford replied "Man can, therefore he will, therefore we must."[12]

COSMIC POWERS

Many of the intellectuals and thinkers that figure in this chapter—Hannah Arendt, Gunther Anders, Hans Jonas, Robert Jungk, and Ossip Flechtheim—were refugees and exiles, denizens of European high culture and displaced scholars in the US. Arendt and Anders were, like Lewis Mumford, convinced of the necessity to reinvest liberalism with a sense of transcendental spirituality and humanity, but also to find new safeguards against the human capacity to act. That there were important links between these actors is not by chance but for situated reasons. In most cases they knew each other, they had studied together, they shared the experience of exile, and they also shared the intellectual spaces of exiles in New York and Chicago.[13] They also shared an interpretation of the post-war period as a continuation of the inherent genocidal tendencies of human civilization. The destruction of European Jewry marked, to them, not the end, but the beginning of a much larger process of human destruction that stemmed from the loss of a future image. There were both Christian and Jewish backdrops to this idea of a loss of

[10] Lewis Mumford, *Values for Survival.*

[11] Russell Jacoby, *Picture Imperfect* (New York: Columbia University Press, 2005).

[12] Mumford letter to Erich Fromm, March 15, 1955, Lewis Mumford Archives. Box 20, folder 1730.

[13] Axel Fair Schulz and Mario Kessler, eds, *German Scholars in Exile* (Plymouth: Lexington Books, 2011). Hartmut Leehman and James Sheehan, eds, *Interrupted Pasts. German Speaking Refugee Historians in the United States after 1933* (Cambridge: Cambridge University Press and German Historical Institute, 1991); Lewis A. Coser, *Refugee Scholars. Their Impact and Experiences* (New Haven: Yale University Press, 1984); Aaron Rabinbach, *In the Shadow of the Catastrophe. German Intellectuals between Apocalypse and Enlightenment* (Berkeley: California University Press, 2001).

Gestalt, outside of secular philosophy.[14] The Holocaust and the Atomic bomb also re-vested notions of good and evil with relevance. After 1945, it was no longer possible to start from the premise of human beings as the carriers of a hopeful or good future. The future posed therefore an altogether different problem of how to contain man's evil. A letter to Mumford from the Christian theologist and international relations theorist, Reinhold Niebuhr, reads "...evil is no longer in the realm of the metaphysical or the mysterious...evil (is) in human behaviour."[15]

Such conceptions that human behavior held the key to understanding good and evil were themselves an important change from previous decades. As we will see in other chapters, behavior became the new fascination of the social sciences and humanities from the early 1950s on. This fascination fell back on templates from the natural sciences and from modern biology, which after World War II began describing humanity as a species, prone to similar laws of autoregulation as other species.[16] This interest would culminate, some years later, in highly deterministic accounts of a human "system" governed by laws of behavior as were other organisms. But in the immediate post-war period, ideas of behavior were, as Or Rosenboim shows, also directly related to idealistic hopes that by transforming human behavior, a new world order could be found. Niebuhr and Mumford were both involved in the Chicago Committee for a New World Constitution, created at the University of Chicago in 1940. The *City of Man*—the title alluding to a man made version of Augustine's God's City—was a pamphlet written by the Committee, introducing the idea of a concrete "build[ing] Utopia" by designing a constitution for so called world government, including control over the Bomb.[17] The Committee was a gathering space for intellectuals believing, in 1945 and 1946, that a new world order required a new commitment to universal values of Mankind.[18]

As Rosenboim shows, the Chicago Committee came out of the feeling that the Bomb challenged the foundational notions of political order, including sovereignty and decision, and that the world had therefore entered a form of anarchy and chaos. She argues that the notion of world order was the product of this feeling, and it deserves to be added to this insight that not only the notion of world, but also the notion of humanity and human power, was at the core of these reflections. In the words of Lewis Mumford, human beings were like petulant children, "playing with sky rockets," failing to see that their firecrackers could destroy the universe. Science and technology had left their bounds, but the human capacity to grasp meaning had somehow fallen behind. A core element, in both Mumford's and Arendt's writings, was the notion of "cosmic powers," the idea that the splitting of the atom had inverted the hierarchy in the natural order of things. There had been

[14] Amin Engel, *Gershem Scholem* (Chicago: Chicago University Press, 2017). Letter, Martin Buber to Lewis Mumford, April 7, 1954, Lewis Mumford's archives, box 8, folder 646.

[15] Behavior research project 1947–1950, document dated December 17 1949, Lewis Mumford's archives, box 4, folder 359.

[16] Robertson, "Total War and the Total Environment."

[17] Herbert Agar et al., *The City of Man. A Declaration on World Democracy* (New York: Viking, 1941).

[18] Or Rosenboim, *The Emergence of Globalism. Visions of World Order in Britain and the United States* (Princeton: Princeton University Press, 2017), 168–209.

a distinction between universal laws and human action. But now there was nothing left in the world that human beings could not influence, and this, to them, rendered the world meaningless.

Hannah Arendt's deeply pessimistic observations of the powers set in motion by the "probe" set on the moon by the USSR in 1959 have somehow been forgotten by intellectual historians, who have preferred to see the exhilaration and optimistic futurism of space exploration.[19] But Arendt saw space travel as the beginning of a fundamental process of wilderness. As planet Earth became the site of destruction, human beings had started looking for other worlds. The exploration of space was not an optimistic search for a new frontier, but a desperate act, an escape from the real world in which human beings could not bare to face their destructive nature.[20] "Cosmic" was Arendt's qualification of a new human reach by which the power of human beings now superseded the powers of laws of the universe. Cosmic implied that human beings could tamper with both space and time, and in so doing, they could undo the physical boundaries of being and escape earth bound existence. Cosmic powers unmade history, because history was the manmade sequence of human events, taking place within the confines of the natural universe. Human beings could now transgress these boundaries.[21]

To Lewis Mumford, writing in 1946, the human condition was dictated by the invention of the super machine, the Bomb.[22] In the wake of this discovery, human beings had allowed the Bomb to establish its rule.

> We have now to devi[s]e, under pressure of the greatest crisis that Mankind has yet faced, the political and moral protective devices that will keep our knowledge not merely from ruining civilisation, but from causing life, in all its organised forms, to disappear from the planet... The question is no longer whether this or that nation can survive. The question is whether Mankind has enough imagination to mobilise, on behalf of peace and cooperation, forces men have hitherto conscripted only for war and destruction. Unless the crisis produces such a dynamic will, Man himself is lost.[23]

Values for Survival, written after Mumford's 1946 letter published in *The Saturday Review*, "Gentlemen you are mad," was prompted by the Atomic hearings in 1946. At these, atomic power was reinterpreted as acceptable and peaceful civil technology and nuclear weapons as the core of a new American defense policy. To Mumford this was the sign that American politics had not only imported the nuclear scientists, but also integrated core elements of national socialism into its polity.[24]

To both Arendt and Mumford, therefore, cosmic powers required a new source of authority, which had to be about the restoration of a sense of end goal. While

[19] See, however, Dennis Cosgrove, *Apollo's Eye, Apollo's eye: a cartographic genealogy of the earth in the western imagination* (Baltimore: John Hopkins University Press, 2001) and Duncan Bell, "Making and taking worlds," in Samuel Moyn, and Andrew Sartori, *Global Intellectual History* (New York: Columbia University Press, 2013), 254–279.

[20] Hannah Arendt, "The conquest of space and the stature of Man" in *Between Past and Future. Eight Exercises in Political Thought* (New York: Penguin classics, 1954).

[21] Arendt, *Between Past and Future*, 58.

[22] Lewis Mumford, *The Myth of the Machine. The Pentagon of Power* (New York: Harcourt Brace, 1970).

[23] Mumford, *Values for Survival*, 3.

[24] Sylvest and van Munster, *Nuclear Realism*, 42–61.

many other writers discussed in this chapter would arrive at the conclusion that saving the future required highly concrete binds on action—constitutions, legal principles, world government—Arendt and Mumford both turned to the future as a form of sacrality or transcendentalism that reestablished a sense of hierarchy in the universe. As all ends had been turned into means in a perfectly instrumentalized notion of progress in the post-war era, the world was a growing meaninglessness: "we can transcend the world, but we do so without sacrality..."[25] In Arendt's thinking, this loss of sacrality, the perfect confusion between ends and means, was the precondition for totalitarianism and the only way out of it was a reinvesting of the end, the future, with some sense of authority.

PREDICTION AS POWER OVER TIME

As the future was reinterpreted, in these writings, from a utopian dream to a problem of political action, the future could also become an imperative for action in a new way, in the meaning of forms of activism, engagement, and militancy. Arendt herself did not venture into futurism. Lewis Mumford, on the other hand, came to an idea of the future as a necessary new pedagogy and form of education of modern man. In 1955, Mumford participated in the Wennergren Center's conference, Man's New Role in Changing the Face of the Earth, and suggested a thematic session on the future.[26] This future had to break with other ways of instrumentalizing and colonizing the future. Both Arendt and Mumford understood the emergence of new forms of prediction after 1945 as part of a totalitarian form of colonization of future time. The idea of cosmic powers drew on observations of the rise to prominence of not only physics but also ballistic engineering, sciences that tampered not only with space, but also with time.[27] It was the turn, in "Christian men" like Nils Bohr, from the legacies of physics as an Enlightenment science to relativist quantum physics that had produced the power over the Atom, and that had also devised the forms of prediction that enabled the Bomb. Physics had been transformed from a science for the understanding of the laws of the universe into a science for the undoing of those laws, hence for the unmaking of the human world. For Mumford, ballistic science and its manifestation in long range weapons had conquered the human future by replacing it with predictability and calculation.[28] The long range as a technological category had thus entered into direct conflict with the moral

25 Arendt, *Between Past and Future*, 73.

26 Lewis Mumford Archives, box 82, folder 61030. Sylvest and van Munster, *Nuclear realism*, 122; Paul Warde and Sverker Sörlin, "Expertise for the Future. The emergence of environmental prediction, 1920–1980", in Jenny Andersson and Egle Rindzeviciute, eds., *The Struggle for the Long Term in Transnational Science and Politics* (Abingdon: Routledge, 2015), 38–63, 47.

27 Mumford refers to Bertrand Russell's 1924 essay on nuclear physics, "Icarus—or the Future of Science," published in the pocket book series *To-day and To-morrow*. It was a response to Haldane's 1923 essay "Daedalus—or Science and the Future," in the same series.

28 Arendt, *Between Past and Future*; Mumford, *The Condition of Man*, 89, 233; Lewis Mumford, *Man: A Programme for Survival* (Abingdon: Abbey Press, 1946); Hannah Arendt to Lewis Mumford, May 20, 1965, Lewis Mumford Archives, Box 3, folder 200.

category of the future. Long range weapons, said Mumford in *Values for Survival*, had insulated human beings from the morality of the future, because they separated the act of killing from the experience of the consequences of that act. Long range weapons had also allowed for time and space to become the realm of disaffected technicians and military aviators. Such separation was to Mumford the culmination of an historic separation between rationality and reason in modernity.[29] Mumford's 1934 book, *Technics and Civilization*, drew the contours of this separation out of time from human experience by describing the invention of the clock in the medieval monastery and of the perspective in renaissance paintings. So, began a rationalization of time which could really only culminate in the state of perfect predictability of the infernal machine. Both Mumford and his intellectual father, H.G. Wells, foresaw the arrival of such total machines.[30] The time world, said Mumford in *The Condition of Man*, was lost, and the predictable replaced God as the source of authority. The Atomic bomb, built on a myriad of complex equations of time and space, had become the master of time, and time was no longer history but a great chain of predictable sequences.[31]

To both Mumford and Arendt, prediction was totalitarian because it concentrated power. In its willingness to control all future outcomes, it annihilated the fundamental plurality of the future. But at the same time, totalitarianism had introduced a dangerous element of unpredictability into the world—because by undoing history, it turned the future into the terrifying sphere of the unknown.

> Mankind is faced, because of the increased scope of action and the loss of history, with unpredictability. Political terror—totalitarianism—was a huge effort in the predictability of human behavior but it fails because it can never be sure of its future. Human plurality is one of the fundamental conditions of human life, in so far as it rests on natality—the fact that the human world is constantly invaded by strangers, newcomers, whose actions and reactions cannot be foreseen by those that are going to leave in a short while. If therefore, by starting natural processes we have begun to act into nature, we have manifestly begun to carry our own unpredictability into that realm which we used to think of as governed by inexorable laws.[32]

As the popular movement against the Atomic bomb began in 1954, widely inspired by Norman Cousin's SANE-manifesto and the Pugwash-movement, the fear of cosmic powers spread into the public imagination. In 1954, Robert Jungk—soon to be icon of the West European peace movement—published a blockbuster book entitled *Tomorrow is Already Here*.[33] The book, published in German as *Die Zukunft hat Schon Begonnen* in 1952, was a description of the megacomputer at RAND, charged with the calculation of all future possibilities. Trusting a machine with the future could, to the deeply Christian Jungk, be nothing more than the ultimate display of hubris. The book was a description of an American cowboy civilization

29 Mumford, *Values for Survival*, 23.
30 See Warren Wagar, *HG Wells and the World State* (New Haven, CT: Yale University Press, 1969).
31 Mumford, *The Condition of Man*, 251.
32 Arendt, *Past and Future*, 61.
33 Jungk's *Brighter Than a Thousand Suns*, on the scientists that had produced the bomb, appeared in English in 1958.

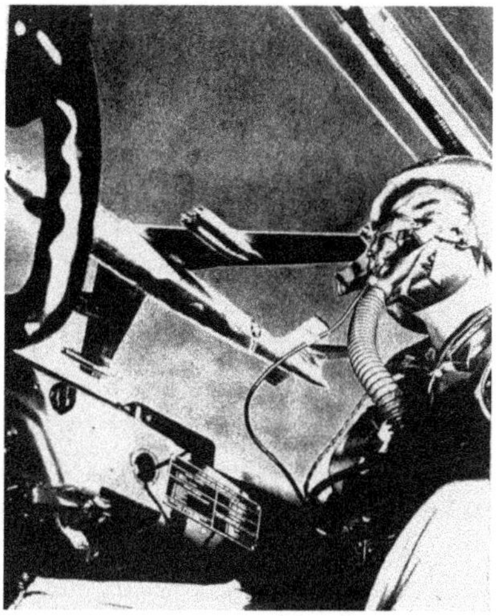

Figure 3.1. Tomorrow is Already Here.
"Stratospheric bomber plane seen from the cockpit of another plane in the platoon".
(Robert Jungk, *Tomorrow is Already Here* (New York: Simon and Schuster, 1954), 61).

that had now added the future to a long series of frontiers to be transgressed.[34] By colonizing future time, cowboys had undone the last territory of God. To Jungk, this hubris had a physical manifestation in the projection into the heavens of young airforce pilots, driven by centrifugal forces in rocket planes, and the book included a dramatic illustration of their contorted bodies (see Figure 3.1).

THE FUTURE IS US

It was Arendt's close friend, Hans Jonas, who in his much later (1979) *The Imperative of Responsibility* would most clearly set words on the gap between the human capacity to act out and the incapacity to control the effects of such action over time. Arendt and Hans Jonas had studied together in Heidelberg and their life long correspondence was marked by their need to understand where Heideggerian philosophy had gone wrong and how the notion of being might somehow be salvaged from its unholy alliance with Nazism.[35] *The Imperative of Responsibility* was Jonas' attempt to restore being through the notion of responsibility, which to Jonas meant the imperative for human beings to act consciously for the future. Jonas has somewhat unfairly been described as authoritarian, but his ideas of a legal bind

[34] Robert Jungk, *Tomorrow is Already Here* (New York: Simon and Schuster, 1954). The book was prefaced by Herbert Agar, editor of the *City of Man*.

[35] Hannah Arendt papers, Library of Congress, Washington (her correspondence with Jonas can be accessed online). Arendt and Jonas disagreed over her treatment of anti-Semitism and Jewish responsibility but they corresponded over long periods of time, see Christian Wiese, "Zionism, the Holocaust, and Judaism in a Secular World," in Tirosh-Samuelson and Wiese, eds, *Order from Disorder. The Legacy of Hans Jonas. Judaism and the Phenomenon of Life,* (Amsterdam: Brill, 2007) 159–93.

in the precautionary principle are another version of the ideas of world government that preoccupied Gunther Anders (Hannah Arendt's first husband) or John Herz (life long friend of Ossip Flechtheim).[36] For Jonas, it is Heidegger's principle "*l'homme est sa fin*" that is inherently authoritarian, and that explains the philosophers' descent into Nazism. To Jonas, the only way of being in the world is to take responsibility for existence. Man, to Jonas, is the only living being capable, through the capacities of his imagination, of imagining consequences and assuming responsibility for them. Futurology, says Jonas, is what can create this sense of responsibility by acting as a systematic form of imaginative foresight.[37]

As such, *The Imperative of Responsibility* was a break not only with Heidegger, but also with Ernst Bloch's three volume epos *The Principle of Hope*.[38] Bloch left Germany in 1938 and returned to German soil in the DDR in 1949. Bloch published *Dass Prinzip Hoffnung* in German in 1954 but the translation into English did not appear until the 1980s.[39] *The Principle of Hope* was firmly anchored in Hegel and Marx and argued that the dream of a perfect future state, in which alienation and class struggle had come to an end, was a precondition for the revolution. Utopia, to Bloch, was concrete, realizable, and both spiritual and scientific. Human beings were latent perfection, guides to the universe and masters of a dialectical process.[40] The Polish philosopher Leszek Kolakowski later saw Bloch's affinity with Stalinism as equivalent to Heidegger's affinity with Nazism, in the idea that "being is revealed only in acts oriented toward the future."[41]

Bloch's notion of utopia first emerged in the 1923 book, *The Spirit of Utopia,* the year after Lewis Mumford's 1922 book, *The Story of Utopia*. In fact the two books played out a central controversy in the notion of utopia, from Bloch's Marxist dialectics, to Mumford's romanticism and Gestalt-driven transcendentalism. For Bloch, utopia was scientific, and there figured in *The Principle of Hope* a somewhat mystical notion of a coming future technology of perfection.[42] For Mumford, utopia was an antimechanistic notion that was inherently about humanity itself, but humanity, in turn, was the real problem. Indeed, utopia could not begin with the notion "I am—we are—that is enough" (the opening line of *The Spirit of Utopia*) as both the "I" and the "We" were what to Mumford had to be completely transformed. *The Story of Utopias* laid the basis for Mumford's constant plea in later

[36] Casper Sylvest, "The Conditions and Consequences of Globality. John Herz' International Politics in the Atomic Age," in *Classics of International Relations: Essays in Criticism*, edited by Casper Sylvest and Peter Wilson, 89–98 (London: Routledge, 2013).

[37] Hans Jonas, *The Imperative of Responsibility. In Search of an Ethics for the Technological Age* (Chicago: The University of Chicago Press, 1985), 26–8.

[38] Arno Munster, *Principe esperance ou principe responsabilite*, (Paris: Le bord de l'eau, 2010).

[39] Mumford was the reviewer on Bloch's 1954 proposal to the English editor, letters from Bloch to Mumford with the original draft in 1954, Lewis Mumford Archives, Box 5, folder 458.

[40] Ernst Bloch, *Dass Prinzip Hoffnung* (Frankfurt: Suhrkamp Verlag, 1954), translated as *The Principle of Hope* (Cambridge MA: MIT Press, 1986). Ruth Levitas, "Educated Hope. Ernst Bloch on Abstract and Concrete Utopia," in *Utopia Studies* 1990, 1(02): 13–26.

[41] Leszek Kolakowski, *Main Currents of Marxism*, Volume 3, *The Breakdown* (Oxford: Clarendon Press, 1978), 420–1, 446.

[42] Ernst Bloch, *The Spirit of Utopia* (Palo Alto: Stanford University Press, 2000).

decades for a notion of the future as a human and organic construct.[43] *The Story of Utopias* began, "how the will-to-utopia causes men to live in two worlds, and how, therefore, we re-read the Story of Utopias—the other half of the Story of Mankind."[44] To Mumford, utopia was not a perfect society, but a new human subject, a united and collective humanity that he referred to as Mankind. To Mumford, there was a dialectics of sorts between the real world, which man had created, often in a destructive impulse, and the inner world, which was the world of images after which people pattern their behavior.[45] The inner world could serve two purposes to human beings: it could be an escape from intolerable conditions, or it could be a space of reconstruction, of "our release in the future." To Mumford, utopia could thus serve two opposite functions of either escapist castles in the air or reformist and rationalist utopias of reconstruction. In the latter, "we consult a surveyor, an architect and a mason and proceed to build a house which meets our essential needs."[46] In 1973, the little known essay "Human Futures," written for the first conference of the World Futures Studies Federation, reiterated this notion of utopia as the fulfilment of human physical and spiritual needs that had to begin with a new humanity, united in a world society or world federation.[47]

Lewis Mumford was a transcendental romanticist, profoundly inspired by Emerson, and a liberal who in 1940 campaigned against American isolationism. The use by the allies of the Atomic bomb in 1945 shocked him.[48] This shock came not foremost from the Atomic bomb over Hiroshima, but from the subsequent testing of an American H-bomb in Bikini Atoll in 1954, and the American decision to use long range weapons as the foundation of defense policy. Casper Sylvest and Rens van Munster have recently argued that Mumford was not a utopian but a realist, and indeed realism, through reason and rationality, figures at the place of hope in Mumford's notion of utopia.[49] But reason, to Mumford, is what must control rationality. Utopia is not a fatalistic hope that better or perfect conditions will present themselves, but rather, the only possible source of sensible conduct. The aspiration to a "house that meets our needs" to Mumford was the basis of a critical scrutiny of the conditions of emergence of better futures: "which conditions must be met." Utopias of reconstruction are thus ways of bringing together the inner and the outer world in a more harmonious whole, and they require for this a work of reform not only of the outer environment, but of human beings themselves. Utopias should not be projections of the utopians ego but they should lead outward—"into the world" and into a "reconstructed environment" of human relationships and institutions.[50] Utopias could not begin from the premise of perfect men, rather, utopia was the necessary work on humanity's imperfections. "It would

[43] In 1973 Mumford participated in the first future research conference with the essay "Human futures."

[44] Mumford, *The Story of Utopias*, 10.

[45] Mumford, *The Story of Utopias*, 12.

[46] *The Story of Utopias*, 15.

[47] "Human Futures."

[48] See Mumford's open letter to the *New York Times*, March 28, 1954. Lawrence Wittner, *The Struggle against the Bomb.* Volume one. *One World or None. The History of the World Nuclear Disarmament Movement Through 1953* (Palo Alto: Stanford University Press, 1993), 66.

[49] Sylvest and van Munster, *Nuclear Realism.*

[50] *The Story of Utopias*, 21.

be so easy, this business of making over the world, if it were only a matter of creating machinery."[51] But "the problem (of utopia) is fundamentally a human problem. The more completely man is in control of our physical nature, the more urgently we must ask ourselves what under the heavens is to move and guide and keep in hand the controller."[52]

MANKIND

To Mumford, utopia was thus a process of reform of humanity, a process that in his view had to take place both at the level of individual values and attitudes, and on the collective level of humanity or Mankind. Utopia, to Mumford, was universal being, and could therefore not be a question of partisanship, specific organizations or fellowship. The only possible level of utopian organization was therefore on the level of a new united, global, humanity. This humanity had to share a new form of consciousness of the world and its future, and this awareness of an inherently shared and universal future was what to Mumford would bring men together into a new collective subject of Mankind.

Mumford's *The Story of Utopias* presented a very different argument here, not only from Bloch's Marxist utopia, but also from the rationalist, indeed eugenicist accounts that dominated liberal concepts of the future in the interwar period (see the next chapter). Mumford's Mankind is not a supreme being, but a transcendental humanity that has reconnected with being and with the recognition of the limits to existence. There was an obvious nostalgic and romantic content to these notions in Mumford's writings.[53] Meanwhile, Mumford's outlook on human civilization was already pretty bleak in 1922. *The Story of Utopias* ended:

> Unless we can weave a new pattern for our lives, the outlook for our civilisation is almost as dismal as Herr Spengler finds it in *Der Untergang des Abendlandes*. Our choice is not between utopia and the world as it is, but between *eutopia* and nothing, or rather, nothingness... If the dissipation of Western civilisation is to cease, the first step in reconstruction is to make over our inner world, and to give our knowledge and our projections a new foundation. The problem of realizing the potential power of the community—which is the fundamental problem of eutopian reconstruction—is not simply a matter of economics or eugenics... if we are to build up genuine eutopias... we must examine anew the idola which will assist us in reconstructing the environment. So we are forced to consider the place of science and art in our social life, and to discuss what must be done in order to make them bear more completely upon the improvement of Man's estate.[54]

Utopia, in the form of a united Mankind, could thus be created through science, but through a new kind of science grounded in human values, and with an edge

[51] *The Story of Utopias*, 251. [52] *The Story of Utopias*, 23, 242, 251.

[53] Mumford wrote the obituary for William Morris. He was also a great admirer of Wells, see Mumford correspondence with the American futurist Warren Wagar, who had written his Ph.D. dissertation on Wells.

[54] Mumford, *The Story of Utopias*, 269.

directed against an instrumental use of technology. The machine figures in Mumford's writings as a reflection of human values and as the image of humanity itself. *Technics and Civilization,* written in 1934, argued that the machine could be "dissolved" so that more human machines could be created.[55] Mumford's despair, after 1945, came from his conclusion that the Atomic bomb was a "total machine" that could not be dissolved, because it undid all forms of reason.[56]

"Gentlemen, you are mad," wrote Mumford in the *Saturday Review* in 1946.

> We in America live among madmen. Madmen govern our affairs in the name of order and security. The chief madmen claim the title of Secretary of state, admiral, senator scientist, administrator, even President. And the fatal symptom of their madness is this: they have been carrying through a series of acts which will lead eventually to the destruction of Mankind, under the solemn conviction that they are normal responsible people, living sane lives, and working for reasonable ends. Soberly, day after day, the madmen continue to go through the undeviating motions of madness: motions so stereotyped, so commonplace, that they seem the normal motions of normal men, not the mass compulsions of people bent on total death. Without a public mandate of any kind, these madmen have taken it upon themselves to lead us by gradual stages to that final act of madness which will corrupt the face of the Earth and blot out the nations of men, possibly put an end to all life on the planet itself. These madmen have a comet by the tail, but they think of treating it as if it were a child's skyrocket. They play with it, they experiment with it, they dream of swifter and brighter comets. Their teachers have handed them down no rules for controling comets, so they take only the usual precautions of children permitted to set off firecrackers. Without asking for anyone's permission, they have decided to play a little further with the cosmic force, merely to see what will happen at sea in a war that must never come. Why do we let the madmen go on with their game without raising our voices? Why do we keep our glassy calm in the face of this danger? There is a reason: we are madmen, too.[57]

As the total machine could not be dissolved, the only way out of collective insanity was an "awakening." Awakening was a kind of existential shock back into sanity, and it is to Mumford of an enduring and pathetic paradox that the only awakened ones in 1946 are the atomic scientists themselves, the men who in their "final throes of dementia" were forced to see the cosmic evil that they had brought about. Mumford was full of contempt for the atomic scientists, including Einstein and Szilard, but he understood, after 1946, SANE as the possible first stage of a new global society of friends, an embryo of a world organization or world federation of Mankind. World government, a UN right to rule over the bomb, was an early demand of the anti Bomb movement. The demand for world government, including demands of a world constitution and a UN police force over the Bomb, united many anti-Bomb organizations until the armaments struggle took off and,

[55] Lewis Mumford, *Technics and Civilization*, 1934, 6, 7, 24, 326–34, 427.

[56] Eugene Halton, *From the Axial Age to the Moral Revolution*, (London: Palgrave Macmillan, 2012). Mumford, "Apology to Henry Adams," Stanford University lecture 1962, published as Lewis Mumford, "Apology to Henry Adams", in *The Virginia Quarterly Review*, 1962, 38(2): 196.

[57] Lewis Mumford, "Gentlemen, you are mad," in *The Saturday Review of Literature*, March 2, 1946, 5–6.

as Rosenboim puts it, bipolarity replaced globality.[58] One of the most ardent supporters of the idea was Gunther Anders, first husband of Hannah Arendt and correspondent not only of Mumford, but also Ossip Flechtheim and Robert Jungk. Witnessing developments in the Soviet Union, many believers in world government, including Mumford, turned rather to the idea of world federalism, the creation of a world parliament that would set the interests of the whole of Mankind above interests of nation states.[59] To Mumford, world federation would be instrumental to the development of a world consciousness that could "transform man at the core" and turn him into the reflection of a peaceful world image.[60] Utopia, to Mumford, was the development of a new personality, a *world being* that could only be created through a purposeful transformation of the mind after a new "world image."[61]

In Mumford's argument, therefore, the only possible utopia is in Man himself.[62] But how then should Man be reformed? Among Mumford's many correspondents was the Marxist humanist and psychoanalyst Erich Fromm. To Fromm, psychoanalysis could perform what Mumford referred to as the "awakening," the turn from life threatening impulses, to life enhancing ones. Both men understood the question of how to change Man as the missing piece in post Marxist thinking, and they were hopeful that decentralized forms of social organization, student and community groups, could turn into proto forms of world organization. They were disillusioned by the advent of the neo Marxist left after 1968. By the late 1960s, their correspondence had turned into two elderly gentlemen's lament over the errant ways of the student movements. The students, wrote Mumford, were obsessed with their own existence, but they had no interest in the world. A tongue in cheek note from Theodore Roszak, whose wife attended Mumford's Apology to Henry Adams lecture at Stanford in 1966, relayed the graffiti on a Berkeley wall: "the Bomb has already dropped. We are the mutants."[63] But both Mumford and Fromm rejected as totalitarian the return of revolutionary thinking in the New Left. Mumford loathed Hebert Marcuse, who saw "no possible reform of man," only a radical disruption. Fromm described Marcuse as a person "whose highest ideal of human progress is the return to pregenital sexuality."[64]

Mumford observed an arm's length distance not only from the peace movement and the student movement, but also from the futurology, future research, or futures studies that by the late-1960s was coming together and for which he was also a reluctant idol. Mumford was annoyed by the vagaries of American future research. A correspondence with Arthur C. Clarke, whose book *Profiles of the Future* took a jab at Mumford's *The Transformation of Man,* ended with a punch:

[58] Rosenboim, *The Emergence of Globalism*, 13.

[59] The world federalists campaigned for a reformed UN system in the early 1950s, advocating a UN with restrained police powers over the bomb and, as such, an effective world government.

[60] Mumford, *Values for Survival*, 52.

[61] Mumford, *The Story of Utopias*, 238–9; Mumford, *The Condition of Man,* 13, 235, 236.

[62] Mumford, *The Condition of Man*, 423.

[63] Theodore and Betsy Roszak to Lewis Mumford, Lewis Mumford Archives, box 71, folder 5502.

[64] See letters from Fromm to Mumford, box 20, folders 1731–33.

> The deeper differences between you and I are, I'm afraid, unbridgeable... What you call life enhancing I call life cheating or life defeating... Your (astronauts) are an aristocracy, chosen and exalted by the Gods... They enjoy the loss of contact with earth bound realities. Their trip and the drug addicts are the same. As for the ecstacies of space travel, have you ever considered this in terms of costs, benefits, and liabilities? Are not the billions of dollars already spent on Skylab missions a slightly excessive price to pay for such limited pleasures as zero gravity athletics? This is aristocratic luxury with a vengeance. The only possible answer to such irrational phantasies is: come down to Earth.[65]

About the same time, Mumford describes Buckminster Fuller's description of a space capsule as the ideal human environment as lunacy. Asked by Edward Cornish to join, in 1972, the Washington-based World Future Society, Mumford politely refused but his handwritten notes on Cornish's draft article, "Predicting the Future," were less polite: "for futurists, the future is a field for more extensive power and greater wealth."[66]

THE INVENTION OF FUTUROLOGY BY A UKRAINIAN JEW IN ATLANTA

But Mumford was the perhaps reluctant link between immediate post-war philosophical notions of the loss of future in the human condition, and the emergent *project* of futurism, which was larger than American futurology.[67] Mumford corresponded on a much more sympathetic note with the emigre scholar Ossip Flechtheim, who coined, in 1942, the notion futurology for a new pedagogical project of teaching the future as a form of mass education in the American liberal arts colleges. "Even if we cannot avoid calamities, a person has the right to know what to expect, what will be the source of his troubles, and what is their place and meaning in the chain of unfolding events."[68] In February 1946 Mumford wrote to Flechtheim to thank him for this idea. "... your suggestion to start teaching the future is well taken. It might open the door for a three dimension history in which past, present and future would all be given weight... "[69] Mumford was an expert to the Ford Foundation on the German humanities, and was also called to testify to the American Committee for the Aid of Refugee Scholars through which Flechtheim arrived in America. Both Mumford and Flechtheim were also personal

[65] Lewis Mumford to Arthur C. Clarke, May 24, 1975, Lewis Mumford's archives, box 74, folder 5720.

[66] Mumford letter to Edward Cornish, Lewis Mumford's archives, May 18, 1976, box 71, folder 5461.

[67] Compare Sylvest and van Munster, *Nuclear realism*, 122.

[68] Ossip Flechtheim, 1945, "Teaching the future. A contribution to the intellectual and moral growth of the participants." Draft outline, Alvin Toffler archives. Published as, Ossip K. Flechtheim, "Teaching the Future: A Contribution to the Intellectual and Moral Growth of the Participants," *Journal of Higher Education*, (Dec. 1945), 16(9): 460–5.

[69] Lewis Mumford to Ossip Flechtheim, February 2, 1946, Alvin Toffler archives. Presumably donated by Flechtheim to Toffler, who seems to have been collecting material for a future study course.

friends of Thomas Mann. Mann helped Flechtheim secure his first academic position in the US.[70]

For Flechtheim, futurology was the *method* by which humanity could be pushed away from the *Abendsland* toward an *Aufhellerung*.[71] Ossip Flechtheim was a Ukrainian born Jew whose first notes on futurology appeared in English in the first years of his American exile. A former communist and life long Marxist, Flechtheim was a first hand witness to the disintegration of the German Left in the Weimar Republic, and joined the resistance movement, Neu Beginnen. This was one of the central groups of the German resistance, created from the destruction of the SPD in 1934. It is worth noting that not only Flechtheim, but also Robert Jungk, came from Neu Beginnen, and that Georgy Lukasz, whose notion of the "present future" was fundamental to East German revisionist futurologists in the mid 1960s (see Chapter 6), was a key influence on the Neu Beginnen manifesto published by the pseudonym Miles in Switzerland in 1934.[72] Neu Beginnen stood for the idea of a new departure after fascism, and for the importance of the idea of the future to the activity of resistance. The motto of Neu Beginnen was *Socialismus oder Fascismus*—but Flechtheim would his whole intellectual life look for the third way, the possible alternative between fixed and dogmatic positions, or between irrational destruction and naive utopias. As an emigre first in Geneva, Flechtheim made lifelong friends with John Herz, Gunther Anders, and Theodor Adorno, who provided him with employment at the Institute of Social Research before his departure to New York. At the Institute, Flechtheim wrote his first criticisms of the theory of history of Marxism.[73] Among the German exiles of 1938, Flechtheim was different, and he would remain different as a self-described *Freidenker und Friedensmensch*—a man of peace and thought.[74] Flechtheim worked temporarily at Columbia with Marcuse but did not obtain a position there nor at the New School nor the Institute for Social Research, and ended up teaching political science at a black college in Atlanta. His first notions of futurology appeared in the college journals *Forum* and *Phylon* between 1942 and 1946. These first writings presented futurology as a scientifically grounded way of engaging with time, and as such as distinct from philosophies of history from Fichte and Hegel to Marx.[75] There was no foreseeable finality to social time, Flechtheim suggested, no human destiny or line of history

70 In February 1946 Mann also wrote to thank Flechtheim for the "brilliant" course outline.

71 Ossip Flechtheim, *Futurologie. Der Kampf um die Zunkunft*, 16.

72 See *Gedankstatte Deutsche Wiederstand* online, *Neu Beginnen,* and Terence Reynaud, *Restarting Socialism. The New Beginning Group and the Problem of Renewal of the German Left, 1930–1970*,(diss. University of California, Berkeley, 2015), in particular Chapters 2 and 5; Mario Kessler and Ossip K. Flechtheim, *Politischer Wissenschaftler und Zukunftsdenker, 1909–1998* (Bohlau Verlag, Koln, 2013), 42–7; Timothy Brown, *Weimar Radicals. Nazis and Communists Between Authenticity and Performance* (New York: Berghahn books, 2009).

73 Ossip K. Flechtheim, "Zur Kritik der Marxschen Geschichtskonzeption" [1939], *Cahiers Vilfredo Pareto*, 1965, 3 (5): 141–58.

74 Biographical note, Ossip Flechtheim Nachlass.

75 Ossip Flechtheim, "History: Theodicy or Odyssey" in *Phylon, the Atlanta University Review of Race and Culture*, 1941, vii (1): 78–88; Ossip K. Flechtheim, "Toynbee and the Webers," *Phylon*, 1943, 4 (3): 248–64 and Ossip K. Flechtheim, "Futurology: the New Science," in *Forum*, 1949, III: 206–9.

could be sketched beforehand. Rather, human destiny oscillated between crisis and progress, and between moments of destruction and moments of creation. The core challenge to the future, he argued, was existence, and it was the singularity of the political animal that he could himself make an informed existential choice on whether to perish with the globe, move to the stars, or start assuming responsibility for planetary survival.[76] Flechtheim thought in the 1940s that the assurance of survival could only be guaranteed by a democratic world federation that could counteract the rise of a global, Wellsian and Bolschevik totalitarian state.[77] By the 1960s, as Flechtheim became a key figure in the German New Left, he understood this totalitarian state as having permeated the Bundesrepublik, the *Atom Staat* that suppressed dissidence and integrated, in Flechtheim's view, core legacies of national socialism.[78]

The early notes on what Flechtheim hesitated to call a new science, and preferred calling a method, pedagogy, or discipline, appeared at a crucial moment in time.[79] They were at that moment entirely peripheral, although there were kind words from Mumford, Thomas Mann, and Aldous Huxley (who had written, in 1949, the novel *Ape and Essence* on the Atomic era).[80] It was the book *Futurologie* (in English, *History and Futurology*) in 1968 that attracted attention to these earlier notes. But Flechtheim's notes appeared at a time of increased relevance for the idea of the future. In the early 1950s, American scientists began experimenting with methods of forecasts and prediction, methods described by Flechtheim as "ein Griff nach der Zukunft" in a spirit of conquest and robbery. Flechtheim probably got the description of these experiments from Robert Jungk. In the early years of the 1950s, a range of critical future works appeared that included not only Mumford's writings and Jungk's *Tomorrow is Already Here*, but also the Dutch sociologist, Fred Polak's *The Image of the Future*. *The Image* argued humanity had lost its guiding star in Christian images of the future. Images of the future, said Polak, therefore had to be replaced, and images could be actively created and conjured in order to set out a constructive role for humanity.[81] To Flechtheim, who had been looking for ways of breaking with what he saw as the deeply pessimistic future images of the nineteenth century, the counter utopias of Spengler, Wells, Toynbee, Huxley, and Orwell were the promise of a new engagement with the future.

Flechtheim's utopia was meanwhile not a moral one, but a scientific and rationalist one. Flechtheim returned to Germany several times in the 1950s, first to work for the Allied forces at the Nurnberg tribunal, then to the Otto Suhr Institut, and finally to Berlin's Freie Universitat on a Rockefeller scholarship. Flechtheim had been selected as part of the Foundation's project to refound German political science

[76] Flechtheim, "History, Theodicy or Odyssey," 87.

[77] "Geschichte der Futurologie," undated, 1940s; documents on the "World State," 1940s, "How Did We Get This Way," and "Dass Futurologie Aufsatz," written in New York in 1940 on the back of a letter from the Committee for aid to displaced German scholars. Ossip Flechtheim Nachlass.

[78] Kessler, *Ossip K. Flechtheim*, 157–220.

[79] Raynaud qualifies Flechtheim's concept of futurology as critical utopia studies, and traces it to Flechtheim's 1939 manuscript. Reynaud, *New Beginnings*, 143.

[80] Aldous Huxley, *Ape and Essence* (Chicago: Dee, 1948).

[81] Fred Polak, *The Image of the Future* (Amsterdam: Elsevier, 1956).

and purge it of national socialism.[82] His book *Futurologie* became the main result of his return to political science.[83] *Futurologie* was no ordinary textbook. It was rather the sum of Flechtheim's reflections on the state of the future, as a continent ripped in two by the Cold War. The division of Germany appeared, in *Futurologie,* as the symbolic grounds for thinking about this larger problem. The future, to Flechtheim, lay somewhere between the two systems, and as such, it had to be freed from ideology and reinvested with a social scientifically grounded sense of critical scrutiny.

The inspiration here was not Marxian philosophy but the liberal sociologist and philosopher, also refugee scholar, Karl Mannheim. Mannheim's core notion—that the non-ideological critique of ideology could be turned against left parties including the communist ones—was a central influence on Neu Beginnen. Utopia, in Mannheim's work, was a philosophy of knowledge that could create awareness for change and therefore lay the foundations of resistance. As such, utopia was distinct from ideology—the dogmatic and non-teleological objectives that were beyond rational investigation. Utopia was a critique of ideology, and futurology for Flechtheim had a critical emancipatory function, which was that of evaluating the rationality of overarching ideological objectives, the posited goal of social development in socialist and liberal societies. The problem of the future, to Flechtheim, was not to produce exact prognosis, but to enlighten the future direction societies were set on so that good futures could be identified and catastrophic ones averted. The goals of contemporary societies—unlimited economic growth through *Marktwirtschaft* in the West, similar by five-year plans in the East—were to Flechtheim unreasonable in their social and environmental consequences. If such objectives could be put to rational scrutiny, they could be replaced by goals more purposeful and more widely shared, and by goals that could permit the avoidance of foreseeable disaster.[84]

To Flechtheim, who remained a socialist his whole life and for the larger part a Marxist, there was no question about the political color of futurology. Futurology, to Flechtheim, was the instrument for the creation of a new kind of global human socialism, a pacifist, democratic, and ecological Marxism the logical conclusion of which was a democratic world federation as the opposite of the Bolschevik world state. From the 1960s on, Flechtheim began thinking of futurology as the systematic method with which to create a "Third way" between the blocs. In 1964 Robert Jungk set futurology at the heart of the West German New Left with the book *Deutschland ohne Konzeption. Am Beginn Einer Neuen Epoche.*[85] Flechtheim also began a series of radio broadcasts, in which he presented futurology as a method of

[82] Flechtheim file in Rockefeller archives, RG. 1.2.7175.

[83] First published as *Futurologie. Moglichkeiten und Grenzen* (Frankfurt: Edition Voltaire, 1968) then as *Futurologie. Der Kampf um die Zukunft* (Berlin: Verlag Wissenschaft und Politik, 1971).

[84] "Ist die Futurologie eine wissenschaft," Ossip Flechtheim Nachlass, and *Futurologie. Moglichkeiten und Grenzen,* 234.

[85] Robert Jungk, *Deutschland ohne Konzeption, Am beinn einer neuen Epoche,* Munchen, 1964. The notion of Konzeption came from *Neu Beginnen* and the 1934 Miles manifesto. A few years later Leszek Kolakowski published *Der Mensch ohne Alternative. Die Moglichkeit und Unmoglichkeit Marxist zu Sein.*

freedom for the Cold War era and escape route from a squeezed middle ground between American neoconservative future research and Soviet long-term planning. Futurology could not be the "*Botschaft* of the Bomb" or "*einen sozial technischen Methode der Generalstrategie plankapitalistischer Krisenverhinderung*," but it had to be an opening of the future as a horizon made up by the possible, the plausible, and the desirable.[86] Such a humanistic future was a "Third Way", a great opening of world power structures.

German futurology, stemming from the divided country, could to Flechtheim embody such a Third Way, and through futurology, German political science could become a real "*Politologie*"—as opposed to its American or French counterparts (see the coming chapters).[87] The disciplinary kernel of this *Politologie* would be the invention of future institutions and polities for humanity, a new *Weltkultur der Zukunft* and a new Gestalt to humanity on the planetary level.[88] As such, political science would be a super science, a metascience charged with a normative reflection on the human world system.

Flechtheim was, like Mumford, a tireless writer of letters, tribunes, and radio talks. He wrote to Willy Brandt, the social democrat who was responsible for taking West Germany into the Atomic era. He corresponded with Bertolt Brecht, with Bertrand Russell, and with Thomas Mann. In the late 1960s and 1970s, Flechtheim and Erich Fromm entertained a vivid correspondence on the reactionary tendencies in the BRD. In the 1980s, Flechtheim turned his attention to ecological issues and clearly understood the 1980s as a profound crisis for humanistic future conceptions.[89]

CONCLUDING REMARKS

Later chapters return to Ossip Flechtheim's idea of futurology, and to the way that the future resurfaced, from the mid 1960s on, in the project of futures studies, a form of counter-expertise to the project of Cold War prediction with strong links to the new social movements. In order to understand this development, the two following chapters will explain the scientist idea of the long term, as linked to a set of distinctly liberal arguments about the future as a problem of prediction and decision, and as directly related to the military and technological category of the "long range."

This chapter has argued that the beginnings of future research can be found in the futurism of Mumford and Flechtheim, which stands as a link from an interwar *Kulturkritik* with roots in enlightenment philosophy, and emerging forms of radicality that would become associated with the second Frankfurt school in the late 1960s. The link was the idea of the centrality of man and humanity in the critical

[86] *Futurologie. Der Kampf um die Zukunft*, 21.

[87] See Flechtheim's objection to Bertrand de Jouvenel's notion of conjecture in 1962, Flechtheim to Bertrand de Jouvenel, July 4, 1964, Bertrand de Jouvenel papers, correspondence files.

[88] *Futurologie. Der Kampf um die Zunkunft*, 103–5, 110, 162, and draft manuscript, "Politik als Wissenschaft," 1953, Ossip Flechtheim Nachlass.

[89] "Ist die Zukunft noch zu Retten," Ossip Flechtheim Nachlass.

notion of the future, as well as the identification of the future as the central sphere of critique and protest in the nuclear age. Importantly, this chapter has shown that the idea that the future was fundamentally associated with human responsibility changed the notion of utopia: if the future could no longer be about a coming possible era of perfection, it had to be about the sum of all the things that human beings do and do not do, the capacity for action and the failures of action. The only possible site of utopian energy at this point was the idea of human beings themselves, as the harbingers of the apocalypse, but also as the sole saviours of the world. The world, in turn, became the reflection of human irrationalities and the lack of future image. By the late 1960s, arguments around the future developed into critiques of the "system"—but to both Mumford and Flechtheim, the future meant new forms of association that could embody a new future consciousness and give birth to a new human subject as Mankind. The only way to the future was to transform human beings, to replant the idea of the future in human consciousness and educate human beings about the consequence of their actions on nature and unborn generations.

4

Futures of Liberalism. The Congress for Cultural Freedom and Futurology as a Transnational Space

FROM THE END OF IDEOLOGY TO FUTUROLOGY: THE CONGRESS FOR CULTURAL FREEDOM

Ossip Flechtheim's notion of futurology as a critical philosophy of history surfaced in the late 1960s as part of the project of futures studies (Chapter 7). Meanwhile, from the 1950s on, the idea of the future was a core element also in liberal debates. This had to do, this chapter proposes, with the reconceptualization of the future as an essentially predictable process of social change. This reconceptualization was part of the return of the problem of social time in the Western social sciences as a consequence of their rejection of Marxist philosophy. Many of the core elements of the post-war social sciences, most notably Parsonian systems theory, Lazarsfeld's behavioral revolution and Rostow's growth theory, were direct products of the attempt to mount a positivist defence to the Marxian theory of history (and future). Nils Gilman describes Rostow's growth theory as a "Marxian theory of historical change, with the class struggle removed."[1] The idea of predictability became an organizing element of those strands of social science known as modernization theory. As Gilman shows, in its assumptions of stage driven processes, modernization theory set forward its own theory of universal and teleological progress. While modernization theory applied itself to global developments, it posited American civilization and the liberal capitalist society as the image of the future.[2]

Modernization theory was, quite like Marxism-Leninism, not a passive but an activist project, which came with a set of policy prescriptions, intellectual vanguards, and political technologies. These were actively circulated and spread in the respective spheres of influence. Future research was part of this production of artifacts and technologies of control. As such, future research became, along with other epistemic constructs in post-war social science that were both scientific theories and concrete devices (such as welfare economics and the prisoner's dilemma theorem,

[1] Nils Gilman, *Mandarins of The Future. Modernization Theory in Cold War America* (Baltimore: John Hopkins University Press, 2003), 64. David Engerman, Nils Gilman, Mark Haefele, and Michael Latham, eds., *Staging Growth. Modernization, Development and the Global Cold War* (Amherst: University of Massachusetts Press, 2003).

[2] Gilman, *Mandarins of the Future*, 6, 12, 16, 26, 42–6.

Walt Whitman Rostow's theory of economic growth, or indeed Operations Research), part of a kit of strategy devices, planning tools, and instrumentalities designed to promote and protect a specific vision of the future.[3]

The chapter sets out the origins of the liberal version of futurology in specific networks of the early Cold War period, by examining one of the key transnational spaces of 1950s and 1960s liberalism, the Congress for Cultural Freedom. Much scholarly attention has been devoted to the Congress, but not to the specific role played by the idea of the future in the debates and discussions within it.[4] The central argument in this chapter is that in its attempt to renew core concepts of liberalism, the Congress was the site for a fundamental shift in the notion of the future, which appeared, through Congress debates and discussions, as an essentially secular construct, a problem of the rational management of progress of social time. Directly related to this reconceptualization was the Congress interest in developing future research as a specific project within the social sciences. For the latter, the chapter stresses the curious encounter between the Ford Foundation, the sociologist Daniel Bell, and the highly enigmatic French political theorist Bertrand de Jouvenel, author of the 1962 book, *The Art of Conjecture*.

AN OPEN vs. CLOSED FUTURE

The Congress for Cultural Freedom was created in 1950 in the context of acute Cold War conflict. The first meetings of what would become the Congress in Berlin, New York, and Paris in 1948, 1949, and 1950 were devoted to the problem of totalitarianism, and to the control exercised by the Soviet Union over cultural and scientific affairs. In the coming years however, the Congress' focus widened to a much larger reflection on the role of the non Marxist social sciences in post-war society. Congress seminars attracted a wide range of scholars, including revisionist Marxists, social democrats such as Gunnar Myrdal, Hugh Gaitskell, and Anthony Crosland, and social liberals, liberals, and neoliberals including Daniel Bell, Raymond Aron, and Friedrich von Hayek.[5]

The Congress was one of several spaces after 1945 that came together around the pervasive notion that historic forms of liberal thinking were in crisis. The idea of *neo*liberalism was present in Congress' proceedings from the 1950s on, denoting the idea that the rate of technological and material progress and the expansion of welfare statist administrations meant that key concepts of liberalism were no longer useful. This applied first and foremost to the notion of freedom, which was reconceptualized within the Congress as a question of "freedom of choice." The link between

[3] Sonja M. Amadae, *Rationalizing Capitalist Democracy* (Chicago: Chicago University Press, 2003).

[4] Francies Stonor Saunders, *Who Paid the Piper. The CIA and the Cultural Cold War* (London: Granta, 1999); Pierre Gremion, *L'intelligence de l'anticommunisme. Le congres de la liberte de la culture* (Paris: Seuil, 1995).

[5] Giles Scott Smith, "The Congress for Cultural Freedom, the End of Ideology and the Milan seminar of 1955," in *Journal of Contemporary History*, 2002, 37 (3): 437–55.

CCF and early strands of neoliberal thinking has been reemphasized in recent historiography, which has also set out a less than obvious link between the Congress and other much more explicitly neoliberal sites.[6] In 1938, the former social democrat, Walter Lippman, had organized his meeting on planning in a welfare statist society, and, in 1947, Hayek created the Mont Pelerin Society of which some leading figures of the Congress, notably Aron but also de Jouvenel, were members.[7] There were important differences between these sites. As Dieter Plehwe and Philip Mirowski have shown, Hayek's MPS grew into a dogmatic neoliberal thought collective. But within the Congress, neoliberalism was only one of several possible answers to the question of what the future of liberalism should look like, and what freedom meant to the post-war era. The dominant motivation of the Congress was not the rejection of welfare statism but the attempt to understand the nature of an *emergent* welfare statist post-war order.

As Giles Scott Smith has suggested, Congress debates were informed by an essentially positive notion of the post-war economic order as a plurality of interests. Most intellectuals in the Congress understood welfare statism as a pacified social order that marked a fundamental break with the radical politics of the interwar period. Most Congress members were also believers in the necessity of at least limited forms of planning and they did not share the Hayekian view that a social order built around the welfare state was as such a threat to freedom.[8] What they did believe, however, was that the post-war period witnessed the birth of a new democratic mass society dominated by a plurality of agents or decision makers, and that the expansion of state administrations and public bureaucracies channelled political will in new and unforeseeable ways. They therefore proposed that this new mass society required an analysis as to what extent such a society could be understood as by nature liberal. This included not only a positive notion of pluralism, as Scott Smith has argued, but also a much more ambiguous reflection on democratic mass politics as a set of potential conflicts of interests and clashes between individual and collective preferences. The question, to many intellectuals in the Congress, was what would become of this mass society, and what future it would give rise to.

The Congress interest in future research was an outcome of a quintessential reflection on the possibilities of control on a new kind of mass society and its inherent temporalities. As such it also has to be put in the context of modernization theory and the end of ideology thesis, according to which Western political culture had left the era of ideological dispute behind and had entered a new epoch

[6] See, for this important literature, Angus Burgin, *The Great Persuasion: Reinventing Free Markets Since the Depression* (Cambridge MA: Harvard University Press, 2012); Philip Mirowski and Dieter Plehwe, eds, *The Road from Mt. Pelerin: The Making of the Neoliberal Thought Collective* (Cambridge MA: Harvard University Press, 2009); Serge Audier, *Néoliberalismes, une archéologie intellectuelle* (Paris: Grasset, 2012).

[7] Francois Denord, "French neoliberalism and its divisions. From the colloque Walter Lippman to the fifth republic," in Dieter Plehwe and Phillip Mirowski, eds., *The Road from Mont Pelerin*, 45–68. As Denord shows, both Aron and de Jouvenel left the MPS precisely over Hayek's rejection of all forms of state intervention.

[8] Scott Smith, "The Congress for Cultural Freedom."

in which social conflict could be solved by new forms of pragmatic or "rational" problem solving.[9] Pierre Gremion notes that it was in response to Hayek's intervention on the future of freedom that Raymond Aron introduced the idea of the end of ideology and the new focus on rational problems. While neoliberalism was not the dominant idea of the Congress, modernization theory was (and there were of course links between these two projects, particularly in a highly ambivalent notion of the mass). Modernization theory was represented in the Congress by the Chicago sociologist, Edward Shils, the French political scientist, Raymond Aron, Daniel Bell, and to some extent the philosopher Michael Polanyi. The notion of an end of ideology appeared in several different guises in the interventions of these scholars, denoting, as Scott Smith proposes, a common element in the idea of a plurality of classes and interests, driven by technological progress and affluence.[10] But while there were important progressive elements to the end of ideology thesis, it also needs to be stressed that the notion of an end of ideology was the core building bloc of the Congress' rejection of Marxism, and the stepping stone for an idea of the future which emphasized the non Marxist social sciences as agents of change and as bulwarks against forms of social chaos.

The end of ideology thesis identified the social sciences as directly involved in the process of setting the overarching objectives of society, and as such, as holding a specific responsibility for the future. This implication of the social sciences in the act of setting objectives led to a discussion within the Congress of the difference between an "open" versus a "closed" notion of the future. As argued by Daniel Bell in particular, the closed future was the future projected by a Marxist Leninist system of five-year plans, which set down fixed objectives for change and closed down the finalities of social development over the long term. A closed future was predetermined on the basis of ideology, and left no space for social science. In contrast, in a liberal society, future objectives were set in an open process which involved a societal dialogue on overarching objectives, and which also left a space for "freedom of choice" over the long term.[11] The core notion of freedom of choice, a concept directly linked to the idea of social science rationality, was introduced to the Congress by Michael Polanyi. In his key note address to the 1955 seminar, Michael Polanyi observed that the ideologies of liberalism and communism had played out their role as the "great rivers of progress" and no longer offered the philosophical codes of conduct for the present. They were not guides to a future that should be taken, but, rather, a set of practical problems ahead that required rational investigation in order to ensure free choice for future generations.[12] As a secular problem, the future was thus directly linked to the concept of an active choice.

[9] See Gremion, *L'intelligence de l'anticommunisme*, 38–40, 156–62, 317; Daniel Steinmetz Jenkins, "Inverse Marxism. Friedrich Hayek, Raymond Aron, and the Congress for Cultural Freedom Seminar in Milan, 1955." Unpublished.

[10] Scott Smith, "The Congress for Cultural Freedom."

[11] See Daniel Bell, *The End of Ideology. On the Exhaustion of Political Ideas in the 1950s* (Cambridge MA: Harvard University Press, 1962 (second edition), 30.

[12] Michael Polanyi, introduction to the 1955 seminar, quoted by Gremion, *L'intelligence de l'anticommunisme*, 154, 166.

The purpose of social science was to contribute to this active choice, and find the conditions for the preservation of freedom over time.

It was the melange in the Congress of, on the one hand, ideological debates around the future as secular progress and the "future of freedom," and, on the other, the concern with social science analysis of the process of social change, which produced the Congress interest in future research. As a consequence of this melange, the future also came to be thought of as a set of potential instrumentalities and mechanisms with which "open" futures could be protected over time. The idea that the social sciences were responsible for the setting of overarching societal objectives was not as such a new conception. The idea of providing a liberal bulwark against Marxism and reaffirm the values of a liberal society through individual choice was a staple of the American twentieth-century social sciences, described by the historian of science, Dorothy Ross, as "pluralist, behavioralist, and statistical models of a liberal world in perpetual flux, yet constantly reiterating its form.[13] The first chairman of the Congress was John Dewey, the pragmatist philosopher who understood social science as part and parcel of the making of an enlightened polity.[14] The future, according to Dewey, was a question of the peaceful setting of overarching societal objectives under the direct overseeing of the social sciences. Importantly, this was to Dewey—and to most scholars in the Congress—a fundamentally moral affair. The social sciences were not objective or neutral, they were on the contrary part of a normative engagement with the future, by defining social problems and deciding on their proper solution.[15]

The choice of Dewey as first Congress President was highly symbolic for precisely the renewed actuality of a pragmatic concept of the future within the Congress, and for emphasizing a new and rational approach to social conflict that did not, however, negate morality—but argued, rather, that social science was an integral part of the negotiation of a new and pluralistic value order. "Rational," in this context, was the opposite of ideological, and reasserted the idea of an historically justified role for the social sciences. As many scholars have argued, this gave the social sciences a direct role in articulating a future vision for liberal society, different in form from that of Soviet society. Just as Dewey was the anti-Marx, the idea of the future as a rational freedom of choice was also the anti-image of Marxist long-term planning.

[13] Dorothy Ross, *Origins of American Social Science* (Cambridge MA: Harvard University Press, 1991), 15.

[14] Dewey himself is the object of a conflicted American historiography, which on the one hand stresses Deweyan pragmatism as part and parcel of an interwar belief in social engineering, and, on the other hand, as part of the making of an enlightened polity. See Brett Gary, "Dueling Deweys: Moralism, Scientism, and American Social Science History," *Reviews in American History*, 1995, 23 (4): 623–30; John M. Jordan, *Machine-Age Ideology: Social Engineering and American Liberalism, 1911–1939* (Chapel Hill: University of North Carolina Press, 1991) 226–32; and Mark Smith, *Social Science in the Crucible: The American Debate Over Objectivity and Purpose, 1918–1941* (Durham: Duke University Press, 1994); Ross, *Origins of American Social Science*, 167–8.

[15] John Dewey, "Liberating the Social Scientist," in *Commentary*, 1947, 4: 378; Richard D. Westbrook, *John Dewey and American Democracy* (Ithaca: Cornell University Press, 1993) 459, 463, 468; Alan Cywar, "John Dewey: Toward Domestic Reconstruction, 1915–1920," in *Journal of the History of Ideas*, 1969, 30 (3): 385–400; Bell, *The End of Ideology*, 249.

The person within the Congress who would spend most time working out the details of such a liberal and open form of engagement with the future through an informed "social" or indeed "rational" choice was Daniel Bell, and it was Bell who introduced the theme of future research within the CCF. Bell had worked for the journal *Common Sense* in the 1940s, edited by Dewey. Between 1960 and 1965 Bell published several essays on future research and the problem of prediction in the American journals *Daedalus* and *The Public Interest*, and he also organized seminars on futurology within the framework of the Congress.[16]

A LIBERAL THEORY OF HISTORY: DANIEL BELL AND THE END OF IDEOLOGY

At the time of the Congress seminar on the social sciences in 1955, Bell, previously a labour journalist with his roots on the Jewish Lower East side, was a new Columbia professor of sociology, recruited by Talcott Parsons. As many of his comrades—Sidney Hook and Irving Kristol in particular—Bell had made an intellectual journey from his days in a social democrat faction of the 1940s American students' movement to embrace a vehemently anti-communist Cold War stance. As Chapter 6 will explain, this "decline of radicalism" contained embryos of both a highly technocratic and a neoconservative position over the 1960s and 1970s, but in the 1950s Bell was a social liberal not very far from the positions of revisionist social democrats such as Anthony Crosland or Hugh Gaitskell.[17]

Bell's 1960s book *The End of Ideology* popularized the notion of an end of ideology, and it also earned Bell a reputation as the main representative of a technocratic generation of Cold Warriors with direct links to the Military Industrial Establishment, which is how *The End of Ideology* was read by the New Left from the mid 1960s on.[18] Chapter 6 revisits this argument and proposes that Bell's interest in the rational management of a democratic mass society ran as the red thread from his end of ideology argument to his plea for social forecasting as a new "decision tool" for post-industrial societies in a 1973 book, *The Coming of Post Industrial Society. A Venture in Social Forecasting.*[19] *The End of Ideology* contained the first embryos of Bell's interest in future research, as a new development in social science that could permit an "open" engagement with the future. In *The End of*

16 The first of these essays was the 1953 "Ten Theories in Search of Reality. The Prediction of Soviet Behavior in the Social Sciences", in *World Politics,* 1953, 3: 327–65 (later reprinted in *The End of Ideology*). Daniel Bell, "The Study of the Future," *The Public Interest*, 1966, 1: 120–1. See CCF seminars in 1970 and 1971, "The Historian between Ethnologist and Futurologist", November 1970, and Bell talk, "Futurology and History", April 2–6, 1971, CCF archives box 474, folder 7.

17 See Howard Brick, *Daniel Bell and the Decline of Intellectual Radicalism. Social Theory and Political Reconciliation in the 1940s* (Madison: Wisconsin University Press, 1986).

18 See Russell Jacoby, *Picture Imperfect. Utopian Thought for an Anti Utopian Age* (New York: Columbia University Press, 2005), 57.

19 Jenny Andersson, "Prediction and Social Choice. Daniel Bell and Future Research," in Nicolas Guilhot and Daniel Bessner, eds., *The Decisionist Imagination* (New York: Columbia University Press, 2018).

Ideology, Bell spoke of a new democratic mass society that had not yet found its future shape. Bell understood post-war society as driven by a process of rising social expectations that were channelled through a new kind of policy state with welfarist ambitions. As such, mass politics after 1945 were different in kind from the violent interest politics of the interwar period, but *The End of Ideology* was nevertheless a fundamental argument for the necessity of developing, also within a liberal society, forms of planning and steering that could ensure that rising expectations were channelled toward rational and peaceful outcomes. *The End of Ideology* began with Bell's argument that mass society was an emergent social "form," which as such had to be distinguished from the mass, as the agent providing this emergent social order with its form. Analysing mass society was a question of understanding the logic of change within the mass.[20] The future of the form was in other words open, and it could not be presumed that the outcome of mass politics would be a repetition of interwar experiences, nor a new democratic polity. The mass as such was neither benevolent nor evil, it was simply in need of guidance. This was a description of mass society that was highly different both from fearful conceptions of the mass, such as those of Arendt and Jaspers, which Bell understood as conservative, and from leftist narratives such as those of Bell's former friend C. Wright Mills. A few years before, Mills had published *The Power Elite*, in which he argued that post-war democracy was being highjacked by hidden power structures in academia, military, and corporate elites.[21] This argument of the emergent "form" of mass society led Bell to argue that that liberal society also needed a future coordination mechanism, a form of planning for the long term that could ensure desirable outcomes.[22] A mass society driven by a new logic of social expectations and by the integration of the masses into society required some way of setting social objectives so that desirable outcomes were guaranteed. *The End of Ideology* suggested that recent advances in social sciences, in particular with Operations Research and systems analysis during the war, had permitted a new approach to social time as a not ideological but pragmatic problem. As social time was no longer moving toward a given ideological objective, time itself had to become the object of rationalist reasoning, and a new and "conscious" approach to the future as a problem of rational action could be found.[23]

This must be read as an argument according to which these outcomes had to be oriented toward a desired liberal form which could otherwise not be guaranteed, and future research emerged as a central instrumentality in working out and reiterating this form. In this capacity, future research was, to Bell, different in nature from Marxist long-term planning, because it was designed not to reduce, but

[20] Bell, *The End of Ideology*, 35–8. See letter from Daniel Bell to the French sociologist Georges Friedmann on "theories of mass society" and "ambiguities of mass society", October 25, 1956. CCF records, box 6, correspondence files.

[21] Bell letter to Mills' daughter Kate Mills on the development of the end of ideology idea in discussions with Mills, August 15, 1996, Daniel Bell papers, box 19, folders 37, 45, 46. Brick, *Daniel Bell and the Decline of Intellectual Radicalism*, 11; Daniel Bell, "The Power Elite Reconsidered," in *American Journal of Sociology*, 1958, 64(3): 238–50.

[22] Bell, *The End of Ideology*, 249. [23] Bell, *The End of Ideology*, 29, 30.

increase freedom over time, by taking into account the foreseeable or imaginable consequences of decision making and evaluating how these contributed, or not, to freedom.[24] The challenge, to Bell, was to put change under conscious direction, not by steering societal change for the long term, but by "facilitat(ing) desired social changes by working out the relationship between decisions and long-term objectives."[25] Future research, in other words, was an equivalent of Marxist long-term plans, an argument that Bell brought to conclusion in the 1972 book *The Coming of Post Industrial Society* which also made a forceful argument for "intellectual technologies" or "decision tools" as the staples of a liberal version of long-term plans.[26]

In *The End of Ideology*, the new tools for a pragmatic approach to time that had been provided by Operations Research and systems analysis appear as a necessary mediation between the masses and the elite. As Gilman points out, it was Daniel Bell who, in *The End of Ideology*, turned modernization theoretical arguments to bear on the Western world. Edward Shils set out the main theoretical categories of modernization theory as tradition vs. modernity in his study on India.[27] Shils described the process of modernization as the "entry of the masses into society," a process that Shils saw as dependent on the emergence of a modernist strata of intellectual elites in the developing world.[28] Adapting Shils' line of reasoning for the Western world, Bell honed in on specific societal elites in Western societies that had, he proposed, a privileged capacity of managing social time due to their rationalist preconceptions. This was in Bell's mindset a new emerging group of Cold War intellectuals, engineers, planners, and systems analysts. Mass society gave these elites a new role—that of steering, as it were, the process of leading mass society toward desirable outcomes, by guiding social expectations and arbitrating between necessary choices and decisions. The ultimate role of such elites, the final chapter of *The End of Ideology* explained, was to ensure that freedom of choice prevailed over the long term.[29]

Echoing Raymond Aron's warning in *L'opium des intellectuels*, which described the turn to "religion" by a post-war generation of French Marxist intellectuals, *The End of Ideology* observed that the exhaustion of ideology deflated the utopian energies necessary to mobilize intellectual elites.[30] As these elites were thus stripped of their religion, they needed something else to believe in, a new social role. Mobilizing Cold War elites required a repositioning of utopian energies, and Bell thus argued

[24] Daniel Bell, "Twelve Modes of Prediction. A Preliminary Sorting of Approaches in the Social Sciences," in *Daedalus*, 1964: 845–80, 870; Daniel Bell, "The Year 2000. The Trajectory of an Idea," in Daniel Bell and Stephen Graubard, eds, *Toward the Year 2000. Work in Progress* (Cambridge MA: MIT Press, 1997 (1967)), 1–17.

[25] Bell, *The End of Ideology*, 229, 249; Bell, "Memorandum to the Working Parties of the Commission for the Year 2000," November 2, 1965. Papers of the CY2000, box 1, folder 3.

[26] Daniel Bell, *The Coming of Post Industrial Society. A Venture in Social Forecasting* (New York: Basic Books, 1999 (1973)), 29, 30, 313.

[27] Edward Shils, *The Intellectual Between Tradition and Modernity, the Indian Situation* (The Hague: Mouton and Company, 1961). Shils translated Karl Mannheim into English.

[28] The title of Bell's first essay on the end of ideology was "The End of Ideology in the West." Gilman, *Mandarins*, 61.

[29] *The End of Ideology*, 401–5.

[30] Raymond Aron, *L'opium des intellectuels* (Paris: Calmann-Lévy, 1955).

for a relocation of utopia from a problem of ideology to a problem of managing secular social time. Ideology in the Marxist sense of "class politics elevated to universal interest" was a product of the past, "a dead end." But utopia, in the way that it had been used by Karl Mannheim, was the progressive spirit to change the social order.[31] The very final words of *The End of Ideology* was a plea for this new utopia as the responsibility of a new group of Cold War engineers:

> the end of ideology is not—should not be—the end of utopia as well. If anything, one can begin anew the discussion of utopia only by being aware of the trap of ideology... There is now, more than ever, the need for utopia in the sense that men need—as they have always needed—some vision of their potential, some manner of fusing passion with intelligence. Yet the ladder of the City of Heaven can no longer be a 'faith ladder', but an empirical one: a utopia has to specify where one wants to go, how to get there, the costs of the enterprise, and some realization of, and justification for the determination of who is to pay.[32]

"Who is to pay" was a crucial turn of words to which we will return in Chapter 6, but Bell's notion of utopia thus contained a plea for the conversion of Cold War intellectuals from the ideological debates about the good and evil of the liberal and communist system, to debates about the rational management of progress and good or bad social outcomes. In these debates Bell foresaw complicated issues of the merging of social expectations and preferences, a substantial operational exercise.

THE FUTURE OF DEMOCRATIC INSTITUTIONS: THE FORD FOUNDATION AND THE FUTURIBLES PROJECT

A predominantly American historiography has understood modernization theory as a uniquely American construct, a product of the applied turn in American social science after 1945 and of the large investments in behavioralism of the big foundations and, in particular, the Ford Foundation.[33] The history of future research illustrates effectively that modernization theory was also a product of transnational circulation, and that the notions of human beings as rational decision makers which came to dominate American social science in the 1950s and 1960s in fact fell back on earlier European legacies. Daniel Bell's essays on future research were in fact renderings and translations of arguments that Bell knew from

[31] Both Mannheim and Polanyi were key to the development of the sociology of knowledge from the 1950s on, beginning in the reaction to the domestication of science and technology in Soviet communism. As such, the arguments of both scholars also played a key role in Congress debates, see Elena Aronova, "The Congress for Cultural Freedom, Minerva, and the Quest for Instituting Science Studies in the Age of Cold War," in *Minerva*, 2012, 50: 307–37.

[32] Bell, *The End of Ideology*, 405.

[33] See Gilman, *Mandarins of the Future*, 43 and 46; Roger Robin, *The Making of the Cold War Enemy. Culture and Politics in the Military Industrial Complex* (Princeton: Princeton University Press, 2009); Mark Solovey, *Shaky Foundations: The Politics-Patronage-Social Science Nexus in Cold War America* (New Brunswick: Rutgers University Press, 2013).

the context around French planning and so called *prospective*. Bell had many contacts with European social science. He acted as a consultant for the International Social Science Council as well as for the Ford Foundation from the mid 1950s on.[34] It was also as a consultant that Bell was sent to Paris by the Ford Foundation's director, Shepard Stone, in 1962 to report on the *Futuribles* project led by the philosopher Bertrand de Jouvenel. As a result of this trip, Bell, Eugene (Gene) Rostow, and Edward Shils would all become members of the *Futuribles* board, which thus turned into a kind of spearhead for modernization theory in Europe.[35]

Futuribles was one of the Ford Foundation's pet projects. Its director, de Jouvenel, had entered into the Foundation's network through the Congress, which was where he met Bell, Shils, Rostow, and Polanyi. Betrand de Jouvenel was a dark blue political theorist.[36] Zeev Sternhell sees de Jouvenel as one of the key intellectuals of French fascism. The first edition of Sternhell's book led to a notorious legal process in the 1980s and to the testimony of de Jouvenels' long time friend, Raymond Aron. Francois Denord has argued rather for de Jouvenel as a central character in French neoliberalism. The main biographer of de Jouvenel, Olivier Dard, stresses the diversity of de Jouvenel's thinking and his trajectory from fascist circles to ecological perspectives in the 1970s. It is clear that de Jouvenel was a somewhat eclectic figure. His books on sovereignty and power had earned him a certain fame in post-war liberal and neoliberal circles, but de Jouvenel became of interest to the Ford Foundation because of his ideas about a new science of political prediction as presented in the book, *L'art de la conjecture* (translated by the Congress as *The Art of Conjecture* in 1962).[37] The son of the French aristocrat Henry de Jouvenel, de Jouvenel was a dispossessed member of the French nobility. Henry's brother Robert was a key figure in French nationalism, and de Jouvenel himself had a past in fascist circles in the 1920s and 1930s, notably with the publication of the pamphlet *L'économie dirigée* with Librairie Valois in 1928. Librairie Valois was a small publishing house established by George Valois. Between 1928 and 1930 Librairie Valois published a number of nationalist or monarchist essays, and in 1930, *Perspectives socialistes* of Maurice Deat. *L'économie dirigée* was a call for a corporatist form of economic and social planning and expressed a deep concern with order.[38] In 1942, de Jouvenel had to flee Paris for Switzerland after a personal friendship with the German Embassador to Vichy, Otto Abetz, turned sour.[39]

[34] Jennifer Platt, *Fifty Years of the International Social Science Council* (Paris: UNESCO, 2002).

[35] Correspondence between Shepard Stone and Daniel Bell, FFA 61-22, grant files "Futuribles," and letter from Bell to Stone June 18, 1962; Correspondence between de Jouvenel and Bell in FFA 62-41 ("Strengthening the Democratic Institutions of Europe and Other Areas of the World"); and letters from de Jouvenel to Bell in Bertrand de Jouvenel's papers, correspondence files beginning in August 1955.

[36] Zeev Sternhell, *Ni droite ni gauche. L'ideologie fasciste en France* (Paris; Seuil, 2013); Denord, "French neoliberalism and its divisions"; Francois Denord, *Néolibéralisme version francaise. Histoire d'une idéologie politique* (Paris: Demopolis, 2007); Olivier Dard, *Bertrand de Jouvenel* (Paris: Seuil, 2008).

[37] Bertrand de Jouvenel, *Du pouvoir* (Genèva: Editions du cheval ailé, 1945); Bertrand de Jouvenel, *De la souveraineté* (Paris: Editions Marie Therèse Génin, 1955).

[38] Bertrand de Jouvenel, *L'économie dirigée. Le programme de la nouvelle génération* (Paris: Librairie Valois, 1928). Zeev Sternhell, *Neither Right nor Left. Fascist Ideology in France* (Princeton: Princeton University Press) 1986, 16, 348; Dard, *Bertrand de Jouvenel*, 95, 100–126.

[39] Dard, *Bertrand de Jouvenel*.

De Jouvenel joined Hayek's MPS in 1953, before joining the CCF in 1955.[40] While de Jouvenel disagreed with Hayek on the role of the state, and thought that the market could be a source of confusion and cultural degeneration in a mass society, he shared with Hayek an overarching concern with authority and order, but in de Jouvenel's terms this search for order was expressed in the idea of pure *politics*, not pure markets.[41] de Jouvenel's close friend was Raymond Aron. Denord has argued that the great French intellectual of the Congress was not de Jouvenel, but Aron, but de Jouvenel exerted a different kind of influence, directly related to his ideas of political prediction.[42] In the first years of the 1960s, de Jouvenel, funded by the Ford Foundation's division for the social sciences, travelled widely in order to gain support for "conjecture" with talks and essays aimed at a high level audience in the American social sciences, and taking place in venues such as the American Political Science Association, the Yale Law School, and the Geneva Institute for Advanced Studies in International Relations.[43] On a journey through American Ivy League campuses in 1960, de Jouvenel also attended the RAND research seminar with the particular purpose of connecting his conjecture to American future research as it was being performed at RAND. The trip was organized by Josselson and Daniel Bell.[44]

The origins of what would become *Futuribles* can be traced to the Congress' 1960 seminar, where de Jouvenel met Wally Nielsen, the Ford Foundation officer for the social sciences. The idea of a "*Looking forward project*" came according to de Jouvenel's diary notes directly from Nielsen.[45] The project was an experimental application of the largely theoretical ideas of *L'art de la conjecture* in actual predictions of the political development of mass democracy. "Looking forward" was a euphemism for a concrete interest, at least on behalf of the Ford Foundation, in methods and tools for studying the behavior of mass democracy. In the first descriptions of the *Futuribles* project, *Futuribles* was described as an "exploration of the evolution of the institutions of government in Europe."[46] But the final grant is classified in the Ford Archives under the title *"Studying the evolution of democratic institutions"* which included the idea of predicting political events and trends in the West and the developing world. In fact the Ford Foundation, which channelled the CIA funds to the Congress, intended *Futuribles* to become the Congress' social science venture, modeled on the template of an American think tank, but based in Europe.[47] The idea was that *Futuribles* would develop a scientific program for the Congress, and that this program would be oriented around the combination of

40 Dard, *Bertrand de Jouvenel*, 329.

41 Burgin, *The Great Persuasion*, 96–7, 113–14, 123–4.

42 Denord, *Néolibéralisme version francaise*, 224–9.

43 See Conference at Yale, December 4–6, 1965, FFA, grant file 62-41.

44 FFA 61-22.

45 De Jouvenel refers to *Futuribles* in his private notes as "the Nielsen project." Bertrand de Jouvenel papers, *Cahier de travail* nr. 100, August 11, 1960; letter from de Jouvenel to Waldemar Nielsen, May 5, 1961, "*Dear Wally, yesterday was a triumph for your idea*..." FFA 61-22.

46 "Description du projet futuribles," January 1961, FFA 62-41.

47 Michael Josselson was the former Cultural Liaison Officer in the Occupied Territories and was the main link between the CIA and the Congress until 1967.

theoretical reflections on the future of liberal institutions with the development of predictive methods intended for political science and international relations.[48]

In the years before, the Ford Foundation had invested heavily in European social science, in particular in France. The American foundations ventured massively into the social sciences from the 1950s on, with ideas of a Marshall Plan for the European social sciences.[49] Think tanks or independent research centers were a preferred modus operandi of the foundations. As Giuliana Gemelli has shown, the Ford Foundation had trouble reaching into French social science, which they understood as torn between the Marxist opium and an old, unmodern, and old-fashioned hierarchy and lack of concern with methods. They were also mindful of developments in French politics, where the productivity missions developed as part of the Marshall Plan after 1950 had escalated into full blown five-year plans under General de Gaulle. The think tank format, similar to a RAND like structure but in Europe, offered a mode of independence from academia and planning that was valuable.[50] It was also the independence of the think tank structure that allowed the Ford Foundation to choose the figure of their choice to lead such a UFO in the French landscape. They investigated several alternatives before settling with de Jouvenel. De Jouvenel was tainted by his wartime experience and had significant problems reentering Parisian intellectual life after 1945. For the Ford Foundation, his status as a free floating intellectual or *electron libre* with a large network in French academia, planning circles, and media outlets was an asset.[51]

The notion of conjecture was a mix of de Jouvenel's fundamentally conservative notions of political theory and his interest in the applied orientation of social science after 1945. De Jouvenel's two treatises on political theory, *Du pouvoir* (1945), *On Power,* begun during his time in Swiss exile, and *De la souveraineté (*1955), *Sovereignty*, written during a Ford-funded visiting professorship at Oxford, were reflections on the devastating effects of post-war politics on the constitutional principles inherited from nineteenth-century liberalism. De Jouvenel deplored the end of monarchy, a political regime which he understood as marked by stability, social peace, and order. Monarchy meant clarity of arrangements as the sovereign, the "Prince," embodied the power of decision and carried the responsibility of an enlightened interpretation of the popular will.[52] The idea of *conjecture* would recycle this concern with order, but also de Jouvenel's post-war interest in economic and social forecasting. De Jouvenel had developed this interest in business cycles, market movements, and conjecture as a journalist during and after the War. At Oxford, de Jouvenel had met several representatives of the emerging British school of

[48] Vincent Guiader, "Sociohistoire de la prospective," Ph.D. diss., Université Paris Dauphine, 2007.

[49] F. Denord, *Néolibéralisme version française,* 114; Ludovic Tournes, *L'argent de l'influence*; Giuliana Gemelli, ed., *The Ford Foundation and Europe, 1950s–1970s* (Rome: Memoirs of Europe, 1999).

[50] Giuliana Gemelli, *Fernand Braudel* (Paris, Odile Jacob, 1995).

[51] The Ford Foundation discussed several alternatives before settling on de Jouvenel, including Fernand Braudel's assistant, Clemence Heller.

[52] See Bertrand de Jouvenel, "Du principat," *Revue Française de Science Politique,* 1964, December issue: 1053–86. Monarchism was a central element in French fascism.

political and economic history, most importantly Peter Wiles and Colin Clark.[53] It was also at Oxford that de Jouvenel met Gene Rostow. Having problems with his reinsertion in academic life as he came back from Oxford, de Jouvenel began publishing a small statistical bulletin called SEDEIS. SEDEIS was mailed out to an eclectic circle of clients in businesses, public companies, planning entities and private persons through the assistance of de Jouvenel's often exasperated wife, Helene. SEDEIS was directly inspired by the beginnings of comparative economic statistical data and growth measures, much of which focused on predictions of the performance of the Soviet economy.[54] Under the label of *conjoncture*, the SEDEIS newsletters mixed statistical and monetary factoids with observations on the economic politics of different nations in order to make informed speculation on world markets. The newsletters also followed the development of forecasting theories and conjectural research in Western economics, and de Jouvenel corresponded with theorists ranging from Wassily Leontieff to Kenneth Arrow.[55] As part of the Ford grant in 1960, de Jouvenel began transforming the SEDEIS newsletter into a series of essays with the title *Futuribles*. The *Futuribles* essays replaced the statistical and quantitative focus on forecasting methods in SEDEIS with qualitative "speculations" on the future. The essays were written by leading social scientists, American modernization theorists, British economic historians, and French international relations theorists, and each essay dealt with either a country or a question of strategic interest to modernization theory. Essays tackled the choice of planning methods in India; experiments with workers councils in Yugoslavia; development planning in Ghana; the future role of the agrarian peasant in Eastern Europe. In fact, the essays were planned under the direct supervision of Shepard Stone, and Michael Josselson.[56]

In 1960, Stone also sent de Jouvenel to Poona in India, where he was to set up an Indian *Futuribles* office. The Indian section of the Congress for Cultural Freedom under the chairmanship of Asoka Mehta was directly inspired by the discussion on planning at the CCF seminar in Tokyo in 1957, where alternatives to five-year plans were discussed by planning experts and growth theorists such as Colin Clark. The Congress took a particular interest in India, where Nehru had

[53] Peter Wiles was a sovietology expert, and Colin Clark was a British economic historian and contributor to the development of the GDP measure and Marshall Plan negotiations, also the editor of the new *Journal of Economic History*. Both became central contributors to the *Futuribles* essays along with the economic historian Michael Postan. See David Engerman, *Know Your Enemy: The Rise and Fall of America's Soviet Experts* (New York: Oxford University Press, 2009); Matthias Schmelzer, *The Hegemony of Growth: The OECD and the Making of the Economic Growth Paradigm* (New York: Cambridge University Press, 2016), 89–92.

[54] de Jouvenel had been active in *La nouvelle revue de l'économie contemporaine*, a key review of economic thinking after the War, the purpose of which was to introduce modern American economic thought into France, in particular forecasting methods. Denord, *Néolibéralisme version francaise*, 213. The first issues of SEDEIS between 1953 and 1954 appeared under the name of *Faits et Conjonctures*.

[55] Bertrand de Jouvenel to Arrow, June 6, 1952 and Arrow to de Jouvenel, August 11, 1952, Bertrand de Jouvenel papers.

[56] Waldemar Nielsen to Bertrand de Jouvenel, June 14, 1961, FFA 61-22. Michael Josselson was the CIA link in the Congress and was exposed as such in 1966. It was Josselson who oversaw the translation into English of de Jouvenel's *L'art de la conjecture* (Monaco: Editions du Rocher, 1962).

created the first Indian five-year plan in 1951, and in Japan, both countries being seen as stages of experiment for a liberal version of long-term planning.[57] The chair of the Japanese group was Saburo Okita, later chair of Japan's OECD Delegation and foreign minister of Japan. The 1957 seminar also included the Jamaican development economist, Arthur Lewis, as well as the Yugoslav economist, Rudolf Bicanic.

The Futuribles essays and the think tank with the same name were the practical illustration of the ideas that de Jouvenel had set out in *The Art of Conjecture*. *The Art of* advocated a new future oriented approach in political science and international relations, a form of forecasting similar to economic forecasting, but for the political realm. The book set out the idea that the future was the result of a number of open possibilities (*futuribles*) that had to be taken into account in decision-making. Conjecture was the act of wisely thinking through these possibilities in order to privilege the futures that were good and avoid the ones that were bad.[58] The key question was thus not probability, but *desirability*, the capacity to actively chose and pursue good forms of development and distinguish these from bad. The original French title of *L'art de la conjecture* was a derivation of the Swiss mathematician Bernoulli's classical work on probability, *Ars conjectandis*. But futures in political and social life were not, *The Art of Conjecture* argued, mere patterns of probable evolutions. Economic forecasts dealt with strict causality assumptions and data that they modeled forwards. But political developments, de Jouvnenel proposed, could not be forecasted scientifically, that was after all the unacceptable Marxist position. This did not to de Jouvenel mean that conjecture was unscientific, but rather that conjecture was a kind of art of the good guesses, a skilful exercise in creating hypothetical forms of causality between possible events and sequences and evaluating these. This "art" of sketching futures from the visible germs of the future in the present, the *futuribles*, required both normative and objective forms of reasoning.

> We define, says Bernoulli, the art of conjecture as the art of evaluating as exactly as possible the probability of things, so that we might always, in our judgements and actions, orient ourselves toward that which would be best, the most suited, the safest and best advised, this which is the role of philosophers' wisdom and political prudence. Our problem cannot be to distribute probabilities between different possible futures unless these futures are first known. But it is not so that possible futures are given to us. On the contrary, they have to be invented by our imagination, through a work of inference by which futures are pulled out like the descendants of known or unknown states of the present. The intellectual construction of the probable future is in the real sense of the word an art. This is what we call here conjecture.[59]

[57] See Engerman, forthcoming; letter from Daniel Bell to Colin Clarke, October 22, 1956, CCF records, correspondence files 1956–57, box 6; Daniel Bell to Michael Josselson, April 6, 1957 and Bertrand de Jouvenel to Daniel Bell, May 18, 1957, on the "Asian group", CCF records, box 403, folder 3. Documents from the Indian CCF committee, Daniel Bell papers, box 35, folders 3, 19, and 53.

[58] de Jouvenel, *L'art de la conjecture*.

[59] *Nous définissions, dit Bernoulli, l'art de la conjecture... comme celui d'évaluer le plus exactement possible les probabilités des choses, afin que nous puissions toujours, dans nos jugements et nos actions, nous orienter sur ce qui aura été trouvé le meilleur, le plus approprié, le plus sûr, le mieux avisé, ce qui est le seul*

Futuribles were not, de Jouvenel argued, facts, and could not, therefore, be simply extrapolated as one would in economic forecasts. *Futuribles* were the possible descendants of the present and the consequences of presently existing choices, decisions, and actions in social life. They were therefore inherently the objects of value judgments and verdicts on desirability and undesirability on behalf of individual actors. But forms of rationality could be applied to the systematic scrutiny of possible futures, in ways that were not, de Jouvenel proposed, so different from conventional forms of explanation in the social sciences. Conjecture was the systematic study of these myriads of possible consequences of the present. The purpose of this analytical exercise was a form of ex-ante evaluation that could carry on the act of decision. De Jouvenel was fond of a quote from Alfred Marshall: "A chief purpose of every study of human action should be to suggest the probable outcome of present tendencies and thus to indicate such modifications of these tendencies as might further the wellbeing of mankind."[60] The same citation figured on some of the working papers from RAND.[61] Meanwhile, de Jouvenel was not uncritical of the rationality assumptions that dominated American experiments with prediction, in particular at RAND. To de Jouvenel, rationality assumptions had limited bearing on prediction in social and political affairs in an era in which the key problem was precisely that rational instincts could no longer be presumed. "*Les instincts rationnels ne semblent pas fiables*". In particular, rationality assumptions could not foresee the "event"—*l'evenement politique*. Conjecture was an alternative way of predicting in social and political affairs, which included the active creation of desirable images for action so that forms of behavior could be influenced beforehand. As will be explained in the next chapter, this was a standing debate around gaming, a debate carried out in the departmental seminars at RAND that de Jouvenel visited in 1960.

The Art of Conjecture was profoundly misunderstood in coming decades as a plea for a pluralistic notion of the future as associated with human freedom. A more accurate interpretation is that de Jouvenel drew inspiration from the language of the Congress and that this language of "freedom of choice" allowed him to dress up and translate the concern with monarchic order and authority from his previous writings into a kind of neoliberal creed. The 1928 fascist pamphlet *L'Economie dirigee* spoke of an undefined "*cadre d'autorité*." In de Jouvenel's notes and drafts for *The Art of Conjecture*, this "authority frame" appears in the idea of conjecture as a mechanism of coordination which can weigh on what he sees as a dangerous

objet de la sagesse du philosophe et de la prudence du politique. Notre problème ne pourrait être de distribuer les probabilités entre les différents futurs possibles que si, d'abord, cet ensemble de futurs possibles étaient portés à notre connaissance. Or il s'en faut bien que les futurs possibles nous soient ainsi "donnés." Au contraire, ils doivent être construits par notre imagination, se livrant à un travail de "proférence" qui les tire comme descendants possibles d'états présents plus ou moins connus. La construction intellectuelle d'un futur vraisemblable est, dans la pleine force du terme, un art. C'est cela que nous appelons ici conjecture." de Jouvenel, *L'art de la conjecture*, 31.

60 See Olaf Helmer, *Social Technology* (New York: Basic books, 1966), 11–13. The citation comes from Alfred Marshall, *Industry and Trade*, 1919, 7. de Jouvenel, undated proposal, FFA62-41.

61 Bertrand de Jouvenel, "Les recherches sur la décision," *SEDEIS*, January 20, 1962.

plurality of coming possible futures in a mass society. At the heart of this lurked the fear of the event, the sudden and irrational move of the masses.

> I propose to look at society as an immense collection of individuals, each the carrier of his own energy, each with his own project... in normal times, the scene of the whole changes most slowly and progressively. But individual vectors do not exercise a convergent pressure. There is a change of state in the chemical sense if these different pressures somehow are regrouped in one and sole pressure point. From there stems the event.[62]

Spontaneous and revolutionary vents were, in de Jouvenel's understanding, inherent possibilities in a mass society that he understood as inherently prone to irrationality.[63] Post-war society was characterized by an infinite mass of individuals that de Jouvenel sometimes compared to a school of fish. Like fish, they might take off in an unexpected direction at a sudden fright.[64]

This irrationality stemmed more specifically from a problem of decision. Mass society was a society in which individuals were to an unprecedented extent free to make a multitude of decisions about their own fate. But political systems contained no mechanism for ensuring what future results would stem from this myriad of uncoordinated decisions and individual desires. In addition, post-war political systems had institutionalized what de Jouvenel saw as a dangerous diffusion of the power of decision. This, to de Jouvenel, led to an important and familiar critique of bureaucracy and planning. De Jouvenel abhorred Gaullism, which he saw as the very opposite of the ideal of the order of enlightened monarchy, in other words as a perversion of the idea of the prince. De Jouvenel saw the corporatism and bureaucratization of the Fifth Republic as a dangerous diffusion of sovereignty and a constant catering to organized interests.[65] He identified planning, and not only Soviet planning but also the five-year plans of the French Commissariat General du Plan, as a new and very particular form of hold on time. The French Plan was created in 1946 as part of the productivity missions of the Marshall Plan. Beginning with the Vth Plan in the late 1950s, the Plan ventured out into general economic planning with five-year plans that were destined to provide the underpinnings of de Gaulle's reform program and intensified industrial planning. The first drafts for *L'art de la conjecture* described the economic and social policy as a "speculation on the future."[66] The effect of this speculation was the creation of a set of unforeseeable and potentially uncontrollable consequences over time. From these reflections emerged a not unfamiliar idea: that the modern welfare state, through its constant desire to meet a myriad of potentially conflicting demands,

62 *Je propose de regarder la société comme une immense collection d'individus, chacun porteur d'une énergie propre, chacun muni d'un vecteur correspondant à son projet propre... En temps normal, la scène de l'ensemble se déforme très lentement et progressivement sous l'effet des composants déformateurs des vecteurs individuels. Mais ces vecteurs qui exercent des pressions simultanées n'exercent pas une pression convergente... il y a changement d'état au sens chimique s'il arrive que les pressions diverses soient regroupées en une seule et appliquées en un point. De ce changement sort l'événement* (B. de Jouvenel, 'Trois conférences sur la prévision' draft, FFA 62-41.

63 See Harold Lasswell, *Power and Personality* (London: WW Norton and Company, 1948).

64 *"un banc de poissons"*, de Jouvenel, "Trois conférences sur la prévision" draft, FFA 61-22.

65 de Jouvenel, *De la souveraineté*; Dard, *Bertrand de Jouvenel*, 205–54.

66 "Sur l'évolution des formes de gouvernements", draft, January 1961, FFA 62-41.

and through its use of bureaucracy and long-term planning as the core technologies of the political, was exercising a new form of power over time. Planning extended the reach of public decisions in unacceptable ways. This raised the problem of freedom again, because once the apparent effects of a decision were manifest in the polity, its consequences had already been carried far ahead into time. The greatest menace to freedom in the post-war age was thus, to de Jouvenel, that future horizons were threatened by the multiplicity and temporal reach of political programs.[67] "Why is it that despite increasing progress and range of merchandises and choice, we feel as if freedom is thwarted and progress runs between narrowing banks? This is a very strange feeling. What is its source?"[68]

THE FUTURE AS SYNTHÈSE AND RATIONAL DECISION IN THE CENTRE DE PROSPECTIVE

Conjecture was, in fact, an idea of *anti-planning*, of finding ways of protecting "pure politics" from the invasive power of long-term plans.[69] The final section of the chapter returns to the problem of conjecture as anti-planning, but a detour is necessary here to show the profoundly technocratic origins of conjecture, and the way in which the notion of the future set in place a strange marriage between a notion of order inherited from the interwar period, and ideas of rational decision taken from post-war American social science and modernization theory.

De Jouvenel was through a set of unlikely circumstances, and a good dose of American interference, the heir to a French project with its roots in the interwar period, *prospective*.[70] *Prospective* developed in the 1950s as a fusion between certain currents of practical philosophy and management theory, focused on the possibilities of rationalizing or "synthesizing" the act of decision. The concept of *prospective* figured in the XVth tome of the new French Encyclopedia, a project begun by the *Annales* historian, Lucien Febvre, before the War and handed over in 1945 to the philosopher Gaston Berger. The volume was entitled *Le monde en devenir*, the coming world or the emergent world, and dealt with the human experience of time. It had three titles, *L'Histoire*, *l'Evolution*, and *la Prospective*. The third section was devoted to the new scientific methods of decision, and introduced core strands of American Operations Research, cybernetics, and systems analysis, to the French context.[71] It was written by Berger.

67 De Jouvenel, "Du principat," *Revue Française de la Science Politique*, 1964, 14 (06): 1053–86.

68 De Jouvenel draft text on the Surmising forum, 1962, FFA 62-51. Let's note the recycling of Polanyi's turn of words: progress runs between distant shores. To de Jouvenel these distant shores were "narrowing banks."

69 De Jouvenel, *L'art de la Conjecture*, 224, 261, 278. Jenny Andersson and Pauline Prat, "Gouverner le 'long terme'. La prospective et la production bureaucratique des futurs en France," *Gouvernement et action publique*, 2015, 3: 9–29.

70 Bertrand de Jouvenel letters to Gaston Berger, January 25, 1956, November 22 and 25, 1955. Bertrand de Jouvenel papers.

71 Gaston Berger and Lucien Febvre 1959, *L'Encyclopédie francaise. Tome XX, Le monde en devenir* (Paris: 1959), 204–12; Gemmelli, *Braudel*, 149.

Gaston Berger was not your ordinary French philosopher. As the *Inspecteur de l'education superieure,* he was the overseer of the reconstruction of the French social sciences after 1945. It was Berger who negotiated the American funding to the so called *Sixième section* of the new social sciences or the "*sciences de l'homme,*" in which the *Annales* school was a central undertaking.[72] Berger travelled with Fernand Braudel to the US in 1957 and 1958. During this trip he met the *parnasse* of American social science. He visited the Ford Foundation's newly created Center for Behavioural Study in Palo Alto (see Chapter 8) and he also used the trip to convince the Ford Foundation to fund his new forward looking history or "anthropology of time."[73] It was the Berger proposal on "forward looking thought" that prepared the terrain for the Ford Foundation's interest in the *Futuribles* project, which they passed on to de Jouvenel after Berger died in a car crash in 1960.[74]

Conjecture in the form designed by de Jouvenel was not by any means identical to Berger's *prospective,* but *prospective* contained an original reflection on the problem of the future as a problem of decision in a mass society. As such it stemmed from interwar notions of technocracy as a necessary bulwark against the failures of parliamentary democracy, and as a particular constellation between French engineers and the Patronat, expressing itself in the idea of management science and rational decision.[75] Berger was not only a philosopher but also an industrialist, the manager of a large industrial fertilizer plant before World War II. His beginnings in philosophy came from what he termed "caractèrologie": the "study (of) an object (the human being) in the objective of knowing how he will behave in a given situation."[76] Caractèrologie was a biologist depiction of human beings as shaped by predictable and classifiable characters or personality types. These were informed by different capacities for action and decision.[77] Berger's first essay *L'attitude prospective* described what he thus labelled a "prodigious biological adventure," focused on the human capacity to make decisions and embrace action.[78] In 1957, Berger created the so called *Centre de prospective* around a group of like minded intellectuals. The purpose of the Centre was to study the situation of human beings in the context of the "general problems" posed by the social,

[72] Brigitte Mazon, *Aux origins de l'Ecole des hautes etudes en sciences sociales. Le role du mecenat americain, 1920–1960* (Paris, La Decouverte).

[73] Letter from Shepard Stone to Gaston Berger, November 2, 1954; letters from Leslie Bradey to Gaston Berger and Shepard Stone, October 25, 1955; and to Stone, December 31, 1955, FFA 51-60.

[74] Obituary of Gaston Berger in the London *Times*, November 14, sent by Nicholas Nabokov to Shepard Stone, November 20, 1960, FFA 51-60.

[75] Gabrielle Hecht, "Planning a technological nation" in Hughes, T., and Hughes, A., eds., *Systems, Experts and Computers. The Systems Approach in Management and Engineering, World War II and After.* (Cambridge MA: MIT Press, 2003), 133–61; Francois Denord and Odile Henry, "La modernisation avant la lettre. Le patronat français et la rationalisation (1925–1940)," in *Sociétés contemporaines*, 2007, 4(68): 83–104, and Paul-André Rosental, *La santé au travail, 1880–1986* (Paris: La Decouverte, 2006) 41–56.

[76] "*étudier un objet afin de savoir comment il se comportera dans une situation donnée*", cited in Guiader, *Sociohistoire de la prospective*, 81.

[77] Guiader, *Sociohistoire de la prospective*, 83; Gaston Berger, *Caractère et personnalité,* 1955. In 1939, Berger published a paper on Husserl's phenomenological notion of consciousness, Gaston Berger, "Husserl et Hume," *Revue internationale de philosophie*, 1939: 342–53.

[78] Gaston Berger, "L'attitude prospective," *Prospective*, May 1958, 1: 10.

cultural, and political consequences of progress. The Centre recycled notions that Berger had developed for the French Employer Federation's managerial research unit, the *Centre d'études et de recherches des chefs d'entreprises*, CRC in the early 1950s.[79] The purpose of the CRC was to promote management studies and business education for corporate leaders. In his papers and talks for the CRC, Berger set out his vision of a near metaphysical entrepreneurial *geist*, a "spirit" of decision, *l'esprit de la décision*, or attitude of the future, *attitude prospective*. This spirit or attitude was not a mere set of methods or tools of decision making, but a question of character, a specific form of rationality that Berger saw as embodied by a particular decisionist elite, the "men of decision" (sometimes also referred to in the proceedings of the CdP as the "*militants de l'avenir*").

The Centre de prospective also incorporated a group that had been close to the French Patronat since the Liberation, the *Conseillers de synthèse*. The *Conseillers de synthèse* were management consultants, equipped with theories of organization, human resources, and professional or industrial hygiene. Among the *Conseillers de synthèse* involved in the Centre de prospective was the social hygienist and *médécin de travail* par excellence, Andre Gros. Gros was close to Papon during the War, but cleared by the Liberation in 1945, at which point he created the *Conseillers* as a management consultancy for the French Patronnat.[80] In 1958, Gros published the book *La reconstruction de l'homme*. Through Gros, the CdP became the direct heir of French eugenics. Gros brought the concept of *synthèse* as referring to a new form of universal or total knowledge from the so called Fondation Francaise pour l'Etude des Problèmes Humains (FFEPH) created in 1940 by Alexis Carrel. *Synthèse* was a tremendously complicated notion, which stands at the crossroads of very different understandings of time, being, and the new "sciences de l'homme" in the interwar era.[81] Carrel was a surgeon, biologist, and convinced eugenicist.[82] The study of human problems in the FFEPH were directly influenced by the racist American eugenicist Albert Wiggam's 1923 book *The New Decalogue of Science*. The publications of the Foundation also make reference to Julian Huxley's *Science and Social Needs*, published in 1935. The Carrel Foundation, in turn, replaced an earlier construction, the *Centre d'études pour les problèmes humains* created in 1937 by Jean Coutrot. Coutrot was one of the founders of *X-crise*, a group of French engineers and economists who promoted scientific management as the solution to "all problems of the human condition," and who set this scientific management in

[79] Statutes, Centre international de prospective, *Prospective*, 1957, 1.

[80] Guiader, *Sociohistoire de la prospective*, 29, 31, 156, 175.

[81] See Giuliana Gemmelli, "Henri Berr, communauté intellectuelle et stratégies institutionnelles. Henri Berr et la Fondation du Centre international de Synthèse", *La Revue de Synthèse*, 1987, 2: 256; Gemmelli. *Fernand Braudel*, 140–54.

[82] *Cahiers de la Fondation francaise pour l'étude des problèmes humains*, nr 3 mars 1945, 13. Alain Drouard, *Une inconnue des sciences sociales, la Fondation Alexis Carrel sur l'étude des problèmes humains* (Paris, INED, 1992); Alexi Reggiani, *God's Eugenicist. Alexis Carrel and the Sociobiology of Decline* (Oxford: Berghahn Books, 2007); Rosental, *La santé au travail*, 56. Carrel's first drafts for the Foundation included the titles "Council for Human Problems," "Institute ofMan", but also the "Center for the Improvement of the Human Race" ("Centre d'amélioration de la race humaine") as well as "Charting the Future". Reggiani, *God's Eugenicist*, 99.

opposition to the democratic experiments of the popular Fronts. At the end of his life Coutrot developed a "transhumanism," a mystique of the future that would follow from what he described as the fully fledged rationalization of the total social structure.[83]

French historians have been long wrapped up in a historiographic dispute about the nature of French fascism and its relationship to the institutions of the Vth Republic. Coutrot is known in French historiography as a *non-conformiste des années trentes*, part of an argument for technocracy as the alternative to the social revolution defended both by fascism and communism. Many *non-conformistes* had links to the radical nationalist and monarchist movements of *Ordre nouveau* and *Action française* and in the 1920s and 1930s. Eugenics, catholicism, and monarchism were all integral parts of French fascism. Eugenics were disqualified after 1945. This does not mean however that eugenic ideas as such disappeared, rather, they traveled into some of the core institutions of the IVth and Vth Republics.[84] The Fondation Carrel would lay the basis for post-war French demographics, with the creation in 1945 of the Institut Nationale d'Etudes Démographiques, INED. Gros was a direct link between the Fondation Carrel and the idea of *prospective*, which from 1960 on would be taken up by the *Plan*. Meanwhile, Gaston Berger was a former resistance fighter, and there were important differences between Gros' totalizing notion of the future and Berger's idea of *prospective* as a kind of phenomenology or "*antropologie du temps*."[85] Berger was also a personal friend of Braudel, and Braudel foresaw the creation within the new *Sixième section* of a chair of prospective anthropology intended for Berger. The chair would create an equivalent to Braudel's own economic and social history, by applying forms of modeling and forecasting to the future dimension of the *longue durée*. Berger died before this project of a new *antropologie du temps* could materialize, and, posthumously, his links to the conseillers de synthese were obscured.[86] It is nevertheless possible to point to clear elements of continuity between the notion of *prospective* and earlier technocratic reasoning, and suggest that this carried over into post-war ideas of conjecture as a form of decision science.

Prospective was to Berger a profoundly elitist construct that echoed Coutrot's transhumanism in its emphasis on a mythical spirit or attitude to the future. The idea of creating a future oriented human character capable of "décision rationelle" through a new comprehensive and totalizing humanistic science, focused on the complete comprehension of man, had clear eugenicist heritage. This applied also

[83] Guiader, *Sociohistoire de la prospective*, 68; Reggiani, *God's Eugenicist*, 66–9, 91. Olivier Dard, *Jean Coutrot, de l'ingénieur au prophète* (Presses Universaires Franc-Comtoises, 1999), 144–56, 223–5, 239–41, 331–3, 382.

[84] Paul-Andre Rosental, *Destins de l'eugenisme* (Paris: Seuil, 2016).

[85] Gaston Berger, *Phenonoménologie du temps et de prospective* (Paris: Presses Universitaires de France, 1960).

[86] The preparatory documents for the *Maison des sciences de l'homme* mention several different projects in anthropology, including the social anthropology of Claude Levi-Strauss, but the only mention of the Centre de Prospective figures on a note from Braudel to Berger in 1960 in which he asks for quick confirmation of the creation of the Center within the MSH. Documents préparatifs de la Sixième Section, Archives of the MSH.

to the particular social group that could carry rational decision, namely expert engineers and managers. These experts were to Berger the offspring between "savants," on the one side, and "practical men" on the other, thus embodying a kind of enlightened and reflected form of action-minded decision. Finally, the notion of *prospective* carried over a crucial element of future crisis from interwar ideas of human degeneration. This crisis was understood by the *conseillers* as being produced by a general confusion and disorientation of man in the context of accelerating progress. This phenomenon was described in the debates of the Center with the concept of *l'embrouillement* or *l'encombrement*, confusion or "crowding."[87] Crowding was a phenomenon depicted with a by now familiar argument as arising from the development of a technologically puissant mass society, in which social change was characterized by a myriad of individual actions without a mechanism of coordination. Such a society produced ample opportunities for clash and crash, collisions of contradictory impulses to action in everything from traffic situations to bureaucratic overload.[88] As technological capacity had increased, the capacity to actively grasp and comprehend a new human situation had reduced, and Man's *will* had lagged behind his new technophysical aptitudes, to the point that he could no longer be characterized as being free. Was it possible, in such circumstances, to talk of the free will and of a subjective capacity to order desires and preferences in a rational way, or had Man in fact lost his capacity to act?[89] Importantly, crowding also denoted a new phenomenon of planetary disorder in relationships between the Western world and what Alfred Sauvy, member of the Centre, would famously describe as the "third world," *le tiers monde*,[90] Algeria and Indochina. These new relationships were described as a clash and rejection of the future images proposed by Western civilization.[91]

As Western Man was thus depicted as being in the process of losing his capacity to grasp the future, *prospective* emerged as the remedy. If Man could develop the "attitude prospective" he would re-emerge as the active pilot of change and regain a capacity to handle the future "actively."[92] In his last writings before his death, Berger proposed this to be the basis of a new futures pedagogy, an education project designed to give children the capacity to adapt to emergent conditions by speeding up the process of human evolution.[93]

[87] Centre International de prospective, Compte rendu de la troisième réunion du Conseil d'administration, September 28, Château de Menars, FFA 57-1128.

[88] "Conséquences générales des grandes techniques nouvelles," *Prospective*, January 1959, 2. Centre International de Prospective "Etudes en cours", FFA 57-1128.

[89] Gaston Berger, "Avant propos," *Prospective*, November 1960, 6: 3.

[90] Sauvy was a demographer, who coined the concept of *tiers monde*, see Alfred Sauvy, *Le tiers monde* (Paris: Presses Universitaires de France, 1952).

[91] "Rapport de l'Occident avec le reste du monde," *Prospective*, April 1959, 3: 11–22.

[92] G. Berger, "L'attitude prospective," *Prospective*, May 1958, 1: 1–11, 3; *Cahiers de la Fondation française pour l'étude des problèmes humains*, March 3,1945, 13. André Gros, "Conséquences générales des grandes techniques nouvelles," *Prospective*, January 1959, 2: 1–10, 6; Berger, "Attitude prospective."

[93] "Centre for prospective anthropology," and "Planning the future". Drafts, Gaston Berger, Centre de prospective, FFA 57-1128.

Berger's death unleashed a power struggle in the CdP between the conseillers de synthese, on the one hand, and a group of planners, led by Louis Armand, Francois Bloch Laine, and Pierre Masse, on the other.[94] While the mysticism around the spirit of decision evaporated, the notion of rational decision as an essential tool of coordination for a modern mass society characterized by a myriad of individual and collective decisions was what would become the central element of *prospective*.[95]

CONJECTURE AS ANTI-PLANNING: THE SURMISING FORUM

De Jouvenel's argument for conjecture as a way of choosing between desirable and undesirable futures left a million dollar question, namely, who would be charged with the intricate task of enlightened speculation on the basis of rational decision? *Conjecture* was in actual fact an argument for a new form of futuristic expertise, which, to de Jouvenel, had to be situated outside the state bureaucracy but have a well developed flare for politics. De Jouvenel's talks and essays in the early 1960s were aimed at the highest level of international political science and international relations theory. The seminars organized at the International political science association, the Yale Law School and Sciences Po brought together the key names of American and European modernist political science (and many names of the CCF): Irving Kristol, Melvin Lasky, Ithiel de Sola Pool, Oscar Morgenstern, John von Neuman, Robert Oppenheimer, Denis de Rougemont, Maurice Allais, Jean Paul Casanova, Stanley Hoffman, Olaf Helmer, Robert Dahl, Seymour Martin Lipset, Paul Lazarsfeld, Karl Deutsch, Herman Kahn, Edward Shils, Eugene Rostow, Jean Claude Casanova.[96] These political scientists were also the particular group identified by de Jouvenel as the experts who as part of their professional responsibility should embrace conjecture as a particular form of explanation of political events. This, to de Jouvenel, was an alternative form of scientific prediction, which, because it relied on expertise, seemed acceptable (this was of course totally different from Marxist prediction, which was a Party construct). If conjecture was not about *fact*, it was nevertheless, to de Jouvenel, a form of explanation, a forward looking reflection which could be falsified by coming events, and which could also be informed by theories and postulates of political science. As such it had, despite

[94] Louis Armand, "Vues prospectives sur les transports," *Prospective*, 1958, 1: 37–43. Armand was the director of the SNCF, which played a key role in the importation of Operations Research and systems analysis into the French planning apparatus. He was also the future architect of the European Coal and Steel Union and the EURATOM program, which integrated prospective or forecasting as a new planning approach in the European Community.

[95] *Prospective* was published between 1957 and 1960. In 1958 the Centre d'études prospective became the Centre international de prospective, a name change motivated by the desired relation with the Ford Foundation. It was renamed Association Gaston Berger after Berger's death in 1960.

[96] Conference at Yale Law School, December 4–6, 1964; meeting of the International Political Science Association, Geneva, September 21–25, 1964; Institut d'études politiques, Paris, April 5–7, 1963. FFA 62-41; Bertrand de Jouvenel papers, box 57.

the minor fact that direct observation was not possible, all the prerequisites of a modern empiricist science. In fact, through the study of possible futures, de Jouvenel argued that political science could leave the dusty halls of "moribund science," old political philosophy and political theory, and become a modern social science as defined by its predictive capacity. This came with a moral charge: "The political scientist must seek to coordinate anticipation."[97] This would make the political scientists into a necessary counter-power to a growing omnipotent bureaucracy, and charge them with the vital function of evaluating desirable futures. De Jouvenel was inspired here by the move to independent conjectural clearing houses like NBER, the way that the economists had taken responsibility for public, but independent, economic forecasts. In contrast to planning, such conjectural clearing houses occupied a vital democratic function outside the state apparatus, independent of the modern princes and their bureaucracies.

De Jouvenel's understanding of freedom as emerging from order and authority and fundamentally threatened by mass society was not dissimilar to Hayek's notion of the market as the main mechanism of coordination, but it drew on another key philosopher, Michael Polanyi. Polanyi set the tone for the 1955 CCF seminar by situating the future as a question of free and rational choice. Polanyi was originally a chemist, born in a Jewish family in Hungary. In Vienna, he followed the so called Vienna circle in physics, mathematics, and chemistry (see the next chapter). Forced to leave Europe, Polanyi came to the UK in order to take up a chair in chemistry in Manchester, and took a leading position there in the anti-Soviet Society for the Freedom of Science. Polanyi's understanding of the freedom of science here is important. Polanyi rejected, as did many other scholars in the Congress, Karl Popper's 1953 assertion that liberal social science had to be value free and was defined by objective criteria of verification and falsification. This was a highly problematic position for liberal intellectuals who thought that social science was an inherently normative enterprise, concerned with setting the social objectives of society (and that it could only so be defended against totalitarianism). Scientific explanation, to Polanyi, as emphasized in the 1951 book *The Logic of Liberty*, cited by both de Jouvenel and Daniel Bell, was not a matter of reference to an external objective reality, but rather, a matter of the subjective experience of trained scientists.[98] This conception lay at the heart of Polanyi's understanding of science, and social science, as an inherent element of order, a kind of order that surfaced both in his idea of tacit knowledge, and in his idea of science as community. Verification was an intersubjective process that depended on a free community of scholars, not on inherent properties in science as such. As such social science was not a neutral or value free enterprise, but had to be a constant reiteration of the value of freedom. Prediction, said Polanyi, was not a test of verification, but rather, an expert statement on the future. To Polanyi, this meant that social science had

[97] Bertrand de Jouvenel "Political science and prevision," *American Political Science Review*, 1965: 59 (1): 29–38.

[98] Michael Polanyi, *The Logic of Liberty* (London: Routledge and Keegan Paul, 1951) cited by Bell, "Twelve modes of prediction, 873; Aronova, 'The Congress for Cultural Freedom, Minerva, and the Quest for Instituting Science Studies'; Gremion, *L'intelligence de l'anticommunisme*, 116.

the task of making value judgments on desirable and undesirable developments, and that these judgments could be made on the basis of rational evaluation. Arguably, it was exactly this position that gained Polanyi the presidency of the Congress for Cultural Freedom in 1955.[99] The idea of conjecture recycled this idea that desirable futures could be identified on the basis of a process of rational evaluation drawing on social science expertise, and that this process was essential for the protection of freedom.

Conjecture drew also on a second notion, the principal reason that Polanyi would later be credited as a neoliberal philosopher, having to do with the way that he would also associate a free community of scientists with the free organization of knowledge and identify the market as the basis for this organization. De Jouvenel first presented his idea of a "surmising forum" or "look out institution" during his visit to the RAND research seminar in 1964. The trip was organized by Bell, and de Jouvenel met, at this seminar, Hasan Ozbekhan, the systems analyst who would later go on to develop the first computer model for the Club of Rome, but also the two mathematicians Olaf Helmer and Theodore Gordon (see the next chapter).[100] De Jouvenel's notion of a surmising forum laid out the basis for a "new constitutionalism" by which conjecture was entrusted to independent expertise in political science and positioned outside the reach of long-term planning.[101] The text on the surmising forum began:

> Policies and programs imply a very serious threat to freedom. It is quite easy for a faction in power to regard some policies and programs as called for by the 'needs of our time' and extremely difficult for the remainder of the community to defend itself against this suggestion.[102]

The surmising forum was an antidote to this condition, by establishing a kind of clearing house for conjecture, not much different from the agencies of conjectural economic forecasting that had been created in the 1950s. De Jouvenel's paper discussed two possibilities for such an agency, the first being a public agency whose independence would be guaranteed by the constitution, and, second, a think tank operating on a "free market for conjecture." His preference was for the second idea. "We need a free trade in conjectures and independent establishments which can be houses of exchange for such products of expertise speculatively employed." With the creation of a "free market for surmises" the freedom of choice between different possible futures would be guaranteed. The surmising forum was of course a sales pitch for *Futuribles*.

[99] Polanyi, *The Logic of Liberty*, 16–17; Esther Lightcap Meek, *Comfort with Reality. Michael Polanyi's Realism and Why it Matters* (Eugene Oregon: Concorde books, 2017); Mary Joe Nye, *Michael Polanyi and his Generation. Origins of the Social Construction of Science* (Chicago: Chicago University Press, 2011) 223; Or Rosenboim, *The Emergence of Globalism*, 223f.

[100] de Jouvenel, "A surmising forum," paper to RAND interdepartmental seminar, November 30 1964, AFF 62-41, de Jouvenel, *L'art de la conjecture*, 343.

[101] Bertrand de Jouvenel, "Sur L'évolution des formes de gouvernements," January 1961, Bertrand de Jouvenel's papers.

[102] Ibid.

CONCLUDING REMARKS

Daniel Bell's evaluation of the *Futuribles* project in 1962 concluded that de Jouvenel's interest in the future was philosophical, and lacked concreteness and application.[103] Ford officers were also, like de Jouvenel's wife, increasingly exasperated by his eccentric character and endemic lack of organization. The American interest in France faded decisively after 1967, when de Gaulle withdrew from NATO. In 1967, several other future research initiatives also caught the Ford Foundation's attention, including the so-called Institute for the Future, discussed in the next chapter, the International Institute for Applied Systems Analysis, IIASA, in Vienna, and a possible European forecasting institute to be directed by the British economist, Andrew Shonfield.[104] In fact, at this point, the Nixon administration was clearly considering the creation of an Institute for the World Future on American soil.[105] As he lost the Ford grant for *Futuribles*, de Jouvenel turned to the French planning apparatus. The Commissariat au Plan took an active interest in the idea of *prospective* as a form of long-term planning from 1965 on, by integrating the ideas of Berger and Masse into its new Long Term Division, where prospective became a form of long-term planning oriented around the capacity to make rational decisions (*choix rationnels*).[106] In 1967, the CIA funding of the Congress was also disclosed, marking the end of nearly twenty years of defending liberalism on the European continent, and, in fact world wide as the Congress set up offices not only in India but also on the African continent. The Congress was restructured into the International Association for Cultural Freedom. One of the first seminars of the International Association was a seminar on futurology organized by Daniel Bell.[107] By this time, Bell had taken future research into the mainstream of American social science through his chairmanship of the so called Commission for the Year 2000 in the Academy for the Arts and Sciences. In many ways the CY2000 was a *Futuribles* venture on American soil, a surmising forum for a rapidly changing American society (see Chapter 6).

Meanwhile, futurology was increasingly the target of a critique to which we will return in later chapters, which understood it as a new form of elite rule over coming time. Having attended the *Futuribles* conference at Sciences Po in 1965 on "the new constitutionalism" (see Figure 4.1), Robert Jungk wrote in the *Sunday Times* of "futuribles at work":

> In Paris this month a hundred wise men, gathered by an organization called *futuribles*, tried without crystal ball to predict the future relationships between governments and the governed. Economists, sociologists, psychologists, politologists, administrators,

[103] Memorandum from Daniel Bell to Shepard Stone, August 11, 1962; letter from Waldemar Nielsen to Shepard Stone, May 1,1966, FFA 62-41.

[104] "Proposal for an Institute of Forecasting Studies" from Michael Young and Andrew Shonfield, November 30, 1967. Ford Foundation archives file L 68–261.

[105] Letter from Will Sutton to Michael Young, June 8, 1968, FFA 68–261.

[106] Pierre Massé, "Prevision et prospective", *Prospective*, 1959, 4: 91–120.

[107] Frances Stonor Saunders, *Who paid the piper. The CIA and America's Cultural Cold War* (London: Granta, 1999).

Figure 4.1. The Future of Political Institutions, Paris 1966.
(Robert Jungk Nachlass.)

jurists and historians from both sides of the Iron Curtain, from Afro Asia, the Middle East and the affluent world spent three whole days playing the 'If... then' game. When Henry VIII divorced Catherine of Aragon he did not know the reformation would follow. *Futuribles,* which was founded by the distinguished philosopher Bertrand de Jouvenel, might have warned him... Despite Marx and Tocqueville, whose presence was conspicuously missed at this gathering, political science is still, like astrology, a speculative art. As one delegate put it, 'Governing is like selling soap, one has always to think of tomorrow's consumers'. *Futuribles* is very good at that.[108]

[108] "Futuribles at work," *Sunday Times* April 18, 1965.

5

The Future as Social Technology. Prediction and the Rise of Futurology

> If we refuse to succumb to... "the new fatalism" of passively accepting new social institutions thrust upon us by an uncontrolled technological explosion, then surely it follows that we must search for a constructive approach which will ensure to us some measure of control over the future of our society.[1]

A GENERAL THEORY OF THE FUTURE

Daniel Bell's understanding that the future could be put under a conscious approach and shaped as a question of active and rational choice was based on actual developments in American forecasting. While Bell was enchanted by these developments in social science, others were troubled. It was the American interest in future research as a quintessential Cold War technology that led critical futurists to object to what they saw as a dangerous colonization of the long term. The super computer in Robert Jungk's 1956 book *Tomorrow is Already Here* drew inspiration from John von Neumann's MANIAC computer that calculated the algorithms of the first intercontinental ballistic missiles.[2] In Jungk's depiction, the super computer was an electronic oracle, charged with calculating all possible future probabilities of human development and replacing all moral notions of the future with machine rationality. As such it was an expression of unforgivable hubris.

The MANIAC computer was developed at Las Alamos by mathematicians and engineers, many of whom would, after 1946, go to work at Project RAND, the new research and development unit of the US Airforce.[3] The purpose of project RAND was to develop new analytical approaches to the problems of future warfare. In the following decades, project RAND became the RAND Corporation, and initial experiments with gaming, modeling, and simulation developed into forms of strategy, planning, and policy analysis for the civilian sphere in what is now a well-known story.[4] The RAND Corporation holds a preeminent position in

[1] Olaf Helmer, *Social Technology* (New York: Basic Books, 1966), 32.

[2] Paul Edwards, *The Closed World* (Cambridge MA: MIT Press, 1996), 122–5, 188–93.

[3] Edwards, *The Closed World*; Fred Kaplan, *Wizards of Armageddon* (Palo Alto: Stanford University Press, 1983).

[4] Sharon Ghamari Tabrizi (Cambridge MA: *The Worlds of Herman Kahn. The Intuitive Science of Thermo Nuclear War*, 2005), 126; Alex Abela, *Soldiers of Reason. The RAND Corporation and the Rise of American Empire* (New York: Houghton Mifflin Harcourt, 2009); Jennifer Light, *From Warfare to Welfare. Defense Intellectuals and Urban Problems in Cold War America* (Baltimore: John Hopkins Press, 2003).

American historiography as the cradle of Cold War science. Among the approaches that were developed at RAND were not only game theory and rational choice theory, but also concrete planning technologies derived from wartime Operations Research, such as cost–benefit analysis and forms of forecasting. These technologies had in common their concern with rationalizing the problem of decision.[5]

American historians have rightly seen RAND as the birth place for a set of approaches to problems of planning and decision making, which carried over a heavy legacy of militaristic thinking into a growing American public administration.[6] It might be argued meanwhile that this was far from an exclusively American story, and that the planning technologies developed at RAND spread from the US into European welfarist administrations, as well as onto a global field. The previous chapter provided insights into the European origins of ideas of rationalizing decision, and argued that future research was a space of significant transnational interest and circulation well before the Second World War. This had to do, the chapter argued, with the specific way in which the problem of decision was associated with a new problem of foreseeing the future of a democratic mass society that might potentially produce a limitless series of desirable and undesirable outcomes. This raised the need for a mechanism within planning systems capable of distinguishing between good and bad futures. This chapter proposes to revisit what Eisenhower famously dubbed the "military industrial complex" in order to examine the specific experimentations at RAND with future research. The purpose of future research was precisely to develop methods and technologies with which to foresee the many outcomes and consequences of decision, so that these could be ordered according to an idea of rationality. Several key methods of prediction were invented at RAND under the label of future research, including, famously, the scenario tool developed by the nuclear strategist Herman Kahn. The key futurist at RAND was however not the flamboyant Kahn, but the much more discreet mathematician Olaf Helmer, and while the scenario tool with its apocalyptic imagery of nuclear holocaust and its standard and deviant worlds is fascinating, the core method of future research was arguably not the scenario tool, but the so called Delphi tool of formalizing expert opinion.[7]

THE FUTURE AS SOCIAL TECHNOLOGY

Both the mathematics and social science departments at RAND were involved in future research, in a quest that started, in the words of the chief RAND futurologist

[5] Phillip Mirowski, *Machine Dreams. How Economics Became a Cyborg Science* (Cambridge MA: Harvard University Press, 2002); Paul Erickson, "Mathematical Games, Rational Choice, and the Search for Cold War Culture", *Isis*, 2010, 101 (2): 386–92; David Hounshell, "The Cold War, RAND, and the Generation of Knowledge 1946–1962" (RAND History Project, 1998).

[6] Most recently Rohde, 2015, *Armed with Expertise*; David Jardini, *Out of Blue Yonder. The Transfer of Systems Thinking from the Pentagon to the Great Society* (Washington, 1996); Light, *From Warfare to Welfare*.

[7] See Kaya Tolon, *The American Futures Studies Movement. Its Roots, Motivations, and Influences* (Ph.d. Diss., Iowa State University Digital Repository, 2011), which includes an oral history interview with Helmer; Ghamari Tabrizi, *The Worlds of Herman Kahn*, 126.

Olaf Helmer, in a search for a "general theory of the future." It did not seem farfetched, in the context of the behavioral revolution, that such a general theory could be found, but at the same time, the very statement of a general future theory is also highly indicative of the particular approach taken to social science at RAND.[8] As argued in the previous chapter, prediction—by postulating law driven or stage driven developments, identifying logical patterns of consequence, or explaining structures as part of a functionalist systems logic—was a latent claim in 1950s social science. Disciplines such as applied psychology, electoral research, and international relations were deeply busy in the 1950s and 1960s with trying to uncover nothing less than the presumed laws governing conduct and behavior in everything from brain cells, traffic jams, social groups and relationships between nations.[9] Modernization theory, as discussed in the previous chapter, was one of the outcomes of this development with its projections of a specific form of liberal capitalist rationality.[10] Another was the search for concrete methods, technologies, and devices intended to shape rational behavior and create foreseeability by actively influencing forms of individual and collective decision making.[11]

As RAND developed in the 1950s and 1960s from a center for experimentation with such predictive techniques into a think tank concerned with much larger questions of planning, policy, and strategy, its focus on developing methods of steering and control were transposed from the military field to the world of social and political affairs.[12] This depended, as several important works have shown, on a very particular take on social science. As Paul Edwards and others have shown, the behavioralist or indeed *behaviorist* conceptions of the behavioral turn were closely dependent on developments in the natural sciences with mechanistic reasoning and the development of the computer. Computer based forms of prediction inspired the important shifts in nuclear science, quantum physics, mechanics, and electrics during WW2. The making of the atomic bomb itself was a gigantic exercise in prediction through a myriad of calculations that would not have been possible were it not for the machine brains and their supreme analytical capacities.[13] Edward's account of the development of Cold War computer culture shows that, following its invention, the computer became more than a machine; it became a metaphor and template for pervasive images of how human rationality ought to function.[14] After 1950 the advances that the computer had produced in the natural sciences led to the idea that similar forms of instrumental rationality

[8] Olaf Helmer, "Science," in *Science Journal* 1967, 3 (10): 49–51, 51.

[9] Heyck, H., 2016, *Age of System*; Edwards, *The Closed World*.

[10] See Nils Gilman, *Mandarins of the Future. Modernisation Theory in Cold War America* (Baltimore: John Hopkins Press, 2003).

[11] Sonja M. Amadae, *Rationalizing Capitalist Democracy* (Chicago: Chicago University Press, 2003).

[12] David Jardini, *Out of Blue Yonder*; Light, *From Warfare to Welfare*; Joy Rohde, *Armed with Expertise. The Militarization of American Social Research During the Cold War* (Ithaca: Cornell University Press, 2013).

[13] Dominique Pestre and Amy Dahan, eds., *Sciences pour la guerre 1940–1960* (Paris: EHESS, 2004); Peter Galison and B. Bernstein, "In Any Light. Scientists and the Decision to Build the Superbomb, 1952–1954," in *Historical Studies in the Physical and Biological Sciences*, 1989, 19 (2): 267–347.

[14] Edwards, *The Closed World*.

could lead to important breakthroughs also in the social sciences. The making of the bomb was hailed as a feat of human ingenuity. In the Manhattan project, science and technology had been brought together around an idea of application and use, as theorists met with engineers and mechanics. In 1950, the American Foundations proposed a "Manhattan project" for the social sciences. This transfer of mechanistic reasoning to the social sciences fell back on the idea that the social sciences were the frontier for a major scientific breakthrough, and that this breakthrough would occur in the area of understanding the mechanisms of problem solving and decision making in human and social behavior.[15]

Future research at RAND began with precisely this optimistic idea that the methods that had been developed as part of Operations Research during the war could now be transposed to the social world, where they might be applied to emergent problems of values, choice, and decision in growing public administrations. As Olaf Helmer put it, if the social sciences with their emerging applied orientation could develop engineering skills for the social world they would be able to find solutions to the wide range of social problems facing contemporary societies and produce "an adequate theory that can enable us to deal with socio-economic and political problems as confidently as we do with problems in chemistry and physics."[16] Advances in computer technology and cybernetics, along with developments in social science toward quantitative surveys and behavioral analysis, had given the social sciences access to the unprecedented analytical capacity and "the kind of massive data processing and interpreting capability that, in the physical sciences, created the breakthrough which led to the development of the atomic bomb."[17] A "general theory of the future" capable of predicting all social problems and pointing to their solution was, to Helmer, within reach. The precondition was that the social sciences actively emulated the advances made in technology and engineering.[18]

What was at stake at RAND was thus not science as the nineteenth century idea of neutral and mechanistic observation, but science as an active intervention in the shaping of the future. This understanding of social science as a purposeful tool of social engineering is clear in the descriptions of the concrete methods of decision experimented at RAND. These were described with terms such as "craft," or indeed, with a term that was present in a number of RAND reports in the early to mid 1960s, "social technology." Social technology was not a new term in American social science, on the contrary, it had been used since the interwar years as a description of an essentially mechanistic approach to the social sciences as a form of social engineering of liberal individualism. From this perspective, social technology

[15] See the Gaither Report: *Report of the Study for the Ford Foundation on Policy and Program* (Detroit, 1949); Mark Solovey, "Project Camelot and the 1960s Epistemological Revolution Rethinking the Politics-Patronage-Social Science Nexus." *Social Studies of Science*, 2001, 31 (2): 171–206, 183.

[16] Olaf Helmer, "Science," in *Science Journal* (London), special issue "The Future of Future Research," 1967, 3 (10): 49–51, 50. See also Olaf Helmer, *Social Technology* (New York: Basic Books, 1966), and Helmer, *The Future of Science* (Santa Monica: RAND, 1967).

[17] Helmer, "Science," 50.

[18] Olaf Helmer and Nicolas Rescher, *On the Epistemology of the Inexact Sciences* (Santa Monica: RAND, 1958), 1–3.

was a positive notion, a reflection of progressive era ideals in American social science.[19] Notions of social technology informed investments into behavioral research in the early 1950s, which referred explicitly to social science as a "'technology of human behavior'.[20] At RAND, social technology referred to the way that predictive technologies were intended to have a specific outcome on the social world by shaping action toward desirable outcomes. Gaming, for instance, was designated a "craft" in contrast to a scientific method, because it aimed at shaping certain forms of behavior.[21]

Specifically, social technology referred to future research, and to forms of prediction that aimed at rationalizing decision making in the social and political field. In 1957, Olaf Helmer wrote an arguably key paper in the history of RAND. The paper, "The Prospect of a Unified Theory of Organizations," argued that the main object of study of the social sciences was the organization. Helmer defined organizations as "variously motivated entities in a flux of decision making" and argued that these existed on a multitude of levels, from the business to the nation, and even, the international system or the world. What held an organization together was the need to make decisions, based on values, preferences, fears, and attitudes. If the mechanisms of these decisions could be understood, they could be improved, and hence decision making, on all relevant levels from the nation to the conflicting states of the international system, could be controlled. Importantly, Helmer proposed that viewing the decision making entity as a collective organization, and not as an individual rational agent, was of huge significance because organizations were held to a different set of rationalities than individual utility maximizing agents. Indeed, organizational decision making stemmed from important problems of attitudes, values, and social or cultural preference. Predicting decision making and future outcomes in an organization therefore required other methods than the ones based on strict rationality assumptions, and Helmer argued therefore that methods such as gaming had to be extended to a much wider set of rationality assumptions.[22]

The Delphi tool of expert opinion was Helmer's solution to the question of what such a technology would look like. Helmer introduced Delphi to a wide audience in the American public in a 1966 Basic Book with the telling title *Social Technology*.[23]

[19] Jordan, *Machine Age Ideology. Social Engineering and American Liberalism 1911–1939* (Chapel Hill: University of North Carolina Press, 2010).

[20] Solovey, "Project Camelot," 176.

[21] RAND Mathematics Division, *Strategic Gaming* (Santa Monica: RAND, 1960); Olaf Helmer and Nicolas Rescher, *On the Epistemology of the Inexact Sciences* (Santa Monica: RAND, 1958). Solovey shows that the infamous Project Camelot was designed as exactly such a model of behavior: if correct mechanisms of insurgency could be found, then the mechanisms of counterinsurgency could also be found and created in, for instance, Latin American populations. Behavioral research in the US took off after Khrushchev declared, in 1960, that the USSR would support national liberation projects. Solovey, "Project Camelot," 176f, 185.

[22] Helmer, *The Prospects of a Unified Theory of Organizations*, RAND discussion paper, April 1957. The paper was published as Olaf Helmer, "The Prospects of a Unified Theory of Organisations," in *Management Science* 1958, 4 (2): 172–76.

[23] Olaf Helmer, *Social Technology* (New York: Basic Books, 1966). Also the scenario tool was widely spread and marketed in books aimed at the general public through Kahn's 1960 book, *Thermo Nuclear War* in 1960 as well as the ensuing volume *The Year 2000*, published by the Hudson Institute.

Helmer had been working on Delphi together with his colleagues Nicolas Rescher and Norman Dalkey since the late 1940s, parallel with experiments on gaming in the mathematics department at RAND.[24] Like the scenario method, Delphi was a central reflection on the knowability of future developments and the possibilities and limits of prediction. Both Delphi and the scenario tool were also reflections on the limits of gaming. Gaming had begun at RAND immediately after the publication in 1944 of John von Neumann and Oskar Morgenstern's book *A Mathematical Theory of Games and Human Behavior*. Known first and foremost for the introduction of the Prisoners Dilemma theorem, *Games and Human Behavior* laid out a set of theoretical prescriptions of the predictability of individual and social behavior. The games presumed that agents had the same probability distribution, and that the preferences of an agent could be ordered hierarchically as a question of expected utility. This hierarchical order of preferences and values was in turn presumed to be transferable as a question of universal rational interest.[25] The postulate of rationality was of course a natural key to prediction. If rationality could be presumed to consist of a logical and therefore foreseeable and transferable hierarchy of preferences, then the behavior of everything from nation states in a war game to actors in a marketplace or the movement of cars in an urban crossing was predictable, and rationality assumptions could be extended to a general theory of human action.

Games and Human Behavior laid, as we know, the foundations for rational choice theory, built on the premise of a universal rational agent.[26] It was the dominance of the concept of rationality produced by gaming that led a first wave of studies of so called Cold War science to argue that it was organized around a hegemonic notion of economic rationality, and the evacuation of situated notions of reason or subjectivity. A more recent strand of studies has shown, rather, that experimentations with gaming and mathematic modeling at RAND were the site of a key debate on what actually constituted human rationality. Importantly, this debate stemmed from the experience of limits to the rationality assumptions in gaming. These experiences seemed to demonstrate that the games were not in actual fact sufficient predictors of human behavior. Experiences with gaming thus opened the door for a much wider set of experimentations with prediction at RAND, with the purpose of complementing rationality assumptions with observations of inductive and subjective behavior, attitudes, values, even culture.[27] Moreover,

[24] Nicolas Rescher, *Predicting the Future. An Introduction to the Theory of Forecasting* (New York: State University of New York Press, 1998), 28–9, 93–7 and footnote 132, 262.

[25] John von Neumann and Oskar Morgenstern, *A Theory of Games and Economic Behaviour* (New Jersey, 1944); "Research Memorandum on Project RAND, "The Military Doctrine of Decision and the von Neumann Theory of Games", Colonel Olivier G. Haywood, USAF RM-528, Olaf Helmer papers, RAND Archives, Santa Monica. On game theory see Robert Ayson, *Thomas Schelling and the Nuclear Age*, 2004; Robert Leonard, *Von Neumann, Morgenstern, and the Creation of Game Theory. From Chess to Social Science* (Cambridge, 2010); Sonja Amadae, *Prisoners of Reason. Game Theory and Neoliberal Political Economy* (Cambridge MA: MIT Press, 2016), 69–76; Edwards, *The Closed World*, 117f.

[26] Amadae, *Rationalizing Capitalist Democracy*, 27–35; Ghamari Tabrizi, *The Worlds of Herman Kahn*, 159–70.

[27] Mark Solovey and Hunter Cravens, *Cold War Social Science. Knowledge Production, Liberal Democracy and Human Nature* (Toronto: Toronto University Press, 2012), and compare Erickson et al., *When Reason Almost Lost its Mind.*

experiences of the limits of rationality assumptions in games led to the idea that predictive technologies could be used as test sites for learning rational behavior, including shared norms of conduct. As demonstrated by Paul Erickson, the suboptimal or zero sum outcomes posited by games were understood as serious limitations for potential real world situations in which a good outcome would require a change of behavior toward cooperation. With the discovery that games could serve a learning function through reiterated processes, the games thus became a kind of learning site for adaptive forms of rationality and experimentations with moves from zero sum to positive outcomes.[28] Another key result of experiments with gaming was the discovery that forms of subjectivity and the human imagination could be mobilized to shape rational decisions. The rationality assumptions in gaming did acknowledge a certain role for subjectivity. Gaming drew on important scripted and narrative elements and even hardliner RAND strategists—such as Albert Wohlstetter—acknowledged the role played by imagination and subjectivity in producing what was in the world of modeling called "artificial" or "synthetic" fact.[29] The idea of synthetic fact was a key epistemological trait of the nuclear world, because in a world of possible nuclear war, nuclear facts could not be observed. Gaming and simulation thus proposed to substitute fact with imagined experience. Sharon Ghamari Tabrizi, the chief scholar on Herman Kahn, has shown that scenarios drew on a crucial element of subjectivity, and on the idea of actively mobilizing the human imagination as a source of, as Kahn put it, alternative world futures.[30] As such, scenarios challenge notions of strict rationality, and they also confirm Peter Galison and Lorraine Daston's argument on objectivity: that both subjectivity and imagination have been core elements in scientist notions of objectivity. The scenario method drew on scripting techniques imported from Hollywood. In contrast to gaming, which posited a limited number of outcomes, its objective was to think up a potentially unlimited series of probable and improbable futures including, famously, the "unthinkable."[31] Scenarios thus shifted the emphasis from the deductive mathematical logic of the games, to inductive reasoning and to the problem of action. Grégoire Mallard and Andrew Lakoff have proposed that scenarios were intended as a kind of future rehearsals or "techniques of prospection," through which possible outcomes of the present could be experimented.[32] Both scenarios and Delphi exercises aimed at the evaluation of possible decisions by outlining a series of hypothetical consequences. These consequences could then be systematically compared and ordered. As such,

[28] Erickson, "Mathematical Models, Rational Choice, and the Search for Cold War Culture," 311f; Paul Erickson, *The World the Game Theorists Made* (Chicago: Chicago University Press, 2015).

[29] Ghamari Tabrizi, 169.

[30] Ghamari Tabrizi, *The Worlds of Herman Kahn*. Lorraine Daston and Peter Galison, *Objectivity* (New York: Zone Books, 2007); Lorraine Daston and Peter Galison, "Fear and Loathing of the Imagination in Science," *Daedalus*, 1998, 127 (1): 73–98.

[31] Ghamari Tabrizi, *The Worlds of Herman Kahn*, 169; Erickson, "Mathematical Models, Rational Choice, and the Search for Cold War Culture," 388.

[32] Grégoire Mallard and Andrew Lakoff, "How Claims to Know the Future are Used to Understand the Present," in *Social Knowledge in the Making*. Edited by Michele Lamont et al., 339–79 (Chicago, 2011), 341.

it was not the representation of the future carried by the scenario that mattered, but the way that it led to purposeful action.

The purpose of Delphi was not, as Helmer would time and time again insist, to predict the actual future. Delphi was a tool for improving decision making. This was the precise meaning of social technology. Neither Kahn nor Helmer were a priori interested in the accuracy of foretelling. Instead it was the communicative aspect of prediction that they found promising. Importantly, they recognized that this parted with conventional understanding of scientific experimentation as informed by objectivity. As Olaf Helmer put it, "The fact that any contingency planning based on *an image thus formed of the future* would directly affect the probabilities of the alternatives of which that image is composed does not invalidate the suggested procedure, but, in fact, demonstrates its usefulness, for it is precisely the foreboding content of unfavorable forecasts that might induce preventative action."[33] While future research at RAND had begun in the spirit of a search for a general theory of the future, what it in fact came up with was not as such a theory of the future, but an idea of prediction as social and political technology.

FROM THE LONG RANGE TO THE LONG TERM

It needs to be proposed here that from the mid 1960s, the purpose of both Delphi and the scenario tool went far beyond preventative action and into a very different problem, which did not have to do with avoiding worst possible outcomes but with inducing desired forms of social action on a whole range of levels of decision making within an organization. In 1964, Helmer and Theodore Gordon published the results of the first large scale Delphi experimentation at RAND in the report *A Long Range Forecasting Study.* The report introduced Delphi to the world and met with immediate attention in a transnational community of planners as a major breakthrough in so called technological and social forecasting.[34]

The concept of long range forecasting conflated the spatial term of the "long range," with the temporal the "long term." This conflation of time and space was not an accident but a result of experimentation not only with Operations Research (OR), but also with systems analysis, at RAND. Both of these approaches were designed to integrate space and time functions.[35] Through a complex process of translation, the technologies that had originally been devised as estimations of a new kind of technological reach over long distances in space became understood as technologies which might also have a bearing on questions to do with forms of control over the long range of time.[36]

Systems analysis had been performed at RAND since the late 1940s. It was introduced at RAND by researchers with direct involvement in the Manhattan project, such as Herman Kahn, who had experimented with the first so called

[33] Helmer, *Social Technology*, 26. My italics.
[34] Olaf Helmer and Theodore Gordon, *A Long Range Forecasting Study* (Santa Monica: RAND, 1964).
[35] Phillip Mirowski, *Machine Dreams,* 17.
[36] See Eric Jantsch, *Technological Forecasting in Perspective* (Paris: OECD, 1970).

Monte Carlo exercises.[37] Monte Carlo exercises were probabilistic experiments with large numbers, numbers so large that seemingly stochastical patterns could be identified. Kahn developed scenarios as literary versions of such patterns.[38] A central influence on systems analysis was the publication in 1964 of the Imperial College professor, Denis Gabor's, book *Inventing the Future*, which proposed that technology could be viewed as an organic system that evolved through specific generations of change. Imperial College had been the central site of experimentation with OR in post-war Britain. In Gabor's book, the process of innovation could be influenced through operational methods of setting specific objectives, values, and goals at key moments of decision.[39] At RAND, systems analysis was like OR (which was a wartime derivation of applied mathematics) quintessentially concerned with military strategy and nuclear defense. The long *range* was a term with a long history in military strategy. A classical problem of probabilistic reasoning was the so called jeep problem, which concerned how to calculate the optimal "range" distance between jeeps and fuelling stations and find the optimal distribution point.[40] World War II saw important breakthroughs in military technology, represented first by advancements in rocket technology and ballistic research, culminating in the invention of long distance missiles, ICBMS.[41] Space travel and ballistics changed the idea of the long range into a series of complicated time space equations, and intercontinental ballistic missiles transformed the problems of strategic warfare into complicated questions of civilian organization, including the need for calculating time spans of warning, evacuation, and response.[42] Another set of predictive issues, however, had to do with the larger logic of the armament struggle, which placed a premium on the necessity to predict the likely evolution of a military technological system. Technological forecasting recycled a notion from the so called Monte Carlo exercises, which was the idea that the development of a technological system followed a given and predictable set of branch points.[43] Branch points were the points of system change, the predicted moments of evolution within a technological system at which new paths of technological change would occur, stretching out like the branches of a tree. From such branch points stemmed innovation and system change, as opposed to systemic inertia. Technological forecasting was first deployed in the question of the likely time frame in which the

[37] Ghamari Tabrizi, *The Worlds of Herman Kahn*, 129–34.

[38] R. J. Williams, "World Futures", in *Critical Inquiry*, 2016, 42: 473–546, 480.

[39] Gabor, *Inventing the Future*, 1964. Gabor was a Hungarian physicist and professor at Imperial College, who argued that the future could not be predicted, but invented, by setting objectives to science policy and technological invention. Earlier arguments for forecasting came from W.F. Ogden, "Prospecting for the Future," in *Social Frontiers*, 1935, 1: 20–22; and Theodore von Karman, "Towards New Horizons," in 1947; and the previous RAND study, Kaplan, Skogstad, Gishik, "The Prediction of Social and Technological Events," in *Public Opinion Quarterly*, 1950, 14: 93–110.

[40] *A Problem in Logistics: The Jeep Problem* (Santa Monica: RAND, 1946); also, *An Experiment in Estimation* (Santa Monica: RAND, 1947).

[41] Kaplan, *Wizards of Armageddon*, 130–1, 135.

[42] Jennifer Light, *From Warfare to Welfare*.

[43] Thomas Hughes et al. eds., *The Social Construction of Technological Systems* (Cambridge MA: MIT Press, 2012); David Mindell, *Between Human and Machine. Feedback, Control and Computing Before Cybernetics* (Baltimore: John Hopkins University Press, 2002).

Soviets would develop a missile system capable of carrying out a nuclear attack on the US.[44] This question became obsolete in 1957 when the Soviets launched, successfully, Sputnik, while an American attempt to launch a missile from Cape Kennedy failed, creating the "missile gap."[45] The missile gap was understood not only as a failure of prediction, but as a failure of social organization (see Chapter 6) and as evidence of the fact that the American state did not sufficiently harness the productive forces of science and technology.[46] In the first years of the 1960s, a range of American activities designed to take active control over the process of public investment and technological innovation began, culminating in Kennedy's decision in 1960 (following the introduction of cost–benefit analysis in the Defense Department) to decree the use of forecasting in the totality of the federal administration.

Technological forecasting built on core elements from OR. OR posited the idea of a field or space for action. In order to control action within this field, both OR and systems analysis made use of devices such as branch charts, relevance trees, and decision trees as ways of sorting a hierarchy of objectives, values, and preferences in the decision making moment. By delimiting variables and identifying correct sequences, forecasting created an illusion of a direct and logical link between a decision and its future result. One of the first large technological forecasts was the PATTERN study at the Lockheed Corporation, in which the evolution of the missile system was understood as depending on values, in the sense of the values of the decision maker and the planning process, as well as of the public and in social acceptance of a new technology. A number of such studies of projecting future resources and technological needs within a given future field appeared in the US in the first years of the 1960s, including at General Motors, IBM, Bell Laboratories, and General Electric.[47]

The forecasting of specific developments in technology thus depended on a much larger set of issues in the social organization, and importantly, in the political system. This conclusion would eventually lead to the term "integrative forecasting," developed by the OECD consultant Eric Jantsch in a report that spent many pages on experiments with the social technologies at RAND.[48] Jantsch described as social technologies the new methods of prediction, which had as their purpose to plan for a time span that was beyond the means of conventional planning. The actual horizon could vary substantially, from five years to a generation like concept of twenty-five to thirty years. Eric Jantsch defined these horizons of time as the kind of time space that is not immediately foreseeable but governed by uncertainty

[44] Michael Gordin, *Red Cloud at Dawn* (New York: Faber, Strauss and Giroux, 2009), 63–88. At RAND, futurological research closely followed Soviet forecasting methods. See Fred Ikle, personal papers, RAND archives.

[45] Ghamari Tabrizi, *The Worlds of Herman Kahn*, 189; Kaplan, *The Wizards of Armageddon*, 135–6.

[46] The Commission for the Year 2000, in its 1967 report, addressed as one of its central themes the decentralized federal structure of the American state and its failure to systematize knowledge between federal agencies and independent expertise. The Kennedy administration had failed in efforts of prediction while the Soviets excelled. See Daniel Bell and Stephen Graubard, *The Year 2000. Work in Progress* (Cambridge: MIT Press, 1967), 43.

[47] Erik Jantsch, *Technological Forecasting in Perspective* (Paris: OECD, 1967).

[48] Jantsch, *Technological Forecasting in Perspective.*

and which can therefore not be planned according to conventional means. The 1964 Delphi study at RAND was the first attempt to transfer the ideas from the field of technological and military forecasting, to a theory of decision making in social and political organization. In the 1964 report, the idea of the long range and the long term were used synonymously, in order to denote what was no longer the future of a technological system, but the range of social trends understood as shaping the future of the US: nuclear threat, urban development, pollution, mining on the moon, man machine symbiosis, global famine, and automation.[49] The report was immediately translated into several European languages and published in French by Bertrand de Jouvenel's publishing house SEDEIS.[50]

FORMALIZING EXPERT OPINION: THE INVENTION OF DELPHI

Delphi focused attention on one of the key epistemological problems of predictive experiments at RAND, which was the problem of expert opinion. As discussed, gaming developed at RAND from a 1940s optimistic idea that it could be used to identify a limited number of foreseeable outcomes of a given situation, to the idea that human behavior and decision making was subject to fundamental conditions of uncertainty. Uncertainty, in this context, defined situations in which one could not pretend to foreknow the possible reactions of other social actors and in which action could not be presumed to be rational.[51] Expert opinion had long been a core strategic concern at RAND, because in the context of simulation and synthetic fact, expert opinion was used as substitute knowledge for actual experience of real world situations.[52] The use of expert opinion, however, also led to reflections on the epistemology of expertise, as critics of gaming argued that the games relied on scripted inputs and scenarios, and that this delegated authority to the expert in an unacceptably subjective manner. As Ghamari Tabrizi has shown, this led to the identification of intuitive judgment as a central factor determining the outcome of the games.[53] As RAND researchers identified the problem of intuitive judgment, they started experimenting with how such judgment could be improved.[54] In 1957 Olaf Helmer wrote to Kahn to offer his point of view on the scenario method as an alternative to war gaming:

> In as much as a war game falls short of a scientific model, according to you it can be no more than pedagogical and stimulative. You say (that the reliability of) substantive results coming out of the game has to be justified like any idea. This in fact applies not

[49] Helmer and Gordon, *A Long Range Forecasting Study*, 1964; Nicolas Rescher, *Predicting the Future*, 28–9, 262.

[50] Helmer's 1967 paper *Social Technology* was translated into French, Italian, Russian, and Swedish.

[51] Soraya Boudia, "La genèse d'un gouvernement par le risque ", in *Du risque à la menace. Penser la catastrophe,* edited by Pierre Benoit Joly et al., 69–88 (Paris: Seuil, 2013).

[52] Ghamari Tabrizi, *The Worlds of Herman Kahn*, 166f.

[53] Ghamari Tabrizi, *The Worlds of Herman Kahn*, 159–70.

[54] Olaf Helmer, *Social Technology*, 11–13; Olaf Helmer, *Analysis of the Future: The Delphi Method*, (Santa Monica: RAND, 1967).

> only to games but to any scientific model whose results *always have to be justified*... Ideally the input into the model would be facts, hence the output reliable, but this is not so. Judgements enter crucially into the model at several points.... This does not make it valueless as a scientific model but what is necessary is to *recognise the existence of such judgement and process it in a systematic way.*[55]

In other words, Helmer drew the conclusion from gaming, that it offered valuable results as a model of behavior, but that it lacked a mechanism of substantiation or verification of subjective judgment. This was, in essence, the task of Delphi.

Olaf Helmer came to the social science department at RAND by way of the Applied Mathematics Panel of the Office of Scientific Research and Development of the War Department in 1946, in which he was a resident mathematician on bombing accuracy. His escape was facilitated by Paul Oppenheimer.[56] The War Department had employed many Eastern European mathematicians and physicists during the War, including John von Neumann and Oskar Morgenstern who developed some of the first Monte Carlo exercises in the Manhattan project. Born in Austria, Helmer had studied with Carl Hempel, the leading figure of the Vienna circle of logical empiricism (or logical positivism).[57] This is a highly significant fact, because the Vienna circle was the site of a central discussion on the nature of scientific truth in both philosophy and physics. Indeed, Michael Polanyi, discussed in the previous chapter, had studied chemistry in Vienna and there laid the basis for his conceptions of science as a free community, and scientific truth as a necessarily subjective question of what these scientists agreed on as the most probable explanation—and not as a falsifiable phenomenon. As Polanyi's biographer, Mary Joe Nye, explains, in this Polanyi came to social science explanation from a completely different perspective from Karl Popper, for whom value statements had no scientific purpose and for whom objectivity depended on falsification.[58] Carl Hempel published in the 1940s and 1950s a series of articles on logics, the function of general laws, and the structure of explanation.[59] The problem of prediction and the structure of explanation ex ante and ex post figured in all of these. Moving, like Einstein and Russell, from the classical positivist assumptions that science was an internally consistent and deductive logical system, Hempel argued that scientific explanation depended on a mechanism of empirical verification. But all forms of verification depended, to Hempel, on the essentially linguistic system in which scientists expressed judgments on truth. All predictive claims had to be logically sustained in an empirical observation constituting objective truth, but, as Hempel believed that most empirical reality was only incompletely observable, in the end,

[55] "Comments on your war gaming chapter," Olaf Helmer to Herman Kahn, October 7, 1957. Olaf Helmer papers, RAND Archives, box 4. My italics.

[56] Olaf Helmer, Curriculum Vitae, in RAND archives, Helmer papers, box 1.

[57] Peter Galison, "Aufbau/Bauhaus: Logical Positivism and Architectural Modernism," in *Critical Inquiry*, 1990, 16(4): 709–52.

[58] Mary Jo Nye, *Michael Polanyi and his Generation.*

[59] "The Function of General Laws in History," 1942, "Studies in the Logics of Explanation," 1948, "The Nature of Mathematical Truth," 1945. "Carl Hempel's Challenge to Logical Positivism" in the Stanford Encyclopedia of Science; A. Richardson,*Carnap's Construction of The World. The Aufbau and the Emergence of Logical Empiricism* (Cambridge: Cambridge University Press, 1998).

objectivity was the product of a form of intersubjectivity in the exchange of views between scientists. One of Helmer's RAND colleagues, Nicolas Rescher, became a leading interpreter of Hempel in so called pragmatic idealism, the idea that theoretical concepts in science can be proved through a pragmatic process of verification in which the interaction between such judgments of different scientists is crucial. Notions of scientific objectivity are thus deduced from the social process of constituting objectivity through intersubjectivity.[60]

Helmer and Rescher first worked on what would become Delphi in 1946 with a series of expert panels, the purpose of which were determining which strategic American cities the Soviet Union would be most likely to attempt to wipe out in a nuclear attack: New York, Chicago, Pittsburg, Philadelphia?[61] The expert panels formulated judgments on the properties of optimal targets and the factors (density of population, proximity to military installations, strategic industries, and the time to rebuild these) that could be expected to figure in a Soviet decision of target. These judgments were then aggregated into a deduction of the likely or probable target. Subsequent Delphi runs were experimented parallel to gaming, they were no longer deployed foremost as ways of finding accurate probabilities but as a specific technology for experimentation in the social world.[62] In 1957, Helmer and Rescher wrote a paper, based on a decade of observations of Delphi experiments, on the "epistemology of the inexact sciences." By the inexact sciences they meant the social sciences, and the paper stated that social science lacked the capacity to produce and verify predictive statements, since they could rarely employ experiments and direct observations. Importantly, they proceeded to argue that this had not to do with the objects of social science as such, but with the lack of methodological precision of the social sciences and in particular, the insufficient attention devoted to the process of verification. All sciences, said the paper, are inexact, because in all forms of science, the process of verification is based at some point on subjective judgment. This was thus not the relevant difference between natural and social science, and therefore forms of experimentation could be developed that permitted forms of verification similar to the experimental situation in the natural sciences but for problems pertaining to the social world. Their Delphi panels, Helmer and Rescher proposed, had the promise of offering such an experimental social situation and a mechanism of verification despite the lack of a directly observable external reality.[63] While future developments could not as such be directly observed, expert statements on the future could.

In the early 1960s, Helmer began, with Norman Dalkey at RAND and the Douglass consultant, Theodore Gordon,[64] to experiment with Delphi as a method

60 In the 1980s, Rescher managed to reconstruct the philosopher Leibniz' cipher machine, a kind of encrypted typewriter, created for Leopold I in Vienna in 1688.

61 *An Experiment in Estimation* (Santa Monica: RAND, 1947); Olaf Helmer and Norman Dalkey, *The Use of Experts for the Estimation of Bombing Requirements: A Project Delphi Experiment* (Santa Monica: RAND, 1951).

62 Sharon Ghamari Tabrizi, "Simulating the Unthinkable Future War," *Social Studies of Science*, 2000, 30: 163–223; Light, "Taking Games Seriously," *Technology and Culture*, 2008, 49 (2): 345–75.

63 Helmer and Rescher, *On the Epistemology of the Inexact Sciences.*

64 Gordon worked on the Apollo project.

for the systematic processing of expert judgment, so as to find ways of translating expert opinion into a set of probabilistic values that might translate as predictive accuracy (see Figures 5.1 and 5.2). In this capacity, Delphi was a form of experimentation, a virtual lab experiment of verification of forms of logical analysis on coming developments. The input to the process was the intuitive knowledge of scientists, and its output was the processed subjective opinion of experts in the form of probabilistic values which translated as predictive objectivity.[65] The importance of Delphi lay in the extraordinary emphasis put on the formalization of the process of extraction of intuitive judgment. Experts, Helmer proposed, were highly skilled individuals, who had among their knowledges also forms of tacit knowledge or knowledge that they did not actively mobilize, but that figured into their judgment as a matter of intuition.[66] Securing expert opinion depended on the way that such intuitive judgment could be extracted, and exploited, in a

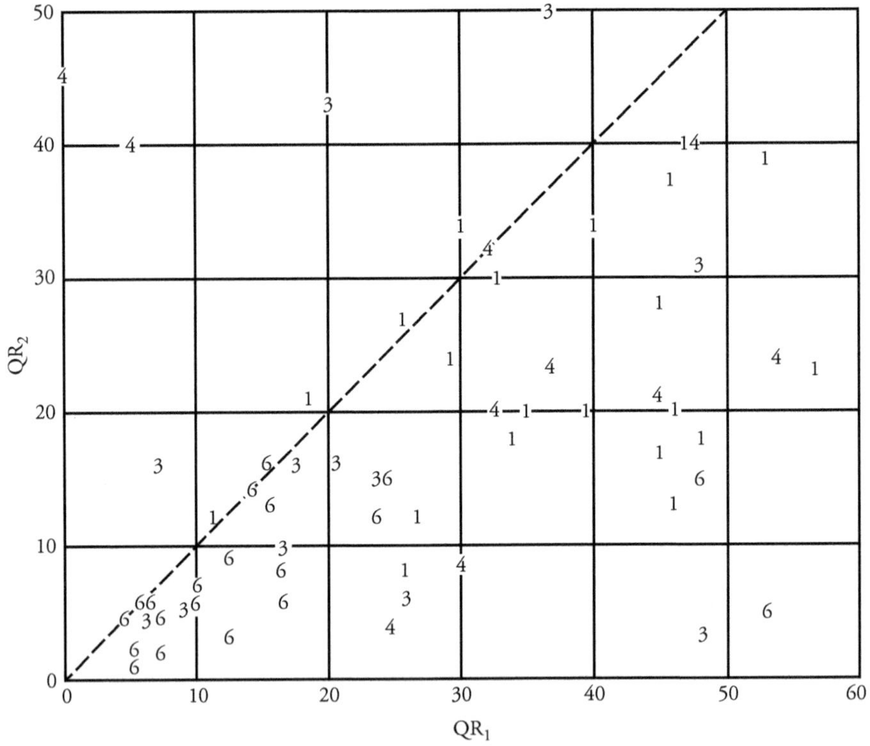

Figure 5.1. Delphi, 1964.

The graph shows reiterated Delphi runs, in which expert opinion clusters over time around an estimated consensus opinion. Questions in 1964 included the likelihood of a Soviet nuclear attack on the US.

[65] Olaf Helmer, "Experimentation in the Nonexperimental Sciences, A New Research Tool," 1953. Olaf Helmer papers, RAND Archives, box 2.

[66] The notion of tacit knowledge was introduced by Michael Polanyi.

	D_1	D_2	D_3	…
D_1				
D_2				
D_2				
⋮				

Figure 5.2. Delphi Matrix.

laboratory like manner. Expert judgment, if extracted in a scientifically sound way, could be used to identify the *branch points of social development* and the available societal options that they indicated.[67] The Delphi panels were constructed as such lab exercises in verification. By reiterating a series of questions and inviting experts to consider the responses of the other experts in order to then modify their opinions, such intuitive judgment was verified through a reflexive process in which expert judgments' were bounced off other expert judgments. And by systematically following the positioning of reiterated responses in a graph, points of divergence or convergence of judgment could be identified. These points could then be mathematically broken down into medians and deciles of agreement or disagreement, with a precision that was presumed to indicate predictive value, but that also allowed for the distribution of opinion to be guided toward the systematic creation of forms of consensus.[68]

Delphi was a controversial technique. It was heavily criticized at RAND in particular by Albert Wohlstetter, who was first of all not convinced by the idea of future research, and secondly, understood Delphi as a dangerous activity of group think.[69] But the performative capacity of consensus creation was exactly what was intended in Delphi. Delphi was not, Helmer insisted, per se an experiment in predicting the future. The future could not, he reassured RAND's direction, be predicted. What could be systematically analyzed was the fundamental uncertainties pertaining to future developments, so as to identify the alternatives facing societies and improve mechanisms of decision at these branchpoints.[70] At this point reaching a level of consensus among experts was desired. Initial Delphi experimentation did aim to find "true" answers to fundamental problems of prediction.

[67] Olaf Helmer, *Systematic Use of Expert Opinion* (Santa Monica, RAND: 1967), 5, 11.

[68] Norman Dalkey, "Some Preliminary Research Results on Delphi." Olaf Helmer papers, box 2.

[69] The problem of decision as related to group think or the socialization of an expert community led, after the Bay of Pigs, to considerable discussion in public administration and policy science. Many researchers at RAND, for instance Fred Ikle and Harry Rowen, participated in Harvard's *Bureaucracy, Politics and Policy* seminar, devoted to the problem of the gap between the intentions of actors and the results of governmental action—the problem of decision. Graham T. Allison's book on the Cuban missile crisis, written between 1966 and 1971, summarized many of these debates. Graham T. Allison, *Essence of Decision. Explaining the Cuban Missile Crisis* (Boston: Little Brown and Company, 1971).

[70] Olaf Helmer, "Long Range Planning," memo to RAND mathematics division, December 13, 1962. Olaf Helmer papers, RAND Archives, box 3.

Put most explicitly on an overhead slide for a presentation by Helmer's colleague Norman Dalkey, if used in a sufficiently formalized and scientific manner, Delphi would allow for the spread of opinion to narrow, and the median, more often than not, would shift toward "the true answer."[71] Convergence of expert opinion hence translated as depicting true probabilities. Both Dalkey and Helmer also realized that the particular usefulness of Delphi was that expert answers could be manipulated, so that forms of desired consensus could in fact be actively shaped. This was, to Helmer, the true value of Delphi—in other words not its predictive capacity, but its effects in terms of formalizing opinion. Presenting this conclusion in his comments on the debate on the future of RAND, Helmer proposed that the Delphi method could be used as a system of scientific world making, a way of constructing integrated forecasts for the development of human society over the next fifty years and creating "super Delphis" of world economic and cultural systems that could "then be manipulated in order to obtain consensus."[72]

SUBSTITUTING PASSIONATE OPINION

Through the 1964 study, Delphi thus went from being a military technology of prediction to a social planning tool. In this new mode, Delphi was part of the set of technologies that were key to the reinvention of RAND as the organization ventured into social research, urban planning, and public policy from 1966 on. The mid 1960s was a period of crisis for the Corporation as shifts in US defense strategy stripped RAND of its role as a Cold War think tank. Paradoxically, this loss of role was to no small extent produced by predictive activities at RAND themselves. In 1966, Nixon took Kahn's depiction of nuclear Apocalypse in *Thermonuclear War* to mean that a nuclear war could not be won, and that the doctrine of Mutually Assured Destruction should be substituted by international regulation and a halt to the arms race.[73] By the mid 1960s, RAND's contribution to military strategy was also increasingly controversial. In 1964 Herman Kahn was portrayed by Stanley Kubrick as doctor Strangelove, the mad inventor of the Doomsday machine. The Doomsday machine was a reference to Kahn's attempt to develop a hypothetical computer algorithm intended to take away the problem of human judgment altogether, by creating a machine-controlled answer of full retaliation for Soviet aggression. Knowing that the response was automatic, the enemy had full certainty of the response—and the political color of government would not matter for security strategy. Erickson quotes Anatole Rapaport upon hearing

[71] Norman Dalkey, "Some preliminary research results on Delphi." Olaf Helmer papers, box 2. In fact Delphi would be heavily criticized inside the Corporation, precisely because it was not a random poll of opinion but a way of shaping opinion, see Harold Sackmann, *Delphi Assessment* (Santa Monica: RAND, 1974), and Harold Sackmann, "A Sceptic at the Oracle." *Futures* (1976) 8, 5, 444–6.

[72] Olaf Helmer memo to Jay Williams on his "A Small World Revisited," November 9, 1961. RAND Archives, Olaf Helmer papers, box 4. Integrated forecasts signified the cross running of variables of economic, technological, and social development.

[73] Herman Kahn, *On Thermo Nuclear War* (New Jersey, 1960).

of Kahn's draft of a Doomsday machine in 1962, "That souped up Clausewitz. It was ghastly... The man has the outlook of a psychopath."[74] In 1965, a massive behavioral research undertaking in the so called Project Camelot was revealed by the peace theorist Johan Galtung to serve the purposes of the War Department, to the shock of many of the participants. By the end of the decade, game theory was blamed for the military failures in Vietnam.[75] A 1968 article in *Life* magazine ran "A Kahn fact is trained to do only one thing: to lead to a Kahn conclusion. The conclusion, in turn leads to the heart of Herman Kahn: the message. And that message, preceded by layers of proof and explanation, and hours and hours of sweat and suspense, when at last unveiled, is Herman Kahn's last surprise. He is not only the oracle, but its most faithful pilgrim; he is not only the preacher, but the most terrified believer in the audience."[76]

As direct talks began with the Soviets from 1966 and 1967 onward, systems analysis, forecasting, and other forms of prediction were reconceptualized from tools with which images of possible enemy behavior could be shaped in a quintessential bipolar logic, to the tools with which possible common and shared images of behavior could be created. In 1972 American and Soviet governments created IIASA, the International Institute of Applied Systems Analysis, and, in the same years, the focus of prediction shifted toward the production of shared norms and the analysis of behavior not in two clashing systems, but in a larger world system with "common" or shared futures.[77] Chapter 8 returns to this story of shared futures, but a final argument needs to be made about the shift of predictive technologies from the military to the social realm after 1965 and their emergence as veritable social and political technologies. In the early 1960s, both Delphi and the scenario technique had been showcased in publications that were aimed far outside the RAND community. In 1966, Herman Kahn made the scenario tool the flagship device of his think tank, the Hudson Institute. In the following year, he and Jerome Wiener published *The Year 2000*, in which the scenario method was used for the first time on civilian problems by conjuring up images of possible developments in a now turbulent American society. From Hudson, the scenario tool was also brought as a tool of corporate planning to Royal Dutch Shell by the enigmatic French engineer Pierre Wack. In a similar process, Delphi was also outsourced from RAND and marketed as a tool of social experimentation in increasingly contested times. Helmer wrote a series of memos to the RAND direction in the mid 1960s where he proposed that research on the future would be a way of reinventing the RAND spirit of social innovation. He suggested that futurological techniques be put to use in new fields of organizational theory and public policy, in which they would be promising tools of system control. "We can apply tested techniques to new fields, urban programmes, education, pollution, arms control, long range forecasts of world conditions."[78] This reflected earlier ideas in the Social Science Division that

[74] Erickson, "Mathematical models" 308. [75] Solovey, "Project Camelot," 185.

[76] *Life Magazine,* December 6, 1968, 119–23.

[77] Rindzeviciute, *The Power of System* 109–12.

[78] "The Future of RAND," memo from Olaf Helmer to RAND Research Council, May 3, 1965. Olaf Helmer papers, RAND Archives, box 4.

modeling and scenario crafting could be used as tools not only for predicting the moves of enemies but for building model societies for the US—and for the world. Systematic studies of US goals and values could be a way of shaping purposeful action and recreating "American utopias." The sinister business of designing warfare could be replaced by the more hopeful task of actively designing global society, in the process reaffirming the sense of public usefulness and service of the Corporation.[79] In other words prediction was now understood as a form of anticipatory evaluation, a way of testing possible future societies and evaluating the desirability of social change. From this perspective, systems analysis was a curious mix of utopian aspiration and technocratic spirit. Applied to the social system, the "branch points" predicted in systems analysis indicated points where alternative societal trajectories could be envisaged as branches stretching out from a tree. From these points, scenarios could be created that allowed for the comparison of alternative envisioned societies. But how could one make sure that, at such points of crucial social choice, the best possible future world was indeed chosen? Here was the real value of Delphi.

Helmer had, with the help first of his assistant Bernice Brown, and then with his fellow researchers Norman Dalkey and Theodore Gordon, experimented with ways of formalizing Delphi techniques in order to obtain the most accurate results and break with group think.[80] Paradoxically, from the very first experimentations, they found that accuracy of prediction depended on the constitution of a community of forecasters who were not experts on the various subject matters involved but rather, experts on the forecasting procedure as such. Delphi was thus experimented with in the closed circles at RAND as a tool for expert socialization. This would have a certain importance as, from the early 1960s on, Delphi exercises no longer focused on the likelihood of enemy attack, but on domestic issues of social choice and the problem of the values and preferences of the American population.[81] The 1964 exercise included 100 scientists, of which 82 were from RAND. In fact, the 1964 Delphi was an exercise in judging the predictive sophistication of a group of professional predictors—verified only by their own positionings. It had thus taken a decisive epistemological step further from Hempel's analysis of the role of intersubjectivity in its analysis of the results of an empirical experiment in the natural world, because it had quite simply suppressed any reference to an empirical element even in the form of specialized knowledge, and made verification an entirely internal question of expert subjectivity. The successful results in creating, within this group of experts, consensus, Helmer and Gordon understood as highly important, because it meant that probabilistic values on virtually any social question could be created through the intermediary of a constituted community of experts in prediction. As RAND was accused, from the mid 1960s, of

[79] J. D. Williams, "Small World Revisited," manuscript, June 21, 1961. Olaf Helmer papers, RAND Archives, box 3.

[80] Olaf Helmer and Bernice Brown, "Improving the Reliability of Estimates Obtained from a Consensus of Experts" (Santa Monica: RAND, 1964).

[81] See Olaf Helmer research notes on Delphi, including undated note entitled "Gathering Expert Opinion," RAND Archives, Olaf Helmer papers, box 2.

technocracy, the question of values factored into debates on social technology. Values were not evacuated from debates at RAND, on the contrary, experiments with game theory pinpointed the question of values as a crucial element of decision, as preferences, it seemed, could not be ordered logically but were determined by factors outside the games. This led to the question not of how will but how *should* players act, a problem that Erickson sees as the root of a separation between the strategist mathematicians at RAND, and mathematicians who, like Rapaport, ventured into the field of peace and conflict studies and left RAND.[82] As experimentation with Delphi continued, and in particular as contestation in American life increased while Helmer and Gordon simultaneously started to imagine cutting loose from RAND in order to create a consultancy based on Delphi, the question of values became crucial. Helmer himself had long recognized that if forms of long range planning were shifted from the field of military strategy into the field of policy, then Delphi would necessarily point towards explicitly normative questions. It was exactly in the field of predicting and analyzing normative and value based problems in the social organization that the great field of application for Delphi could be found. It was here that policy makers were confronted to complicated issues of coordination, priority, and choice. Moral choices, Helmer argued, were not for scientists to determine, but such choices could be rationalized, in the interest of making "judgmental expertise" as *objective* as possible. For instance, were Delphi to be used in the field of social affairs, accuracy required making sure that expert panels did not involve concerned individuals or groups as experts on their own condition, particularly if they were potentially radical. This would be the case, Helmer foresaw, if Delphi were applied to the problem of race relations. More reliable forecasting judgments are obtainable in this case from experts "once removed, that is from social psychologists and other specialists who have made a detailed study of the circumstances, the potentialities, and desires of the group in question." Using such detached expert opinion would be a way of "disciplining speculation," and of making sure that the "most objective" statements pertaining to possible futures were reached, as the "emotional involvement" of those actually concerned "is likely to bias their view of the future and cause them to substitute wishful thinking for objective forecast."[83] Helmer began experimenting for such situations, which he referred to as "adversary Delphis," with Delphi exercises which aimed not at the creation of consensus, but at the clarification of opposed views so that issues of choice could be visualized. Delphi, applied to value laden issues, could be used to manage and experiment, in a formalized and scientifically methodological and rational way, what were essentially questions pertaining to the desirability of specific developments and questions for which the policy process seemed inapt. Here a final step was taken, in which Delphi moved from processing judgments on probable future developments, into the field of making judgments on the desirability of these developments, and arriving at forms of

[82] Erickson, "Mathematical models," 303.

[83] "Gathering expert opinion," and "Notes on economic planning," RAND Archives, Olaf Helmer papers, box 2. Helmer draft, "Adversary Delphi."

consensus around a future deemed, on the basis of expert opinion, to represent the best possible outcome.

As Chapter 4 shows, the distinction between probability and desirability had first been made by Bertrand de Jouvenel in *The Art of Conjecture*, and de Jouvenel was also one of the eight Europeans (along with Erik Jantsch) who participated in the 1964 Delphi run. De Jouvenel had also pioneered the "lookout institution," the idea of a horizon scanning think tank. In 1966, Helmer and Gordon, using Delphi as their pitch, created the so called Institute for the Future with funding from the Ford Foundation and the National Science Foundation. The board of the Institute included Daniel Bell, Henry David of the National Science Foundation, Helmer, and Gordon.[84] The Institute for the Future was dedicated to systematic and comprehensive studies of the future, and to promoting "understanding concerning technological, environmental, and societal changes and their long range consequences." Concentrating research into simulation models and Delphi research, the Institute would educate decision makers in forecasting techniques and develop an "anticipatory culture" for politics. "As change quickens in tempo and widens in sweep, the risks and opportunities that confront us call increasingly for expanded efforts to lead the course of events, rather than be led by them."[85] The first big study of the Institute for the Future was a forecast of the future values of the population of Middletown, Connecticut, in a Delphi study where no actual Connecticut residents were included, and experienced forecasters instead acted out the presumed values of the population.[86] The research program in the late 1960s addressed the topics that would also be at the center of the activities of the so called Commission for the Year 2000 (see the next chapter)—the future of the American family, the future of race relations, and "organisation theory as an extension of the mathematical theory of games into a general theory of social conflict".[87]

The Institute for the Future also sold Delphi to a range of private clients, among whom were some of the major Cold War corporate players. In 1966, Helmer and Gordon produced, for the American steel corporation, Kaiser Aluminum, the Future Game in which Delphi was adapted to a board game in which players could push variables up and down on a two scale metric composed of lists of questions determining the probabilities of, for instance, a great industrial strike in the US pushing labor costs up, or a revolution in an aluminum producing country cutting off supply (see Figure 5.3 and Figure 2.1 in Chapter 2). The Future Game was a promotional gadget, distributed to Kaiser Aluminum managers for Christmas,

[84] In 1970, these were also on the editorial board of the new journal *Futures* (created in 1969). See *Futures*, 1970, 2 (04).

[85] Institute for the Future, brochure, 1966. RAND Archives, Olaf Helmer papers, box 5. The Board of Trustees of the Institute for the Future included Paul Ylvisaker, Ed Quade, Daniel Bell, Ithiel da Sola Pool, futurists John McHale and Alvin Toffler, and the OECD forecaster Eric Jantsch.

[86] Institute for the Future, *Development of Long Range Forecasting Methods for Connecticut: A Summary.* July 1970. RAND Archives, Olaf Helmer papers, box 5. A similar Delphi had been conducted by RAND in Pittsburgh in 1966, with forecasters acting out the values of key segments of the population: housewives, teenagers, cultural elites and the poor. RAND, *A Use of Simulation for the Study of Future Values* (Santa Monica: RAND, 1966).

[87] *Institute for the Future, A Brief Description*, April 1969. RAND Archives, Olaf Helmer papers, box 5.

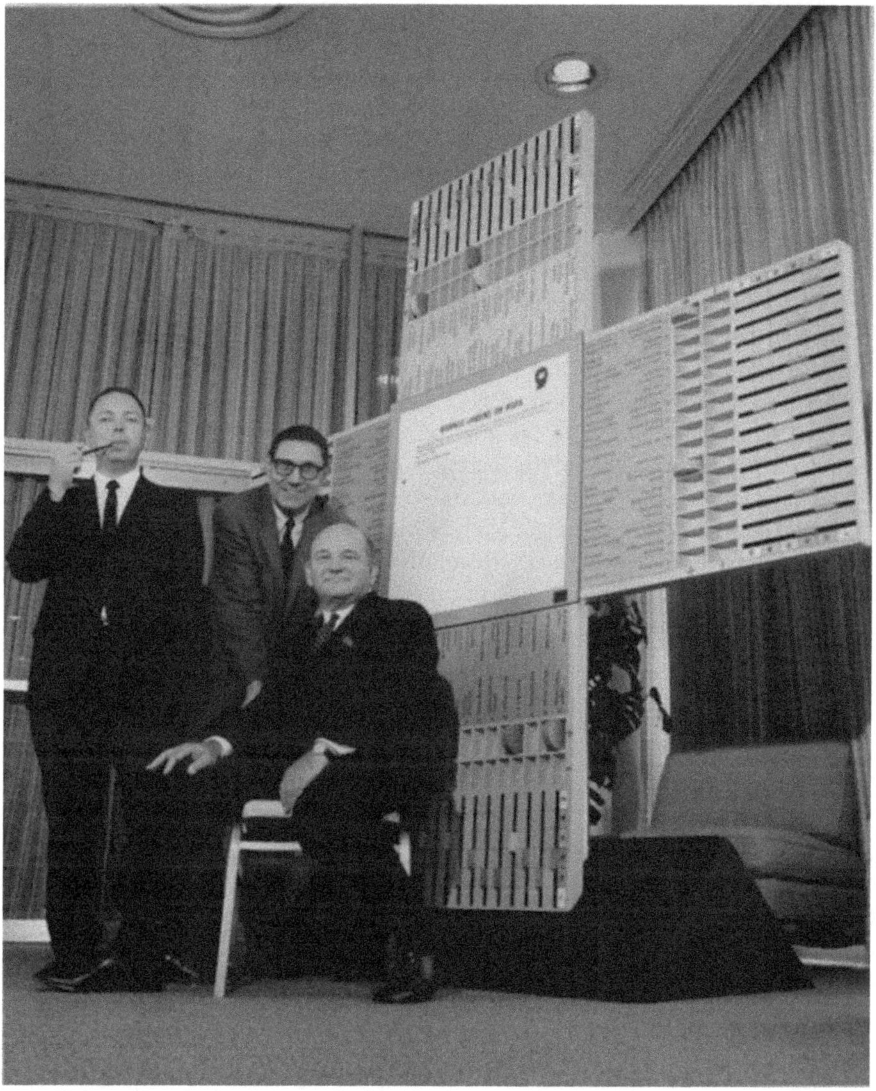

Figure 5.3. Theodore Gordon and Olaf Helmer at RAND in front of the Future Boardgame.

but several large American corporations made use of management and strategy games as ways of rehearsing future corporate environments at this point; indeed it was also in this context that scenarios began to be used by Royal Shell from the mid 1960s on.[88] Helmer continued to work on the sophistication and formalization of Delphi in the years to come, and Delphi developed both into

[88] Jantsch, *Technological Forecasting in Perspective*, lists a range of American companies who started experimenting with such management games in the mid 1960s.

extensive lists of all possible cross-correlations in a matrix of probabilistic values, and into attempts to boil such cross-correlations down to a limited number of variables.[89] In 1967, Helmer became a Professor of management and computer science at UCLA. He then began work on how to automatize Delphi through a net of connected computers—D net—through which forms of expertise could be linked up so that immediate Delphi runnings could be performed of any future relevant question, and put at the disposition of business leaders or Congressmen.[90] In his last writings, Helmer proposed that all issues that raised potential conflicts of interests or values could be addressed through the systematic mobilization of expertise in Delphis and adversary Delphis, and that even the presidential State of the Union could be reinvented as a systematic accounting of "the major options available to our society and the course of action that might be pursued."[91]

Theodore Gordon meanwhile, the Douglas consultant who had experimented with the first Delphi run with Helmer in 1964 and co-launched the Institute for the future, realizing "he could make a buck on this," ventured to create a number of different consultancies in the coming years based on Delphi. The successor of the Institute for the Future is the Millennium Project, a Washington based think tank, which has fulfilled Helmer's dream of an automatized Delphi man-machine in the shape of a global network of nodes of futurists that stand ready to provide expertise on issues concerning all aspects of world development (see Chapter 9).

CONCLUDING REMARKS: TRAVELING DELPHI

Predictive experimentation at RAND laid the basis for a very specific conception of the future as a category of rational decision, the "long term." Through this conception of the future as a matter of optimal preference, the future became a question of an unabashed form of expertise, as expert opinion transpired to be the mechanism that could assure a level of rationality in political and social decision making. The next chapter follows up on this conclusion by tracing the social technologies experimented with at RAND into the so called Commission for the Year 2000, chaired by Daniel Bell, but a central point needs to be made here. Through their paradoxical but fundamental awareness of the performative or self fulfilling role of predictive technologies, RAND researchers arguably modified significantly the idea of expertise, from that of a neutral observation to that of active intervention.[92] This experience shaped, I propose, the post-war notion of prediction. Prediction, from the rise of scientific positivism onwards, was based on the idea that social science could capture law bound and stage driven social developments. But at RAND, designing the future depended on an eclectic range of repertoires,

[89] Theodore Gordon, "Cross-Impact Matrices: an Illustration of Their Use for Policy Analysis." *Futures*, 1969, 1 (6): 527–31.

[90] "Proposal for an Institute for the Future," Olaf Helmer papers, RAND Archives, box 4.

[91] "Report on the Future of the Future of the State of the Union." Olaf Helmer papers, RAND Archives, box 5.

[92] Olaf Helmer, *The Future of Science* (Santa Monica: RAND, 1967).

which varied from the hard core rationality assumptions of initial experiments with gaming, to the expert panels gathered through Delphi, and the future rehearsals of the scenarios. Many of these methods did not at all deny the essentially normative or moral problem of the future, rather, they proposed that such concerns could be dealt with by replacing passionate debate with a rational and logical ordering of probable and desirable developments, and with a systematic comparison between decisions and their logical outcome. The future was thus a question of identifying optimal outcomes. In its proposition that expertise could in this manner be applied to the foremost value laden issues of society, that of choosing a desired future, Delphi was nothing less than a reinvented tool of technocracy.[93]

As Jennifer Light has shown, RANDs gradual exit from the field of military thinking and increased engagement in urban and social policy from the mid 1960s onwards was directly related to the Civil Rights struggle and the urban riots of 1964. In this context, the tools developed at RAND for predicting the actions of irrational communist regimes and jungle guerillas were redeployed as anticipatory warning systems for counterinsurgencies and urban riots at home. RAND created a City office, in New York. As events of the mid 1960s turned the security problem from the outside to the inside of American society, the tools experimented at RAND, gaming, simulation, and modeling, were deployed as the means with which to detect and foresee forms of unrest or even "civil war" at home.[94] At the same time, they also gained notoriety on the global level. For instance, the international relations theorist Ithiel de Sola Pool, closely associated with RAND futurologists and member of the Commission for the Year 2000, developed the war games from RAND into experiments in information technology as a way of controlling liberal publics in various parts of the world.[95] Meanwhile, the terms social technology, Delphi, and forecasting were spread to international planning circles through Erik Jantsch' report, *Technological Forecasting in Perspective*. The report was written for the OECD's Science Policy Committee, and argued that European administrations had to take up the challenge from the American policy sciences in order to increase the foreseeability of economic, social, and technological developments. Jantsch defined both Delphi, and the Look Out institution discussed in Chapter 4, as "social technology." Delphi, Jantsch argued, had permitted a new and scientific understanding of decision making and the possibility of ordering values within social organizations, including the political system.[96]

[93] Frank Fischer, *Technocracy and the Politics of Expertise* (Newbury Park, CA: SAGE, 1990).
[94] Light, *From Warfare to Welfare*, 63; Rohde, *Armed with Expertise*, 136–41.
[95] Light, *From Warfare to Welfare*, 166.
[96] Eric Jantsch, *Technological Forecasting in Perspective*; Matthias Schmelzer, *The Hegemony of Growth* (Cambridge: Cambridge University Press, 2016), 245–52.

6

Predicting the Future of American Society
From RAND to the Commission for the Year 2000

The future belongs to the masses, or to the men that can explain things simply to them.[1]

THE END OF IDEOLOGY THESIS REVISITED

In 1964, Daniel Bell became the president of the so named Commission for the Year 2000 in the American Academy of Arts and Science. The members of the Commission for the Year 2000 were an eminent group of American intellectuals, modernization theorists, Cold Warriors, and former RAND scientists: Walt Rostow, Samuel Huntington, Ithiel da Sola Pool, Albert Wohlstetter, Paul Ylvisaker, Herman Kahn, and Zbigniew Brzezinski. Among its members were also several leading progressives who would by the late 1960s find themselves in the neoconservative camp: Daniel Moynihan and Irving Kristol. In addition, the Commission included the anthropologist Margaret Mead, most known for her study of adolescent culture and sexuality in *Coming of Age in Samoa*, and less well known for having participated in anthropological studies of Cold War populations, as well as the sociologist Lawrence K. Frank and the psychologist Eric Erickson.[2] This chapter proposes that the Commission for the Year 2000 was a central site for the transfer of the social technologies from RAND into a wider reflection on the future of American politics. It suggests that Bell used the Commission to put future research to use in a large scale Delphi exercise on the future of an American society that he understood, by the mid 1960s, as caught in a set of future tensions.

American historians have described the 1960s as the great "age of contradiction," as the confidence in an affluent society clashed with a set of emerging tensions in American politics. The first half of the 1960s was an era in which progressives saw a chance of finally eliminating social problems, through the active use of rationalist social science. At the same time, the intensity of social change in 1960s society created apprehensions, astutely described in scholarship as the "anxieties of affluence," the fearful sense that consumerism, mass culture, and the erosion of working class

[1] Jacob Burkhardt, cited by Daniel Bell in *The End of Ideology. On the Exhaustion of Political Ideas in the 1950's* (Illinois: The Free Press of Glencoe, 1960), 13.

[2] List of confirmed and solicited participants, American Academy for the Arts and Sciences, records of the Commission for the Year 2000, box 1.

culture was contributing to a cultural crisis in American society.[3] The notion of social trends, used not least in Bell's work and the 1972 book *The Coming of Post Industrial Society*, was a marker of these apprehensions. "Trends" denoted the idea that social change was displaying a new phenomenon of scale, and that forms of mobility in many different areas might produce transformative effects on society as a whole. Many of these trends—poverty, problems in youth socialization, and the evolution of race relations—were not at all new. But by the mid 1960s, they were increasingly understood as a set of joined up causal relations, the consequences of which might interact over time and risk shaking historically grounded ideas of American modernity. By the mid 1960s, Bell stood alongside a range of other emblematic American scholars such as Robert Dahl, Seymour Martin Lipset, and Talcott Parsons, whose work became quintessentially concerned with the problem of stabilization and control of the political system.[4] That the term system figured preeminently in their work, now to describe the political organization, was an illustration of the fact that by the mid 1960s a wide range of systems theories dominated the social sciences. But it also testified to the fact that experimentation at RAND had filtered into the very mainstream of American political science.[5] As the "long term," the category produced by space engineering, ballistics, and technological forecasting at RAND, shifted meaning and became a term that denoted the key trends that were in the process of shaping American politics, other notions from RAND were also reinvested with significance, for instance the idea that social change happened through predictable and controllable branch points.

As Brick also suggests, the "optimism of the mind" of progressives in the first half of the 1960s began to falter by 1964 and 1965, to no small extent due to the return of contestation in American social life.[6] These years of the mid 1960s were key years in American political history, marked by the rise of the Great Society programs and new ambitions in welfare policy, the civil rights revolution and rapid and particularly black urbanization. To many liberal intellectuals, understanding themselves in these years as progressives, these were quintessentially positive developments, but they also opened the question of what kind of society would be the result of the process that modernization theory had described as the "entry of the masses into society."[7] In the years of 1964–1967, there were violent clashes between black populations and police in several American cities, sparking fears both of forms of native "tribalism" in American society, and of a white middle class backlash to the civil rights revolution. Leading scholars, including Bell, interpreted this as the sign of a return of interest politics in political life and as a dangerous social rejection of rationality. Modernization theory came into open crisis from its confrontation

[3] Howard Brick, *The Age of Contradiction. American Thought and Culture in the 1960s* (Ithaca: Cornell University Press, 2000); Daniel Horowitz, *The Anxieties of Affluence. Critiques of American Consumer Culture 1939–1979* (Amherst: University of Massachusetts Press, 2004).

[4] Brick, *The Age of Contradiction*, xii, 19, 33.

[5] Jennifer Light, "Taking Games Seriously," in *Technology and Culture*, 2008, 49 (2): 348–75.

[6] Howard Brick, "Optimism of the Mind. Imagining Post Industrial Society in the 1960s and the 1970s," in *American Quarterly*, 1992, 44 (3): 349–80, 349.

[7] Daniel Bell, "Twelve Modes of Prediction. A Preliminary Sorting of Approaches in the Social Sciences," *Daedalus* 1964, 3: 845–80, 862.

with military failure in Vietnam.[8] But modernization theory was an inherently tension ridden enterprise all along. In many ways future research, with its search not only for representations of the predictability of social developments, but also for the actual levers with which these developments could be influenced and controlled, was the product of these tensions. As Nils Gilman has argued, modernization theorists of the 1950s posited American society at the apex of world developments and as the carrier of a particular image of the rational capitalist future. The American polity, modeled on the progressive era writings of Dewey and reproduced in the accounts of much of 1950s political science, was to this extent the very opposite of a global and tribal mass society prone to various forms of irrationality. But as Gilman puts it, if American society was the embodiment of a completed form of modernization, then there was also only one way that it could go. By the mid-1960s, the preoccupation of modernization theorists with traditionalism and forms of nationalism and national character in the global arena was projected onto domestic developments in American society.[9] From the mid-1960s on, future research turned its gaze inward to the trends of American society and became a reflection on the hidden futures of this society, and on a modernization process which no longer seemed to have a clear direction.

Daniel Bell modified his understanding of mass politics significantly in the course of the 1960s, in what can only be described as a turnaround of the assumptions of the end of ideology thesis. *The End of Ideology* had, as argued in Chapter 4, an ambivalent, yet optimistic tone in its outlook on a coming mass society heading toward a likely process of social peace and pragmatic compromise between a plurality of interests. By the mid-1960s, Bell was increasingly skeptical about the end of ideology thesis, and in 1970, he declared to a seminar on futurology of the Association for Cultural Freedom that it was false.[10] Bell's 1973 magnum opus *The Coming of Post Industrial Society* argued that the relatively stable structures of industrial society and its foreseeable patterns of social change were in the process of a radical transformation—a state that Bell labeled, following an emerging set of writings by revisionist Marxist scholars in Europe, post-industrialism. The post-industrial society, to Bell, could not be grasped or controlled by the linear means of planning, but required foresight, a new kind of forward looking intellectual technology which included long-term indicators, technology assessment, and the analysis of interrelated social, economic, and political trends.[11] It is striking that most scholarship on Bell has been concerned with the rather optimistic vision of capitalism that underlay the 1973 book, and not with what was arguably the central tenet of the book, namely the idea of forecasting as a social and political

[8] Gilman, *Mandarins of the Future*, 203f.

[9] See Rohde, *Armed with Expertise*, 139; Michael Latham, *Modernisation as Ideology* (Chapel Hill, 2000), 67.

[10] International Association of Cultural Freedom, Seminar on Futurology, 1970, CCF records, box 403; see also Bell's revisiting of the thesis of the post-industrial society in "The Coming of Post Industrial Society", *The Educational Forum*, 1976, 46 (04): 4, 574–79.

[11] Daniel Bell, *The Post Industrial Society. A Venture in Social Forecasting* (New York: Basic Books, 1999 (1973)).

technology for post-industrial mass society.[12] Meanwhile, Bell's idea of forecasting as a technology for the crafting of rational decision stood in a direct continuity with the argument in *The End of Ideology*—that a political system driven by rising social expectations in the masses needed some kind of counter balance, some measure of judging and anticipating the effects on its future form. In *The Coming of Post Industrial Society*, Bell's 1960s argument had developed into the notion that a post-industrial society was marked by inherent clashes of values and preferences between different social groups, and that this created a new situation of conflict in liberal society. This conception brought to the fore the ambivalent and latently pessimistic notion of the mass that had informed the end of ideology thesis.

The Commission for the Year 2000 has not attracted much attention from American historians, possibly because in the end it was a failed enterprise. The Commission never finished its final report and proceedings imploded over the increasing turmoil in American society with the Vietnam protests and the rise of the New Left. Meanwhile, the Commission was arguably a key site for the translation of future research into a notion of liberal planning, and it is also highly indicative of the way that future research marked a bridge from modernization theory's assertive stances on social development in the Western world, to much more concerned reflections on a future that could no longer be taken for granted.

SOCIAL CHANGE AS A DELIBERATELY PLANNED PROCESS: FROM PLANNING TO PREDICTION

As he took presidency of the Commission in 1964, Daniel Bell was in the process of becoming a living hub in transnational exchanges around future research and forecasting. Bell is a towering figure in American historiography, to do with his personal trajectory from radical thought in the 1940s, to budding neoconservatism following his bewildered reaction to the student protests at Columbia in 1968.[13] But Bell was also a tireless transnational broker, whose interest in planning brought him far into circles of liberal and social democrat planners in Western Europe, as well as, as the next chapter will explain, revisionist and reform communist planning circles in Eastern Europe.

The transnational activity around the concept of post industrialism marked a shift or second mode in ideas of planning, as the social theories of Bell and others met with planners' visions of forecasting as a new political and social technology for complexity, forms of interrelation between economic, social, technological, and cultural change, and feedback mechanisms. In the same year, 1964, that the AAAS created the American Commission for the Year 2000, the French government set

[12] Brick, *The Age of Contradiction*; Howard Brick, *Transcending Capitalism. Visions of a New Society in Modern American Thought* (Ithaca: Cornell University Press, 2006).

[13] Howard Brick, *Daniel Bell and the Decline of Radicalism. Social Theory and Political Reconciliation in the 1940s* (Madison: Wisconsin University Press, 1986); Malcolm Waters, *Daniel Bell* (London: Routledge, 1996).

up a similarly forward-looking committee, the *Groupe 1985*.[14] Through the *Groupe 1985*, *prospective* entered into the French planning system as a tool for *décisions rationelles*, rational decision. The *Groupe 1985* introduced conjecture, Delphis and scenarios into the heartland of the French state.[15] Bell, who remained in close contact with French planners such as Pierre Masse and Jacques Delors, was the bridge between these two commissions, and both commissions developed key reflections on 1960s societies marked by automation, social trends, and dramatic value change. In actual fact the *Groupe 1985* and the CY2000 followed a very similar logic: just as the Commission for the Year 2000 would eventually break down over the Vietnam protests and what Bell sarcastically referred to as the "me-me generation," the Groupe 1985 also turned into an elitist expression of shock at the apparent rejection of affluent society that was 1968. The first report of the *Groupe 1985* was optimistic, enthused by the new tool of *prospective* as a way of extending planning rationalities into the "long term" (a twenty-five-year horizon, compared to the five-year horizon of the *Plan*). The second report meanwhile, appearing in 1972, was much more pessimistic and did not hide its disdain for the young generation, the students, and the universities. In between the two reports, the idea of the uses of future research changed profoundly. To the second report, *prospective* was no longer a mere planning tool, but a strategic device for foreseeing destructive value revolutions, and for implanting new and common images of the future in a French public that now appeared in a planners' view as deeply suspect.[16]

In transnational circles, Bell was known for his notes on forecasting and future research. *The Coming of Post Industrial Society* was eventually published in 1973, but it resumed thoughts and arguments that Bell had experimented within his preferred essay form since the publication of *The End of Ideology* in 1960. The first notes on post-industrial society were compiled for a Salzburg Seminar in 1959 and argued that a shift was ongoing from manual labor to forms of technical labor.[17] *The End of Ideology* introduced the ideas of intellectual technologies capable of having a bearing on social time. In a 1967 essay in *The Public Interest*, Bell proposed to see the social "system" as something that was now truly becoming reachable for social science rationality. He argued that the process of social change had speeded up to a point where it was possible to make direct observations of changes that historically had not been visible within the span of a generation, and that moreover, such social changes had also become amenable to forms of deliberate intervention. The openended "form" was now a determined "system". *The End of Ideology* had argued that new and scientific approaches to social time derived from operations research, systems analysis, and cybernetics had turned the problem of utopia into a question of the rational management of choices, decisions, and values. Bell's notes on post-industrialism took this argument further by arguing that post-industrial societies were marked by a fundamentally new approach to technology

[14] In the same year, the British Social Science Research Council had also created a forecasting commission on the next thirty years, including Michael Young, Andrew Schonfield, and Marie Jahoda.
[15] Commissariat General au Plan, *Refléxions pour 1985* (Paris, 1964).
[16] Commissariat Général au Plan, *La France face au choc du futur* (Paris, 1972).
[17] "Notes on Post Industrial Society", 1959–60, Daniel Bell papers, box 14, folder 23.

as intellectual technology; a new and conscious application of technology to societal decision making. Technology, Bell argued, in his first address to the Commission, was in the process of being transformed from a specific machine or invention, to a series of applications to social problems. "Technology is a systematic, disciplined approach to objectives, using a calculus of precision and measurement." This included "intellectual technologies" or "decision tools" such as the new methods in futurology. "Instead of a machine technology, we will have, increasingly, an intellectual technology in which such techniques as simulation, model construction, linear programming, and operations research will be hitched to the computers and will become the new tools of decision making."[18]

The purpose of intellectual technology was to solve the social problems of the post-industrial age. Its growing role corresponded to a shift in social power relations. Where *The End of Ideology* ended in a plea for a new utopian spirit among Cold War engineers, the 1967 essay spoke of a new kind of technocracy in the "technicists" of a highly educated white collar nation. The technicists were not, Bell insisted, a new version of Saint Simon's technocrats, because they did not themselves wield power. Rather, technicists were taking on an indispensable role as providing inputs to a growing political arena in need of new forms of formal and technological tools of decision making because of growing problems of interdependence and feedback.[19]

It is not surprising that these notes fell on fertile ground in a growing transnational community of forecasters, who arguably saw themselves exactly as such technicists and as the helpers of political decision. In 1969, forecasters met at the OECD seminar in Bellagio around Eric Jantsch's 1967 report *Technological Forecasting in Perspective*, and in the year before, they had met in Tokyo on the initiative of the Japan Techno-Economic Society. The Japanese interest in forecasting is important: Japan had gone through a process of remarkable growth and speedy industrialization under American dominance in the 1950s, and in the 1960s, Japan was included in new planning notions of the Western world as the "advanced" industrial nations. Advanced referred to post-industrial patterns of production, organized around white collar work and technological automation, as well as around value changes toward consumption and leisure. Importantly, what distinguished Western industrial societies from the socialist ones was the difference in planning rationalities toward "open" or "closed" conceptions of the future. From 1969 on, "long range forecasting" was a mark for a new kind of liberal long-term planning which drew on scenarios, Delphis, decision trees, and branch charts, and which often times included management methods taken from the corporate sphere and aimed at setting out common visions of socio-industrial development. In Japan, forecasting became a planning tool for "multi channel society"; a Japanese term describing exploding communication, innovation, and cultural changes. As such it drew on direct contributions from Japanese companies such as Toyota and

[18] Daniel Bell, "The Year 2000. The Trajectory of an Idea," in Bell and Graubard, eds, *The Year 2000. Work in Progress* (Cambridge MA: MIT Press, 1967) 1–17, 5.

[19] Daniel Bell, "Notes on the Post Industrial Society (1)," *The Public Interest*, 1967, 6: 24.

the public railway company, the Shinkansen.[20] The Japanese immediately translated Jantsch's report (which brought the Delphi study at RAND to international attention), and Bell used his presence at the 1968 forecasting seminar in Tokyo to take notes for his book project.[21]

Bell had become an avid student of future research in the years that followed the notes on the scientification of social time in The *End of Ideology*. In fact, he read all the key works of futurism, beginning with Dennis Gabor's *Inventing the Future*, and he also imagined turning these into course work at Harvard.[22] His position on the *Futuribles* board allowed him to draw conclusions from the hundred or so *Futuribles* essays that had been produced by Bertrand de Jouvenel's venture, and in addition, Bell followed closely experiments with gaming, simulation, modeling, and forecasting at RAND and NASA. Bell was not at all uncritical of much of this activity, on the contrary, he understood much of it as dangerously limited, encountering "rational fallacies" and reproducing machinistic notions of a closed system.[23] For this reason, from the smorgasbord of predictive attempts available, it was very specific forms of prediction that caught Bell's interest. This had to do precisely with the idea of social technology, in other words with the notion of future research as a way of foreseeing the consequences of public decision. In 1964, Bell presented the evaluation of the *Futuribles* enterprise that he had conducted for the Ford foundation on the request of Shepard Stone in the essay "Twelve Modes of Prediction."[24] "Twelve modes of Prediction" introduced all the central themes of the later 1972 book. It proposed to see future research as an emergent reflection on the futures of the social system, and as a powerful tool for foreseeing social trends, provided specific methods of prediction were tied to the larger systems theories that had been developed in American social science. If future research could be tied to a theory of the social system, it could, in Bell's view, reproduce what had been done in technological forecasting: identify the relevant sequence and range of decisions and sort between priorities, values, and preferences, in such a way as to identify strategies for achieving social objectives and sort good outcomes from bad. Future research, Bell argued, could be developed into a much needed governmental anticipatory mechanism. After all, said Bell, if other social entities such as the big corporations developed forecasting as tools with which to foresee interrelationships between new technological trends and products, estimates of costs and outputs, then so should any government concerned with new forms of socio economic interdependence.[25] "Why does one seek to predict? This is an era in which society has become future oriented in all its dimensions; a government has to anticipate future problems, an enterprise has to plan for future needs."[26]

[20] Eric Jantsch, "Technological Forecasting at National Level in Japan. Notes from a Brief Visit," in *Technological Forecasting and Social Change*, 1970, 2: 325–7. See also special session on Japanese forecasting, "Perspectives on Multi Channel Society," in *Challenges from the Future. Proceedings from the Kyoto Conference in Future Research* (Kyoto: Japan society for futurology, 1970), 293–385.

[21] Notes on Japanese society; Daniel Bell papers, box 3 folder 36; box 31 folder 8.

[22] Reading list and possible syllabus on future research, Daniel Bell papers, box 15, folder 18.

[23] Bell, "Twelve Modes of Prediction," 869.

[24] "Twelve Modes of Prediction" was also published in French as one of the *Futuribles* essays.

[25] Daniel Bell, "The Study of the Future," in *The Public Interest*, 1965, 1: 119–30, 121.

[26] Bell, "Twelve Modes of Prediction," 869.

The essay "The Study of the Future" in the first issue of *The Public Interest* in 1965 argued that future research held the potential for a new form of planning, devoted to the creation of the best possible conditions of happiness for the great mass of people living in a welfare society.[27] As such, it was, Bell argued, in a line of argument that followed closely de Jouvenel's linkage of conjecture and freedom of choice, inherently linked to the idea of increasing freedom over time, by setting forth representations of the future consequences of decisions and comparing these in terms of their desirability. From this perspective, future research was a new kind of planning, which could also help create awareness of consequences over time in the public and therefore weigh on rational social expectations.[28]

> Can we, with full awareness of the problem of choosing between conflicting values... find some way of choosing the best planning process that is consonant with our belief in liberty? The function of planning is not just to set forth goals and alternatives and means of achieving these. Equally important and usually neglected are the specifications of costs and benefits, the reallocation of burdens, and the probable consequences of different kinds of actions. The true function of the planning process is not to designate the most appropriate means for given ends, but to predict the possible consequences, to explicate the values of a society, and make people aware of the cost of achieving these.[29]

Bell was particularly enthusiastic about de Jouvenel's concept of conjecture, as a method that did not pretend to predict, but rather, to explain social changes and "identify forms of control on transformations of a given situation."[30] He was also enthusiastic about Herman Kahn's scenario method, which Bell saw as a concrete way of illustrating alternative futures with the purpose of influencing both policy makers and public opinion. The Hudson Institute prepared several working papers for the CY2000, including a series of memos which attempted to adapt the standard and deviant worlds from Kahn's *Thermonuclear War* to a domestic American situation. Bell showcased Herman Kahn's scenarios as examples of "conjecture as high art."[31] If de Jouvenel's conjecture was a way of putting political scientists to work drawing up elaborate guesses about what would happen under what given circumstance, then Kahn's scenarios could be understood as the direct application and visual form of these conjectures, by outlining futures that might come into being under given conditions and provided certain forms of action were taken. Scenarios were possible "guides to policy makers in sketching their own responses to the possible worlds that may emerge during the next decade."[32]

Meanwhile, Bell reserved his most elaborate praise for the Delphi technique, which he understood as having successfully shifted the focus of long range forecasting from exercises focused on military technology toward representations of a social

[27] Daniel Bell, "The Study of the Future."

[28] Daniel Bell, "Twelve Modes of Prediction," 847, 852. Bertrand de Jouvenel, *L'art de la conjecture*, (Monaco, 1962) and Bertrand de Jouvenel, 1964, "Evolution of the Forms of Government."

[29] "Twelve Modes of Prediction," 870.

[30] "Twelve Models of Prediction," 847.

[31] Bell, "Twelve modes of prediction," 861.

[32] Bell, "Twelve modes of prediction," 866; Herman Kahn, "Alternative world futures," Hudson Institute discussion paper, April 1964, CY2000 papers.

and political system. "The Study of the Future" ended with an in depth discussion of the 1964 Delphi exercise at RAND—a "sophisticated use of expert talent to look at the future." The shortcomings of Delphi, meanwhile, were that Delphi panels had so far focused on the likelihood of single events, and failed to use prediction in a systems logic. The Delphi exercise had depended on the premise that the United States and the world remain essentially the same system. This, to Bell, could not be presumed, because it was the systems logic itself that needed to be foreseen. The challenge of future research was therefore to predict dominant forms of movement and evolution within both a domestic social and political system, and in a surrounding international system. If a technique of systematizing intuitive judgment on future developments, thereby laying out an array of possible futures, could be combined with the creation of models representing these systems, then prediction would become a powerful tool for desired forms of social change.[33] "Though this may not create the changes themselves, it will at least anticipate their direction and effects, and plan accordingly."[34] Bell's enchantment with Delphi reiterated here his end of ideologyidea, that of an enlightened technocracy at work on setting out the objectives, decisions, and consequences of future society, and in this capacity, working out liberal society's future form.

A SENSE OF NATIONAL PRIORITY

As he gave the first address to the Commission in 1964, Bell introduced the Commission itself as a large scale Delphi, a "controlled prospective experiment" shaped as a number of expert hearings on the core questions of the American future.[35] In line with the idea that such expert opinions should have a bearing on public opinion and decisions by creating a measure of visibility for future developments, the first proceedings of the Commission were published in the 1967 *Work in Progress* volume, and this was followed by several issues in the Academy journal *Daedalus*. The entirety of the proceedings and essays were also collected in volumes that were sent to forecaster networks and planning centers all over the world.[36]

The 1967 volume took the shape of a great catalogue of problems pertaining to the future of US society, in a fascinating play of mirrors of problems and trends situated on the inside of the domestic American "system," and trends in the outside world. About half of the essays to the Commission concerned domestic changes in the US, while the other half involved high ranking international relations scholars such as Eugene Rostow, Ithiel da Sola Pool, and Samuel Huntington, whose essays

[33] Bell, "The Study of the Future," 124. In his foreword to the political scientist Harvey Perloff's book *The Future of US Government*, Bell cited Delphi as a promising approach to the determination of social futures through the extraction of expert knowledge, and in July 1965 Bell wrote to Olaf Helmer asking him for more papers on futurology that he might send out to the members of the Commission. Daniel Bell, "Foreword," to Harvey Perloff, *The Future of US Government. Toward the Year 2000* (New York: Braziller, 1971) 1971). Daniel Bell letter to Olaf Helmer, July 12 1965. RAND Archives, Olaf Helmer papers, box 2.

[34] Bell, "The Study of the Future," 122.

[35] Bell and Graubard, eds., *Work in Progress*, 32.

[36] Send out lists of CY2000 proceedings, CY2000 papers.

portrayed a new international system in which the former threats of Soviet Russia and Maoist China were being replaced by a fragmented and multipolar world order, a world in which the leading role of America was far from clear.[37] The ongoing changes in the American state with the creation of the Great Society programs were in a preeminent position among the problem areas in the domestic system of the US. These were understood as being at the heart of a major dislocation of power, from states, markets, and citizens, to a new federal government and the presidency. Alongside this development, commission debates placed a tremendous emphasis on social mobility, defined not least by the integration of the African-American population in the aftermath of the Civil Rights revolution. As the Commission started out in 1964, the year of the Civil Rights Act and Johnson's declaration of the War on Poverty, this process of social mobility seemed directly linked to expanding state action, in a new relationship between public and individual power. What Bell labeled "the diffusion of the few to the many" was a fundamentally different description of mass society than Shils' "entry of the masses into society," the formulation that had laid much of the basis for the end of ideology idea. In mid 1960s society, 42 percent of Americans went to college. What would happen to intelligence in such a society?[38] And what would be the place of the American Negro in the aftermath of a rights revolution that had "unleashed a new set of expectations" on public policy?[39] These questions reflected a fundamental anxiety, namely, that the American polity was changing and that the outcome of this process might not be a recognizable liberal form but rather, a new version of the future.

At the heart of Commission exchanges, Bell placed the hypothesis that American society was for the first time in history in the process of becoming a genuinely communal society, but that as such, it lacked a shared sense of national priority and a common image of the future.[40] Like space research, future research could, suggested Bell, be used as a way of creating a "genuine national society," by giving meaning to profound forms of social change.[41] Of particular relevance, Bell thought, were forms of prediction that could show emergent forms of change in national character and in the forms of behavior associated with a particular culture or nation. National character was a core concern in modernization theory, and Bell took this from the sociologist David Riesman. In 1950, Riesman published *The Lonely Crowd*, and in the first years of the 1960s he taught classes on national character in the modernization process at Harvard, and Bell, collected the notes for his work on the Commission.[42] Modernization theorists thought that the process of modernization could be traced from national character, and key works of modernization theory reiterated conceptions of American national character as steeped

[37] Eugene Rostow, "Thinking about the Future of International Society," in Bell and Graubard, *The Year 2000. Work in Progress*, 310–14; Samuel Huntington, "Political Development and the Decline of the American System of World Order," in *The Year 2000. Work in Progress*, 315–17; Ithiel da Sola Pool, "The International System in the Next Half Century," in *The Year 2000, Work in Progress*, 319–22.

[38] *Work in Progress*, 32. [39] *Work in Progress*, 56.

[40] Bell, *The Coming of Post Industrial Society*, 248.

[41] Bell, "The Study of the Future," 120f.

[42] David Riesman, 1950, *The Lonely Crowd. A Study of the Changing American Character* (New York: Doubleday, 1952); Riesman lectures, Daniel Bell papers.

in a specific form of individualism. The problem for the CY2000 was therefore how a new process of mass mobility and expanding state action transformed national character, thereby changing the very meaning of America. The question that Bell put to the Commission was how a society dominated by a number of disparate and fragmented social trends such as the breakdown of agriculture and homesteading, massive urbanization, and the gradual end of segregation might collectively arrive at a sense of future priority.[43]

The historian Daniel Rodgers has argued that the conception of being a national society, but not sharing a national future was a central product in American social theory following the breakdown of the sense of unity forged by the Cold War by the mid 1960s. As such, it preceded what Rodgers refers to as the great fracture and situates it in the Reagan era of the 1970s and early 1980s.[44] Put in this context, the Commission for the Year 2000 displayed a peculiar and transitional sense that forms of change were eminently controllable through the prism of rationality, and yet, were slipping away from rationality's hold on such notions. This feeling of slipping away was directly related to observations of a new logic of state action, setting in motion a new and somehow foreign relationship between decision makers and citizens. The Great Society programs had introduced a new level of ambition in the heartland of the American state, that of transforming, through the programs on poverty, community action, urban renewal, and antidiscrimination, the fate of a generation.[45] In so doing, they set in place a new logic of public action, at the expense, or so Commission proceedings suggested, of other forms of action in a liberal society. "More and more people are coming into society, and as claimants, are making effective demands on it." This raised a question that was addressed in Commission proceedings both as a problem of governmental rationality and practice, and as a fundamentally moral problem of the nature of the social contract. What was the "relevant social unit," the adequate social structure for dealing with problems in a rational way, as the boundaries between states and citizens, individual and public action, but also federal government, states, and corporations changed?[46] And in a time of increased public action and social claims, what was the relevant meaning of equality and freedom? The process of becoming a national society required a new "commitment to directed social change," the creation of a sense of overarching value and priority.[47]

Like so many of Bell's undertakings, the Commission was not entirely his own idea. It was first proposed to the AAAS by the Depression era social psychologist Lawrence K. Frank, previous chair of President Hoover's 1933 Commission for Social Trends.[48] Frank's description of the Commission in the proposal to the

[43] Bell, "The Trajectory of an Idea"; Daniel Bell, "Preliminary Memorandum, October 22, 1965," in Bell and Graubard, eds., *The Year 2000. Work in Progress*, 17–20.

[44] Daniel Rodgers, *Age of Fracture,* (Cambridge MA: Harvard University Press, 2013).

[45] Alice O'Connor, *Poverty Knowledge. Social Science, Social Policy and the Poor in Twentieth Century US History* (Princeton NJ: Princeton University Press, 2009); Michael Katz, *The Undeserving Poor. From the War on Poverty to the War on Welfare* (New York: Pantheon Books, 1990).

[46] Rostow, in *Work in Progress*, 39, and Bell, *The Coming of Post Industrial Society*, 301.

[47] *Work in Progress*, 22.

[48] *See Recent Social Trends*, 1933; Jordan, *Machine Age Ideology*, 181.

AAASs projected his experiences of the Great Depression onto 1960s American society. Just as in the 1930s, Frank proposed, the rate of social change of the 1960s was such that it might distort the American "character-structure." Avoiding such negative effects required increased planning. "If we are to maintain a free social order in the face of the discontent and anxiety we will probably provoke, we must attempt the Promethean task of renewing our traditional culture and reorienting our social order as a deliberately planned process."[49] But Frank also proposed that a national commission for the future be devoted to setting out a new sense of national priority, a forging of collective objectives based on a new social and political philosophy for the 1960s.[50] In 1965, the Academy journal, *Daedalus*, held a seminar including Bell, at which Carl Kaysen called for "something between a taskforce and a utopia." The seminar description said "What kind of society do we want to be in 1975–1985? And what are the steps that we need to take in the coming decade to bring this image to reality?"[51]

In fact, there had been a full range of attempts to address questions of national priorities and national future in the recent past. In 1960, in a context of acute Cold War struggle, president Eisenhower appointed the so called President's Goals Commission in order to establish a list of national priorities. Such lists of national priorities were created by the CIA's Office for National Estimates, and William Bundy, the security advisor to Kennedy, also wrote a chapter for the Goal's Commission. In the context of the Goals Commission, the problem of national priority was now transformed into the problem of identifying the central priorities for American politics.[52] Created at the height of Cold War tension, the Goals Commission was an attempt to extend this reflection into a larger one that would mobilize Americans around recreated feelings of national unity and collective belonging.[53]

By 1964 and 1965, the Cold War was entering into a new stage of thaw, and such feelings of Cold War unity against a joint enemy were eroding. At the same time, the first half of the 1960s had seen a range of initiatives aiming to develop new forms of planning in science, technology, and energy resources for the purpose of national objectives. This spread from the field of science and technology into queries about the inputs of social science and technoscience on the American state. The Carnegie Corporation, which funded the CY2000, was a central site for this transfer. In the years before the creation of the Commission, the Carnegie Corporation had funded several AAAS conferences on the uses of science and technology in American society, the future of race relations, and the future of intellectual institutions, activities that also regrouped many of the intellectuals of the

[49] Memorandum from Frank to Hudson Hoagland, January 1964, cited in Bell, "The Trajectory of an Idea," 9.

[50] Frank, Proposal for the Commission for the year 2000, in CY2000 records.

[51] Bulletin of the American Academy for the Arts and Sciences, May 1965, 8, in Lewis Mumford's archives, box 1, folder 83.

[52] *Goals for Americans. The Report of the President's Commission on National Goals* (New York, 1960); see in particular William P. Bundy, "A Look Further Ahead," 360–72.

[53] Eisenhower foreword, *Goals for Americans.*

CY2000.[54] Carnegie also held a series of conferences on the inputs of social science to the political process, as well as on the future of race relations.

RATIONAL SOCIAL CHOICE

Work in the Commission thus began in the optimistic spirit that forms of social science expertise could be applied to a reflection on the key trends in American society, from which would emerge a rationally grounded sense of national priority and ordering of future objectives. While the Commission never produced a final report, among the outcomes were nevertheless several key illustrations of a feeling of a future unfolding in US society. These included Kahn's and Jerome Wieners 1967 *Toward the Year 2000*, in which the scenario method was now applied to domestic developments and not least to race relations; the political scientist Harvey Perloff's book, the *Future of US Government*, which proposed that the Great Society programs risked not only strengthening the federal structure of the American state at the expense of the states, but also of introducing tensions in the social contract between communitarian ambitions and principles of individual freedom as rooted in the American character and constitution, and Bell's own *The Coming of Post Industrial Society*.[55]

Bell's first statement to the commission spoke of the necessity of a new "organization of rational decision" and in contrast to Frank's idea of a founding fathers document for the 1960s, he proposed that the main purpose of the Commission should be to outline a new decision theory or "theory of moral choice" for American politics.[56] Futures research, he argued in a draft note for the Commission, could be used for the threefold purpose of finding solutions to key social problems and setting out overarching social objectives, but also identifying the possible consequences of dealing with such problems, and, through such a reflection on consequence, find a measure of distinction between desirable and undesirable social objectives.[57] Future research was "a systematic effort to anticipate social problems, to design new institutions, and to propose alternative programs for choice."[58]

This stemmed from his understanding that a communal society introduced a new problem in a liberal polity, which was that of merging individual and collective preferences together in ways that did not breach the social contract. A communal society, as described within Commission debates not only by Bell but also by scholars such as Daniel Moynihan and Zbigniew Brzezinski, was a society in which an expanding public administration increasingly made decisions in the place of markets and individuals, and in which the production of good was increasingly a public good, created for welfare purposes. As more and more decisions in society were made by government, this placed a new premium on the act of public choice.

54 Records from the Commission for the Year 2000, Carnegie Corporation of New York, Series III 1 A-B, box 391–2.

55 Kahn and Wiener. See Bell, Foreword to Perloff, *The Future of US Government*, ix–xvii.

56 Bell, "The Trajectory of an Idea," 4–6.

57 Future research, notes, CY2000 papers box 1.

58 Bell, "The Trajectory of an Idea," 10.

Commission proceedings began with the shocking observation that "more than half of national income was now distributed by government, without conflict" in the non communist countries. The expansion of public responsibility, raised to Bell, a new question in the American polity: "Will we have to forego individual decision for the communal enterprise?" and "What is the meaning of free choice, when so many choices are group based rather than individual?"[59]

These statements on communal society are highly revealing of Bell's reinterpretation of the relationship between the mass and the future of the social form in post-industrialism. The logic of a communal society was that it did not once and for all settle the social expectations of different social groups toward a state of social peace, as the end of ideology thesis had proposed, but that rather, it set in motion a spiral of growing claims on the state.[60] As not all claims could reasonably be provided for by governmental action, at certain points they would clash, and social expectations were thus now understood as inherently confrontational. "Hence the problem of social choice—how to reconcile conflicting individual desires through the political mechanism rather than through the market, becomes a potential source of discord."[61]

From this perspective, Bell's suggestion of forecasting as a particular intellectual technology took on a meaning that was in fact much more specific than the idea of future research as a new kind of anticipatory planning, because Bell suggested that the points of collision between different expectations were the "decision points" in the social system. Decision points were "points of decision making—because they are the points of conflict."[62] At these points of collision, arbitrations between different claims needed to be made, and the decisions taken at these points would (like investments in key technologies) set in motion a new set of consequences and claims, and thus lead to system change. It was therefore of the essence that these points could be foreseen. In the 1972 book, Bell developed this argument into the proposition that forecasting was a necessary tool for a conflict prone post-industrial society, by solving the problem of social choice, and transforming "social choice" into "rational social choice."[63] It is noteworthy that "rational" here takes the place of "collective."

The problem of social choice was introduced in the book *Social Choice and Individual Values* by the economist Kenneth Arrow in 1951. *Social Choice and Individual Values* was based on Arrow's experiments with gaming in the mathematics department at RAND, with the purpose of finding out how individual utility preferences could somehow be combined with a collective welfare utility. Behind this lay the question discussed in the previous chapter: what kind of planning mechanism would be acceptable in a liberal society, unwilling to engage with fixed or "closed" long-term plans but also in need of an efficiency mechanism for social action. Arrow's theory of social choice was built on the so called impossibility theorem.

[59] Bell, "The Trajectory of an Idea"; Daniel Bell, "Preliminary memorandum, October 22, 1965," in Bell and Graubard, *The Year 2000. Work in Progress*, 17–20, *Proceedings*, 32.

[60] *Work in Progress*, 22.

[61] "The Trajectory of an Idea," 6; *Work in Progress*, 22.

[62] *Work in Progress*, 48.

[63] Bell, *The Coming of Post Industrial Society*, 305–7.

The impossibility theorem was a game theoretical exposition of the impossibility of logically moving from the range of individual preferences in a mass society to a collective or social choice. As this proved impossible within game theoretical assumptions of strictly rational actors, Arrow's conclusion was that any kind of collective decision making mechanism was bound to infringe the principle of individual utility. Democracy was an arbitration between essentially suboptimal outcomes. Just as Walt Rostow's *The Stages of Economic Growth. A Non Communist Manifesto* (1960) was a demonstration of the fallacies of Marxist planning, Arrow's theory of social choice was a mathematical defense of liberal democracy as organized around the preeminence of individual utility preferences.[64]

Meanwhile, Arrow argued that certain forms of social choices were necessary in order to uphold a limited, welfare mechanism. The social choice theorem was part of the development of rational choice theory into a budding school of thought around social and public choice. In contrast to public choice theory, the heydays of which came in the aftermath of the perceived failures of the Great Society programs and in particular the Community action program (which were understood as having pervaded incentive structures and set in place new "group claims"), social choice theory did foresee a necessary space of intervention, but only on the premise that this left a significant terrain to individual and market based decisions.[65] Bell's suggestion that forecasting represented a technical and empirical solution to Arrow's impossibility theorem, by orienting collective preferences toward something that could be identified as a rational social choice is therefore interesting because it shows how the progressive concern with forms of welfarist planning in American politics was only possible through a simultaneous reflection on how such welfare choices could be constrained in order to control their long-term effects. In Bell's idea that the balance could be found through the application of rationality figures, moreover, a, by now, familiar notion that only by a measure of outside expertise and judgment on consequences as desirable or not, could an inherently conflictual social choice be transformed into a "rational" one.

The 1973 book made a complicated argument about social indicators as a quantitative measure of social change and as a form of "calculus of consent" (a term borrowed from James Buchanan) by monitoring the social trends that Bell thought revealing of emergent changes in the social system, and therefore of possible decision points.[66] By mapping out key social trends, social indicators could make statements on possible conflicts in values and goals within the "system," and help make decisions on priority and choice between different social programs. In so doing, they could solve the problem of social choice, by a measure

[64] Kenneth Arrow, *Social Choice and Individual Values* (New York: Cowles Commission, Wiley and Sons,1951); Amadae, *Rationalizing Liberal Capitalist Democracy*, 83; Gilman, *Mandarins of the Future*, 13; Latham, *Modernisation as Ideology*, 30, 34–5, 50, 67.

[65] *Work in Progress*, 27.

[66] Bell, *The Coming of Post Industrial Society*, 306–7; Karl Deutsch, "Towards an inventory of basic trends and patterns in comparative and international politics," *American Political Science Review*, 1960, 54 (1): 34–57; Seymour Martin Lipset and Paul Lazarsfeld, "The Psychology of Voting," in *Handbook of Social Psychology*, 1954, 2: 1124–75.

of rationality that to Bell was directly linked to quantitative measures of cost efficiency and a desirable result on social trends per investment in each area. The trends in American society, Bell argued, were in danger of displacing decision from the two spheres that had historically guaranteed mechanisms of rational decision, namely, the market (through the use of the price mechanism), and the individual (through his knowledge of his preferences). In a state of affairs in which such choices were increasingly sidelined, the social choice could only be rational—and therefore, legitimate within a liberal polity—if it was performed through some mechanism that guaranteed desired and efficient outcomes.[67]

Bell went as far as to suggest that a systematic process of forecasting consequences of decision would therefore solve a classic dilemma of liberalism, the problem of conflict between collective and individual preferences. Arrow's social theory can be placed in a long line of arguments first traced by Condorcet in the so called voting paradox. The novelty in Bell's line of reasoning lay in his understanding that decision tools could provide a neutral and technological instrumentality to quintessentially value based decisions. As argued in the previous chapter, the core meaning of the term social technology was how to apply forms of rationality to mass decision making, in which one could not be sure that the outcomes of the decision process were desirable. Chapter 4 traced these ideas to European technocratic circles of the interwar period. It needs to be argued that Bell, through his application of de Jouvenel's notion of conjecture, translated these ideas into a theory of the possibilities of control of post-industrial society. It was also these arguments on the need to find forms of control on growing public action (present already in 1964—in other words before the great backlash against the community action program)—that led not only Bell but also other scholars in the Commission onto budding neoconservative ground, where they gave a new lease of life to what can only be described as a profound concern with technocracy. The scholarship on Bell is divided in its understanding of Bell's transition from progressivism into neoconservatism, and on how to qualify his great interest in systems theories ("machine systems, economic systems, social systems, and perhaps eventually, political systems").[68] The main scholar on Bell, Howard Brick, proposes that Bell was misrepresented as a technocrat by C. Wright Mills and the late 1960s student movement, and that the critique failed to recognize that Bell believed that all decisions in contemporary society were profoundly value based and were moral decisions.[69] This is certainly what Bell himself thought.[70] Meanwhile, the essay "Twelve Modes of Prediction" spoke unashamedly of forecasting as a new intellectual technology with which to control the system, and of "the new role of military technology as constitutive of political

[67] Bell, *The Coming of Post Industrial Society*, 301.

[68] Bell 1965, cited by Brick, *The Age of Contradiction*, 132.

[69] Brick, *The Age of Contradiction*, 124–6, 132; Brick, *Daniel Bell and the Decline of Radicalism*, 12, 72, 82, 94, 105.

[70] Foreword to second edition of *The End of Ideology*; notes on C. Wright Mills in Bell's papers, box 19, folders 37, 45. Bell correspondence with Howard Brick in Daniel Bell papers, box 19, folder 27.

decisions."[71] If we consider, furthermore, Bell's infatuation with Delphi, then it becomes clear that it was precisely in the idea that forms of expert judgment could be applied to the problem of values so that moral decisions could be arbitrated on the basis of an external principle of rationality that was the very meaning of "social technology" and that also underpinned the concept of a rational social choice. As seen in Chapter 5, the purpose of Delphi was not only to bring expertise to bear on value judgments, it was to create a quasi scientific and formalized process through which, by creating systematic comparisons between decisions and their expected outcomes, core future matters were relayed to expertise. This was an understanding that went much further than identifying social science as an input to the process of problem solving—it put the task of judging and formulating societal objectives in the hands of experts. It has to be argued that this line of reasoning both translated an inherently pessimistic element of the end of ideology thesis since the mid 1950s, and that it was also based on a figure of thinking by which the desired choices of the mass were the carriers of latent and dangerous forms of collision and future crash. Social choices could not in themselves be expected to reflect a rational order of decision or a logic of preferences that guaranteed a good future.

PEOPLE WHO CAN READ TRENDS

According to Bell's line of reasoning, the particular relevance of future research therefore was that it could be used in order to establish images, scenarios, and expert statements of possible outcomes, and consequences, so that these could be systematically compared and integrated at the point of decision, hence making the decision rational. "The shaping of conscious policy requires the men with the skills necessary to outline the constraints ahead, to work out in detail the management and policy procedures, and to assess the consequences of choices."[72] The trouble with American politics, then, was that despite successful experimentation at RAND, the American political system contained no mechanism for the arbitration of inherently moral decisions with a crucial bearing on the nation's future and that the liberal political system had to this extent fallen behind developments in both socialist and corporate planning.

One of the first arguments for the CY2000 came in an article for *The Public Interest* entitled "Government by Commission." The essay proposed, in a line of reasoning directly influenced by de Jouvenel's critique of Gaullism, that in the wake of the big federal programs, there was the risk of an unprecedented concentration of power in the American presidency, and of the multiplication of public decisions and far reaching programs without any clear view of their "linked up" effects over time. No government, Bell argued, could allow itself to be passive "in the face of rapid changes which erode older social forms." But American government contained no agency responsible for considering such changes in the warranted

[71] "Twelve modes of prediction," 867.

[72] Bell, *The Coming of Post Industrial Society*, 311.

20 to 30 year perspective, or for considering the "linked effects of different aspects of government policy." "Perhaps most importantly, at a time in which we must begin consciously to choose among alternative futures to establish priorities of what must be done—for it is only an illusion that we are affluent enough to take care of all our problems at once—we have no forum which seeks to articulate national goals and to clarify the implications and consequences of different choices. The Congress is not such a forum."[73]

That American politics was in need of a new decisionist agency was a feeling shared within the Commission by a range of intellectuals also connected to *The Public Interest*. *The Public Interest* was created in 1965 with the purpose of discussing progressive reform, and in particular, the automation question.[74] In 1964, President Johnson appointed the Automation Commission, a major national inquiry that had the double purpose of discussing the uses of intellectual technologies in government and administration, and examining the effects of automation on employment and poverty in American social life. There were hopes on behalf of liberal intellectuals that the Automation Commission, which made use of forecasting methods, would function as a consensus panel and come up with a shared sense of priority between trade unions and business around the relevant goals for science and technology. Instead, the Automation Commission became the site for a major controversy between American labor and industry. Howard Brick proposes that the concept, post-industrialism, in the writings of David Riesman and the early notes of Daniel Bell, was "unabashedly progressive in spirit, imaging a future based on modern cosmopolitan ethics and achievements of advanced technology." Post-industrialism was, he suggests, a joint intellectual project of liberals and the New Left, until these were estranged in the late 1960s, and post-industrialism became, for the latter, associated with alienation. For the trade unions, automation was a process of technological rationalization that threated the working class with the specter of unemployment. For liberal observers, automation sparked other fears such as the titillating question of what an idle mass might turn its attention to when work was no longer the core value of national community.[75] Importantly, the automation debate disenchanted conservative leaning liberals and former social democrats who understood themselves, in the mid 1960s, as "meliorists" and moderate progressives. Irving Kristol, the coeditor, with Bell, of *The Public Interest*, later described the experience of the automation debate as central to the move towards neoconservatism. The "automation scare," inflated by "left wing sociological ideas" led to the founding of the journal as a site for the restoration of rational progressivism and a belief in individual opportunity that constituted "public interest."[76]

[73] Daniel Bell, "Government by Commission," *The Public Interest*, 1966, 5: 3–10, 5, 9.

[74] Brick, *The Age of Contradiction*, 4, 100.

[75] Howard Brick, "Optimism of the Mind," 349; Brick, *The Age of Contradiction*, vii, 3–14.

[76] Irving Kristol, "American Conservatism 1945–1995," in *The Public Interest*, fall 1995, 121, 80–85; Brick, *The Age of Contradiction*, 34, 98: Alan Brinkley, "The Problem of American Conservatism," *The American Historical Review*, 1994, 99 (2): 409–29, 422; Maurice Isserman and Michael Kazin, *America Divided* (New York: Simon and Schuster, 2000), 50, 117–21; Vaisse, *Neoconservatism*, 3, 8, 31, 37; Angus Burgin, *The Great Persuasion. Reinventing Free Markets Since the Depression*, (Cambridge MA: Harvard University Press, 2011), 123.

To Bell, who was a member of the Automation Commission, it was an example of a failure of exactly the kind of anticipatory intelligence that to his mind, a post-industrial society was in need of. The Automation Commission had contained reflections, such as governmental responsibility for unemployment and negative income tax, which would give an entirely new role to the federal state and thereby change the foundations of the American polity by setting in place a new set of public expectations on the future. There was the risk, he argued, of commissions becoming a governmental organ for manipulating public opinion, instead of debating rational choices.[77] It was also the experience of the Automation Commission that led Bell to conclude that all decisions in post-industrial society were inherently moral decisions. In 1963, forecasting had been mandated in the federal administration by Kennedy, as part of a parcel of new planning tools and technologies including program budgeting and new forms of policy analysis for the growing federal administration.[78] The experience of the Commission on Automation was that program budgeting and other management tools were not enough. There was still the question of prioritizing between different program areas and dealing with essentially value based and moral choices. These, to Bell, could only be handled through a sense of future consequence.

This critique extended to the Great Society programs as a whole. In fact, it was the lack of foresight, Bell argued, that had created the need for the Great Society programs in the first place. Using Moynihan's study of the disintegration of the black family as the specific example of a problem that demanded new forms of anticipation, Bell argued that the occurrence of unoccupied male blacks in urban areas had been eminently foreseeable since the end of sharecropping in the 1930s.[79] The problems in focus of the Kennedy and Johnson administrations had therefore really been unrealized problems of the future for some time, and political structures urgently needed a rational sense of forecast in order to stop emerging problems from developing into yet unforeseen ones.[80] Among such presently unforeseen problems were now those that might result from unprecedented government action, from the "linking up" of effects of social policy programs in different areas and from the creation of a new set of expectations on the American state.

This reflection is inseparable from the debate conducted, in 1964 and 1965, in the pages of *The Public Interest* by not only Bell but also Daniel Moynihan and Irving Kristol, and which became increasingly critical of the Great Society programs as driven by communitarian claims and not by rational investigation. The Commission for the Year 2000 was appointed in 1964, the same year that Johnson held his Great Society speech and launched the War on Poverty. The announced intention behind the programs was to transform the fate of a "generation,"

[77] Daniel Bell, "Government by Commission," 5.

[78] Jardini, *Out of Blue Yonder*; Light, *From Warfare to Welfare*; Otis Graham, *Toward a Planned Society. From Roosevelt to Nixon* (Palo Alto: Stanford University Press, 1976).

[79] Daniel Moynihan, *The Negro Family, the Case for National Action* (Washington: US Department of Labor, 1965).

[80] Bell, "The Trajectory of an Idea," 10.

in other words to have a lasting effect on American society. President Johnson's 1964 speech at Howard University, drawing to a large extent on the as yet unpublished Moynihan report, spoke of the need for an extensive and "long-term" commitment to improving conditions in the ghetto.[81] For Bell, and many of the members of the Commission for the Year 2000, this kind of new "long range" policy ambitions in the heartland of the American state ran the danger of exercising a new kind of power over the future, by laying the basis for decisions that could produce a "distortion of expectation," or even, an erosion of the American "character structure."[82]

In this context, futures research thus provided an answer to a problem of an escalating cycle of government and citizenship claims, by turning problems of future priority into a matter of experts in public policy. The answer to irrational social decisions was, as suggested by Daniel Moynihan in the pages of *The Public Interest*, the professionalization of public policy, putting decisions in the hands of an enlightened administration where it could be performed in consensus and not in conflict. Professionalization to Moynihan, was predictability, by mobilizing the great industry of discovery in the social sciences, and by employing people in federal government who could "read trends."[83] In the first proceedings of the Commission, several other intellectuals (Brzezinski, Bell, Perloff, and Rostow), similarly argued that the growing role of specialized interests and group claims demanded a new kind of governmental structure, in which expertise on policy problems had an entirely new role.[84] This changed a line of argument around the so called missile gap after the Soviet launch of Sputnik in 1957, which had insisted that American society needed to develop forecasting capacities in science and technology to compete with the Soviets. The forecasting institution proposed by Brzezinski, Rostow, and Bell now resembled de Jouvenel's Look Out institution, the surmising forum of political science expertise on desirable futures. In the words of Zbigniew Brzezinski: "a new system of representation, overseen by a weighing of interests performed by a computing agency and situated outside of the legislative process."[85] Behind Brzezinski's proposition lurked the phantom notion of a coming "service state," which might create structures that would constrain future action, and in which forms of individual choice had disappeared. Bell himself seems to have thought that such forms of policy expertise needed to be balanced by new forms of influence on public opinion for instance through scenarios, in a Deweyan process by which public preferences were changed in the active light of desirable consequence.

[81] Carol Horton, *Race and the Making of American Liberalism* (Oxford: Oxford University Press, 2008), 172–4.

[82] Kristol, "American Conservatism 1945–1995," 81.

[83] Daniel Moynihan, "The Professionalization of Reform," in *The Public Interest* 1965, 1: 6–14.

[84] Brzezinski in *Work in Progress* 35; Perloff in *Work in Progress* 36. On missile failure at Cape Kennedy, *Work in Progress*, 42.

[85] Rostow, in *Work in Progress*, 46; Brzezinski in *Work in Progress*, 53.

FUTURE CRASH

As the CY2000 published its *Work in Progress* report in 1967, Stokely Carmichael aligned black power with the Cuban revolution and the Black Panther movement put the final nail in the coffin of modernization theory. In 1968, the Vietnam protests broke out and the Cold War intellectuals that Bell had had such high hopes for became the target of a cultural backlash. As the art of prediction thus entered into a profound crisis of public legitimacy, the purpose of future research changed meaning. Work within the CY2000 went from its initial reflection on the preconditions for forging a sense of national priority, to the understanding that no such clear sense of national unity and common future could be found, and understanding the future was therefore first and foremost a way of speculating on various forms of unfolding crisis. Among the problems defining the American future from 1964 were worries and disturbances that the Commission at this point regarded as side effects and pathological reactions to change and described with the terms of post-war psychology as forms of sociogenic pathology. This included, for example, problems in youth behavior, discussed in the Commission by Frank and Erikson, or the rise of the Beatniks. Another central question was the future of race relations. The seminar in the Carnegie Corporation on the future of the American Negro had asked whether the African American population, involved in a massive process of urbanization, would, like previous waves of immigrants to the American cities, integrate, or whether black urbanization would concentrate and turn the American cities into ghettoes.[86] Senator Moynihan was a member of the Commission and a preliminary version of the Moynihan Report, detailing the erosion of black family kinships under the rise of a new matriarchy, was discussed at length in the Commission.[87] "A country in which one in ten are Negro is different from one in which the ratio is one to ten, and in which most Negroes live in the rural South."[88] Moynihan's observations would be taken further in one of the scenarios produced by Kahn and Wiener in their 1967 book *Towards The Year 2000.*

Towards the Year 2000 was one of the major outcomes of the Commission with its famous projection of a "standard" world with a number of possible deviations. In it, Herman Kahn posited Arrow's impossibility theorem as a fundamental problem for living together in a post-civil-rights era in which a range of communitarian claims seemed to be exploding prevailing understandings of the social contract. How could liberal futures be ensured in a society in which individual utility maximizers (personified in Kahn's vulgarization as Bill, Tom, and Hank) had to decide together, but where one could no longer be sure of who Bill, Tom, and Hank were? The book included a scenario on black power and the future of black Muslim men. Would the American Negro adapt to affluence and consumerism, along with the

[86] Carnegie Corporation, "Future of the American Negro," Daniel Bell papers, box 3, folder 28; and see IACF seminar in 1967, Bell papers box 14 folder 15.

[87] Moynihan, *The Negro Family; Work in Progress*, 213; Horton, *Race and the Making of American Liberalism*, 134, 141.

[88] Moynihan in *Work in Progress*, 56.

already commenced pattern of black urbanization and middle classification, or turn into a violent guerilla fighter?[89]

By 1967 and 1968, the problem of black power men seemed to apply also to a wider set of value clashes in the American public. The disassociation of youth from the structures of the affluent society and the growth of juvenile delinquency had been a much discussed problem in behavioralism and social psychology since the 1940s and 1950s, discussions that were well represented in the Commission through Frank, Kai Erikson, and Margaret Mead. While there were already critiques of the pathologization of youth and delinquency in these decades, by the late 1960s the notion of alienation and of a young generation in revolt against the affluent society became directly associated with the New Left. Theodore Roszak published *The Making of a Counterculture* in 1969, confirming feelings of a growing societal divide between the majority population and the young. Roszak's book did, for the question of youth, what Michael Harrington had done for the question of poverty in 1964, indeed it contributed to reshaping the debate on the social problems of American society from one which focused on residual issues or "pathologies," to one which focused on new *trends* rupturing fundamental forms of social continuity.[90] In the same year that Roszak published *The Making of a Counterculture*, Margaret Mead held a series of lectures, based on observations that could be traced back to her first anthropological studies of teenage culture in *Coming of Age in Samoa*, where she described human society as entering into a stage of crisis and instability due to the fundamental transformation in outlooks on the future between the old and the young generation. The stable transfer of future anticipations in traditional "forebearing" societies had been lost in societies were the young had no authority to rely on and no way of committing to the future image produced by modernity. Such a gulf between generations was a fundamental source of cultural crisis, shifting the future from a "continuation of the past" into a "radically different continent" and pushing the young towards potentially violent outbursts. The young were thus no longer recognizable children of the past generation, but fundamentally alien inhabitants of an unknown continent ahead.[91] Mead presided, in 1971, at the American Anthropological Association's Symposium on Cultural Futurology, in which she began arguing for a new anthropology of coming generations.[92] That was a major turnaround from Mead's background in wartime research and her commitment, in the 1950s and 1960s, to the idea that cultural and anthropological studies should be of use for consolidating liberal societies also in peacetime, which was what had led her into the CY2000.[93]

[89] Kahn and Wiener, *The Year 2000. A Framework for Speculation*, 206.

[90] Theodore Roszak, *The Making of a Counterculture* (New York: Basic Books, 1969); Michael Harrington, *The Other America* (New York, 1964). See Daniel Horowitz, *The Anxieties of Affluence* (Boston, 2004), 143–50.

[91] Margaret Mead, "The Life Cycle and its Variations. The Division of Roles," in *Work in Progress*, 239–44; Margaret Mead, *Culture and Commitment. A Study of the Generation Gap* (London: Bodley Head, 1970), xii, 66, 83.

[92] The symposium was devoted to a highly New Left debate on the rise of utopian future images in the black and red power movements.

[93] Peter Mandler, *Return from the Natives. How Margaret Mead Won the Second World War and Lost the Cold War* (New Haven: Yale University Press, 2013), 177–84.

The events of 1968 were a final blow to the idea of using social science to forge a common sense of the future. As the Commission published its final report in 1974, the turmoil in American society was formulated by Bell in terms of a number of burning future questions. Just as in the New Deal era, "the institutions we set up now will live for the next thirty years," and required therefore, a fundamental reflection on long range social questions. Among these were now not only the extension of federal and presidential power and new forms of "non market forms of decision making," but also the rise of plebiscitary and violent politics driven by group marches to Washington.[94] The report of Lawrence Frank's working group, appointed by Bell in order to find a "theory of human value change," began "no one can deny the antics and a deliberately planned posturing, the esoteric language and dress, the erratic and often bizarre behaviour, the use of drugs, and the many criminal acts and vandalism exhibited by so many of the 'New Generation'."[95]

CONCLUDING REMARKS

By the time it was dismantled, in 1974, the Commission had become the stage for a clash of different views on the future as inherited from the last three decades of American social science. Leading members ventured onto emergent neoconservative ground, while others broke their previous engagements with the behavioralism of the 1950s and 1960s. At the same time, Bell had tried to integrate voices of the New Left in the Commission, in particular through the psychologist Leonard Duhl. The records from a seminar in 1970, at which Talcott Parsons was present as the new president of AAAS, reveal open conflict: (Duhl) "Parsons occasionally offered an idea or two." "No point in calling him (Frank) names... The spirit of the fifties is being expressed by Bell. In psychoanalytical perspective we witnessed a rigid superego projecting on someone else repressed qualities."[96] In 1976, as Bell published his personal conclusions from the CY2000 in the paper "The Next Twenty Five Years," he lamented the rejection of social science in mass populations and the erosion of rationality within the social sciences themselves (a theme that Bell also turned into a pet project of the International Association for Cultural Freedom).[97]

While the Commission for the Year 2000 was in many ways a spectacular failure, overtaken by unpredicted developments that far extended its collective imagination, the Commission's work was hailed in planning circles in Japan, Europe, and more surprisingly, Moscow, as an ambitious attempt to use forecasting for the overarching questions of the social objectives of society. The activities in the Commission attracted the attention both of Japanese forecasters, and of the group in the Soviet Academy of Sciences responsible for cybernetics and future planning. The latter

[94] *Report of the Commission for the Year 2000,* (Cambridge MA: AAAS, 1974) 37–42, 41.
[95] Lawrence K. Frank, draft, 1967, "The Life Cycle of an Individual," CY2000 papers, box 5.
[96] "Summary of proceedings, Individual and the Life Cycle," CY2000 records, box 5.
[97] Daniel Bell, "The Next Twenty Five Years," 1976, draft, Daniel Bell papers, box 15, folder 14.

resulted in the translation into Russian, for closed circles, of Bell's *The Coming of the Post Industrial Society*, and in Talcott Parson's trip to Moscow in 1974.[98] In 1976, the Japanese Toyota Foundation brought Bell, as a consultant in futures research, to the OECD's Interfutures program, which used futures research to model the future of world markets and in particular emerging relationships between the industrial and the developing world.[99] A few years after the final report, ideas introduced within the CY2000 debates also found their way into the debates of the Trilateral Commission, which also regrouped intellectuals from the *Futuribles* venture, solicited by Bell for the CY2000: Michel Crozier, Samuel Huntington, Zbigniew Brzezinski. To the Trilateral Commission, the extension of public action had rendered democracy ungovernable through social overload. What mattered was thus protecting decision making processes from the perverse effects of democracy.[100]

[98] Correspondence files, CY2000 records, box 7.

[99] Andersson, "Shaping the future".

[100] Zbiegnew Brzezinski, Samuel Huntington, Michel Crozier, and Jojo Watanuki, *The Crisis of Democracy. Report on the Ungovernability of Democracy to the Trilateral Commission* (New York: New York University Press, 1973).

7

Bridging the Iron Curtain. Futurology as Dissidence and Control

Futurology: "Systematic and critical analysis of future issues"

from the West German *Brockhaus Encyclopadie*, vol. 6, 1968.

Futurology: "Term which denotes the attempts of bourgeois scientists and planners in imperialist states to prognosticate future developments in capitalism"

from the East German *Kleines Politisches Worterbuch*, 1967.[1]

DREAMS OF AN OPEN FUTURE

Daniel Bell's 1973 book, *The Coming of Post Industrial Society*, was profoundly inspired by Bell's twenty and more years of observations of Marxist thought in the East bloc, and by his enduring interest in the future of the Soviet system. Bell's first reflections on the future stemmed from his critique of theories of Soviet behavior. His 1958 essay on the fallacies of predicting the evolution of the Soviet regime introduced some of the elements of the convergence theory that would be developed in Bell's, *The Coming of Post Industrial Society*.[2] The previous chapter discussed *The Coming of Post Industrial Society* in the context of liberal debates, in which it stands as an attempt to solve the classical problem of liberalism—the joining together of individual and collective preferences—by developing forms of prediction. Future research, to Bell, was a liberal equivalent of long-term planning and a potential solution to the problem of social choice. But *The Coming of Post Industrial Society* was also a central observation on the development of key "trends" of convergence between capitalist and Soviet society. As the previous chapter explained, post-industrialism, in Bell's interpretation, was a new stage of industrial society, in which stable class relations of factory production were giving way, and in which an emerging educated managerial class was increasingly replacing the industrial working class also in the communist system. This class was increasingly involved in the governance of political and social affairs and in executing what Bell saw as a shift

[1] Ossip K. Flechtheim, *Futurologie. Der Kampf um die Zukunft* (Köln, 1968), 8.

[2] Daniel Bell, "Ten Theories in Search of Reality: The Prediction of Soviet Behavior in the Social Sciences", in *World Politics*, 1958, 10(3): 327–65.

David Engerman, *Know Your Enemy. The Rise and Fall of America's Soviet Experts* (Oxford: Oxford University Press, 2009), 186.

from planning to forecasting in an increasingly futuristic governmental mode. In Bell's post-industrial society, the future was driven by the spread of human creativity, value revolutions, and education. These drivers were common to the "advanced industrial" nations, a category that now included the communist world.[3]

Convergence theory was a child of modernization theory in its description of regular patterns of development, trends common to the blocs, and maybe to the industrialized world as a whole. First and foremost of these trends was value change, correlated with the end of work as a consequence of automation. The idea of an end to work inspired both hopes and fears under liberal as well as communist regimes. Bell, the frequent borrower, not only leant on the work of the French Marxist sociologist Alain Touraine, but also on his contacts with the group of Czechoslovak social scientists in the Prague Academy of Sciences under the leadership of the philosopher Radovan Richta.[4] The publication in English of *Civilisation at the Crossroads* in 1969 (published in Czech in 1966 as *Civilizace na rozcesti* and spread in papers in Czech, English, German, and French in 1967 and 1968) led to hopes that spring had come to the communist world. These hopes were crushed as the tanks rolled in on the streets of Prague in August 1968. The Richta group, which set the future at the heart of its discussions of the Scientific and Technological Revolution (STR), became the center of transnational debates on forecasting and future research from 1966 and 1967 on as the symbol for another future for the East bloc or "Socialism with a human face."

The members of the Richta team were sociologists, philosophers, psychologists, urbanists, economists, and management theorists. The problems of STR, post-industrialism and convergence created a space for new forms of circulation between East and West. The precondition of this activity was the rehabilitation of forms of future research in the socialist countries. In 1966, 1967, and 1968, All Union Meetings of socialist forecasters were held in Kiev, Moscow, and Marienlyst, and during these years socialist forecasters could also participate in Western networks. These networks were held together by the idea of forecasting as a social technology for advanced industrialism, and although the precise meaning of this term could vary, its dominant message of using forms of future research as an intervention into social and economic decision making was shared on both sides of the Iron Curtain. Exchanging knowledge of methods and technologies of future research was thus possible. Between 1967 and 1972 the transnational activity in this field was enormous, with seminars and conferences, a flood of publications in the *International Social Science Journal*, the new journals *Futures* and *Technological Forecasting and Social Change*, and several edited volumes of translations on both sides of the Iron Curtain. From 1967 journals appeared in the East bloc with titles and content similar to Western ones, for instance the Czechoslovak journal *Trend*, the East German *Analyse und Prognose* (compare the French *Analyse et prévision*),

[3] Bell, *The Coming of Post Industrial Society. A Venture in Social Forecasting* (Cambridge MA: MIT Press, second edition, 1976); Howard Brick, "Optimism of the Mind. Imagining Post Industrial Society in the 1960s and the 1970s," in *American Quarterly*, 1992, 44 (3): 349–80.

[4] Radovan Richta et al., *Civilizace na Rozcesti* (Prague: Svoboda, 1966).

and articles on forecasting and future research were also published in the Russian journal *Vyprys Filosofie* (Problems of Philosophy).[5]

Egle Rindzeviciute has shown that the focus on "common" or "global" problems created a platform for the creation of what she describes as a new technocrat elite that straddled the Iron Curtain. The focus of this elite was the complex problems of governance and steering a world marked by problems that defied the nation space due to their fundamental nature of interdependence and complexity.[6] Before 1966, when talks began between Soviets and Americans, the idea that the different systems encountered similar problems was ideologically impossible. But as Rindzeviciute shows, the promise of the so called policy sciences, meaning the range of approaches that allowed for an expertification or scientification of the problems of political organization, including forecasting and system analysis, was that they could address issues of the rationality of the political system outside of the ideological arena. Neutral policy expertise made forms of collaboration between the two systems possible, emphasizing their practical similarities while not shaking doctrinary notions of ideological distinction. The purpose of this elite, Rindzeviciute proposes, was to create norms of mutual concern that could increase predictability in international affairs. Prediction served as a site of exchange of data and methods in areas ranging from nuclear arms control to the modelling of climate and energy supply. Soviets and Americans collaborated on the creation of the International Institute for Applied Systems Analysis, IIASA, eventually set up in 1972.[7] IIASA was in fact the culmination of five years of cross curtain exchanges around the fields of forecasting and future research. Governmental exchanges were paralleled by circulation and mobilization between the social movements that the Cold War also gave rise to.[8] The first World Future Research conference was held in Oslo in 1967 with the participation of Soviet forecasters and with the Richta group in a preeminent position.[9] The idea of the conference, initiated by the global peace movement, was to use future research to strike a metaphorical bridge across the Iron Curtain (see next chapter). This idea of a bridge guided both the creation of IIASA and many other transnational initiatives.[10] In 1968, Ossip Flechtheim, back in West Germany at a Rockefeller funded chair in the Freie Universität, published

[5] Joakim Radkau, *Geschichte der Zukunft. Prognosen, Visionen, Irrungen in Deutschland von 1945 bis Heute* (Munchen: Carl Hansen Verlag, 2017).

[6] Egle Rindzeviciute, *The Power of Systems. How Policy Sciences Opened up the Cold War World* (Ithaca: Cornell University Press, 2016), 2–3.

[7] Egle Rindzeviciute, "Purification and Hybridisation of Soviet Cybernetics: The Politics of Scientific Governance in an Authoritarian Regime," in *Archiv für Sozialgeschichte*, 2010, 50: 289–309.

[8] Matthew Evangelista, *Unarmed Forces. The Transnational Movement to end the Cold War* (Ithaca: Cornell University Press, 1999).

[9] Johan Galtung and Robert Jungk, eds., *Mankind 2000* (Oslo, 1969). The Mankind 2000 volume was the international introduction of the works of the Richta group, see Radovan Richta and Ota Šulc, "The Perspective of the Scientific and Technological Revolution," 199–244; also, Radovan Richta, "Die wissenschaftlich technischen Revolution und die Alternativen der modernen Zivilisation," in *Futurum*, 1968, 1: 205–28.

[10] Leena Riska-Campbell, *Bridging East and West: The Establishment of the International Institute for Applied Systems Analysis (IIASA) in the United States Foreign Policy of Bridge Building, 1964–1972* (Helsinki: Helsinki University Press, 2011), 108–9.

the book *Futurologie*, which proposed that futurology was a "Third way" between the blocs. A critical social science outlook on the future could free up a radical or utopian space between liberalism and Marxism and break up the system logic of the Cold War.[11] In the same year, Flechtheim created the journal *Futurum* in order to publish the Richta group as well as East German prognosticians of the so called *Wirtschaftsprognosen*, the writings of the Polish *Polska 2000* group of sociologists, and the Yugoslavian *Praxis* group, created around the journal with the same name.[12] In 1970, Soviet and Western forecasters met at the Seventh World Congress of Sociology in Varna around the common notion of future research as social technology for the solution of all pressing world problems: peace, hunger, human needs. The result was the creation of an official East West Committee for Future Research.[13]

Rindzeviciute proposes that the transnational activity around the policy sciences introduced an element of openness into the socialist, and more specifically, Soviet world. The ideas carried by the systems approach, which emphasized the uncertainty of social developments, contributed to the incorporation of political technologies that in her view led to the eventual opening up of the Soviet system through the integration of a new autonomous expert culture.[14] While I think that this is an important argument, I also think that it downplays the very complex process of East–West translation around the difficult category of the future. Rindzeviciute highlights the apparent paradox in that both Western and Soviet regimes turned at the same time to the new tools of policy science, Operations Research, cybernetics, and systems analysis. This can be explained with reference to the important transnational circulation around these tools and by the governmental interest in forms of prediction as social technology on both sides of the Iron Curtain. But the rules dictating this process of circulation were not the same in the socialist countries as in the West. Forecasting, future research and futures studies carried a similar debate on the problem of steering the direction of social change. It also re-enacted the crucial debate on the future as a category of science vs. imagination in a debate that mirrored key assumptions of the relative closed or open nature of social time in both systems. But while the regime interest in control between East and West might

[11] Ossip Flechtheim, *Futurologie* (Frankfurt: Surkamp Verlag, 1969), 275, 286, 299, 306; Ossip Flechtheim, "Futurologie als Brucke," Radio Free Europe, 1969, Ossip Flechtheim papers.

[12] *Futurum. Zeitschrift fur Wukunftsforschung, herausgegeben von Ossip K. Flechtheim*, Berlin, nr 1 and 2, 1968, and Flechtheim, document "Futurists of the East bloc", August 15, 1972, which describes the Richta group as having come closest to embodying a global vision of human social democracy, a space "between Marx and Masaryk"; Flechtheim, "Warum futurologie?", in *Futurum,* 1968, 1: 3–23. The Praxis group marked, more than anything, the face of revisionist Marxism, but is given little space in this chapter due to the fact that only the philosopher Mihail Markovic would become a member of the World Futures Studies Federation and this in the 1990s in a very different context of Serbian nationalism.

[13] International Sociological Association, Transactions of the 7th world congress in sociology, Varna, September 8–14, 1970, "Contemporary and Future Societies: Prediction and Social Planning," and ISA Bulletin, "Research Committee nr 7, Future Research." Archives of the Research Committee 7, possession of Markus Schulz, NYU.

[14] Egle Rindzeviciute, "A Struggle for the Soviet Future: The Birth of Scientific Forecasting in the Soviet Union," *Slavic Review*, 2016, 75 (1): 52–76.

have been similar, the limits for the future debate were hugely different under liberal and authoritarian regimes.[15] The next chapter discusses the Western creation of futures studies, which defined the future as a crucial space of resistance against forms of Cold War prediction by making a radical call to the human imagination. The present chapter demonstrates that the debate on the future as a site for the utopian imagination began in fact in the East bloc in the mid 1950s—and closed with a whimper in 1968. In their return to an idea of the future as a human creation concerned with values, needs, and image, revisionist socialist forecasters had a direct influence on Western futures studies. In international contexts, their understanding of the future could be anchored in a long historical humanistic heritage, but in their own contexts, socialist future research existed in a space squarely defined by Marxism Leninism and its prescription of the future as a singular and law-driven entity. Future research, in the East bloc, was shaped on a plane between the two poles of tight regime control and dissent. On this plane, a multitude of positionings were possible, as illustrated in this chapter by the personal trajectories of some of those socialist forecasters who were most active in international networks.[16]

The turn to revisionist Marxism and reform communism (these should not be conflated as they included very different positions vis a vis the possibility of reform of the socialist system) began with the thaw after Stalin's death in 1953. The Khrushchev era saw the rehabilitation of certain forms of social science, in particular sociology, some economics, and strands of political science.[17] The period from the mid 1950s therefore marks the period of socialist future research, as a combination of revisionist postulates—ranging from tacit critiques to open dissidence—and as a set of new empirical questions and categories of observation with direct links to the future as a question of problem solving, decision making, and planning in the socialist economies. After 1968, much of this open ended future debate was dead, and futures research was reined in by the USSR into an ideologically sanctioned form of forecasting as essentially economic and technological long-term planning, *prognostik* or *prognostica*.[18] But in the 1953 to 1968 period, future research in the socialist bloc was a world of rich arguments about the importance of the future to human existence. This chapter deals therefore with this era of socialist futures research, through the prism of the role played by East European socialists in transnational networks in which they were central in bringing out their revisionist notion of the future as a human category and manmade vision of social change, a vision that in the end they could oftentimes not pursue.

[15] Mitchell Dean, "Liberal Government and Authoritarianism," in *Economy and Society*, 2002, 31 (1): 37–61.

[16] See James H. Satterwhite, *Varieties of Marxist Humanism. Philosophical Revision in Post War Eastern Europe* (Pittsburg: University of Pittsburg, 1992).

[17] Martine Mespoulet, "La renaissance de la sociologie en URSS (1958–1972). Une voie étroite entre materialism historique et 'recherches sociologiques concrètes'," *Révue d'histoire des sciences humaines*, 62–5, 70–5; Martine Mespoulet, "Quelle sociologie derriere le Rideau de fer?" Cairn 3-1-10; Vladimir Shlapentokh, *The Politics of Sociology in the Soviet Union* (Westview Press, 1987).

[18] Viteszlav Sommer, "Forecasting the Post Socialist Future. From Futurology to Prognostika", in *The Struggle for the Long Term in Transnational Science and Politics. Forging the Future*, edited by Jenny Andersson and Egle Rindzeviciute (London: Routledge, 2015), 144–69.

A NEW FUTURE HORIZON: THE POLSKA 2000 GROUP

The concept of Marxist humanism or Marxism with a human face was coined in an English language edited volume with the title *Human Socialism*, published in 1967 by the German philosopher Erich Fromm.[19] The volume revisited Marx' early manuscripts, the *Economic and Philosophical Manuscripts of 1844*, which had just appeared in new translation in English and Russian. The rereading of the early manuscripts allowed Marxist, Christian, and liberal socialist intellectuals to return to an original Marx, and inscribe Marxism in an Enlightenment legacy of humanist philosophy. The centrality in Marx's thinking of Man and the "full unfolding of all his potentialities" was now placed at the centre of revisionist debates.[20] The Human Socialism symposium brought together interventions from Fromm, Marcuse, Leopold Senghor, Adam Schaff, Ernst Bloch, and Bertrand Russell. Among the less well-known authors were several intellectuals active in futurist networks from 1967 on, including the leading philosopher of the Yugoslav Praxis group, Mihailo Markovic, and the Polish futurologist Bogdan Suchodolski.[21]

"Open" or humanistic Marxism was a large strand of ideas that dominated sociology and philosophy and that took place in the space between what recent East European historiography defines as revisionist Marxism, including open dissidence and outspoken critique of the communist system, and reform communism. While revisionist Marxists rejected Marxism Leninism while holding on to a core of Marxist thought, which led many of them into dissidence, reform communism was a reflection on late socialism or advanced socialism and the need to improve the functioning of socialist society in particular by new management methods.[22] From 1968 on, reform communism and revisionism would part ways, but they shared until then a concern with the future as a central horizon of human activity. At the heart of the attempt to create a Marxism with a human face stood a shift in emphasis from the socialist project to the notion of Man's condition and existence within socialism.[23] The central philosophers of human Marxism, icons of the Western New Left by 1968—Leszek Kolakowski, Georg Lukasz, and Erich Fromm—all began within the Marxist tradition, although their trajectories would then diverge.[24] Their core problem was not to do away with Marxism, but to revisit the problem of emancipation in the context of regimes exerting unprecedented forms of domination. The central question for these authors was whether the project

[19] The latter term is often attributed to Radovan Richta, but there was a variety of arguments around human Marxism, Open Marxism, or human socialism. See Erich Fromm, ed., *Socialist Humanism, an International Symposium* (London: Penguin Press, 1967).

[20] Fromm, "Introduction," in *Socialist Humanism,* edited by Erich Fromm, 9–19.

[21] Ibid. Bogdan Suchodolski, "Science, Technology and the Future," paper for the UN conference on technology and the future, 1979.

[22] See Viteszlav Sommer, "Are We Still Revolutionaries?," in *Studies in East European Thought*, published online March 2017.

[23] Jan Mervart, "Czechoslovak Marxist Humanism and the Revolution," *Studies in East European Thought*, 2017, 69 (1): 111-26; Satterwhite, *Varieties of Marxist Humanism.*

[24] Tony Judt, *Reappraisals.* Fromm remained both a Marxist and a communist, while Kolakowski left Marxism after 1968 as he went into his British exile.

of socialism had contributed to the creation of a fuller and more whole socialist person, or whether it had recreated totalitarian and oppressive structures of work and bureaucracy. The reopening of the Marxist vocabulary allowed them to reintroduce the theme of alienation, now put in the context of the loss of life control in the factories of the socialist state. There were direct parallels here between the rediscovery of the theme of alienation in Eastern and Western debates. Herbert Marcuse, the iconic thinker of the second Frankfurt school and author in 1964 of *One Dimensional Man* (which was, as the next chapter explains, a fundamental influence on Western futures studies) had escaped prosecution in Germany in 1934. He went from the Institute of Social Research at Columbia, where the Frankfurter Institute had found refuge during the war, to work for ten years for the Office of Intelligence Research in Washington before returning to Columbia as a fellow in the Russia Institute.[25] Ossip Flechtheim, who stands as a link between a liberal critique of ideology based on Karl Mannheim and the revisionist Marxist notions of Marcuse and Kolakowski, had written his Ph.D. thesis on the KPD. Like Marcuse, Flechtheim was accepted as a refugee scholar in the US because of his in depth knowledge of Soviet communism.[26] Alienation, to Marcuse, was a constant threat to emancipation. The forces of science and technology that shaped freedom in a new age of affluence and plenty were also the forces that recreated new forms of alienation in the post-industrial society.[27] The only way out of this was a new revolutionary praxis, an escape from forms of reiteration.[28] For Fromm, this mechanism of liberation was psychoanalysis, for Bloch, it was in the principle of hope and active citizenship. Praxis was a new and utopian dialectics, a constant form of social critique of the distance between the objectives of socialism and human reality.[29]

The shift operated, in human Marxism, from the *project* of socialism to the conditions of existence of the socialist *person* led into a diverse set of interrogations into the potentially open ended nature of social change. From the mid 1950s on, East European scholars turned the process of change into a problem in its own right and thus began to question the idea of a stage driven and foreseeable process. This shook the epistemological world of Marxism Leninism. Revisionist Marxist scholars re-evaluated not only the relationship between the dialectic process and its outcome, they also rethought the concept of revolution, as in Richta's emphasis on

[25] Tim B. Muller, *Krieger und Gelehrte. Herbert Marcuse und die Denkssysteme Im Kalten Krieg* (Hamburg: Hamburger Edition, 1991).

[26] Flechtheim and Marcuse were on the same ship, received by the American refugee committee on the same day in New York. Papers of the American Committee in Aid of Displaced Scholars, New York Public Library, folders Flechtheim and Marcuse. Flechtheim, "Marxismus, futurologie und Dritten Weg"; and radio talk, "Futurologie, eine Brucke zwischen Ost und West," Hessischer Rundfunk, April 15, 1967"; Flechtheim, "Marxian and Non Marxian Views on The Future," Ossip Flechtheim Nachlass.

[27] Marcuse, "Socialist Humanism," in *Socialist Humanism,* edited by Erich Fromm, 97–106.

[28] Ernst Bloch, "Man and Citizen According to Marx," in *Socialist Humanism*, edited by Erich Fromm, 200–6.

[29] Marcuse, "Socialist Humanism." It was the Praxis group that would take this position furthest, see Satterwhite, *Varieties of Marxist Humanism*, 174.

the STR as an ongoing revolutionary process taking place in the present.[30] They pinpointed the distance between Party and society through a set of critical writings on bureaucracy and the ruling elite, and they put forward a lightly painted, positive picture of an emerging new and creative socialist personality not much different in life style and values from that of consumerist workers in the West. The future re-entered Marxist thinking through their writings, as a presentist horizon linked to profoundly humanist notions of existence, being, and phenomenon. In Poland and Czechoslovakia, revisionist Marxist scholars reengaged with forgotten concepts, including even the concept of utopia, which Marx and Engels had of course famously dismissed as an unscientific, metaphysical concept. Utopia, to Flechtheim drawing on Bloch and Lukasz– was a necessary sphere for an emancipatory dialectics, as only through utopian consideration could alternative social realities become imaginable.[31] It was thus the basis for a critical epistemology.

This resituating of the future, from a linear and dogmatic vision prescribed by the equivalent to natural laws to a potentially open ended horizon of change, was the core of revisionist debates. Its implications were enormous. A future opened up from Marxism Leninism was a future open to a plurality of different social goals of developments. How to chose between such different goals, in a political context where the setting of the Goal was the undisputed Party prerogative? If Goals were displaced from Party doctrine to empirical undertaking, could they be rationally evaluated or openly discussed? Were there, indeed, similar problems in communist society to the liberal problem of choosing between or combining individual and collective values, preferences, and needs? If collective and individual needs were in conflict, how could long-term goals be settled?[32] In axiological Marxist debates, values were the "ideal" social subject. But if decisions and social goals were also taken to be value based, there could conceivably be not only a plurality of values but also a plurality of social goals and possible decisions. And if revolution was, as Richta suggested, not a matter of a future endpoint, but of ongoing, constant developments in a high technological and scientist society, then the revolution required new forms of participation and involvement of both socialist citizens and expert intellectuals in the realization of the project.[33] Importantly, if the future was not proscribed but both described and scrutinized, then it could also be an empirical category of the social sciences. This opened the door to what would turn out to be a liminal and ultimately dangerous confrontation between Party and futuristic expertise.

The premise of Open Marxism was the relative emancipation of philosophy and social science that followed the 20th Party congress in 1956. The Congress saw the

[30] Sommer, "Are We Still Revolutionaries?"

[31] Satterwhite, *Varieties of Marxist Humanism*, 57, 69–70. Kolakowski to Flechtheim, November 9, 1977, and November 23, 1977. As indicated by the correspondence with Flechtheim, Kolakowski abandoned all hopes that such utopian energy could find a space within Marxism. Flechtheim and Kolakowski had very different takes on Bloch, whom to Flechtheim was a source of inspiration while Kolakowski's verdict on Bloch (as well as on Marcuse) in *Main Currents of Marxism* was without mercy.

[32] Satterwhite, *Varieties of Marxist Humanism*, 115.

[33] Sommer, "Are We Still Revolutionaries?"

rejection of the cult of Stalin. It also contained an overture to the social sciences as it humbly declared that there could be many roads to socialism in different countries and that the process of political and economic transformation could not be fully foreseen. It also pointed out the important task in overcoming the gap between ideological work and practical communist construction.[34] In the coming years, the relative thaw introduced by Khrushchev allowed for the return of rehabilitated social science disciplines, in most places in strict empirical and concrete form. As social issues were settled by Marxist doctrine, there was little need for the social sciences before 1953, and core areas of social science thinking disappeared through the purges of the interwar period.[35] From 1956, certain parts of sociology, economics and even political science reappeared in Eastern Europe, and achieved a certain distance from ideological premises in what Satterwhite calls "an opposition to external laws and their predetermining role in favour of an emphasis on the creative role that humans play in actively shaping their new reality."[36] As sociologists returned to assume a role as experts in social matters, they proposed that sociology could make a contribution distinct from ideology, and they proposed also, that Marxist Leninist assumptions of social development were in fact open to scientific examination. Questions pertaining to the future of socialist society could thus be one step removed from the end point.

It was this analytical separation out of ideology and science that produced the revitalization of Marxist debates in the 1950s and 1960s, and which also returned the future to the forefront of sociological thinking in the East bloc, as a matter of human horizon and a problem of human existence. As an empirical category and a potential field of action, the future now became thought of as a set of concrete social problems of trends, values, life styles, and living conditions, or "quality of life," that afflicted not only capitalist but also socialist society and could therefore potentially be studied through Western methods that included social indicators, consumer research, management studies, and opinion research.[37] These developments were followed carefully from our Western lookouts: in 1960 Daniel Bell travelled as a Ford emissary to Poland, where the Gomulka regime was reluctantly watching the renaissance of Polish sociology. He met with sociologists and journalists including Adam Schaff, Julian Hochfeld, and Andrej Sicinski.[38]

Malgorzata Masurek has shown that Polish sociologists in the Warsaw Academy of Sciences were forerunners in adapting open Marxism postulates into a project of empirical investigation which included Western methods such as, in particular,

[34] Nikita Khrushchev, *Report of the Central Committee of the Communist Party of the Soviet Union of the 20th Party Congress* (Moscow: Foreign Languages Publishing House, 1956).

[35] Martine Mespoulet, "Quelle sociologie derrière le Rideau de fer?" Cairn 3-1-10; Susan Weissman, "The Role of Purges and Terror in the Formation of the USSR," *Critique*, 1999, 27 (1): 145–57.

[36] Satterwhite, cited by Mervart, "Czechoslovak Marxist Humanism," 4.

[37] Malgorzata Masurek, "Between Sociology and Ideology. Perception of Work and Sociologists Advisors in Communist Poland, 1956–1970," in *Edition Sciences Humaines*, 2007, 1 (16): 11–31.

[38] "Polish journey, 1960," Daniel Bell papers; Daniel Bell to Shepard Stone, June 2, 1960 and August 10, 1960 on the Polish journey, FFA 56-21.

Lazarsfeld's psychosocial surveys and, importantly, opinion research.[39] Polish scholars had good access to Western publications from the mid 1950s on. Adam Schaff, Julian Hochfeld, and Andrej Sicinski were central actors in transnational networks, especially in UNESCO's International Social Science Documentation Center in Vienna, led by the Marxist philosopher Adam Schaff.[40] In 1956, Polish scholars traveled to France to study the French Plan and its recent experimentation with long-term forecasting and conjectural research under the influence of Jean Forastié.[41] They came back, as Lukas Becht proposes, "infected with contemporary ideas of long term planning and socio cultural change as it was debated in France." From 1967 on, UNESCO championed forms of futurology as part of its emphasis on a cross-divide interrogation in the social sciences.[42] The problem of a common or shared future thus followed on the organization's previous interest in a universal history of Mankind. Julian Hochfeld was the key intellectual in orienting Polish sociology toward a new empirical investigation of the living conditions and life experiences of Polish workers. Notions of living conditions, life styles, values, and needs became part of an empirical project of humanization of labour, and investigating the "many sided development" of the individual. This was by no means a harmonious process: in 1956, workers' councils were introduced into Polish factories under the observation of sociologists, and, from 1957, the Gomulka regime started to tighten management methods in order to get rid of "slack." Sociologists of the work process were ordered to confirm expected results. Sociologists were thus re-drawn back into *sociotechnika*, management as the social technology of factory life.[43]

Opinion research played a specific role in Poland as a vehicle of forms of empirical investigation into life styles, hopes, and expectations of urban and rural populations. This included the crucial problem of their emergent images of the future. One of the most prominently transnational Polish sociologists was Andrej Sicinski.[44] Sicinski began his research in the public opinion research centre of Polish television, an

[39] Masurek, "Between Sociology and Ideology."

[40] Katia Naumann, "East Central European Experts in International Scientific Institutions: Research Planning in the International Social Science Council and the European Coordination Center for Research and Documentation in Social Sciences (Vienna Centre)," forthcoming in *Planning in Cold War Europe*, edited by Sandrine Kott et al. (Munchen: de Gruyter, 2011).

[41] Lukas Becht, "From Euphoria to Frustration. Institutionalising a System of Prognostic Research in the People's Republic of Poland, 1971–1976." Unpublished, and Becht, personal communication to the author.

[42] In 1958, a French Polish seminar on public opinion research was held in Warsaw with the participation of Lazarsfeld, Stein Rokkan (chair of the ICSS), and Jan Stoetzel. See Andrej Sicinski, "Surveys of Media of Mass Communication Public Opinion Research Center," in *Polish Sociological Bulletin*, 1961, 1–2.

[43] Satterwhite, *Varieties of Human Marxism*, 61; Masurek, "Between Sociology and Ideology," 13, 16, 19, 24.

[44] Andrej Sicinski studied sociology under Ossowsky at the Warsaw Academy of Sciences. He remained in the Academy as the Secretary of *Polska 2000* until 1984, with the exception of a year as a Ford fellow in the US in 1968–1969 (when several other Polish sociologists lost their positions). Sicinski resigned from the Council of the World Futures Studies Federation in 1985, having been denied travel abroad. Andrej Sicinski, CV, and letter to Eleonora Masini, February 1, archives of the World Futures Studies Federation, Jim Dator papers.

organization referred to with the efficient abbreviation OBOP: *Osrodek Badanya Oponii Publicznej przy Polskim Radiu i Telewijzji.* OBOP was created in 1958 on the model of French opinion research, and could, as Masurek describes, enjoy a highly independent status, producing data that were often at odds with the party line. From the early 1960s on, this research center conducted opinion survey studies of the Polish population and its exposure to new forms of mass media culture. It conducted comparisons between the urban Warsaw population, and rural populations, in order to learn about differing cultural needs.[45] Citing Marshall McLuhan and Roland Barthes, Sicinski described the role of opinion research as understanding how mass media contributed to shaping images of the future in socialist populations and creating new cultural audiences.[46] The original purpose of the center was however a more specific one: OBOP was created to analyse the mass of public correspondence that came into the television authorities from the Polish public, "pointing out problems requiring speedy solutions, such as administrative shortcomings, the needs of particular categories of the population and so on."[47] In 1967, Sicinski was charged together with Jan Stralecki (sometimes Strzelecki) with the creation in the Warsaw Academy of Sciences of a Commission for the next thirty years of Polish society, *Polska 2000.* In 1967, forecasting had been decreed official "social technology" in the Soviet Union and the first All Union meetings had taken place. In 1967 appeared also the work in progress volume of the American Commission for the Year 2000, as well as the first report of the French Planning Commission's *Groupe 1985.* The same year, Polish forecasters met in Tarda in an apparently enthusiastic meeting that became the starting point of Polish futurological studies.[48] Within Polska 2000, created in 1969, opinion research and empirical investigations of life styles was developed into a research undertaking into the problem of "quality of life" in the STR.[49] Polska 2000 took on board Western notions of consumerism, mass media culture, and value change as part of the investigation into what was cautiously described as an emerging new socialist society defined by a plurality of social groups and forms of individualism, and an emerging division of labour between experts, intellectuals, and populations.[50] Life style research, said Sicinski in 1979, was about understanding the forms of meaning attached by different social groups, on the individual and collective level, to life. It could thus explain the choices of behaviour of individuals, how these made sense of social reality and how they actively chose from a "repertoire" of values and

[45] Andrej Sicinski, "Surveys as Media of Mass Communication of the Polish Public Opinion Research Center," *International Communication Gazette*, 1963, 9 (3): 237–41.

[46] Andrej Sicinski, "Recent transformations in the role of writers," in *Diogenes*, March 1, 1973, 21 (81): 70–87.

[47] Andrej Sicinski, "Public Opinion Surveys in Poland," in *International Social Science Journal*, 1963, 15: 91–110, 93. Schaff and Ossowski were both on the board of OBOP.

[48] Andrej Sicinski, "Polske studia futurologiczne," in *Kultura i Spoleczenstwo*, 1967, 2 (11): 243–4 (cited by Lukas Becht).

[49] J. Szczepanski, Andrej Sicinski, and Jan Strzelecki, "Changes in the Way of Life in Socialist Poland in the Light of Contemporary Hypothesis Concerning Changes in Social Structure," in *A Long Term Model of Consumption* (Warsaw, Ossolineum, 1970), 80–154 (in Polish and cited in Sicinski 1979); Andrej Sicinski, "Les études prospectives en Pologne," in *Analyse et Prévision*, 1973, 16 (1–3): 197.

[50] Sicinski, "Recent Transformations in the Role of Writers."

decisions, thus influencing the social trajectory of the nation as a whole. Life-style research was about the interplay between the "objective possibilities of the development of a human being," and "subjective life satisfaction."[51] Different subjective views on meaning and life satisfaction could thus be used to characterize social groups within socialist society and their life aspirations. "Maybe in the future, in socialist society, creativity will constitute the basic criterion."[52]

Becht situates Polska 2000 in the midst of a Polish "War on Prognosis," in which Sicinski consciously brought in de Jouvenel's notion of futuribles and Daniel Bell's work on the Commission for the Year 2000 in order to counteract a regime demand for scientific forecasting. The concern, to humanistically oriented futurologists, was to find a model of future socialist culture, organized around the whole person. Sicinski's idea of creativity as a question of cultural audience and subjective perceptions of the meaning of existence placed the future as emerging from images and desires in ordinary people, and as such, as in a constant state of tension with socialist leadership. In 1969, Sicinski and Jan Strzelecki began a series of studies for UNESCO's International Social Science Council and the UN University on images of the future in socialist populations. These studies aimed to understand how images of the future were formed, and under what conditions they could be actively influenced (through psychosocial technologies such as opinion polls). The studies contained a potentially subversive element in the way they sought to contrast images of the future dormant in populations, with images of the future of leaders. Sicinski collaborated with the Norwegian peace researcher and philosopher Johan Galtung and the French opinion researcher Jan Stoetzel on the volume *Images of the Year 2000*. This made systematic comparisons between images of the future of Western and socialist populations, and at a second stage, compared the allegedly peaceful images of these with the aggressive images of their leaders.[53] In the foreword, Sicinski explained that the future, a previously unreachable continent, could now be studied, by virtue of sociological examination of ordinary peoples hopes and fears.[54]

Polska 2000's reflection on the future of socialist man developed over time into an interrogation of the conditions of emergence of a post-socialist future, anchored in images of change in socialist populations and differences between human needs and their satisfaction.[55] An article by Sicinski in 1978 on systems analysis explained

[51] Andrej Sicinski, "Theoretical Assumptions of Empirical Research of Specific Ways of Everyday Life (Styles of Life)," in *Greek Review of Social Research*, 1979, 35: 67–74, 69.

[52] Ibid.

[53] Johan Galtung and Jan Stoetzel, *Images of the World in the Year 2000* (Vienna: European Coordination Center, 1970). Duhautois, *Etudes sur le futur et conscience globale* (Ph.D. Diss. Paris: Centre d'histoire de Sciences Po, 2017), Chapter 3.

[54] Andrej Sicinski, "The Future: A Dimension Being Discovered," in *Images of the World in the Year 2000*, 121–59; Andrej Sicinski, "Peace and War in Polish Public Opinion," *Polish Sociological Bulletin*, 1967, 2: 25–40 (abstracted in English); Andrej Sicinski, "Dallas and Warsaw: The Impact of A Major National Political Event on Public Opinion Abroad," in *The Public Opinion Quarterly*, 1969, 33 (2): 190–6; Andrej Sicinski, *Dominant and Alternative Life Styles in Poland: An Outline* (United Nations University, 1985).

[55] Andrej Sicinski, "How is a Vision of a Desirable Society Possible Today?" in *Visions of Desirable Societies* (Oxford: Pergamon Press, 1983), 101–8.

that a system (a metaphorical biological system) could not survive an increasing inner tension resulting from the refusal to satisfy core values. If values developed in one way and the system functioned in another, inevitable system breakdown would follow. "A need of a given system is that property because of which a defined state of an environment of that system is a necessary condition of the undisturbed functioning of the system in the environment. If a need is not satisfied, that condition is not met, which results in the functioning of the system being disturbed." Interestingly, the article ended with the observation that a researcher, an expert, could start a dialogue with the system by changing its frames of reference.[56]

CIVILIZATION AT THE CROSSROADS AND THE FUTUROLOGICAL SOCIETY OF THE PRAGUE SPRING

From its appointment in 1965, the Richta group became the beacon of future research and the hope of socialism with a human face. The Richta group was appointed within the Institute of Philosophy and Sociology of the Czechoslovak Academy of Sciences to study "the human and social implications of the Scientific and Technological Revolution" and was first and foremost a reflection on planning. Richta was not a dissident, his purpose was to revise Marxist postulates and create the philosophical foundations for a higher stage of socialism as distinct from Marxism Leninism and Stalinism. This meant, as Sommer shows, developing a reflection on new tools of planning which would have as their purpose to deepen all aspects of the STR (Scientific and Technological Revolution) in social life and thus harness the forces of science and technology for advanced socialism.[57] In this manner, Western visions of post-industrialism would be met by a vigorous socialist management revolution, the promise of which was the emancipation of socialist man through automation and creativity.

Richta's texts, which pinpointed both the rise of a managerial and technologically educated class, and the necessity of forecasting as a form of future oriented planning, were remarkably similar to "bourgeois visions" of post-industrialism. Indeed, Bell was very familiar with Richta's writings, citing them extensively in the foreword to the second edition of *The Coming of Post Industrial Society*.[58] The foreword contained Bell's lament for the crushing of the Richta group, as well as his outraged description of the Moscow ban on his own work as "bourgeois." Bell's *The Coming of Post Industrial Society* was translated into the socialist bloc in 1974 and 1975 as a consequence of a controversy created by Raymond Aron's notion of post-industrialism as a gradual reduction of class conflict. The concept of post-industrial society thus became an object of study for ideological research on capitalism and convergence. The translation of *The Coming of Post Industrial Society* appeared in

[56] Andrej Sicinski, "The Concepts of "Need" and "Value" in the Light of the Systems Approach" (*International Social Science Council*, 1978), 17 (1): 71–91. 73.

[57] Sommer, "Are We Still Revolutionaries?"

[58] Bell, *The Coming of Post Industrial Society*, xxv.

the so-called White Series, published by the Central Party Committee, for Party use only. The Polish edition, published in 1975, was provided with a foreword introducing the reader to the right interpretation.[59]

That there could be in this way a correspondence between liberal and socialist accounts of the STR is explainable through the productivist orientation that informed both Richta's and Bell's work. While there was a profound humanist orientation to Richta's emphasis on creativity, creativity and scientific growth played a rather ambiguous role both as what would free human beings from alienation, and as the forces that needed to be harnessed for productive purposes in the STR. Arguably Bell's work embodied the same tension. There were important differences between the revisionist critique and Richta's vision of the STR. Marcuse, in his 1967 chapter for Erich Fromm's book, described visions of post-industrialism as an example of the appropriation in both East and West of reifying forces of sciences and technology into a new project of alienation. STR, to Marcuse, was thus a rival project to Marxist humanism, because of the productivist use put to science and technology.[60]

Meanwhile, the publication in English of *Civilisation at the Crossroads* in 1969 was a sensation, and the book was read as proof that the communist system was changing from within.[61] The difference between Richta's work and that of official socialist forecasting was blatantly clear to Western observers. The historian of post-fordist thought, Kristian Kumar, present at the 1970 Sociological Congress in Varna that launched the joint East West Future Research Committee, reviewed the English translation in 1969. Kumar wrote:

> Whatever the similarities of substance, in one respect Eastern European students differ sharply from their counterparts in the West. Their futurologies must be somehow Marxist. Since their societies are based on a Marxist ideology, and since the claim is that the Marxist theory of social development accounts 'scientifically' for the general direction of social change, all social forecasting has to couch itself in Marxist terminology and concepts. With monotonous insistence, therefore, Marx is invoked as the first, and in many respects only, scientific futurologist.... Scientific futurology is in fact the theory of Marxism. One must not underestimate the real intellectual—and political—difficulties involved here. If the socialist revolutions of this century have overcome the fundamental contradictions of social development, then there should be no real problems about the main outlines of the future. Obstacles and delays there will be, no doubt, but the basic societal form exists for the steady evolution of the fully communist society. The straitjacketing tendency is obvious. It demands a high degree of intellectual sophistication to be able to say something illuminating about contemporary social changes while sticking to the Marxist framework. My impression is that few of the futurological discussions from Eastern Europe manage to break out of the straight jacket. Ritual obeisances and incantations of Marxist terminology throttle the attempt to come to terms with the novel features of industrial societies. All the more

[59] Becht, "From Euphoria to Frustration," 5 and Becht, ongoing doctoral research; Bell, *The Coming of Post Industrial Society*, xxviii.

[60] Marcuse, "Socialist Humanism."

[61] Radovan Richta, ed., *Civilisation at the Crossroads: Social and Human Implications of the Scientific Revolution* (Prague: International Arts and Sciences Press, 1969).

> impressive, then, is the lengthy study by Radovan Richta and a research team from the Czechoslovak Academy of Sciences entitled *Civilisation at the Crossroads*.[62]

Indeed Kumar pinpointed the very core of the message of *Civilisation at the Crossroads*, namely, the idea that automation was "freeing man altogether from direct participation in the production process. It relieves him of his role as a mere cog in the machine system and offers him the position of inspirer, creator, master of the technological system..."[63]

Richta's message of creativity as emancipation and post-industrial society as a new set of economic relations organized around man was a revolutionary contribution to Marxist theory. As Sommer describes, Richta situated the idea of revolution in the present: the first stage of socialism had brought about an industrial society, which was however still defined by the industrial division of labour, the fragmentation of work, and a bourgeois bureaucracy. The STR was the promise, for Richta, of mature socialism, of a complete revolution in which man was free and alienation disappeared. Perhaps the most subversive message in Richta's notion of the STR was his hope that automation would lead to a new socialist person, a "*real* development of human beings". Post-industrial society was a socialist society in which "every individual has an opportunity to use the powers of scientific knowledge and shape his or her existence based on a real human sense of life."[64]

There were several critical elements to Richta's work. The idea of transcending industrial labour was a deeply threatening one to socialist regimes that were, in the period from the late 1950s to the mid 1960s, preoccupied by faltering production numbers and blaming a lack of factory discipline to worker slack and poor management methods.[65] The prospect of an idle working class was no less a specter in the socialist world than in the liberal one (in the West, the "automation scare" also triggered notions of the end of work, the beginnings of drug abuse, boredom, psychosocial pathologies, and chronic unemployment). The idea of creativity as the fulfilment of a full and potentially autonomous personality also held revisionist potential. Meanwhile, Sommer proposes that it was Richta's notions of planning as drawing on new forms of democratic participation in the Prague spring that was most difficult for the regime to accept.[66] The Richta group was charged with the development of "conscious" planning methods for the STR. But while Richta understood this as demanding a new participation of socialist citizens, the regime interest in forecasts emphasized a new kind of total planning through the production of a myriad of indicators. This included indicators measuring progress in science, aimed at making science part of a totally planned process.[67] The contrast between this idea of forecasting as intensified long-term planning, exceeding the five-year

[62] Kristian Kumar, "Futurology, the View from Eastern Europe," *Futures*, 1972, 4 (1): 90–5, 91.

[63] Kumar, "Futurology," 93.

[64] Richta (1963) cited by Sommer, "Are We Still Revolutionaries?"

[65] Pekka Sutela, *Economic Thought and Economic Reform in the Soviet Union* (Cambridge: Cambridge University Press, 1991), 49f.

[66] Nancy Oreskes and John Kriege, *Science and Technology in the Cold War* (Cambridge MA: MIT Press, 2014), 411–13.

[67] Vitezslav Sommer, "Are we still revolutionaries?"

plans, to incorporate a total future of socialist society and Richta's philosophical message of a post-industrial era as human emancipation and self-consciousness was not lost on socialist forecasters.

In 1967, two members of Richta's team, Miloš Zeman and Ota Šulc attended the All Union Seminar on Forecasting in Kiev. The year before, forecasting had been decreed a necessary tool for the realization of STR in the totality of the Union of Socialist Republics.[68] This followed Kennedy's declaration of programme budgeting for the totality of the federal administration in the US. Ota Šulc was an economist at the University of Economics in Prague. He developed his idea of "integrated forecasting" as a form of forecasting that combined technological, economic and social forecasting into a kind of meta prognosis of the STR and its permeation in socialist society.[69] Šulc was however also instrumental in introducing forms of Western future research to the socialist bloc. In the late 1960s, Šulc wrote several articles and books in Czech introducing concepts of Western futurology in the Czech context, and he also wrote articles in the English speaking journal *Technological Forecasting and Social Change* about the possibility of integrating economic, social, and technological forecasts into forecasts of possible goal and value conflicts in the STR, using Delphi techniques.[70] In 1968, Šulc founded the Czechoslovak Futurological Society (CFS), which played a key role in the Prague spring as an open discussion society on future issues in socialist society.[71] With the Society as his base, Šulc started teaching futures studies. The courses included a wide range of Western futurists such as Denis Gabor (author of *Inventing the Future*), Robert Jungk, Bertrand de Jouvenel, and Ossip Flechtheim.[72] Šulc was also part of the editorial committee behind the journal *Trend*, and embarked on a long-term economic prognosis of the Czech economy. As a consequence of the Soviet invasion in 1968, the Futurological Society was dissolved. In the subsequent purge, Richta was allowed to maintain his academic position but in his apology had to abandon the revisionist elements in his theory of the STR, and these were reinterpreted into what Sommer succinctly refers to as a "legitimation narrative of late socialist dictatorship."[73] In 1970, Richta was appointed the new director of the

[68] Gordon Rocca, "A Second Party in Our Midst. The History of the Soviet Forecasting Association," in *Social Studies of Science*, 1981, 11 (2): 199–247.

[69] Sommer, "From Futurology to Prognostika".

[70] Ota Šulc, *Futurologie: Přehl. literatury a informací* (Prague 1968); Ota Šulc and Milos Zeman, *Futurologický slovníček* (Prague 1969); both cited in Sommer, "From futurology to prognostika"; Ota Šulc, "A Methodological Approach to the Integration of Technological and Social Forecasts", in *Technological Forecasting and Social Change* 1969, 1: 105–108. Šulc published an almost identical article in 1986, "Integration of Scientific Forecasts. Methodology of Integration of Scientific Forecasts in The Process of National Science Policy Making", in *Technological Forecasting and Social Change*, 1986, 30: 251–60.

[71] Letter from James Dator to Ota Šulc, April 30, 1969, James Dator papers; Flechtheim, *Futurologie*, 299, and Futurum, "Futurologie Klub in Prague", 1968, 2: 334.

[72] Letter from James Dator to Ota Šulc, April 30, 1969, and from Šulc to Dator, May 21, 1969. Ota Šulc, course outline, *Futurologicka Spolecnost*, James Dator archives.

[73] Sommer, "Are We Still Revolutionaries?" Richta would be described in highly critical terms by his former team members after 1989, as a Viteszlav Sommer, "Scientists of the World Unite! Radovan Richta's Theory of Revolution," in Elena Aronova and Simone Turchetti, eds., *Science Studies during the Cold War and Beyond. Paradigms Detected* (London: Routledge, 2016), 203.

Institute for Philosophy and Sociology in the Academy of Science, and charged with producing forecasts for the management of the STR within an explicitly Marxist Leninist framework.

A Marxist Leninist approach to the STR included using forecasting as a veritable tool of social technology, an integrated instrument for shaping a socialist scientific and technological life style.[74] "Integrated" meant a form of planning based on indicators from all sectors of socialist economy and society—economic, social, and scientific.[75] The Richta team was brought into a joint Czechoslovak-Soviet research group on the STR, which published the *Man-Science-Technology* volume in 1970, in which the official interpretation of the STR was codified. Presenting this work at the International Sociological Association Congress in Varna, socialist forecasters broke with all critical notions from the *Civilisation at the Crossroads* volume.[76] Šulc published several papers on integrated forecasts, in which the interrogation into possible value and goal conflicts in socialist society changed into an emphasis on total planning and forecasting as an instrument with which all relations between technology, economy, and society could be forecasted precisely. In 1972, Šulc presented integrated forecasting as social technology, a form of social prognostiks that could create a "universal structure under optimal conditions."[77]

The clampdown on the Richta group in 1968 also led to what Sommers calls a definite ban on the notion of futurology, used until then by Czech forecasters along with "futures studies" or "futures research" and including the plural s in futures (see the next section). From 1970 on, no East European forecasters could write about future research without reiterating the critique of "bourgeois futurology" and its difference in nature to the scientific prognostika of Marxism Leninism. Ota Šulc, like the Russian forecaster Igor Bestuzhev Lada discussed in the next section, was forced to engage in an ideological denunciation of his previous interest in alternative predictions and stress the difference between Western futurology and Marxist Leninist forecasting.[78] As part of this denunciation, all

[74] Ota Šulc, "Contribution to the Methodology of Forecasting of Life Styles," paper to Bucharest conference, 1973, archives of the World Futures Studies Federation, James Dator papers.

[75] As discussed in the previous chapter, the notion of integrated forecasting circulated also in Western planning circles, in particular through Eric Jantsch's paper for the OECD.

[76] The core elements of *Man-Science-Technology* were also presented by Ota Šulc in an article in *Futures* in December 1973 on futures research in Czechoslovakia as the continuation of the work begun within the Richta group, Ota Šulc, "Futures Research in Czechoslovakia," *Futures*, 1973, 5 (6): 573–9. The article will have struck a chord for those readers of *Futures* who were knowledgeable about the Richta group, as Šulc's text includes a reference to Kumar's introduction of *Civilisation at the Crossroads* in the same journal in 1969.

[77] Šulc, "Integrated Method of Forecasting"; Šulc "Futures Research in Czechoslovakia"; Šulc, "Contribution to the Method of Forecasting of Life Styles." Šulc folder, James Dator archives.

[78] Sommer quotes Šulc's article *Marxist-Leninist Prognostika in the Struggle Against Bourgeois Concepts of Future Studies* which was written as a conference paper for the Third Czechoslovak-Soviet Symposium of Philosophy in October 1970. It described the most important future studies methods (scenarios, Delphi) as bourgeois, and ideologically distinct from *prognostika*. This text represented Šulc's apology, while his earlier papers for *Technological Forecasting* and *Futures* discussed both Delphi and scenarios as useful tools of integrated forecasting. Richta himself had to denounce Western futurology in *Krize perspektiv buržoazní společnosti* ("The Crisis of the Perspectives of the Bourgeois Society") in the monthly *New Idea* (1975).

similarities between socialist forecasting of the STR and liberal visions of the STR became obscured and tangential.

As Richta's critical humanist notion of Marxism was purged, a philosophical version of futurology was replaced with the statistical production of integrated planning indicators conforming to Marxism Leninism. The Futurological Society was dissolved along with other civil society activities of 1968. Sommer tells a fascinating story of how *prognostika*, acceptable in its emphasis on economic indicators, management methods and even market mechanisms, became a pillar of late socialism after 1970, as part of a hierarchical system of expertise for the socialist economy. What had begun thus as a revisionist project of futurology of a reform minded intelligentsia, of introducing notions of alternative development, humanism, and realization of a genuinely socialist man turned into a state-led project of future making, the aim of which was to "replace criticism and thinking about future alternatives with a technocratic expertise," charged with the "authoritative formulation of the goals of society."[79] In 1972, Ota Šulc, corresponding widely with Western futurists in an attempt to get a fellowship in the West, became the head of the prognostics department in the Institute for Philosophy and Sociology.[80]

IN RUSSIAN THE WORD FUTURE EXISTS ONLY IN THE SINGULAR

"In Russian the word 'future' exists only in the singular", ended a laconic text by the Soviet futurist par excellence, Igor Bestuzhev Lada, written in 1976 for the English-speaking journal *Futures*.[81] Bestuzhev Lada was well placed to make this statement. In 1971, forecasting as a tool for the comprehensive planning of science and technology was declared an object of cooperation between the USSR, GDR, Bulgaria, Romania, Czechoslovakia, Poland, and Hungary.[82] Within the official framework of the STR, forecasting was the quintessential social technology, a technique of total planning aimed at realizing goals and objectives of socialist regimes and the accordance between projection and reality. As a technique of total planning, forecasting was a top down technology–economy–society metaplan, which came with the creation of a directed network of forecasting departments, institutes, and societies in every branch and sector of the socialist economy.[83] As the President of the Soviet Forecasting Assocation, Bestuzhev Lada was instrumental in setting this network up.

The Czech historian Michal Kopecek uses the term consolidation regimes to describe the way that social science was reined in as a means of consolidating state power after 1968, and turned into a form of governmental policy expertise.

[79] Sommer, "From Futurology to Prognostika.", 160.

[80] Letter from McHale to Šulc, October 27, 1972. Jim Dator entertained a wide correspondence with East European futurists as part of his plan to set up the Hawaii Center as an East West center in futures studies. Letters from Dator to Šulc and to the Romanian Pavel Apostol, July 24, 1972.

[81] Igor Bestuzhev Lada, "Futures Research in the Soviet Union," *Futures*, 1976, 8 (2): 181–5, 181.

[82] Šulc, "Futures Research in Czechoslovakia."

[83] Rocca, "A Second Party in Our Midst."

This put a premium on policy science, management studies, and economics. As a technology for shaping the long term after desired prognosis, forecasting allowed, indeed, for a tight hold on temporality.[84] Kopecek's argument about consolidation regimes is different from the interpretation offered by Rindzeviciute, who proposes that policy expertise brought a level of openness into Soviet governmentality by virtue of an, at least partly, independent technocrat culture. These explanations are not as such mutually exclusive, and forecasting included both efforts at independence, and a highly hands on brutality in particular after 1968.

The reigning in of the Richta group meant that the presence of East European futurists in the networks of future research changed. Some Polish and Czech forecasters, producing empirical, economic, and statistical work presented as consistent with Marxism Leninism could remain in transnational circles but, after 1968, the Eastern European presence became dominated overall by Soviet future researchers of the Soviet Forecasting Association. These were essentially of two strands: the official planning delegation, represented by the mathematician Gennadev Dobrov of the cybernetics section of the Kiev Academy of Science, and the forecasting section of the Soviet Sociological Association, represented by the sociologist Igor Bestuzhev Lada. Cybernetics was an integrated part of Soviet planning. But as indicated in the previous section, forecasting stood in a highly schizophrenic relationship to planning. On the one hand, forecasting was intended to provide a scientific underpinning to planning by creating a multitude of indicators that could testify to the scientific nature of long-term plans. On the other, forecasting was an, at least partly, autonomous activity, which had as its function to forecast possible alternatives to, and anticipated consequences of, decision making. This "pre-planning" is clearly how socialist forecasters themselves understood their role, but after 1968, such open reflection on the decision clashed directly with the imperative of demonstrating its scientific nature.

Igor Bestuzhev Lada was an historian and sociologist, a survivor of many purges who managed to be an active sociologist through the long period from the 1950s to the 1990s. He was still active in future research into the 2000s as a consultant for the Washington based think tank the World Future Society.[85] In 1970, Bestuzhev Lada became the first president of the joint Future Research committee of the International Sociological Association, created in Varna and set up along the principles of the ISA, with one president from the West and one from the Eastern bloc.[86] Bestuzhev Lada was in many ways a perfect representative of Rindzeviciute's neutral policy expert, the "rider on the storm." In fact he was a Soviet version of the Expert.

The proclamation of scientific socialism saw a certain acceptance of the idea of expertise, as a different source of authority than Party, in the Soviet Union. Forecasting was such an area of expert activity and the production of prognostiks

[84] Michal Kopeček, "The Rise and Fall of Czech Post-Dissident Liberalism after 1989", in *East European Politics and Societies*, 2011, 25(2): 244–71.

[85] Igor Bestuzhev Lada, CV, in James Dator papers.

[86] ISA Research Committee nr 07, bulletin.

depended, for the first time, on forms of external expert activity and even consultancy. Importantly, this activity had limits and those limits were firmer in the USSR than in Czechoslovakia or Poland. Bestuzhev Lada's position as an expert forecaster with one foot in transnational networks and the other in Moscow is highly illustrative of these limits.

While in other East European countries, socialism with a human face debates had by the 1960s challenged orthodox Marxism Leninism with varying results, regime control in the USSR was too tight for such philosophical debates even to occur. The multitude of reports that emerged from Russian scientists in the years after 1967 and well into the 1980s were grounded in Marxist teleology and dismissive of Western bourgeois futurology, portrayed as aimed at predicting *distant events* without the scientific grounding in the objective social laws of Marxism. Western future research was repeatedly described as unacceptably subjective, a recycling of "expert visions" of unplanned and spontaneous market capitalism.[87] Both notions of "distant events" and "subjectivity" were crucial signifiers of a complicated logic of translation. In actual fact, forecasting had a long and complex history in the USSR, as indeed Bestuzhev Lada pointed out himself in a set of audacious writings for a Western audience in the journal *Futures*. The first generation of forecasting was labeled "pre-planning" and emerged in the Soviet Union in 1927–28 in the context of Lenin's New Economic Policy. Pre-planning was a mathematical and philosophical reflection on the activity of choosing and setting the goal, among a theoretical possible number of different goals.[88] Pre-planning clashed with the first five-year plan, created by Stalin in 1928, and most of the mathematicians and philosophers of this interwar moment perished in the first wave of purges. The purges brought home the notion that Soviet society had one Goal of development, that this Goal was set by the Party, and that social affairs followed the iron laws described by Lenin in his interpretation of Marx' *Grundrisse* and political economy.[89] As the five-year plan defined a strict temporal horizon and scientized this according to Marxism Leninism, other notions of the future became impossible.

Forecasting was rehabilitated after Stalin's death in 1953. Destalinization permitted the cautious reintroduction of social science in the USSR, but as a strictly empirical science devoted to "concrete social research" on time studies and the composition of the working class in the classless society.[90] Meanwhile, the reintroduction of social science included the possibility of a new futuristic expertise. It is here that Igor Bestuzhev Lada, not engaged in any manifest dissident activity, but an empiricist, somewhat conservative, possibly mysticist and mainly convinced communist sociologist is interesting, as part of a careful probing of limits through the vehicle of expertise.[91]

87 Bestuzhev Lada, "Utopias of Bourgeois Futurology".
88 *Planovoye Khozisystvo*, 1928, cited in Egle Rindzeviciute, "A Struggle for the Soviet Future."
89 Stephen Fortescue, *Science Policy in the Soviet Union* (London: Routledge, 1990), 17–18.
90 Mespoulet, "Sociologie en URSS."
91 Shlapentokh, *Soviet Intellectuals*.

Bestuzhev Lada's CV included publications with the opaque titles of a "Theory of the Evolution of the Universe," a "Theory of Anthroponimics," and "The Conceptualization of the Philosophy of History in Progress."[92] His career had begun as a student of history in the Institute for International Relations in Moscow. The Institute for International Relations was a hotbed of Party power, which trained civil servants, economists, and policy analysts. Upon graduation, Bestuzhev Lada pursued a doctoral dissertation with the title "History of World Social Thought" in the Institute of History in the Academy of Science. In the 1950s, he developed a keen interest in science fiction, and wrote a novel about the ideal future of Mankind. This novel was inspired by the 1957 science fiction novel *Nebula Andromeda*, written by the paleontologist, Ivan Efremev.[93] *Nebula Andromeda* was hailed as a master piece of post-Stalinist Soviet science fiction. The novel described the space ship Tantra, embarked on the communist colonization of distant galaxies. It sported several perfect heroes, including the so named Darr Veter, director of the Global Space Agency and (Soviet) representative to the Great Circle of Intergalactic Civilizations. The Great Circle was composed of scientists exchanging information, and when one of these takes an experiment too far and causes disaster, he is corrected by the dire punishment that scientists cannot return to Earth. In 1967, the novel was filmed as *The Andromeda Nebula* at Dovzhenko film studios.

Nebula Andromeda marked the beginnings of a new genre of post-Stalinist science fiction, because it ventured into the previously banned territory of the distant future (in the novel illustrated by space travel) and also portrayed Soviet scientists as heroes of the construction of a new global civilization. According to Bestuzhev Lada himself, he came to the idea of future research from his research for this novel, and he seems indeed to have singlehandedly introduced the idea of future research into the Soviet Union. It seems that his ambition was the projection of a new kind of scientific utopia of the Soviet Union, by compiling sociological observations of trends in the world future. As utopia was a shunned concept which would later be applied to bourgeois futurology, such scientific fiction could probably be understood as a testing of a different mode of thinking about the Soviet future, with the difference however that it did not take place within the realm of science fiction, but in science, as form of a "metahistory" or sociological portrayal of a distant ideal society. In 1956 and 1958, Bestuzhev Lada wrote a manuscript in three volumes entitled *Profiles of the Future*, which was intended as scientific future research, a "substitute for science fiction." The manuscript proved scandalous and unpublishable, but as he finished this manuscript, he began working on the idea "in principle" of a new science, the science of the future, and would apparently do so for the next few years.[94]

[92] Bestuzhev Lada CV, and Bestuzhev Lada "Letter from a Russian Futurist," November 8, 1986, James Dator papers.

[93] Ivan Yefremov, *Andromeda—a Space Age Tale* (Moscow: Progress Publishers, 1959).

[94] Bestuzhev Lada, "Letter from a Russian Futurist."

Bestuzhev's letter in the context of a bid for president of the World Futures Studies Federation, retrospectively written in 1986, describes his early approach to this new field of research as explicitly normative, devoted to the idea that future research could be used as a form of problem solving by virtue of which all problems of socialist society including unemployment and narcotics use could find a rational solution, and the ideal society thus realized. Of course, in the 1960s, such problems did not exist in socialist society, and socialist society was per definition the ideal society. Bestuzev Lada's first international publication, the official introduction to Soviet forecasting published in the *Unesco International Social Science Journal* issue devoted to futurology, later resumed in Toffler's 1972 interview for *The Futurists*, set out a different course as it carefully avoided any mention of the normative dimensions of future research and described forecasting as the scientific activity of following the progress of plans and setting down the "likely consequences of their fulfilment or non fulfilment." The paper also stated the key difference between Western and Soviet forecasts: while in the West, forecasting could take the role of planning and identify goals and objectives of policy, in the socialist system, planning was a higher form of setting down objective, scientific and conscious goals of development. Forecasting was not planning, but aimed at improving the scientific standards of the latter, by strictly adhering to the scientific theory of the future as proscribed by dialectical Marxism and Lenin. Forecasts, he explained, could not attempt to influence the future actively, but rather shape forms of scientific and public opinion on the future so that the scientific and objective basis for the Plan could be realized.[95] The paper went on to argue that all future judgments that did not depart in dialectical materialism or scientific communism were pure metaphysics, and gave a dangerous and subjective role to expert opinion.[96]

The publication of this paper in the UNESCO journal in 1969 occurred at a crucial moment in Bestuzhev Lada's career. In the previous year, he had become the president of the Forecasting Section of the Soviet Sociological Association. This marked the end of a struggle over the nature of forecasting between sociologists of the Institute for Concrete Social Research and planners in the Committee for Science and Technology (chaired by the *eminence grise*, Dzhermen Gvishiani). The end of the struggle meant the definite domestication of forecasting, from an, at least partly, independent and expert driven activity contributing to a reflection on the goals of planning (pre-planning) to that of a direct auxiliary to planning in all areas (prognostics). In 1967 and 1968, says Bestuzhev, future research was discredited "because of the understanding that future research as prognosis was a function of

[95] In English, as "Forecasting, An Approach to the Problems of the Future," 526–34, 528. Interview with Bestuzhev Lada, Toffler Archives. Bestuzhev Lada, "Introduction to Systems Analysis of Social Forecasting as a Category," paper to Third World Future Research Conference, Romania, Bucharest, in Ossip Flechtheim's papers, and interview with Bestuzhev Lada, Circular letter of the World Future Research Conference in Bucharest nr 1, Eleonora Masini papers.

[96] Igor Bestoujev Lada (French spelling), "La prevision, une des methodes de l'exploration de l'avenir," in *Revue International des Sciences Sociales*, 1969, 11 (4): 563–74; see also Bestoujev Lada, "Les recherches sur la prevision sociale en URSS," in *Cahier du centre d'études et de recherches Marxistes* (Paris), 1968, 63, (this journal published reprints in French from *Vyprosy Filosofii*); Bestoujev Lada, *Essai de futurologie* (Moscow: Editions du progrès, 1985), 14–15.

any science and must be developed within the framework of all existing sciences."[97] In other words, future research was not a science of its own but a tool for the realization of the STR. A new field devoted to the category or temporal category of the future was not possible (indeed the UNESCO paper describes this as a hopeless "*histoire d'avenir*" defined by Western utopian writing).

The 1967 decree put a halt to the idea that forecasting could be a somehow independent activity oriented at debating different possible future routes. Gvishiani, who plays a central role in Rindzeviciute's book as the transnational entrepreneur of the ideas of Operations Research and policy science across the Iron Curtain, was the son in law of Kosygin. The purpose of forecasting as introduced by the Science and Technology Committee of Gosplan in 1966 was to revitalize a moribound Soviet economy through strategic transfer of technology and management methods from the West within the context of what Slava Gerovitch has described as "overtake and destroy."[98] Gvishiani was the Soviet representative in high level transnational forecasting activities, including the meetings of the Club of Rome and IIASA. This brought him into direct contact with American forecasting methods. These, the "decision tools" of Operations Research, systems analysis, and cost–benefit analysis, were interpreted by the Brezhnev administration as having achieved significant cost control through their simulation of market mechanisms in the federal state apparatus in the US.[99]

This direct regime interest changed a field that had, in the period from the late 1950s, centered on the reintroduction of the banned idea of pre-planning. As part of his efforts to construct Soviet future research as a new scientific field, Bestuzhev worked, before 1967, on the development of a national forecasting system, which would work out indicators for the long term and which would be coordinated by a special scientific council of forecasting comprised by representatives of all branches of knowledge (in other words scientists) in order to work out preplanning recommendations for government and industry. This scientific council would be complemented by a special research institute, and importantly, by a scientific society, the Forecasting Association, which united all futurists of the country and would function as a partly independent consultancy to Gosplan.[100] It also included the idea, which Rocca compares to the futurological societies of the Prague spring, of open future debate. Of this, said Bestuzhev Lada in 1986, no information filtered abroad, but clearly some information did, because in the mid 1980s several Western doctoral dissertations and articles emerged that described the nature of forecasting in the Soviet Union as an activity distinct from planning and as holding

[97] Bestuzhev Lada, "Letter from a Russian futurist"; Fortescue, 21–43, 60, 94.

[98] Slava Gerovitch, Mathematical Machines of the Cold War: Soviet Computing, American Cybernetics and Ideological disputes in the early 1950s, in *Social Studies of Science*, 2001, 31(2): 253–87.

[99] Rindzeviciute, *Power of System*, 36–47, 52–72. In 1970, Gvishiani oversaw and prefaced Eric Jantsch' volume, *Technological Forecasting in Perspective*, into Russian. In the following years, the journal *Technological Forecasting* opened its pages to Russian forecasters, cyberneticians, and planners. Gvishiani's own *Trajectories of the Future* was translated from Russian and published in English in 1972 by the Foreign Technology Division of the Wright Patterson Air Force Base in Ohio.

[100] "Letter from a Russian futurist."

a certain hope for Soviet reform. The first of these, written by RAND experts and sovietologists such as Fred Ikle, were part of an American attempt to follow the development of planning techniques in the Soviet Union. Americans were impressed that the Soviets knew how to actively control value change in society. They described an area in which an authoritarian regime seemed to have certain advantages, by laying down indicators for desirable social developments.[101]

Other studies gave a more complex picture. An article in the academic journal *Social Studies of Science* in 1988 under the name Gordon Rocca (according to the biography an intelligence officer) comes indeed close to Bestuzhev Lada's own descriptions. Rocca describes the fate of the Soviet forecasting association, created as an independent agency to conduct normative and problem-oriented research, which included indicators that would allow for following consequences of political decisions, and suggestions of alternatives to decisions. In this capacity, forecasting was debated at the All Union seminar in Kiev in 1966.[102] It appears that the ambition to create an association of independent scientific forecasters was a step too far, and that the emergence of an independent scientific field debating the quality of Party decisions was unacceptable. The Forecasting Association was dismantled. After this, only forecasting as planning was acceptable, and Gvishiani set up a planning vision of a forecasting system, with units in each sector and branch but piloted not by independent forecasters but by Gosplan. In 1970, Bestuzhev Lada tried his chances at visiting the first conference of futures research in Kyoto in Japan (see Chapter 7). The conference was devoted to futures studies as a new scientific field, and the Kyoto meeting was a step toward the creation of a world federation for futures studies. The Soviet Union was not an official member of this until after Glasnost, but somehow Bestuzhev Lada was able attend its conferences. On his return to the USSR from Japan in 1970, Bestuzhev Lada was faced with the threat of imprisonment and exclusion from the Party. His *mea culpa* was the article "Utopias of Bourgeois Futurology" in the newsletter of the Washington based World Future Society, which expressed a probably genuine view that Western futurology had strayed from a normative engagement with societal problem solving in favour of "visions of eternal capitalism." Notions of the affluent society and consumer society were empty labels to hide the social problems created by capitalism and futurology was but a set of meaningless and subjective expert visions.[103]

[101] Fred Charles Ikle, "Social Forecasting and the Problem of Changing Values, with Special Reference to Soviet and East European Writings," in *Futures*, 1971, 3 (2): 142–50; see also Robert Randolph, "Social and Technological Forecasting in the Soviet Union," in *Futures*, 1976, December: 485–95, 485. In 1975 there was an American Soviet agreement to collaborate in the area of social forecasting.

[102] Rocca, "A Second Party in our Midst." Bestuzhev Lada himself described Soviet forecasting in several articles in *Futures* and *Technological Forecasting*, Igor Bestuzhev Lada, "Futures Research in the Soviet Union," Igor Bestuzhev Lada, "Futures Research in the USSR, part II: 1981–1985," *Futures*, 1986, October: 628–37.

[103] Bestuzhev Lada was, if anything, a convinced communist, even after 1989. Igor Bestuzhev Lada, "Utopias of Bourgeois Futurology" in *The Futurist*, newsletter of the World Future Society, December 1970. He had published the same text in the Soviet weekly of world affairs, *New Times*, on August 12, 1970. He also published, in Russian, "Concepts of Modern Futurology" in a volume entitled *Crisis of Bourgeois Concepts on the Future of Mankind*.

Bestuzhev Lada's account of Soviet forecasting in the journal *Futures* in 1976 laconically stated:

> By comparison with the West, the role played by social goals, plans, programmes, projects—decisions in general—is much more substantial in the USSR, since all of these are by nature state decisions. As a rule, a decision is a universally binding directive or law, and must be undeviatingly complied with. *Great significance is attached to the scientific validation of decisions*, the reduction of the danger of subjectivism, and de-optimization. In this respect, a forecast, together with an analysis and diagnosis, is assigned the important function of providing the scientific basis of the decision. *The need is for forecasts which precede the taking of a decision*, evaluate progress in implementation, and assess in advance its expected consequences.[104]

But it was in the capacity of forecasting or prognostics as "a set of quality indicators for an ideal society" that Bestuzhev Lada brought "social prognostiks" or social forecasting to the Research Committee number 7 of the International Sociological Association. In the transnational context, Bestuzhev Lada was able to reintroduce the notion of normative or problem solving forecasts, but without reference to Soviet society and applied instead to the area of global problems and "alternative civilisations" or "desirable societies" on the world level. This observation allows us, in fact, to return to Rindzeviciute's argument, as her book shows that the focus on "shared" or "global problems" such as disarmament, pollution, energy, development or famine became, after 1970, a way for Soviet scientists to talk about the future without engaging in an explicit and lethal regime critique. The focus on common problems of Mankind and universal goals of humanity thus allowed forecasters, modelers, and systems analysts to partake in international settings and share in methodological debates. In these settings, they could use systems analysis to create projections of an open vs. closed system in ways that were really metaphorical descriptions of the future of the communist system.[105]

FUTURES STUDIES AS DISSIDENCE: MIHAIL BOTES AND THE CENTER FOR METHODOLOGICAL FUTURE RESEARCH IN BUCHAREST

If it was difficult to conduct future research in post-Stalinist USSR, it was positively lethal in Ceausescu's Romania. Paradoxically, Romania was the country where there was, under the dictatorship of Nicolae Ceausescu, an outspoken

[104] Bestuzhev Lada, "Futures Research in the Soviet Union," 182. In 1997, Bestuzhev Lada wrote an article in *Sociological Research* lamenting the fact that empirical and problem oriented forecasts, aimed at improving the quality of bureaucratic decision making, had never been possible in the Soviet Union, and that what had become, instead, the final result of 1950s sociology was the senseless production of indicators. Igor Bestuzhev Lada, "Why I Did not Write the History of the Institute of Sociology," *Sociological Research*, 1997, 36 (4): 89–95.

[105] See letter Eleonora Masini to Bestuzhev Lada, May 2, 1988, "Joint Research Project on Alternative Civilisations"; Sicinski "Research Project on the Universality of Human Values in Past, Present and Future," in James Dator Archives; Rindzeviciute, *Power of System*.

regime interest in future research, but unfortunately an interest that also led to the active prosecution of futurists.[106] Ana Maria Catanus has described the fate of future research in Romania as a complicated play between official and unofficial forms of future research.[107] The Ceausescu regime made active use of forecasts, simulations, and models as tools for the building of a nationalist communist Romanian economy. Future studies were introduced in Romania as part of the import of Western methods and, in particular, management studies during the relative liberalization that followed Ceausescu's take over in 1966. This included an opening for both the Western policy sciences and the ongoing work on global simulation and modeling in the UN system. As a collaborative project with the UN and staffed by Western trained mathematicians, Ceausescu set up CEPECA, a new center for management techniques, the aim of which was to develop economic tools for developing societies and give them the tools with which to take the step from underdevelopment to development. Ceausescu saw Romania as the avant garde of the developing world, situated in a new global space between the Second and the Third world and defined by the idea of self sufficiency from Soviet communism. CEPECA became the platform for the introduction of prospective analysis and modeling of the Romanian economy. The head of the center was later minister of education and member of the Club of Rome, Mircea Malitsa.

Malitsa was a key figure in the import of Western future studies into Romania, with translations of futurists such as Alvin Toffler, Radovan Richta (Romania did not take part in the Warsaw pact invasion of Prague in 1968), John Naisbit, Edward Cornish, and Herman Kahn in the edition *Ideii Contemporanii.*[108] As Catanus shows, their exposure to Western methods of future research, modeling and systems analysis, led Romanian forecasters to initiate a debate on communism as an open or closed system. As future research developed as an academic activity under a, at first, benign dictatorship in Romania, it became a reflection on the possibility of plural future developments within the communist system, applied to ideas of different national roads of socialism, and possible divergent evolutions over time in communist society.[109]

In 1972, Romanian futurists held the Third World Future Research Conference in Bucharest under the auspice of Ceausescu.[110] The theme of the conference was the "common future of Man" under both systems.[111] A group of Romanian futurists under the direction of the mathematician Mihai Botez proposed to the conference

[106] In my interviews Eleonora Masini mentions intense surveillance and a very fearful atmosphere. Letter, James Dator archives about the Securitate surveillance of Botez.

[107] Ana Maria Catanus, "Official and Unofficial Futures of the Communist System," in *The struggle for the long term in transnational science and politics,* edited by Jenny Andersson and Egle Rindzeviciute, 169–89.

[108] See Mircea Malitsa, *Contemporanul cronica anului 2000* (Bucharest: Editura Politica, 1969).

[109] Pavel Apostol, "Marxism and the Structure of the Future," in *Futures*, 1972, September: 201–10, and Pavel Apostol, "Viitorul," in *Editura Stiiientifica si Enciclopedica* (Bucharest, 1977).

[110] *Viitorul Social. Management Science and Futures Studies in Socialist Roumania.* Special issue, World Future Research Conference in Bucharest 1972.

[111] Conference programme, "Third World Future Research Conference September 4–10. The Common Future of Man" (*Viitorul comun al oamenilor*), Bucharest, Socialist Republic of Romania, 1972; "Third World Future Research Conference. Announcement" 1–2, 1973. Spectacul de Gala, September 7, 1972, James Dator archives.

the creation of an International Center for Methodologican Research of Future and Development Studies.[112] The Center was pitched to Ceausescu by Johan Galtung during a personal visit in 1974. The idea was that the Center would work with the newly created World Futures Studies Federation and produce methodological research on world future problems with multinational teams. The Center was active from 1974 to 1977, the year in which Botez also lost his position and ventured into active dissidence.[113]

The Center for Methodological Research was intended to be the heart of management studies in Romania, and the center of a developing axis with the Third World. The Center worked with the National Institute for Science Technology and Development Studies in India and the Center for Economic and Social Research for the Third World in Mexico, both of which were important sites for developing forecasting, technological assessment, and reflections on socio economic models for the developing nations.[114] Its role was defined in one of the published newsletters as defining forecasts for each "development stage" and working out the conditions under which the national socialist model of Romania could be applied to Third World countries.[115] Forecasters held a special role in Ceausescu's vision of self sufficient development strategies, and the document "Ethical Commandments of Forecasting" produced in 1976 by the Center stated that the forecaster researcher "must put his forecasts to the benefit of the whole nation and to the problems of differences in wealth between the developed and the developing world. He must deliberately work out a strategy aimed at reducing these inequalities."[116] The core to this strategy was to counteract dominant images of Western modeling. In 1978, the Center produced one of the key counter images to the Club of Rome's *Limits to Growth* report, which was unacceptable to the regime in the light of Ceausescu's policies of forceful and brutal industrialization (the message of a halt to industrialization of the Limits report was unacceptable also to a large part of the developing world, see Chapter 8). A group of researchers in the Center, presided over by the now minister of education Malitsa, wrote the counter report *The Learning Report*, which argued that while there were limits to an ideological Western model of capitalist development, a socialist model based on STR had no given limits. Science, technology, and learning drew on inexhaustible forms of human creativity.[117]

The other leading futurist, Mihai Botez, turned future research into a platform for active dissidence. Botez began to understand official forecasts as creating a false

[112] Ionita Olteanu, "Researches on Future and Development in Romania," no date, James Dator archives. Ionita Olteanu was an economist who left Romania in 1985 and started doing future simulations for Siemens in West Germany. Olteanu to Dator, January 24, 1989.

[113] Mihai Botez, *Introducere in prospective* (Bucharest, 1971).

[114] International Center for Methodology of Future and Development Studies, newsletter, January–December 1984. James Dator papers.

[115] "Statement on Following up Activities to the Rome conference," 1973, James Dator archives.

[116] Constantin Ionescu and Mircea Ioanid, "Forecasting and Ethical Commandments," paper to WFSF conference in Dubrovnik in 1976.

[117] Malita, Bodkin, Elmandjra, *No Limits to Learning. Bridging the Human Gap. The Learning Report of the Club of Rome* (New York: the Club of Rome, 1978). In 1976 the Center also participated in Unitar's study, *Models for Achieving a New International Economic Order*, see Chapter 8. 1978.

image of reality while in fact they had catastrophic effects on Romania's future as its industrial policy destroyed the Romanian countryside.[118] In 1977, Botez left for the US, but he returned to Romania convinced that official forecasts had to be corrected by other publicly available images of the future. In 1979, he began sending open letters to the Party on the disastrous effects of industrialization on the exhaustion of raw materials, outside dependency on energy and currency, the destruction of peasant life in the Romanian country side, and ensuing famine. He also began broadcasting his criticism of official forecasts on Radio Free Europe. "The general strategy of development in Romania is wrong and is having devastating implications on Romania's future. This situation is generated by unrealistic economic forecasts and incorrect estimates of the country's resources and needs. The government is ignoring these facts and we continue to live in an atmosphere of unreality."[119] The broadcasts resulted in constant harassment by the Securitate. Despite this, Botez continued to publish articles in which he expressed his critique of the communist system inside a metaphorical language of mathematic formulae of predictions of system behavior. Botez' 1972 paper "Some Observations Regarding the Man Society Interaction," argued that man was both a product of society, and the creator of this society. Man and society should therefore be modeled as two separate systems, which would permit modellers to ask about their systemic interaction over time. Modeling, to Botez, was more democratic to forecasts because in a model, systems dynamics could be openly discussed. In contrast to a "monologue of forecasts" that aimed at setting out an image of objectivity, models did not have a "forecast operator," the human agent that could distort the image of the future. Models were, Botes argued, non-monological rhetorical devices that could be used to create a dialogue between the model and its audience (i.e. the Romanian public). If such modes of interaction between the models and their subjects could be created, there could also be a necessary atmosphere of rivalry between different models and debates. "I feel that were those man institutions social relationships placed under this angle of research, the possibility would be opened for a real correlation between understanding, exploration and action."[120] As Botez was pushed into dissidence, he became convinced that a communist system would in fact never allow for such open futures. In 1977, he published a paper in the journal *Policy Science* entitled "Cooperative Management of Force Induced International Situations—An Exercise in Formal Modelling," which argued, in mathematical equations, that the rationality of a decision depended on the number of active decision makers. A single decision maker would produce a perfectly

[118] In the Romanian version of "East-European Intellectuals and the National-Communist State: A View from Bucharest," published in 1993 in Bucharest under the title "Intelectualii din Europa de est," 119. Translation by Mihaela Ghisa. See also Mihai Botez, "A view from Eastern Europe", in *Technological Forecasting and Social Change*, 1984, 26: 121–6.

[119] Mihai Botez, "East European Intellectuals and the National Communist State," *Praxis International*, 1988, 3: 350–9, and Botez, interview on Radio Free Europe, "Romania: Stalinism in one country," 1988, cited in Catanus, "Official and Unofficial Futures," 181.

[120] Mihail Botes, "Some observations regarding the man society interaction," in archives of the world futures studies federation, Rome conference, James Dator papers. Mihail Botes, "A systems vision in futures research." Undated draft, Dator papers.

irrational decision.[121] The text "Undesirable vs. Desirable Societies," produced for the WFSF in 1983, similarly argued that a type A society was a society in which a desired future image could be created, projected, and shared by a plurality of participants. In a type B society, the future was determined by a select number and imposed by brutal force. Type B societies were societies of permanent future crisis. Botez also embarked on a highly audacious interview project with ordinary Romanian people about their visions and desires for the future.[122] In 1987 Botez was sent into internal exile.[123] His analysis of the communist system as a "second world" was published in Romanian in 1997. The second world, to Botez, was not a stable system but characterized by a set of disturbances. It did not conform to a specific historical law, but was held together by a nationalist political will. This will suffocated critique and free expression in a system that could never be stable.[124]

CONCLUDING REMARKS: FROM FUTUROLOGY TO PROGNOSTIKA

As revisionist socialists returned to the problem of the future, they brought back to life an abandoned utopian emphasis on the future as a central category of dissent and resistance. Projections of "open" vs "closed" became metaphorical descriptions of regime dynamics, and models were virtual allegories of citizen–regime interaction. As socialist forecasters thus reinvested the future with radical content, they projected a potentially open ended field, a space defined by human creativity and dreams of human fulfilment. As they brought back a concern with image and *gestalt* from historical philosophical legacies, they understood such images as having an important function in projecting hope and aspiration for a new socialist world. After 1968, such dreams of a human futurology were crushed by the dominating idea of forecasting as a tool of total planning in a vision of post-industrialism that was now harshly economistic. *Prognostika* was, as Vitezslav Sommer has shown, a management tool, a question of setting the long-term indicators for a high modernist "socialist society" in which was included, in the 1970s and 1980s, expert culture, management reforms and both consumption culture and a degree of market mechanisms. It was precisely as a management tool and a tool of market making, expert culture, and consultancy that future research would survive in the East bloc after 1989 and become a carrier of neoliberal reform.[125]

[121] Mihai Botez, "Cooperative Management of Force Induced International Situations, an Exercise in Formal Modeling," in *Policy Sciences*, 1977, 8: 455–68.

[122] Mihai Botez and Marina Celac, "Undesirable vs. Desirable Societies" (UN University, 1983).

[123] Ana Maria Catanus, "Breaking the Barriers of Romanian Conformism. Dissent and the Scientific Critique of Communism in Mathematician Mihai Botez Thinking," in *History of Communism in Europe*, special issue: "Avatars of Intellectuals," 2011, 2: 345–68.

[124] Catanus, "Official and unofficial futures", 185.

[125] See Johanna Bockman, *Markets in the Name of Socialism. The Left Wing Origins of Neoliberalism*, (Palo Alto: Stanford University Press, 2011); Gil Eyal, et al., *Making Capitalism without Capitalists: Class Formation and Elite Struggles in Post-Communist Central Europe* (London: Verso, 1998).

8

The Future of the World. The World Futures Studies Federation and the Future as Counter Expertise

> There is a danger that a better, more complex and informed grasp of things to come might become the monopoly of power groups served by experts in the new branch of futurism. Such a dangerous development is already well underway. At least four-fifths of work in this field has been ordered and financed by governmental departments, military establishments, or large corporations... Most developing nations seem to accept that their future lies in catching up with the present of the developed nations. Only the developed nations are defined as autonomous in the sense of having their own future. This means that it is in the power of the rich nations to define and refine the future and to propagate their images... This is power—he who has insight into the future also controls some of the present. For that reason it is absolutely essential that futures research is internationalized as quickly as possible... In general, to counterbalance and to control the new intellectual tools of anticipation, prognosis, and self-fulfilling predictions, a democratization of "future research" seems of great urgency. The one-sided use of technology and forecasting... can lead us right into new forms of totalitarianism. If we tamper with the time ahead of us, as we have already done with the space around us... if we spoil the future as we have spoiled the environment, then we are in for an epoch of despotism and desperation—a tyranny of a new modernistic type... This must not happen. The future belongs to all of us, not to small oligarchic groups or interests.[1]

TAKING FUTURE RESEARCH TO THE WORLD

In 1967, a conference was held in Oslo. The conference, held in a stunningly beautiful location overlooking the Oslo fjord, was entitled "Mankind 2000." The purpose of the meeting was nothing less than to find solutions for all of the world's great problems: hunger, urban sprawl, human alienation, war. The Mankind 2000 meeting was convened by the Norwegian sociologist and peace researcher Johan Galtung and the West German journalist Robert Jungk. Both Galtung and Jungk

[1] Robert Jungk and Johan Galtung, in Jungk and Galtung eds, *Mankind 2000* (Oslo, PRIO, 1968), 367–78, 378.

were icons of the global peace movement: Galtung was the whistle blower of Project Camelot and the creator of the Peace Research Institute in Oslo, and Jungk was the bestselling author of the history of the Manhattan project, *Brighter Than a Thousand Suns*.

1967 and 1968 were the high point of future research. By the late 1960s there existed several competing organizations and institutes for the future, including de Jouvenel's *Association internationale de futuribles* in Paris, Ossip Flechtheim's *Zentrum fur Zukunftsforschung* in Berlin, Robert Jungk's *Bibliothek fur Zukunftsfragen* in Salzburg, and the RAND outcrop, the Institute for the Future in Palo Alto. In 1967 the Council of Europe also created a research group for the future and in the year before, the Czech Richta group and the Polish group under Andrej Sicinski started working. UNESCO published, in the following year, a special issue of the International Journal of Social Science on futurology, and so did the popular journal *Science*. The prominent Czechoslovak Richta group was present in Oslo, and so were scholars with key positions in Soviet planning as members of the cybernetics group of the Soviet Academy of Science. Western futurists included the RAND futurologist Olaf Helmer, as well as Bertrand de Jouvenel, Fred Polak, and Ossip Flechtheim. Jungk's introduction to the conference stated that almost all of futures research had been conducted in the "idea factories" and "tanks" of the armament effort. The question was whether future research could somehow be turned into an effort to help the peaceful forces of the world. "In calling a conference dedicated to peace and development in the next decade, the organizers of the conference pointed to a new and urgent direction for futures research. Could the new intellectual tools of information technology, systems analysis, operational research, forecasting, anticipating, scenario writing, and futures creation be used on civilian problems? What then were the most important needs, what the resources, the human implications and the goals of such future shaping strategies?"[2]

If future research was to become part of an effort to solve all problems unfolding in the world future, the efforts of both blocs were needed and Jungk proposed that the two dominant strands of Marxist and positivist futures research had a common denominator in the idea of future research as social technology or "social prognosis." As shown in the previous chapter, it was as "prognosis," in other words as a planning technique, that forecasting had been accepted by Moscow as part of the rehabilitation of forms of social science and Soviet forecasters also used the term social prognosis to describe predictions of "universal" or "world" problems in transnational contexts. The Russian interest in forecast as social prognosis had followed developments in the US where forecasting was also described with the term social technology. In other words, future research as a technique for the shaping of the social world was common ground beyond ideological difference.

At the same time, the idea of future research as a technique for solving world problems had a certain radicality that surpassed Cold War competition. The title of the conference, Mankind 2000, expressed the hope of a new unified humanity beyond bipolarity. The idea of using future research as a dialogue or "bridge"

[2] Robert Jungk, preface to Robert Jungk, and Johan Galtung, eds, *Mankind 2000* (Oslo: 1968), i.

between the blocs was also timely. In 1966 and 1967, a number of efforts appeared that tried to break up the locked positions of the blocks in the name of a common world future. In 1967, preparations were underway for the creation of the Club of Rome, and many futurists were either members of the Club or personally acquainted with its initiator, the Italian industrial consultant Aurelio Peccei. Negotiations were also ongoing between American and Soviet interests, led by Shepard Stone and Germen Gvishiani, for the creation of the Institute for Applied Systems Analysis, IIASA, in Vienna. IIASA was created in 1972, with the aim of operating indeed as a "bridge" across the Iron Curtain and developing systems analytical approaches to "common" or "world" problems, similar to how the Club of Rome would focus on computer modeling as the solution to what they labeled the "world problematique."[3] In the year before the Prague spring, East European futurists were still at some liberty. 1967 and 1968 were the high points of future research and for a renewed optimism in planning, including the idea that entire world developments could be foreseen and planned for. The Mankind 2000 volume, published in 1968 by Jungk and Galtung and distributed widely in futurist networks, became a staple of future research. The report presented the effort at cross-curtain collaboration as a manifest success. Through the conference, Eastern and Western futurists had discovered a mutual interest in future research as something that could indeed solve all the world's current problems. As Western and Eastern futurists discovered a shared sense of purpose, they emerged, in the words of RAND mathematician Olaf Helmer, as a "new breed of modern day constructive utopians, who will invent not only better futures, but the social instrumentalities of attaining them".[4]

The idea of future research as a form of problem solving on the global level hid, however, profound differences. The Mankind 2000 conference was the first scientific manifestation of what was by the late 1960s coming together under the label "future(s) studies." The chapter examines future studies as a central form of protest against Cold War world order and proposes that future studies carried a manifest utopian dimension for the Cold and post-Cold War era with its projection of the need to transcend bipolarity and create a field of action on the global level. Future studies were a rejection of futurology, although as we will see this rejection was by no means clear cut. They embodied certain key epistemological principles, the most important one being that the future could not be predicted, but had to be actively created. Future studies also insisted that the future was not *one*, but always plural, as, to futurists, the world had many different possible futures.

This was both a philosophical postulate and an empirical problem. By the late 1960s, the assumptions of modernization theory—that world developments followed a predictable trajectory with foreseeable outcomes—were in crisis. The first

[3] Egle Rindzeviciute, "Purification and Hybridisation of Soviet Cybernetics: The Politics of Scientific Governance in an Authoritarian Regime," *Archiv für Sozialgeschichte*, 2010, 50: 289–309; Leena Riska Campbell, *Bridging East and West: The Establishment of the International Institute for Applied Systems Analysis (IIASA) in the United States Foreign Policy of Bridge Building, 1964–1972* (Helsinki: Helsinki University Press, 2011), 108–9.

[4] Helmer quoted by Jungk, preface.

element of this crisis was the disqualification of the presumed opposition between modernization and traditionalism as the two possible futures of the global mass. By the 1960s, the decolonization process had thoroughly shaken such assumptions. Where modernization theorists saw elements of world chaos, futurists saw embryos of alternative world futures that embodied hope, resistance, and a promise of global emancipation. Futurology was a reflection on a bipolar and dichotomous world order in which movements and actions could be predicted as part of a struggle between two systems. Futures studies, on the other hand, were an active reflection on a multipolar, interdependent, and truly global world.[5] As such they also rejected the idea that Western socio economic models could be applied to the developing world, and engaged instead in various activities designed to unleash or put in motion indigenous, alternative, and dormant future models for the developing world. Futures studies stood in an activist mode to this projected multiplicity of world futures. If the outcomes of the process of world development could not be proscribed and predicted as implied in an overall notion of modernization, then the range of emergent world futures had to be studied in a great catalogue of possible developments. This was a profoundly normative undertaking, and as futurists set out to design and promote "visions of desirable societies," the problem of desirability that had been discovered in early predictive experimentation came back to bite its own tail.

Desirability was a central problem in futures studies, and as shown in Figure 8.1, the Mankind 2000 symbol linked desirable futures to possible and realizable futures in a holy trinity. Futures studies were a radicalization of the first wave of futurism. As discussed in Chapter 3, 1950s and early 1960s futurism had a nostalgic and romantic streak, through which futurism appeared as a project for the restoration of a human civilization cut loose from history by the disruptive forces of war, science

Figure 8.1. The Mankind 2000 Trinity of Possible, Desirable, and Realizable Futures.
(Mankind 2000 letterhead, Mankind 2000 materials, Committee for Nuclear Disarmament and Peace archives, box 700.)

[5] See Johan Galtung, "On the Future of the International System" (formally published in the *Journal of Peace Research*, 1967, 305–33), in R. Jungk and J. Galtung, *Mankind 2000*, 1968, 12–41.

and technology. Reconstituting the human experience of *being*, was imagined as an active process drawing on innovation and design. As such it had a radical component, although this radicality differed significantly between the romantic notions of Lewis Mumford and the techno-utopianism of Marshall McLuhan. But post-war futurism drew on a historic legacy of liberal and Christian concepts of human existence. As we have seen, the emphasis on a rupture and the idea that there were no longer any mobilizing images of the future was central to the idea of a pervasive crisis of human existence in the first wave of futurist writings by Jungk, Polak, and Mumford. The influence of critical systems theories, ecologism, and revisionist Marxism from the late 1960s on changed this nostalgic dimension to futurism, which developed from its post-war reflections on the future as *being*, into a critique of the world as *system*. Meanwhile, it can be proposed that reflections on system, world order, and future transposed the phenomenological notion of being to the aggregate level of the world. The world system was, to futurists, an artifact, a product of human design. Composed of a set of antagonistic relationships and fractures, it was the mirror image of an also fractured humanity. Changing this world system meant changing humanity.[6]

THE IMAGE

Systems analysis, ecologism, and peace research were all fundamental inputs to futures studies as they developed from the mid 1960s on. Systems analysis was a highly complex body of thought, composed both of mechanistic and organic notions.[7] It had a wide range of applications. Systems tools reiterated, in many ways, classical tensions in social science of the world as malleable or fixed, reflected in notions of a closed vs. an open system. Systems theory also stood in a complicated relationship with emerging notions of globality. As systems analysis influenced networks of planning by the late 1960s, its postulates of a closed vs. open system, prone to equilibrium or disequilibrium, betrayed ideas of world and world order as static or dynamic. The Club of Rome report in 1972 popularized ecological systems notions that had much longer origins in biology and climatology.[8] Parallel to this development and driven by intellectual developments in development economics, international relations theory, and peace and conflict studies, was the projection of the planet-world as a social system, a constituted fabric of social relations in an interdependent whole. As future studies transposed forecasting methods to the social and political system of the world, they carried a systems logic to the global level.

[6] Compare Or Rosenboim, *The Emergence of Globalism* (Princeton NJ: Princeton University Press, 2017), 1–15.

[7] See Hunter Heyck, 2016, *Age of System*; David Mendell, *Between Human and Machine. Feedback, Control and Computing Before Cybernetics* (Baltimore: Johns Hopkins University Press, 2002).

[8] Donatella Meadows et al., *The Limits to Growth* (Washington: Club of Rome, 1972); Elodie Vielle Blanchard, *Les limites à la croissance dans un ordre global* (Ph.D. diss, Paris: EHESS, 2011); Peter Moll, *From Scarcity to Sustainability. Futures Studies and the Environment: The Role of the Club of Rome* (Brussels: Peter Lang, 1991).

While most academic works on systems analysis have understood it as an engineers' view onto the social world, systems analysts could mix in a remarkable utopian quality in their conceptions of planning and system design. Systems analysis helped shift the focus of future research from the East West dimension to the North South divide, and as a consequence, the problem of development began to be thought of as a systemic imbalance, a suboptimal outcome of the sum of world relationships. According to systems theorists such as the fascinating Armenian born Hasan Ozbekhan, who designed the first world model for the Club of Rome, the system's logic imposed the view that development in one part of the system corresponded to underdevelopment in another. Ozbekhan was a software engineer from the Systems Development Corporation in Santa Monica, but his ideas of a World Plan that could set the skewed nature of the world right went far beyond ideas of social technology as they had dominated future research at RAND (indeed they were also too radical for the Club of Rome).[9] Furthermore, if problems of war, hunger, and environmental collapse were problems of disequilibrium within a systems logic, then it was also possible to project a future state of equilibrium at a point further down the axis of time. The relevant question then became how the system could be bumped from one state to another.

This was a crucial question not only for systems analysis but also for world order studies. Notions of "world" and "world order" exploded in frequency in the period from 1945. As Rosenboim shows, they were carriers of deeply loaded notions of political organization, moral order, and human destiny.[10] Mark Mazower and Duncan Bell have proposed that notions of world order, originating in late nineteenth century and interwar discourses of civilization and empire, reproduced notions of biological harmony and white imperial moral order.[11] But in the period from the mid 1950s on, world order designated a plethora of initiatives to rethink and remodel the world into a utopian and global category. Among many world associations, world societies, and world federations and societies we can count the Quaker Societies of Friends, the World Order Education Project, the World Institute, Friends for the World, World Councils, the World Order Fund, and Harold Lasswell's World Order Model Project. Not all, but many of these, were religious and mostly associated with the global peace movement, including the ecumenical World Council of Churches, and the Quaker World Friends Society. In these, the notion of Mankind expressed utterly symbolic meaning as a question of profound spiritual unity or world consciousness. While these initiatives fell back in many cases on older legacies of world government and world federalism, in the 1950s and 1960s

[9] Hazan Ozbekhan, *The Predicament of Mankind* (New York: Club of Rome, 1970).

[10] Rosenboim, *The Emergence of Globalism*, 2–18.

[11] Mark Mazower, *Governing the World. The History of an Idea* (London: Penguin Books, 2012), 97, 99; Akira Iriye, *Cultural Internationalism and World Order* (Baltimore: John Hopkins Press, 1997), 7; Duncan Bell, ed., *Victorian Visions of Global Order. Empire and International Relations in 19th Century Political Thought* (Cambridge: Cambridge University Press, 2007).

they need to be described as openly utopian projects that aimed actively to find mechanisms of world change.[12]

Important here was the shift from ideas of a world order, to ideas of a dynamic world system. World order studies reflected the idea that the system was an organized global hierarchy made up of power relationships between nation states, or even between classes in a global division of labour. Peace studies were an old area of philosophical interest. But World Order Studies were an outcrop from so called conflict studies, a field of behavioural investigation created by the Ford Foundation in the 1950s, in particular around the Center for Advanced Studies in Behavioural Science in Palo Alto. In the 1960s, conclusions from conflict studies married peace research to become a new field of peace and conflict research.[13] The focal point of study changed, from the idea of prevention of war to the altogether different problem of creating enduring peace. This was understood as relying on a very different temporal logic, and it therefore drew on a new future horizon. Where conflict studies had asked the question of what was needed to prevent war, as an undesirable but highly probable state, and come up with various notions of successful and unsuccessful strategies and games, peace research asked how peace, as an, on the contrary, improbable but deeply desirable state, could be achieved. What would have to change in the current system for it to promote peaceful values? As such, peace and conflict studies projected a future horizon as a distant goal, a long-term horizon which was far beyond Cold War strategy and situated in the sphere of imagined desired goals.[14] Implicit in both notions of system and world order was thus a notion of temporality and direction, as the system was structured around an overarching value, objective, or indeed image, which was either a source of stability, or a potential source of radical discontinuity and the basis for a shift from one order to another.

In peace and conflict research, quite like in development studies, postulates of modernization theory were turned on their head, as value change was no longer understood as the outcome of a given sociotechnical process but as an undetermined, conscious, and fundamentally social process depending on an active choice of future. The "image" shaped both the status quo of the Cold War world, and its potential for radical transition, as world order reflected the inner psyches and value systems of those human beings who had shaped the world in their image. As both world system and world order were understood as made up of "psychosociological" values, this world image was in fact the reflection of humanity. Aggressive people shaped an aggressive world, while peaceful people might create a world different altogether. As a great volcano of world-order activities erupted from 1955 on, they

[12] Adam Freeman, "The World Order Model Project," unpublished; Frank Fischer, et al., *Handbook of Critical Policy Studies* (Edward Elgar, 2015). There were plenty of direct contacts between the Mankind 2000 project and WOMP, see correspondence in Jungk's archives with Sam Mendlowitz and the later journal *Alternatives*.

[13] See Paul Erickson, *The World the Game Theorists Made* (Chicago: Chicago University Press, 2015), 163–73.

[14] Kenneth Boulding, Seminar on the Resolution of Conflict, abstract of the first meeting, February 14, 1956. Kenneth Boulding papers, box 41.

had in common a not unproblematic amalgamation between social psychological descriptions of the workings of individual human beings, and projections of Mankind as a collective entity suffering also from serious behavior disorders. Where the first generation of futuristic thinking emphasized a process of pedagogical reform of Man himself, futurists such as Johan Galtung would launch large scale value studies of global populations and their future images.[15] Some elements of future studies developed into virtual global psychotherapies.

THE FUTURE AS RADICAL IMAGINATION

As demonstrated in Chapter 3, many futurists came to futurism from the conclusion that there were no longer any mobilizing images of the future. Indeed, this is what led them to conceptualize the future as a problem of active human design and as something that had to be reinvented in order to return humanity to a sense of time, history, and orientation. From this point, future studies took the (neo)utopian idea of the future as a fundamental category of action for the Cold War world further and into the field of social movement activism. The intellectual historian Samuel Moyn has argued that utopianism changed focus after 1945, as World War II had discredited historical utopias of liberalism and communism. To Moyn, the struggle for human rights emerged as a substitute utopia, a conversion of previous dreams of model societies that could no longer mobilize humanity.[16] At the same time it can be argued that utopia, in the sense of a calling for action in the name of a better future and as a necessary escape from "the end," was an integral element in 1960s and 1970s social movements—pacifism, feminism, post colonialism, ecologism, post-Marxism, New Age communitarianism. These movements were fundamentally committed to the possibility of radical system change, and often appealed to interests beyond nation, projected on a universal or global scale.[17] They had in common a systems critical element which permitted them to think of world problems as problems not only of global power relations, but as problems of human design and irrationality.

Meanwhile, they also placed utopia—the imagined world and the process of reaching it—within humanity itself, and so future studies were a continuation of Lewis Mumford's notion that utopia was the process of forging a new futures-oriented world consciousness. While the first wave of futurism in the early 1950s made vague declarations of future pedagogy and world federation as the tools with which to shape this consciousness, future studies were quintessentially concerned with the techniques and methods of future crafting. Futurists saw utopia as having two logical steps. First, it depended on the radical deconstruction of existing futures, in other words the escape from existing projections of power balance and status quo. Second, as a result of such radical deconstruction, new images of the

[15] See Johan Galtung, et al. *Images of the World in the Year 2000.*

[16] Samuel Moyn, *The Last Utopia. Human Rights in History* (Cambridge MA: Harvard University Press, 2010).

[17] Akira Iriye, *Global Community: The Role of International Organizations in the Making of the Contemporary World* (Berkeley: University of California Press, 2002).

future could be created that might act as radical imperatives to undo what futurists understood as hegemonic forms of expertise that constrained world futures, and replace these with a new kind of global future participation.

Where the idea of scientific prediction, as discussed in Chapter 5, was based on a pre-eminent conception of rationality, future studies identified the human imagination as the source of alternative worlds and as the inspiration for a new set of methods. The problem of the future, as put by the science fiction writer Arthur C. Clarke, was a problem of the "lack of imagination."[18] Technical solutions and knowhow to deal with human needs ranging from the basic to the advanced were already in place in the 1960s world—or at least, they were confidently predicted to be in place in the coming decade. Solving future problems was thus not a question of technology, but a question of the ability to project imaginative solutions onto world problems. Clarke was not present at the 1967 conference, but his science fiction was an important influence on future studies and in 1962, Clarke published the book, *Profiles on the Future, an Inquiry into the Limits of the Possible*, on futurists and their methods of future research. The very concept of alternative worlds is important here: alternative worlds were the worlds that could not be forecast by scientific reason but could be reached through the act of imagination. All forms of activities that could act as triggers on the human imagination were therefore acceptable and laudable.

Robert Jungk, in a series of writings in the 1960s, argued that future research had to draw on the creative imagination, and should have the task of imagining radical departures from the sets of continuities of the present.[19] Art, phantasy, and imagination could bring about a new "state of mind" capable of conjuring a different future. "Creative imagination is not content with extending, combining, or negating already existing trends. It attempts, by breaking out of the existing system or counter system, to strike out on a completely new course breaking radically with prevalent concepts. The creative imagination gives rise to a new era."[20] In other texts, notably in dialogue with Erich Fromm, Jungk argued that fantasy and imagination were the only remaining forms of resistance.[21]

As illustrated by the influence of Clarke, there were direct links between future studies and science fiction. This link was stronger in the US, where Clarke's screenplay to *2001, A Space Odyssey* was discussed as a genuine attempt at futurism.[22] Several

[18] Clarke cited by D. Livingston, "The Study of Science Fiction as Forecasting Methodology," *Proceedings of the International Conference in Future Research,* Kyoto, 1970, 71–9.

[19] "Phantasie und Zukunftsforschung", Robert Jungk Nachlass, box 7.

[20] Jungk, "The Role of Imagination in Future Research," *Proceedings of the International Future Research Conference,* Kyoto, 1970, 1–7, 6.

[21] Undated newspaper clipping, *Neue Deutschland Zeitung,* "Immer wider Neu Beginnen"; Press release, "Phantasie und Zukunftsforschung," Kosmos Pressedienst, March 8, 1970; Undated transcript, Jungk and Erich Fromm in dialogue. Robert Jungk Nachlass, box 7, folder 4.

[22] See D. Livingston, "The Study of Science Fiction as Forecasting Methodology," *Proceedings of the International Conference in Future Research,* Kyoto, 1970, 71–9.

Andrew Butler, "Futurology," in *Oxford Handbook of Science Fiction,* 2011, 521. Clarke understood himself as part of futurological thinking, while, in contrast, Isaac Asimov refused the idea of prediction. Asimov's dark visions of humanity and his plea to create a "law of robotics" governing man–machine relationships fell outside of futurology.

science fiction writers were members of the World Futures Studies Federation and the World Future Society (created in Washington in 1972).[23] Science fiction was of course not as such a protest against Cold War world order.[24] Much of Cold War science fiction was a reproduction of technological trends and visions of human powers extended (Clarke is a good example of precisely this, and Clarke embraced the notion of futurology, while for instance Isaac Asimov or Stanislav Lem rejected futurology).[25] For European futurists, science fiction was one of a number of mind altering techniques or "jumps of the imagination" that they identified, along with journalism, theatre, or psychoanalysis, as having the power to break the "strait-jackets" of the present and move beyond the boundaries of rationality.[26] As such it was part of what Jungk called "social fantasy" and identified as having a function of critical epistemology. As seen in Chapter 2, the struggle against the bomb from the late 1950s included the idea that the armament process was determined by a set of technological and scientific logics that could only be broken through the imagination. A telegram from Gunther Anders to Jungk in preparation of the Easter March against Atomic weapons in West German Dalem in 1959 reads "only if we are not afraid of truth, but on the contrary bring up our courage to use the horizon of our fantasy so that we can imagine what we could create if we were to regard remote peoples and future*s* as our neighbours..."[27] Like Jungk, Anders, the defender of world government, thought that world problems were only solvable through the creation of a new world community, and the links of love and friendship creating this community had first to be imagined.

At the time of the Mankind conference in 1967, the notion of the imagination had gone through a significant radicalization, following the publication of Marcuse's *One Dimensional Man*. The Mankind 2000 conference included a number of futurists who were, like Jungk and Ossip Flechtheim, central to the European and in particular German New Left.[28] For them, imagination was an anti systemic force. *One Dimensional Man* included a call to the imagination as the only way of breaking out of the constant reification of reality in high capitalist society. "Fiction calls the facts by their name and their reign collapses."[29] *One Dimensional Man* was the conclusion of reflections around utopia, imagination, and system that Marcuse

[23] Stanislav Lem, *The Futurological Congress*, (New York: Houghton Mifflin Harcourt, 1985 (originally published in 1971, published in English in 1974)).

[24] See Sonja Fritzche, East Germany's "Werkstatt Zukunft": Futurology and the Science Fiction Films of "defa-futurum" in *German Studies Review*, 2006, 367–86.

[25] John Hall, *Apocalypse. From Antiquity to the Empire of Modernity* (London: John Wiley & Sons, 2013), 209–20. Rebecca Lemov, "Hypothetical Machines. The Science Fiction Dreams of Cold War Science," *Isis*, 2010, 101 (2): 401–11; Sharon Ghamari Tabrizi, *The Worlds of Herman Kahn* (Cambridge MA: Harvard University Press, 2005).

[26] Jungk, "The Role of the Imagination in Future Research."

[27] ... *sodass wir vorstellen können was wir anstellen könnten*, Gunther Anders to Robert Jungk, 1959, Robert Jungk Nachlass, box 17. Holger Nehring, *Politics of Security. British and West German Protest Movements and the Early Cold War* (Oxford: Oxford University Press, 2013), 235f.

[28] R. Jungk, and H.J. Mundt, *Deutschland ohne Konzeption? Am Beginn einer neuen Epoche* (Munich, 1964); Elke Seefried, "Towards *the Limits to Growth*? The Book and Its Reception in West Germany and Britain, 1972–73," in *Bulletin of the German Historical Institute London*, 2011, 33 (1): 3–37, 26.

[29] Herbert Marcuse, *One Dimensional Man. Studies in the Ideology of Advanced Industrial Society*, (New York: Beacon Press 1964), 62.

had begun in Frankfurt before the exile of the Institute for Social Research, with the aim of inscribing Husserlian and Heideggerian phenomenology within the dialectical tradition—in other words situating the notion of *being* within a Marxian systems logic.[30] Marcuse's notion of the Establishment came back in some of the more critical futurists' labeling of RAND futurology as "establishment futurology," designed to complete the transition to one dimensional man by obliterating any human capacity to imagine a different future. "I am convinced that as soon as we can predict human behavior, we have reached the one dimensional society..." The opposite of establishment futurology was "critical futurology"—part of a "cultural revolution... (to) bring out the agency of Man," and opposing the way that "dominant cultures tried to extrapolate themselves and their interests into time." Critical futurists were not social engineers such as the social technicians of the RAND Corporation, but rather, "somebody who plays a role in the whole process of the liberation of Man from the ties of his destructive, authoritarian and repressive society."[31] For futurists of this radical persuasion, future research could not be part of planning, in which social changes were directed and steered in relation to economic and technological processes, but was rather a radical infusion of civil society organization and community work and an element in the organization of grassroots social movements within the broader New Left.

Chapter 9 returns to the divisions between the European New Left and an emerging American libertarianism in future studies. Jungk was involved in a range of social movements including the peace movement and the Green movement, but not a Marxist. He describes, in an undated letter, his understanding of future research as revolutionary in the sense of Thomas Kuhn's conception of scientific paradigms, and Marxist future research as one orientation in a field of critical currents. Van Steenbergen on the other hand was a Marxist, member of the Dutch Catholic Churches Left movement and the so called Werkgroep 2000 which protested against the institutionalization of future research in planning in the Netherlands through Jan Tinbergen.

RESHAPING ACTIVISM: FUTURE RESEARCH AND SOCIAL SCIENCE

Future studies were the product of a particular constellation between the new systems critical approaches in the social sciences, many of which were, like peace and conflict studies, avatars of Cold War Science, and new forms of activism in the global peace movement. Peace research was both an academic discipline and global militancy, as peace research institutes and journals had a direct link to the

[30] Martin Jay, *The Dialectical Imagination. A History of the Frankfurt School and the Institute for Social Research* (Berkeley: University of California Press, 1996), 212–17; Douglas Kellner, "One Dimensional Man. Introduction to the second edition," in Herbert Marcuse, *One Dimensional Man* (Abingdon: Routledge, 1991), 11–13.

[31] Bart van Steenbergen, "Critical and Establishment Futurology," in *Proceedings From the International Future Research Conference*, Kyoto, 1970: 93–103, 101.

organization of the antinuclear struggle in 1966 and 1967. As such future studies were an attempt to hold together a research undertaking that in fact straddled two directly opposite sides of the Cold War divide, and the first conference in Oslo included not only futurists from both Western countries and the East bloc, but also both futurologists with a background in war strategy and futurists from the peace movement. It followed from this state of affairs that no easy consensus on what "social prognosis" really meant could be found among the futurists that gathered in Oslo. Not all futurists shared the belief that future research was part of a new Leftist anti Establishment crusade, nor that it should have as its main role to launch a cultural revolution against the forces of science and technology. An indignant letter from the father of technological forecasting, Eric Jantsch to Robert Jungk reads, "Wenn wir uns in dem uns gemeinsam interesserienden Gebiet der Zukunftforschung nicht treffen konnen ohne dass Sie ihre gesamte Welt mitbringen und mich dieses Schlamassel mit hineinzuziehen versuchen, dann muss ich zu meinem Bedauern zu Hause blieben": "If we cannot meet to discuss our common interest, future research, without you trying to draw me into your whole mess of a world, then with much regret I shall stay at home."[32]

The first world future research conferences that took place between 1967 and 1973 were a magnificent epistemological battlefield as futurologists and futurists clashed on where future research should be placed ideologically, and how it stood in relation to social science, planning, and activism. The list of participants in the 1967 conference included Kenneth Boulding, Edward Cornish (President of the World Future Society), Peter Croose (secretary of the Teilhard du Chardin Foundation), Henry David (of the National Science Foundation), John Dixon (of the Education Division of Xerox), Ossip Flechtheim, Galtung, Glagolev, Theodor Gordon (now Director of Advance Space Stations and Planetary Systems at Douglas Aircraft Company in California), Olaf Helmer, Jungk, the psychotherapist Stanley Lesse, John McHale (Director of the World Resources Inventory), Hasan Ozbekhan, Fred Polak, Andrej Sicinski, John Voss (of the American Academy of Arts and Science), and Arthur Waskow (from the Institute for Policy Studies, Washington). Among preliminary participants were Lewis Mumford, Erich Fromm, Harold Lasswell, Dennis Gabor, and Nicholas Sombart. Among these futurists were a first group of liberal thinkers linked to military and governmental activity and American behavioral research. They understood future research as part of a piecemeal social engineering for social welfare purposes, but their roots could often be found in military establishments such as RAND. A second group were revisionist Marxists who saw future research as critical utopia studies, a dialectical comparison between ideological objectives and realities of human existence. This included most of the Western new Left, including the Christian ecologist Jungk, as well as the Richta group. The latter, in turn, had certain affinities with a third group, which included prominent theorists of planning, including Hazan Ozbekhan and the Dutch Jan Tinbergen. Both saw future research as a value-oriented form of metaplanning or World Plan, concerned with the overarching objectives of world development, and

[32] Eric Jantsch, letter to Robert Jungk, September 9, 1967. Robert Jungk Nachlass, box 7.

based on a systems' view of planetary interaction. In addition, the first conferences included a motley crew of participants who were journalists, psychologists, neuroscientists, computer scientists, or consultants.[33] Futurists had, in sum, totally different ideas of the relevance of future research for the world—but they shared a strategic interest in techniques and methods.

The core of the early conferences was the question of the relationship between scientific prediction—futurology—and futures studies as a normative and utopian project based on the imagination. This debate focused on the crux of whether future research was a science, an art, or a craft. An argument existed between Flechtheim, the original father of the concept of futurology, and Bertrand de Jouvenel, the inventor of *conjecture.*[34] Flechtheim's notion of futurology did not denote an academic discipline, but an alternative to the grand theories of history of liberalism and Marxism, both of which he understood as falsely dressing up ideological goals as scientific ones. The purpose of futurology was to show that both liberalism and Marxism projected objectives that were unfit for human ends, and then proceed to invent other and more congruent societal objectives.[35] In 1969 Flechtheim created for this purpose the Zentrum Berlin Zukunftsfragen, which tried to bring together West European and East European futurology in Berlin. Flechtheim's perspective was thus most different from the distinctly liberal argument of conjecture put forward by de Jouvenel, who saw conjecture as an "art" of political prediction and as belonging in the sphere of policy advice and expertise through "look out institutions."[36] As discussed in Chapter 4, the idea had initially been discussed at a RAND seminar between de Jouvenel, Helmer, and Ozbekhan. In 1972, de Jouvenel became the first president of the World Futures Studies Federation, but de Jouvenel was heavily criticized at the 1967 conference for the liberal leanings of conjecture.[37] Fred Polak had moved from the conclusions of his 1956 book, *The Image*, to consider the role of future images in the planning process. Constructing images of the future translated, in the activities of Polak's institute, HIFI, in Hague, as the setting of the "goal of goals," the highest hierarchical objective of social development. The goal of goals was the desired, possible, and realizable utopia towards which all of social action should lead.[38] HIFI was put out of competition by other Dutch planning initiatives, in particular the Central Plaan created by Jan Tinbergen.[39] HIFI was nevertheless intended as a very different institution than

[33] "List of participants, International Future Research Inaugural Conference, Vuksenasen, Oslo, 12–15 September 1967," Robert Jungk Nachlass, box 31.

[34] Letters between de Jouvenel and Flechtheim, July 4 and 24, August 18, 1964, May 5, 1966. Bertrand de Jouvenel papers, correspondence files.

[35] Ossip Flechtheim in *Mankind 2000.*

[36] "The Lookout Institution," 1967, Robert Jungk Nachlass, box 30.

[37] Letter from the Romanian Delegation to the UNESCO Director General, May 16, 1972; letter from John I. Forbes, UNESCO undersecretary, to Pavel Apostol, August 9, 1972 UNESCO archives, box 1972/001 A506(498)71 *Federation mondiale des études du futur.*

[38] Fred Polak, "Towards the Goal of Goals," in *Mankind 2000,* 307–31. See Fred Polak, *Prognostics: A Science in the Making* (Amsterdam: Elsevier, 1971).

[39] Jenny Andersson and Anne Greet Keizer, "Governing the Future: Science, Policy and Public Participation in the Construction of the Long Term in the Netherlands and Sweden," in *History and Technology*, 2014, 30(1–2): 104–22.

de Jouvenel's Look Out institution. The setting of the goal of goals was a matter of social dialogue between social scientists, planners, policy makers, and citizens. It took place through a process that Polak considered scientific, because it made use of social science rationality, but also normative, as it led this rationality to "unswervingly committed ends." For Polak this made normative planning (forecasting) an alternative, and in fact metascience, to established social science. Social science, following in the footsteps of Comte, Weber, and Parson was totally inapt in dealing with coming, and not yet existing developments.

> For social science, tomorrow does not really exist. The future cannot be observed, nor at present be verified. The future is unknown and unknowable. Social science has no clear criteria for assessing trends and their goals, no valid instrument for justly arbitrating between optional social preferences and cultural priorities. It cannot choose without bias and prejudice, nor give any responsible direction, without discrimination, to anyone of different courses of action. It can do no more than impersonally, dispassionately, and neutrally try to explain what *is* happening and perhaps in part why, but not participate in discerning, let alone deciding as to what might happen, and even less what should happen. It can under no circumstances go any further than to examine what eventually may be the most effective means to best reach a given end, taken for granted. About the ulterior ends themselves it has to keep utterly silent... It cannot function as a model builder or shape shifter, it keeps resolutely to the antiquated positions of the 19th century economist, and the field is abandoned to the free play of other forces.[40]

The ultimate consequence of the successful exportation of Parsonian systems theory from the US to the European continent was that social science, which had developed understandings of the historical conditions of past revolutions, had given up on the preconditions of possible future value revolutions. Listening rather, to the pleas of sociologists such as C. Wright Mills, futures research should bring back into social science the world of normative affairs and act for "willful and controlled changeability": changes of the social system in compliance with an ideal preconceived image of the future. "That cannot be described as an 'art' any more."[41]

The idea that futures research had to be a critical metascience of social science and act as the shaper of essential forms of social change was a postulate that Polak shared most notably with Johan Galtung, but also with the American sociologist John McHale. John and Magda McHale founded the Center for Integral Studies in California in 1966. The Center was based on inspiration from Kenneth Boulding's vision of the social sciences as integrated disciplines.[42] We will return to the Center for Integral studies in the next chapter, as it was one of the early future consultancies focusing on "exploring the infinite potential of man" by recourse to management techniques, holistics, and neuroscience. Boulding, a pioneer in conflict research as well as ecological and human economics, wrote, in 1956, the book, *The Image*, in which he presented his alternative to Parsonian systems theory. The human system was not, to Boulding, a set of functional and rational relationships, but structured

40 Polak, "Towards the Goal of Goals", 328.

41 Polak, "Towards the Goal of Goals."

42 Center for Integral Studies, presentation, McHale collection, James Dator archives.

by love and reciprocal feeling.[43] Integral studies strove to unite the disciplines and all areas of human ingenuity around an active exploration of the potential of Man. As argued by McHale, the social sciences, in their applied and behavioral turn, had made social change into their object of study, but they had not tried to create it. The social sciences represented, therefore, a quintessentially pessimistic project, devoted to human anxieties and fears and to the fundamental limitations to human experience, and not to the actual area of interest—the limitlessness of human potential. For instance, social science had developed quintessentially pessimistic theories of post industrialism (such as the one in process by Daniel Bell), which depicted change as the breakdown of established value systems, but not as creative newness and value invention. Futures research had to invert these postulates, so as to ensure the "availability of multiple choices for the greatest number of men." "The future may be literally as we choose to view it, and the conscious degree to which we may materially control our future is quite unprecedented. Our need, therefore is to widen the process and objectives of social and cultural forecasting so as to expand rather than diminish our range of choices and options."[44] From this perspective, futures research was a radical "social design," a "software" through which "we may apply our developed technological capacities to the fullest advantage." Chapter 9 returns to the John and Magda McHale's idea of Man as full of potential and a "cosmonaut of the future," but from this perspective, a central role of futures research should be therefore accorded to social innovation, to the understanding and redesign of social forms and to the exploration of new forms of social organization and new communities, such as the new utopian populations springing up in Western youth collectives or new models of development for the developing world.[45]

DATA-IN-BEING

Future studies were conceived as a kind of counter expertise, a counter hegemonic project to Cold War prediction. For critical or radical futurists, the postulates of future research were thus turned on their head, so that the idea of social technology became a question of using forms of future knowledge as a way of actively shaping and "willing" coming developments. This meant that no events or trends could be regarded as predetermined. Radical futurists rejected not only the idea of prediction, but also the idea that the future could be studied by recourse to established forms of observation and that there was any such thing as a future fact. They turned de Jouvenel's notion of *futuribles* into the significantly different idea of "data-in-being." Data-in-being was different from ideas of artificial or synthetic fact, as produced

[43] Kenneth E. Boulding, *The Image* (Ann Arbor: University of Michigan Press, 1956); Philippe Fontaine, "Stabilizing American Society: Kenneth Boulding and the Integration of the Social Sciences, 1943–1980," in *Science in Context,* 2010, 23 (2): 221–65.

[44] John McHale, "Problems in Social and Cultural Forecasting," *Proceedings of the International Future Research Conference*, Kyoto, 1970, 9–17, 16.

[45] McHale papers, James Dator archives.

by gaming, simulation, and scenarios. Artificial facts were forms of hypothetical fact deriving from observations of experimental social situations and intended to complement rationality assumptions as to the regularities of human behavior. Data-in-being were forms of fact that might trigger new social situations. In this they were similar to *futuribles*, but to de Jouvenel, *futuribles* were the potentially threatening factoids hiding revolutionary sparks in the global mass. For Robert Jungk, who saw future research essentially as a form of social experimentation, fact and data as conventionally understood was historically grounded in past experience. Such forms of knowledge were hopelessly reiterating, therefore, "something that is already dead" and by reproducing this dead body into the social science analysis of present and future society, it condemned the future to the past and made it impossible for social science to contribute to the analysis of new evolutions. Future research required, instead, metadata, "data-in-being," by which he meant forms of fact capable of discerning unfolding changes in the value structure of societies. Data-in-being incarnated hopeful social trends. Data-in-being permitted the identification of emergent value revolutions that futurists might then seek to amplify so that important world transformations could take place and world futures freed. Data-in-being were, as Jungk would later explain with typical 1980s language, "weak signals" of coming cultural revolutions.[46]

By the second world future research conference, held in Kyoto in 1970, the divergence between the "Establishment" forecasters from RAND, the OECD and *futuribles*, and the group of radical futurists had developed into a veritable schism. The second conference statement began, "Many future researchers in their aim to be taken seriously lack in intellectual courage. Many of today's scientific anticipations and projections are not much more than extensions of the present."[47] Kyoto, the city of temples, was a symbolic location (it was originally intended to hold the conference in Hiroshima) and the conference involved leading Japanese pacifists. As a result of Kyoto, the radical futurists gained a decisive upper hand in the process of creating a world federation for future research. The committee charged with the task of creating the federation argued that future research was not trend forecasting, but social change, through the active invention of the future.[48] Galtung laid down the word at the second conference: future research was a "prescriptive social science," which would function like architecture in the active design of new worlds. "Prescriptive future research is like architecture, it stipulates values to be realized, then goes ahead to do the job, on the drawing table (the theory, the blueprint), at the level of the model (the utopian community), in full scale reality (as an effort at large scale implementation)...The [architect] transcends past and present trends, he creates, he breaks apart invariances, he makes what has so far been thought an impossibility

[46] Jungk, "The Role of Imagination", 7. [47] Jungk, "The Role of Imagination."

[48] Bucharest Newsletter no. 1 of the Continuing Committee of the World Futures Research Conference, signed by de Jouvenel, Arne Sorensen, Miro Constantinescu, and Pavel Apostol; Memorandums 1, 2, and 3 of the Continuing Committee for Future Research (written by Eleonora Masini and in Masini's possession); UNESCO Archives, 1972/001 A506(498)71 AMS.

a living reality."[49] Prescriptive social science did not conceal its ideological content (as did would-be scientific forms of prediction), but proclaimed it.

> Prescriptive research can only be meaningful within an effort to create the future now, in other words through practice, through action... In predictive future research the role as an observer may be sufficient... in prescriptive future research this is not enough. Testing of a theory can only be done by creating a new reality: the research... has to be translated into some kind of action. For that reason the prescriptionist appears not only as an ideologist because of the emphasis on values, but also because he is forced to be an activist as opposed to the scientism of the futures researcher, removed from social action in the ivory tower of a thinktank.[50]

The futurist was thus a future activist. Nothing could be farther removed from such a future activist than the idea of prediction: "To predict is to lay the future in a strait jacket."[51]

THE ANTI-RAND: UNITING WORLD SOCIAL MOVEMENTS

The ivory tower was RAND, and, as its opposite, Galtung posited the idea of a democratic world federation for the future. The Wold Futures Studies Federation was eventually created in 1973, and the writing of its statutes confided to the Romanian futurist Pavel Apostol, but the blueprint was drawn up by Galtung: a federation for the world future should serve to democratize futures research and put it at the disposition of global publics. "It is hard to imagine a field in which elitism, even in the guise of professionalism, would be so dangerous as in futures research. Time is the new medium of conquest just as much as space was in the past." Through this colonization process, strong nations and their elites—"high priests of the future," housed in the "citadels" of intergovernmental organizations such as the OECD, NATO, or the Council of Europe, forced existing patterns onto the future of the developing world. "This is what happens if one extrapolates from present conditions." By "lay[ing] claims to future time territory [such elites] make binding decisions for future generations today... they displace the center of gravity in decision making away from the future and towards the present and thereby deprive future generations of an autonomy that is rightfully theirs." To democratize future research meant to transform it from "the monopoly of some people... (to) a truly shared activity, belonging to everybody who wants to enrich the future and himself by adding that forgotten dimension to his life."[52] In addition, democratization meant to move from prediction of the probable future

[49] Johan Galtung, 1970, "On Future Research and its Role in the World," *Proceedings of the International Future Research Conference,* Kyoto, 1970. Published by Japan Society for Futurology, 103–17, 105.

[50] Galtung, "On Future Research and its Role in the World, 104.

[51] Ibid.

[52] Galtung, "The Future of Future Research," in *Challenges from the Future. Proceedings from the International Future Research Conference*, Kyoto, 1970: 106–119, 110.

to the exploration of the many different possible futures of world development. This included the creation of alternative images and models of development in the advanced nations and the developing world alike, and the experimentation of alternative modes of social organization. "In other words the task would not be to explore criteria for selecting one, but to explore how simultaneous realization of a multiplicity of futures would be possible." Such plurality meant a "higher form of world democracy," of which the world federation was the custodian of sorts, spreading methods of future research to the global level and involving world populations in future creation, for instance through a world newsletter or a tele-satellite system that could transmit a Channel of the future. Finally, future research should be renamed futures studies, reflecting notions of plurality and openness.[53]

The WFSF was thus created as a model of the future, its very organizational form of a decentralized, network like structure of a federation intended to act as a vehicle of world future consciousness and incarnation of a supreme form of world democracy. "If futures research is to be organized, should that organization be modeled after the patterns of the past, or be in itself a model of some kind of future we would like to project?"[54]

This idea of a world federation fell back on highly complex historical legacies around world federation and the international peace movement. Jungk, the best-selling author of *Brighter than a Thousand Suns* and one of the first Western intellectuals to visit Hiroshima after 1945 was a figurehead of the international peace movement. In the latter, feelings of a fractured humanity played a particular role. The peace movement understood peace as a universal value of all Mankind. But the peace movement was itself split in two between the liberal Confederation for Disarmament and Peace, and the Soviet-sanctioned World Peace Congress.[55] As a result, in their search for a universally shared value, pacifists found peace, but in their movement, they reified the same divisions that had constructed the Cold War world. Many peace activists were deeply troubled by this and they looked for ways of overcoming these divisions.

Mankind 2000 was initially a "project" concocted by Jungk and Kenneth Lee and James Wellesley Wesley (both Quakers) at the 1964 London meeting of the Committee for Nuclear Disarmament. The 1964 meeting channeled much of the British New Left debate and made a central bid to the UK Labour party to push it to embrace disarmament.[56] The idea of the "project" was to create an organization that could unite the two peace movements around the idea of a common and shared future for all of Mankind—in other words, around a notion of the future that transcended Cold War rivalries and super power competition.[57]

[53] Galtung, "The Future of Future Research" 107.

[54] Galtung, "Future Research and its Role in the World," 103.

[55] Lawrence Wittner, *The Struggle against the Bomb, Volume II, Resisting the Bomb, 1954–1970* (Palo Alto: Stanford University Press, 1997). Matthew Evangelista, *Unarmed Forces. The Struggle to End the Cold War,* 144–6.

[56] Holger Nehring, "National Internationalists. British and West German Protests against Nuclear Weapons, The Politics of Transnational Communication and the Social History of the Cold War, 1957–1964," in *Contemporary European History*, 2005, 14 (04): 559–89 14 (4).

[57] "CND, Mankind 2000," and document marked "The Project," in records of the Committee for Nuclear Disarmament and Peace, vol. 695–700.

In 1964, the first organized conference for peace research had been held. A few years later, in 1967, the antibomb movement created by Bertrand Russell and Joseph Rotblatt, Pugwash, was scheduled to hold a meeting with the Soviet Peace Congress and its chairman Igor Glagolev. It was Glagolev who suggested the names of the Soviet scientists that represented future research, who were all members of the Peace Congress. The initial idea was that conferences for the world future would be held in direct proximity to Pugwash meetings.[58]

The idea of a world federation reflected a long-standing hope in the international peace movement of creating a genuine world society that could bypass nation states and form allegiances to the higher community of Mankind.[59] The two peace congresses in Hague came together around the idea of a world society for peace. In the interwar period, such notions led to the creation in the UK of a Union of World Parliamentarians. In 1937, liberal pacifists created the Campaign for World Government. Dreams of world federation also went back to the interwar-period attempts with world societies, for instance the creation of a world organization for all organizations in the "World Palace" in Mons, Belgium—the Mondaneum. Mondaneum was the creation of the peace activist and Nobel Prize Laureate Henri La Fontaine and the bibliographer and early information theorist, Paul Otlet. It housed the so-called Union of International Associations, of which Mankind 2000 became a member. As shown by Mark Mazower, international associations were understood since the 1870s to incarnate a specific and necessary universal consciousness, the proverbial "World Brain" depicted by H.C. Wells.[60] Created in 1910, the Union of International Associations participated, through La Fontaine, in the founding of the League of Nations and the International Commission for Intellectual Cooperation, ICI. Much of this activity around cultural cooperation and intellectual exchange went into the founding of UNESCO in 1945, with the declaration, in the UNESCO constitution, that "since wars begin in the minds of men, it is in the minds of men that the defenses of peace must be constructed."[61]

As the idea of World Councils, World Societies, and Councils for Mankind came back in the 1950s and 1960s, the idea of universal consciousness took expression in the idea of "Mankind," as denoting a humanity united by sharing an image of a peaceful future. The Pugwash movement, which channeled much of the hope for a new kind of world society, famously urged human beings to "remember your

[58] Letters, James Wellesley Wesley to Robert Jungk 1966, Summary of Decisions Reached at the Mankind 2000 International Meeting, May 25, 1966. Letter, Chairman of the Soviet Peace Commission (Committee) (Igor) Glagolev, dated April 4 1967, Robert Jungk Nachlass, box 31; Seefried, *Zukunfte*, 194.

[59] See Lawrence Wittner, and P. van den Dungen, "Peace History. An Introduction," in *Journal of Peace Research*, 2003, 46 (04): 363–75. After WW2, the world federalist movement sought to push the UN system in the direction of a federal system, with forms of representation based on world citizenship, a world police force, and world law. Both Mumford and Jungk were world federalists, and Jungk upheld a lifelong correspondence with Gunther Anders, principal advocate of world government, former student of Husserl and Heidegger, and first husband of Hannah Arendt.

[60] Mazower, *Governing the World*, 104–10; Paul Otlet, *The Annual of International Life* and Paul Otlet and Raymod Rayward, *International Organization and the Dissemination of Knowledge. Essays of Paul Otlet* (Amsterdam: Elsevier, 1990).

[61] Iriye, *Cultural Internationalism*, 147.

humanity, and forget the rest. If you can do so, the way lies open to a new Paradise; if you cannot, there lies before you the risk of universal death."[62] But by the 1960s, hopes both for Pugwash and for a more genuine form of world government in the UN system had died down. The Pugwash movement, consisting of the elite of nuclear scientists and acting on world leaders, had failed to mobilize world publics against the Bomb, and by the mid 1960s much pacifist hope in the non-aligned world had also been shattered.[63] India began its nuclear programme in 1967.[64] Parts of the peace movement thus understood itself as the avant garde in social movements and networks of activism on the world level—bypassing the outmoded structures of world politics.

The formulation of the future as a "shared concern" of people living in all parts of the world and in particular under both systems, which could be found in the 1967 conference introduction statement by Jungk and Galtung came directly from the 1964 project and contained a clear echo of other 1950s and early 1960s initiatives such as SANE or the world federalist charter.[65] The first SANE conference in 1961 was entitled "World Society in the Nuclear Age" and included a questionnaire to leading scientists "Can human consciousness make the quantum leap that seems required of it? What can be undertaken to realize the spiritual resources of Mankind? How can we modify social structures so as to meet the needs of a developing global civilization? What are the steps that could be taken towards disarmament and is the role of the United Nations moving toward violence or a disarmed world?" In fact, the "project," as such, had two specific connotations. The first was to create a kind of world exhibit of the future, in order to spark the public imagination by showcasing what alternative worlds might actually look like. Mankind 2000 was first thought up as such an exhibit of the "near future of Mankind" and proposed to the Labour government.[66] It was not, as such, a unique idea. Harold Lasswell's World Order Model Project had, with the same purpose, reinventing the social planetarium as an exhibit of a desired world, a peaceful international order.[67] Other organizations, such as the Women's International Peace League had also worked with this idea of subverting the purpose of the world exhibitions that had promoted forms of national rivalry from the nineteenth century.[68] As the British Labour

[62] Russell-Einstein manifesto, 1955. [63] Jungk doc on Pugwash, and Jungk in 1964.

[64] Itty Abraham, *The Making of the Indian Atomic bomb. Science, Secrecy and the Post Colonial State* (London; 1998); Kenneth Lee, "Non Alignment as Applied to Peace Organisations," in *Our Generation against Nuclear War*, 1964: 73–4.

[65] SANE invitation to Robert Jungk, July 6, 1961. Robert Jungk Nachlass, box 25.

[66] International Future Research Inaugural Conference, "The Near Future of Mankind, 1970–2000"; R. Jungk, "A Plea for Social Imagination," *Our Generation against Nuclear War, An International Quarterly Journal*, 1964, 2 (3): 9–14; Mankind 2000 Preparatory International Secretariat, March 23, 1966; Mankind 2000, "The Early History," Robert Jungk Nachlass, box 31; "Libérer la parole pour construire le future, comment on devient futurologue." Interview with Robert Jungk by M. Chaillou, 1968; Letter from James Wellesley Wesley to Ossip Flechtheim, April 27, 1966, and letters from James Wellesley Wesley to Robert Jungk, September 1, 1966; February 24, 1967; April 29, 1967. Robert Jungk Nachlass, box 31.

[67] Harold Lasswell, "The Study of the Future: The Idea of a Social Planetarium," 1970. Adam Freeman,"The World Order Model Project", unpublished.

[68] Sibylle Duhautois, *Etudes sur le futur et conscience globale* (Ph.D. Diss, Paris: Centre d'histoire de Sciences Po, 2017).

government rejected the call to disarmament, leaving a large part of the new Left severely disillusioned, the Mankind 2000 exhibit never materialized. As will be developed, models and simulations would serve this purpose instead, visualizing and exhibiting possible futures, and in 1979, several futurists contributed to an exhibition of "Things that Do not yet Exist" in Paris, which included a section on how to create a world without war.[69]

There were many other such initiatives to use exhibits to spur public awareness and create forms of consciousness: Pugwash began with Joseph Rotblat's travels on the American continent with an Atomic train. The second objective of the Mankind 2000 project was to create a world federation that could diffuse a shared global future consciousness and create a direct link between citizens and the world future. In the first preparations this was described with the term " 'lookout' institution," but it was arguably a very different lookout institution from de Jouvenel's conjectural center, and it was much closer to the rival notion of a world look out institution or "institution vigil" that Hasan Ozbekhan had initially sketched for RAND. By gathering all futurists and their knowledge of world futures, Mankind 2000 would provide a necessary counterbalance to the military think factories of the Cold War and warn ahead of threats to human survival.[70] A slightly different take was that, in the spirit of the Union of Associations, Mankind 2000 was to unite all social movements under the umbrella of the shared world future.

The second convenor of the Mankind 2000 conference, Johan Galtung, would infuse the idea of world organization with a system's rationality. Galtung came to future research from peace research, of which he was, with Kenneth Boulding, one of the main architects. In 1965, Galtung created PRIO, the Peace Research Institute in Oslo, and a few years later the *Journal of Peace Research*, which published many essays from the world future congresses.[71] Galtung modelled the World Futures Studies Federation on his experiences from peace research. Peace research was an outlier of international relations theory, opposed to the realist theories of power politics that had been the basis of the international relations discipline as it came together in the 1950s and 1960s.[72] It saw the world as constituted by a multitude of properties and shaped by images and values. Peace, or conflict, was the result of social psychological imbalances stemming from the distorted values and self-images of groups or subsystems such as world leaders. In a 1959 article in the *Journal of Conflict Resolution*, Kenneth Boulding wrote, "The images which are important in international systems are those which a nation has of itself and of those other bodies in the system which constitute its international environment. At once a major complication suggests itself. A nation is some complex of the images of the persons who contemplate it, and as there are many different persons, so there are

[69] "Things that Do not yet Exist," Robert Jungk Nachlass.

[70] Records from meeting of the Mankind 2000 Committee June 6–7, 1967; Stichtung Mankind International, July 1968, Robert Jungk Nachlass, box 31.

[71] Galtung was also instrumental in setting up futures studies in the UN system and the UN University in Dubrovnik from 1972.

[72] See Stanley Hoffman, "An American Social Science, International Relations," *Daedalus* 1977, 106 (03): 41–60.

many different images. The complexity is increased by the necessity for inclusion, in the image of each person or at least of many persons, his image of the image of others. This complexity, however, is a property of the real world, not to be evaded or glossed over. It can be reduced to simpler terms if we distinguish between two types of persons in a nation—powerful, on the one hand, and the ordinary, on the other."[73] The international system could be transformed by working out increasingly sophisticated images (images of love and reciprocity) and spreading these among "the ordinary," but it could not be considered stable, nor could it be accurately predicted. In fact its complexity was immense: "the variables of the system consist of the innumerable dimensions of the images of large numbers of people, and the dynamics of the image are much more complex than the dynamics of mechanical systems. This is because of the structural nature of the image; it cannot be represented simply by a set of quantities or variables. Because of this structural nature, it is capable occasionally of very dramatic changes as a message hits some vital part of the structure and the whole image reorganizes itself."[74]

The whole image reorganizing itself was a question of first order system change, in other words, the replacing of one, violent, image with images of peace and love. The mix of language between spiritualist and rationalist notions was typical of Boulding, the Quaker who spent his whole life trying to marry rational social science investigation with religious ideals of a good and desirable society. Boulding had developed the notion of image in a 1956 book entitled quite simply *The Image*. *The Image* was Boulding's rebuke of Parsonian systems theory. Boulding was a profoundly unorthodox economist who had begun his studies with John Maynard Keynes in Oxford but was refused a doctorate and transferred to Chicago where he engaged in a controversy with Frank Knight. For Boulding, economics as a mathematical science could not be separated from communicated values and feelings that guide behavior in a human system. It could certainly not be elevated to a supreme form of rationality. Parsonian systems theory to Boulding had put economic exchange relationships in places where there should be love and reciprocity. The system, to Boulding, was one that worked through learned forms of experience, and it was held together by positive or negative images of the future. The concept of the image came from Boulding's interest in what he called from the early 1950s a "general systems theory":

> ...the behaviour of any organisation or organism at any moment depends on the nature of its image or view of the universe in two respects. It depends on the image of the field in which the organisation itself believes to be placed. This might be called, with some hesitation, the image of fact. This includes the images of space and time structure, and the organization's state and position in the field. It includes also an image of the system in which the organisation finds itself, that is an image of relationships, of cause and effect, of action and consequence. The image of the field is not enough to determine behaviour. There must also be an image of values. The essential concept of

[73] Kenneth Boulding, "National Images and International Systems," in *Journal of Conflict Resolution*, 1959, 3 (02): 120–31, 121.

[74] Boulding, "National Images and International Systems," 128.

> an image of values is that of a rank ordering of the field, so that some elements or states are perceived as worse than others... it is sufficient to determine behaviour if we can order the possible alternative states of the organization in such a way that puts one state first and all the others second. The behaviour then consists of moving to the best possible state.[75]

In this manner, a general systems theory was, to Boulding, a "unified science of Man," a science that would explain and create, peaceful behavior in the world system.[76] In 1954, Boulding was instrumental in setting up the Center for Advanced Studies in the Behavioral Sciences in Palo Alto. The Center, of which the first fellows in 1954 included Boulding, Anatole Rapaport, Ludwig von Bertalanffy, and Paul Lazarsfeld but also the unknown Dutch sociologist Fred Polak, incarnated Boulding's dream of an institute that could identify general laws of human behaviour in the social sciences. Boulding took this idea of general laws governing an open system (in fact a living organism), from von Bertalanffy.[77] If a universal systems theory could be found, and the social sciences be unified around a theory of human behavior, then a positive, reciprocal, loving, and cooperative human value system could be created and humanity turned into the kind of self-correcting and harmonious organism that figured in von Bertalanffy's writings. It was Boulding who brought von Bertalanffy to Palo Alto. Boulding understood a general systems theory as an application in social science of the Quaker notion of humanity as a World Society of Friends, in other words a "system." He returned from California with his notes for *The Image*, and a draft proposal for an application of general systems theory in an interdisciplinary center for conflict resolution. The Center for Conflict Resolution at Ann Arbor lay a conceptual stone for the development of systematic peace research from the late 1950s. At Ann Arbor, Boulding and Rapaport turned the prisoner's dilemma theorem on its head, and started games with the purpose of finding strategies for collaboration and shared conduct. The conclusion from these experiments was that games arriving at the *best possible outcome* (enduring peace) required integral system change, in other words a radical change in rank preferences. Such a change could only occur if players agreed on common utility, in other words a shared and common interest beyond the zero sum.[78]

Fred Polak's book *The Image*, discussed in Chapter 2, played a key role of transition here. Upon arrival in Palo Alto, the Boulding family found that the Center had housed Polak in their garden shed. Taken with sympathy for the former Jewish refugee, it was Boulding's wife Elise Boulding, life-long pacifist and president of the Womens

[75] "Theses on the Present Threats," 1958, Kenneth Boulding papers, box 6.

[76] "A Unified Science of Man," draft, 1954. Kenneth Boulding papers. box 5.

[77] *A General Theory of Systems*, the founding thoughts of which were first published in *Filosofische Blätter* in German in 1937, presented at the University of Chicago after Bertalanffy's exile in 1939, and widely spread in English only in 1968. Ludwig von Bertalanffy, *General System Theory* (New York, 1968), 40. See also Kenneth Boulding, "General Systems Theory—the Skeleton of Science," *Management Science*, 1956, 2(3): 197–208. Letters to Lionel Robbins, February 11, 1954, to Thomas Carroll of the Ford Foundation, February 26, 1954, and to von Bertalanffy, February 11, 1954. Kenneth Boulding papers, box 5.

[78] Erickson, *The World the Game Theorists Made*, 173.

International Peace League, who translated the manuscript for *The Image* from Dutch to English, learning Dutch for the purpose.[79] As Kenneth Boulding went from the publication of his own book to become active, through the Quakers, in the global peace movement, he used the message of "image" as an argument for the construction of a new world community with a shared image of peace.

MODELS AS MICRO-UTOPIAS

Following in Boulding's footsteps, Galtung set out his theory of the international system as multi-dimensional, multi-polar, and multi-actor, and influenced by social psychological processes that were in essence transposed from applied psychology to human behavior, and led, in Galtung's interpretation, to what he labeled "rank disequilibrium." Galtung came to peace research and future research from the idea that such epistemological undertakings could act as a bridge or Third Way between the two blocs by focusing on the values that united the world. Observing the decolonization process and the non-aligned movement, Galtung was an advocate of the turn to multi-polarity and systems theory in international relations (IR) theory, but for Galtung, the emerging world system also had a spiritual component in the non-violence of Gandhi and the Confucianism of the Chinese, which is presumably why Galtung does not figure prominently in the canon of IR, just as Boulding's message of the need to turn economies toward the fostering of love and reciprocity has been marginalized in the history of economic thought.[80] Rank disequilibrium was a problem of asymmetrical relationships of status and need. As the world system reflected fundamental dynamics of social psychology, stable or unstable self-images and self-assertion explained forms of peacefulness or aggressivity, as demonstrated in the recent past by countries such as Germany and Japan, and presently by Korea, China, or the American black power movement.[81] Peace—and conflict—were thus values related to a sociotechnical and psychological process of world dominance and submission, in which images of the future and phenomenological notions of self and being were given the utmost importance as structuring elements of the world system. In the mid 1960s, Galtung, together with his wife Ingrid, the French opinion researcher Jan Stoetzel, and Andrej Sicinski embarked on two large scale value surveys, the first comparing values of ordinary people and their leaders in West and East Europe, and the second focusing on the images of the world in the year 2000 held by young people all over

[79] Elise Boulding preface, to Polak, 1956, *The Image*. Kenneth Boulding letter to his mother, October 10, 1954. Elise Boulding directed the Womens' Internal League for Peace, WILP, in which concepts of the world future had been discussed since the mid 1950s, see Duhautois, *Etudes sur le futur et conscience globale*.

[80] T. Weber, "Gandhi, Peace Research and Buddhist Economy," in *Journal of Peace Research*, 1999, 36 (3): 349–61.

[81] Johan Galtung, "Violence, Peace, and Peace Research," in *Journal of Peace Research*, 1969, 6 (03): 167–191, 188; Johan Galtung, "A structural theory of violence," *Journal of Peace Research* 1964, 1 (02): 95–119.

the world.[82] The first aimed to promote the idea that the Cold War was an elitist and technocratic conflict, which clashed directly with the shared values of ordinary people on both sides of the Iron Curtain. The latter depicted the young of the Western world as the "neomodern makers of new civilization" and carriers of a new cosmopolitan world politics, which clashed with that of their nation-oriented decision makers and political leaders. The latter interpretation was crucial as Galtung launched a series of courses for the UN University in Dubrovnik in future studies, intended to educate the world's young populations in the methods of future research.[83] A similar cosmopolitan form of world subjectivity was emerging too from an increasingly integrated web of world organizations, organized from the local chapter to the world federation. As the world became a global system of world federations—*igos, ingos*, and *super ingos*—conflict would evaporate and the system become peaceful. For Galtung this process was already in place, with world associations rapidly outnumbering the world's nation states.[84] A world federation for the future, consisting of integrated local future societies and organizations, would in essence be this new world community's highest form.

Galtung also took Boulding's and Rapaport's experiments with positive sum games further into the idea that models could be used as a kind of micro-utopia, a way of designing and testing model societies and alternative worlds before their realization. Specifically, models could be a way of setting a new image, and then examine the conditions of its realization. As peace was not a learned value and not even an actually existing empirical phenomenon in the Cold War world, it had to be visualized and imagined in order for a new set of peaceful systemic relations to occur. From this perspective, the grand activity of modeling, prediction, and simulation changed significance from actual forms of prediction, and became triggers of the imagination and representations of non-existing but deeply desirable conditions.

The militant ambition in futures studies came from the interlinkage between futures studies and the peace movement, but it also fell back on a strand of behavioralism, in which a central concern from the 1950s on was to create new forms of interdisciplinary and problem-oriented approaches. Peace and conflict research grew, as discussed, from notions of a generalized systems theory as something that could allow for imagined solutions to conflicts in human behavior. In discussions of the Palo Alto and Ann Arbor seminar, models appeared as a particular epistemological device, occupying a central middle ground between, on the one hand, the abstract theorizing and ideal type assumptions of economics and international relations, and, on the other, the empirical and survey-oriented investigations promoted by Lazarsfeld and others. Models, for Boulding, Lasswell, and Galtung, were both test labs and pedagogical tools, with which a non-empirically observable future could be depicted so that new images, objectives, and values capable of carrying systemic change could be forged. As argued in Chapter 4, models were always intended as devices for shaping behavior. For futurists, models became

[82] Galtung et al. *Images of the World in the Year 2000*. Duhautois, *Etudes sur le futur*, 124–5.
[83] Papers of the WFSF, Dubrovnik course, 1974–78, Eleonora Masini papers.
[84] Galtung, "The Future of the International System."

virtual utopias, a kind of future test lab.[85] Galtung, for all his critique of the "ivory tower" futurists, was particularly impressed with the scenario technique developed by Herman Kahn, and by its adaptations at the hands of the international relations theorist Ithiel da Sola Pool. Scenarios, to him, contained visions of alternative worlds and technically sophisticated imagination techniques for their visualization.[86] Models were architectural versions of images of the future, and if a variety of future worlds could be offered up and experimented with safely, then modeling was a technology for the deepening of world democracy as alternative worlds could then be put on display in models and offered as a matter of choice to the range of world populations.[87] The utopianism was in the model. A young Johan Galtung explained these assumptions to a manifestly perplexed interviewer for a grant with the Rockefeller foundation in 1957, stating that he wanted to travel to the United States in order to study with Lazarsfeld and learn mathematical modeling for the purposes of developing world peace in the footsteps of Gandhi.[88]

THE WORLD PLAN

In this capacity world models were part of a set of repertoires which from the late 1960s on were directly concerned with creating images of a better world. An additional application of future studies as a way of solving problems within the system was world plans. Within the early conferences of the World Futures Studies Federation were a group of planners with direct links to the Club of Rome and UNITAR, hubs in the late 1960s and early 1970s for world modeling. Hasan Ozbekhan was a former RAND forecaster and chief scientist of the Systems Development Corporation in Santa Monica.[89] Armenian, born in Turkey and educated at the London School of Economics, Ozbekhan was closely associated not only with RAND but also with the Club of Rome. He participated in the 1969 Bellagio planning seminar, organized by the forecaster Eric Jantsch.[90] The same seminar in 1967 saw the birth of the Club of Rome, as a product initially of discussions between Peccei and Alexander King, the head of the OECD Science and Policy Unit. Ozbekhan was charged with writing its first world model, entitled, *The Predicament of Mankind*.[91]

To Ozbekhan, modeling was a way of imagining plural futures in a complex and dynamic system which included, importantly, values as a dynamic factor of

[85] Elise Boulding and Kenneth Boulding, *The Future. Images and Processes* (New York, London: Sage, 1995).
[86] Galtung, "The Future of the International System."
[87] Galtung, "On Future Research," 107.
[88] Grant interview with Johan Galtung, November 15 1956, Rockefeller Archives Center, RF R6 22 GC 1957.
[89] The Systems Development Corporation was a consultancy created by the RAND Corporation in 1957 to develop software for complex computer systems.
[90] Eric Jantsch, *Perspectives on Planning* (Paris: OECD, 1970).
[91] Hasan Ozbekhan, *The Predicament of Mankind. Quest for Structured Responses to Growing World Wide Complexities and Uncertainties. A Proposal* (New York: Club of Rome, 1970).

potential system change. At Bellagio, Ozbekhan suggested that planning, dominated until the 1960s by forms of extrapolation, must take into account the fundamental factor that the future might be different from the present. "The future must fill the whole, vast and empty canvas with imaginings, with wishes and goals and novel alternative configurations that somehow possess reality and present shared, or at least shareable, values." The planning process, he argued, in this and a number of writings that circulated between the OECD, RAND, the Club of Rome, and the networks of futurists, had to be rethought from that of excavation of law-bound developments, to that of an active process of "imaginative futures creation." Modeling was a tool in the "willing" of the future and the active design of system change.[92] The first draft for the Club of Rome, *The Predicament of Mankind*, spoke of the need to reject positivist science, and develop an "ethic of the human condition."[93] The idea of an ethic of the human condition became the Club of Rome's working procedure in the creation of the "world problematique" following the 1972 report. The world problematique was an inventory of global problems, deduced from a Delphi panel of experts. The Club of Rome dismissed however Ozbekhan's draft version of a world model. This model incorporated global value change as the dynamic component of the system—in other words, it postulated the necessity of political and social changes on the world level in order to solve the "predicament." People would, Ozbekhan thought, adapt their behavior in accordance with system needs, and better world dynamics could be created through political intervention.[94] A prerequisite of this was that people were informed about the predicament of the system, and models could serve here as tools of the global imagination.

Ozbekhan's model was replaced by three generations of world models developed by Jay Forrester at MIT (World I, World II, and World III). Dennis Meadows, head of the computer modeling team, had been working closely with Forrester at MIT. Forrester's World Models, which were in fact later versions of a model that he had initially developed for the purpose of processing goods in the large warehouses of a manufacturing firm in Boston, did not incorporate value change as a dynamic variable, only possible technological advances, which were nevertheless not sufficient to prevent the "overshoot and collapse" scenario that the Meadows report *The Limits to Growth* projected as the result of population growth. The determinism in both its Malthusian and technological message contributed to its reception in 1972 as a harbinger of the Apocalypse, while its neo-Malthusian message, interpreted politically as the need for global population control also sparked outraged reactions in particular from the developing countries.[95] Ozbekhan would go on to consider planetary and world problems such as world hunger as a result not of limited

[92] Hasan Ozbekhan, "Toward a General Theory of Planning," in Eric Jantsch, ed., *Perspectives on Planning* (Paris: OECD, 1970), 47–155.

[93] Ozbekhan, *The Predicament of Mankind.*

[94] Club of Rome, *The Predicament of Mankind.*

[95] Elodie Vieille Blanchard, "Technocornucopian Futures versus Doomsday Futures. World models and the Limits to Growth," in Andersson and Rindzeviciute, *The Struggle for the Long Term* (London: Routledge, 2015), 92–115; Moll, *From Scarcity to Sustainability.*

resources, but of a human failure in envisioning a different organization of the system of world production and distribution.[96]

In the discussion of planners like Ozbekhan, Polak, and Jan Tinbergen appeared the key notion that the world needed a better overarching development objective, a "goal of goals" or a desired, possible, and realizable utopia towards which all of world social action should lead.[97] The task of planners was to identify and formulate this goal, so that strategies for its achievement could be created. Jan Tinbergen was awarded the Nobel Peace Prize in economics in 1969 for his work with macroeconomic modeling. In the first half of the 1970s, following the voting of the UN Assembly of the New International Economic Order (NIEO) in 1974 (see the next chapter), Tinbergen worked closely with UNITAR in proposing a new UN structure which would benefit the Third World by developing new forms of planning that would move beyond the development–underdevelopment divide. In 1970, Tinbergen delivered a series of lectures to UNITAR emphasizing the "need to look ahead to a future world order," and in 1976, he wrote the report *Reshaping International Economic Order* for the Club of Rome. The future, Tinbergen argued, was a planning problem. It was a problem of setting desirable objectives for world development, or, in Tinbergen's words, a "preference schedule." The purpose of a preference schedule was to work out the goal of a given socio-economic structure, in this case the world. This goal, to Tinbergen, had to be the maximization of global welfare. Maximizing global welfare required a major distribution of world resources and also the end to armaments so that productive resources could be transferred from warfare to global welfare. Developing arguments from the Group of 77 of the non-aligned countries, Tinbergen proceeded to argue that there was an "optimal decision level" for world decision making. This reiterated, in a planner's jargon, in effect the idea of world government, including developing a UN mechanism of long-term world planning, modeled on Ozbekhan's notion of a global lookout institution or "institution vigile."[98] As the sixth UN General Assembly signed, in 1974, the UN Charter on the Economic Rights and Duties of States, which included the right to self-determination and autonomous choice of socio economic model for the developing nations, NIEO was rapidly becoming the heart of a struggle for transforming the United Nations from developmentalism to Third Worldism, having as its purpose a profound transformation of the world "system."[99] In Tinbergen's 1976 report, a number of leading dependency theorists re-posed the problem of how to "bump" the system. Which world order could meet the needs of global population and future generations?[100] RIO suggested an

[96] Ozbekhan, "The Role of Goals and Planning in the Solution of the World Food Problem," in *Mankind 2000*, 117–150.

[97] Polak, "Towards the goal of goals." See also Erwin Lazlo, *Goals for Mankind: A Report to the Club of Rome on the New Horizons of Global Community* (New York: The Club of Rome, 1977).

[98] Jan Tinbergen and UNITAR, *Towards a Better International Economic Order*. 1970; Jan Tinbergen, *Reshaping International Economic Order* (New York: Club of Rome, 1976).

[99] See Nils Gilman, "The New International Economic Order: A Reintroduction" in *Humanity*, 2015, 6 (01): 1–16.

[100] For instance, the Egyptian dependency theorist Samir Amin and the Pakistani development economist Muhtad Al Hacq, see Al Hacq, *The Poverty Curtain* (New York: Columbia University Press, 1976).

entirely reshaped world system organized around human needs and the basic idea that humanity had only one future: "Mankind's future depends upon it coming to terms with these differences, with developing a new understanding and awareness, based on interdependence and mutual interest of working and living together. Recent discontinuities in the process of change has placed Mankind at the threshold of new choices. In choosing between them, it will have to accept that perhaps contrary to previous time, it has just one future, or no future at all."[101]

THE FUTURE WORKSHOP

As futurists rejected scientific prediction, they turned the models and forecasts developed by futurology on their head and used them as tools with which to imagine possible exits from the existing system. An important part of the radical and utopian content to future studies was thus in the methods, and in the idea of the instrumentalities and technologies of the imagination. The best example of this was the so-called future workshop, experimented by Robert Jungk as a veritable anti Delphi. The future workshop (*Zukunftswerkstätte*) was inspired by the Argentinian educator Paulo Freire's social pedagogy, which aimed to help Latin America's poor population reach self-awareness or self-consciousness and also inspired masses of young European social workers from the 1960s on.[102] As Freire taught people to read and write and shape their fate, Jungk taught people how to free themselves from their future sorrows and liberate their inner future hopes (see Figure 8.2). The future workshop used tools of radical and dialectical deconstruction and psychotherapy. A workshop had three phases, the grievance phase and verbalization of fears of the future (*what are you most afraid of?*), the phase of articulating the most desired futures (*how would you most like things to be?* The phase of articulating utopias), and finally, the phase of realization, in which the concrete processes of possible change and obstacles standing in their way (*what would have to be different for this future to be realized?*) were pinned down.[103] This method followed Jungk's first thoughts on the social imagination as a particular kind of social technics in his experience from the Committee for Nuclear Disarmament, and the ideas that had informed peace research as a kind of inverted strategizing, *what are the necessary steps for a world without war*? Jungk's paper "A Plea for the Social Imagination" for the CND in 1964 spoke of the social imagination as a kind of "applied speculation, which can be used by critical social theory to show that there is no fatal course of events and set out to draw concrete blueprints for the future, which then allows us to attack all the obstacles standing in the way of this future. This method allows us to understand the difficulties and possibilities which are present in any new social development and give us a sort of imaginative preview of

[101] Jan Tinbergen, ed., *RIO: Reshaping the International Economic Order*, 23.
[102] Pauolo Freire, *Pedagogy of the Oppressed* (New York: Heder, 1968).
[103] Robert Jungk, *Future Workshops: How to Create Desirable Futures.* (London: Institute for Social Invention, 1987); Jungk, "L'atelier du futur," in *Analyse et prévision,* 1968.

Figure 8.2. Future Workshop, 1984.
(Robert Jungk Nachlass.)

the future and so clarify ideas of what the desired future will be. Such concretizations have an educative value, and they can be useful as a sort of social technics. One does not have to fear the risk of totaliarianism, but rather, as social technics it would work on the level of the psyche of the individual and make our generation conscious of the future."[104]

The future workshop was the product of these thoughts, which Jungk also developed as a series of radio conversations for Deutsche Rundfunk in 1959.[105] The first documented workshop was held at a music festival in Klagenfurt, and concerned how music could be given a transformative role in capitalist society. From 1968 on, Jungk held workshops with his protesting students in the sit-ins at Freie Universität in Berlin, and Zukunftswerkstätten then became a veritable social movement of their own in Austria and Germany, as Jungk led workshops for employees of large companies, habitants of areas targeted by urban regeneration, hospital patients, etc. From the 1970s on, Jungk clearly thought that he had invented a technology that could solve key problems of participatory democracy and visited not only RAND,

[104] Jungk, "A Plea for the Social Imagination," 1964.

[105] Proposal for Deutsche Rundfunk, 1959, and Jungk letter to Flechtheim, undated, 1960, Jungk Nachlass, box 7. Unfortunately there is only one letter of what seems to have been a larger conversation between Flechtheim and Jungk on future research as dialectics or social technics.

but also the research department at IBM in order to tie the future workshop to emerging information communication technologies.[106] Jungk's own institutional creation, the Futures Library or Zukunfts Bibliothek created in Salzburg, had as its purpose to gather all available documentation on world futures, so that citizens could be actively informed about future developments.[107]

The future workshop resembled in many ways, in its formalization of steps, questions, and scrutiny, not only a session of psychotherapy but also an inverted Delphi procedure, the difference being of course that the experts were not professional forecasters or realist international relations theorists, but ordinary people. Delphi had impressed futurists with its methodological sophistication, although some of them voiced their fear of the power of such a tool in the hands of military elites. As Delphi spread from RAND to a wider community, experiments began with its conversion as a tool for the experimental exploration of alternative futures. Psychologists Charles Osgood and Stuart Umpleby at the University of Illinois conducted a large scale computer-led Delphi with their students, performed on the Programmed Logic for Automated Teaching Operations machine, Plato. Plato was designed to explore different future possibilities, and learn how students with pessimistic or optimistic worldviews understood events presented by the computer as desirable, or undesirable. The objective of the game was to lead each player to his personally most desirable outcome. In 1968, "Plato talked for the first time..." The computer had produced tape recorded words and could now record and project messages about the future on a screen.[108]

This illustrates a tension that will be taken up in the coming chapter, namely, the close links between futurists' concern for world improvement, and their ideas of human exploration and individual consciousness. Over time, the latter would take over as futurists reformulated the objectives of future research as to "free the potential of Man."

CONCLUDING REMARKS

In their overall rejection of scientific futurology and prediction, the future was not, futurists argued, a question of extrapolation of current trends, nor was it a derivative of the actions of a rational Cold War subject. It was an active human construct, a question of normative desires and values, and could only be reached through the transcendental process of the human imagination. Futurists focused on problems of values, image, and objectives that they thought could break the world out of a one way street of social science rationality. In this, they took the utopian ideas of

[106] See Jungk talk, "Indonesia in the Year 2000," Kuala Lumpur 1973, and correspondence with Yezehkel Dror, RAND, and IBM research department. Robert Jungk Nachlass, box 29.

[107] Zukunftsbibliotek, leaflet, Jungk Nachlass, box 17.

[108] Stuart Umpleby and Charles Osgood, 1968, "A computer based system for exploration of possible futures for Mankind 2000," Mankind 2000; and Stuart Umpleby, "The Illinois Delphi Exploration of Possible Futures," in *The Journal of Aesthetic Education*, 1970, 4 (1): 129–32. See letter from Umpleby to Jungk, August 22, 1968. Robert Jungk Nachlass, box 29.

Mumford and others, and argued that the future could only be saved through a reinvented and peaceful humanity, capable of remaking the world in its image. While futures studies drew on the futurism of the early Cold War era, it added to this a concern with method, social instrumentalities, and concrete tools of realization. Many of these were, paradoxically, the products of futurology, modernization theory, and the behavioral revolution in the social sciences, but these now became part of a highly critical notion of the system, and system change. The great paradox of this was that the utopianism of futurism was, in the end, also dependent on the predictive techniques that postulates of rationality and the experiments with modeling and simulation had enabled. For some futurists, such techniques were tools to contain troubling future developments, but for others, they were aids to the imagination, as they seemed to allow for concrete representation of possible world futures, and they could be used therefore in subversive manner.

Meanwhile, as all utopian categories, the future mobilized by futurists was a reflection of the power structures of the world that it tried to reform. Futurists, in their claim to possess a special link to the future, stepped onto inherently powered ground. Futurists saw themselves not only as students of the future, but as *midwives* of the future. Inspiring, hopeful images of the future, capable of saving the world from disaster, were out there in the minds of people but they needed to be delivered through some form of cataclysmic mechanism. And as futures did not per se exist, but had to be created through processes of mind release and the taunting of the world imagination, futurists invented a highly prominent role for themselves as the saviours of the future world. In the coming decades, future studies would forget some of its assumptions of the pressing need for world transformation, as the motivations for future midwifery changed fundamentally from the quite desperate perceptions of impending Apocalypse in the 1950s and 1960s, to the professionalization of futurists that took place in the 1980s and 1990s.

In the existing literature, the mid 1970s have been understood as marking the peak of a utopian moment inspired by Third Worldism, human rights discourse and radical alternative notions of modernization. Most of these utopian visions would fail in the following decades. The Third World's ability to act as a collective agent, which marked the years between 1968 and 1974, was more shortlived than hoped. Leading Third World countries and leaders also deceived Western social movements in their aspiration to imitate Western models of development rather than traveling back to those premodern utopias that circulated as tropes in Western social movements from the late 1960s on. India developed the bomb. China engaged in a radical strategy of industrialization. The next chapter proposes a different explanation for the decline of utopian energies of the 1970s, having to do with the erosion of the systems thinking that fueled radical globality discourses of the 1960s, and with an intellectual history turn from efforts to transform the world system, to efforts to transform humanity itself. This relocation of the world future from the outside to the inside of the human universe came with a notable shift in futures research, as the kind of future reform movement discussed here began to increasingly resemble a new form of global futuristic expertise, equipped with the theories of the day of the late 1970s and 1980s. This shift in futurism is important, I suggest, in terms of illustrating the links between the failure of the utopian projects of the 1970s and the ensuing rise of what might be called forms of proto-neoliberal thinking in world visions of the 1980s and 1990s. Such liberal visions stemmed from the failure of 1970s utopianism and took over much of the radical energy that had infused the former.

9

The Futurists. Experts in World Futures

FROM SYSTEM TO SELF

The World Futures Studies Federation was finally created in 1973. In the year before, a second world organization for the future was created, the World Future Society, located in Washington DC and presided over by the American business man Edward Cornish. The WFS developed into a continent-wide organization with local chapters, oftentimes consisting of businesses, entrepreneurs, and consultants. It was thus a very different organization from Galtung's dreamt-up federation of world citizens. In the US, futurism never turned into the planning technique for the post-industrial society that Daniel Bell had hoped for; rather, its links to proto forms of neoconservative and libertarian thought in the 1970s and 1980s must be emphasized.

Future research developed, in the course of the 1970s, from a utopian Cold War activism, into an activity of paid futuristic advice. The chapter explains how this was possible, and the consequences that it had for the future itself. As futurologists, future researchers and futurists came together in not one but several professional organizations by the late 1960s and early 1970s, they entertained the hope that future research could be organized into a new field of expert activity. The systems critique and rejection of establishment that characterized futures studies from their inception in the late 1960s, and which caused the many rifts running through the World Futures Studies Federation discussed in Chapter 7, took significantly altered routes as the 1960s turned into the 1970s, 1980s, and 1990s. Systems analysis, the ontological mode that allowed futurists to see the world as a profoundly unbalanced system with built in eschewed dependencies, began running out of steam in the wake of what was arguably its biggest success, the publication of the *Limits to Growth*-report in 1972. The *Limits to Growth*-report launched a major global future controversy. In the first half of the 1970s, a number of counter reports and competing world models appeared. The models were epistemological sites for acting out the struggle between the different visions of global temporalities that had characterized the post-war period and that were by the 1970s in a state of collision. Models re-enacted the division between discourses of modernization and stage-driven developments of the 1950s, alternative and pluralistic notions of world development of the 1960s and 1970s, as well as emergent notions of a Western-driven process of neoliberal globalization. The models also reflected the inherent limits of these world visions. What was considered in the model as static or dynamic was not a mere technical issue but continued to reflect existential notions, as it put the search-light on the question of what was changeable and not in the world system, and moreover, on what was the core variable of future change—human value change, technology, or the finite nature of resources in a planetary system?

As demonstrated in the previous chapter, future research carried a key debate on the possibility of rebooting the world system by setting a better image or objective of world development. This was a deeply normative issue, as the world was understood as reflecting the fundamental values of humanity and the "system" was thus not a somehow external reality but the direct reflection of human beings themselves. In subsequent years, the consensus around the idea of the future as a "common" problem for this world system and shared concern for otherwise widely different efforts broke down. Futurists were centrally involved in the heated debates over global modeling and they were also central to the rejection of the message of a world with limits that characterized the rest of the 1970s and 1980s.[1]

This rejection came from many different directions, and as such it followed the schisms of future studies as they had come together in the period from the late 1960s. The most important rejection of *Limits to Growth* was the Bariloche report, inspired by Latin American dependency theory. The Bariloche report focused on the perceived neo-malthusianism of *Limits to Growth* and its opposition between environmental concerns and the need for development in a world with fixed boundaries.[2] The message of the Bariloche report was instrumental to the UN's crafting of the New International Economic Order. NIEO marked the apex of the non-aligned movement—the Bandung idea that the Third World could chose a future and development model of its own. Several leading futurists—Robert Jungk, Johan Galtung, Eleonora Masini, and Sam Cole—were directly involved in the debate on global models that followed.[3] In the early years of the 1970s, the links between the WFSF, a radicalized UN system, and the Club of Rome, were manifest. In 1971, the UN agency UNITAR initiated a future research commission tasked with mobilizing the tools of future research for the solution of world problems. UNITAR meetings in 1971, 1972, and 1973 were important in consolidating the group of futurists also involved in the construction of the World Futures Studies Federation.[4]

Meanwhile, other futurists participated in forms of future research that were opposed both to the Third Worldist message of NIEO, and the environmentalist message of the Club of Rome. In 1976, the OECD launched its own future

[1] See Elodie Vielle Blanchard, *Les limites à la croissance dans un monde globale. Projections, modélisations, réfutations* (PhD diss., Paris: EHESS, 2011).

[2] Graciela Chichilnisky, et al., eds, *The Bariloche Report* (Spectrum, Utrecht University Press, 1978); Sibylle Duhautois, *Etudes du futur et conscience globale* (PhD Diss, Paris: Centre d'Histoire de Sciences Po, 2017), 301–4.

[3] Sam Cole, *Global Models and the International Economic Order* (Unitar, Pergamon Press, 1979); Sam Cole et al., "Scenarios of World Development," in *Futures*, 1978, 10 (1): 3–20, Elke Seefried, *Zukunfte* (Munchen: de Gruyter, 2016), 293f.

[4] See Philippe de Seynes foreword in Cole, *Global Models*, viii–1; and Duhautois, *Etudes sur le futur*, 187f.

research program, the so-called Interfuturs project, in which several futurists of the "Establishment" kind were employed as consultants: Daniel Bell: French prospectivistes, Bernard Cazes and Jacques Lessourne; the Japanese planner and future foreign minister, Saburo Okita (Okita, Bell, and de Jouvenel had met at the CCF seminar on Problems of Growth in Tokyo in 1957).[5] The OECD reinvented itself in the 1970s as the overseer of a process of globalization that it feared might run counter to the interests of the Western world.[6] In so doing, the organization was a core site for emerging economic discourses centered on the need to protect a liberal version of global interdependence. In order to counteract what organizations saw as a biased use of dramatic and deterministic images in global modeling, Interfuturs made use of Kahn's scenario method and French prospective analysis, both of which it understood as tools with which positive and assertive images of the future of the Western world could be created. Such images might counteract pessimistic notions of scarcity, collapse, and world rivalry, and restore a Western future confidence.

Kahn and Wiener themselves, in the mid 1970s at work at the increasingly neoconservative think tank, the Hudson Institute, put the scenario method on display as a methodological alternative to modeling, with the argument that scenarios placed a premium on the human factor. Human beings could construe other and different futures while computers simply extrapolated current trends. By the mid 1970s this was a core neoconservative American argument against the message of *Limits*, which was perceived in certain American circles as an "attack on the American way of life."[7] The Club of Rome did not include any Americans, and Aurelio Peccei's plea to Nixon to launch a transatlantic axis on responsibility toward the future failed.

These debates on the desired direction of globality introduced a splinter into the world of futurism. Meanwhile, these radically different conceptions of world development had a surprising common element in the rejection of the determinism in *Limits* and its failure to address the "human component." As discussed in the previous chapter, the Club of Rome had evacuated the complex issue of human values from the analysis in *Limits* by rejecting Hasan Ozbekhan's initial proposal, *The Predicament of Mankind*.[8] The final report ruled out the possibility of sufficient value changes and political changes in the Western world and proposed no solution to the predicted collapse other than technological improvement and population control, both understood essentially as new tools of a technocratic world management. A large part of the controversy after *Limits* was concerned with the inherent

[5] Andersson forthcoming, "Shaping the Future of World Markets," in Sandrine Kott et al., eds., *Planning in Cold War Europe* (Munchen: de Gruyter Verlag, 2018).

[6] Samuel Beroud and Matthieu Leimgruber, "A Pilot Fish Ahead of the Sharks? The Changing Fortunes of the OECD During the Long 1970s," unpublished, 2014; Matthias Schmelzer, "Born in the Corridors of the OECD. The Forgotten Origins of the Club of Rome, Transnational Networks and the 1970s in Global History," *Journal of Global History*, 2017, 12: 26–48.

[7] See William Nordhaus, "World modeling from the bottom up," IIASA research papers 1975; Interview with Anthony Wiener, *Information Bulletin from the Continuing Committee for Future Research*, nr 7, 1972, Dator papers.

[8] Hazan Ozbekhan, *The Predicament of Mankind* (New York: Club of Rome, 1970); see Geoffrey Vickers, *Freedom in a Rocking Boat. Changing Values in an Unstable Society* (London: Penguin, 1972).

pessimism of the message and its negligence of possible human change.[9] In the years following the report, the Club of Rome itself would address this factor through several publications that included leading figures of the WFSF. In other venues, futurists put forward the idea that futures studies was precisely the method that could add the study of the neglected human factor. The idea of the system, which had carried an important radicality in the idea that the future had to be understood as the aggregate consequences of system relationships, now left futurism. Meetings at UNITAR saw the more radical futurists rejecting entirely the idea of "system" from the *Limits* report, as an example of a deterministic shying away from the core question of human responsibility and as leaving, therefore, the human factor to the futurists. Coming from the UNITAR meeting in 1971, Robert Jungk scolded the *Limits to Growth*-report as "*Kassandra mit dem Computer*." Jungk was not, as we know, fond of computers, the "electronic brains" that possessed no moral skills and could not be entrusted with the future. Against the apocalyptic scenario of *Limits to Growth* he argued that the human imagination would always find ways of creating "new beginnings."[10] New beginnings was a slightly breathtaking recycling here of the name of the resistance group that Jungk had joined on his return to Nazi Germany as a student in the 1930s (see Chapter 3).

The same seminar saw another futurist, the Hawaiian James (Jim) Dator explain to Aurelio Peccei of the Club of Rome that *Limits* had its own limits in its exclusion of fundamental human change. It was therefore a poor work of futurism, since futurism was concerned with the core question of *humanity*. "How can we look into the future expecting that change cannot occur?" A decade later, the same Dator would enthusiastically proclaim: "The global depression inspired by the pessimistic future outlook of environmentalism is over! The idea of the future is very strong and positive again."[11]

The conflict between the planner's view of the world system and the more radical futurists' view of spiritual or harmonious forms of human development split futurists firmly in two fractions. Eric Jantsch, the father of technological forecasting (Chapter 5) wrote several angry reviews of the field in the new journal *Futures*, dismissing what he now referred to as the "black art" of futures studies, uninterested in the coming collapse of the world system and religiously enchanted with the human being herself. There was not, to Jantsch, anything radical in this, rather, the rejection of rationality had fostered a negligence of human responsibility.[12]

[9] On the reception of the *Limits to Growth*-report, see Elke Seefried, "Towards *The Limits to Growth*? The Book and Its Reception in West Germany and Britain, 1972–73," in *Bulletin of the German Historical Institute London* 2011, 33 (1): 3–37; Jenny Andersson, "Choosing Futures: Alva Myrdal and the Construction of Swedish Futures Studies, 1967–1972," *International Review of Social History* 2006, 51 (2): 277–95; Vielle Blanchard, *Les limites à la croissance dans un monde globale*, 452–536.

[10] Jungk, "Kassandra mit dem Computer"; Jungk in *SudDeutsche Zeitung*, "Immer wieder neu beginnen," Robert Jungk Nachlass, box 17.

[11] Eleonora Masini letter to James Dator, "thank you for sending The limits to the limits to growth, which I will pass on to Peccei." June 9, 1972. James Dator letter to Wendell Bell, undated, 1988. James Dator papers.

[12] Eric Jantsch, "The New Testament," *Futures*, 1971, 3 (1): 68–72.

The chapter also highlights a tangible separation between American and European futurism, as American and European versions of New Leftism, social movements, and counter culturalism took different directions. Recent works have highlighted the emergence in the 1970s US of what Daniel Rodgers calls "psychoscience," Fred Turner a cyber-inspired counterculture, and Patrick McCray "visioneers," and which focused on Bay Area communities of hippies and nerds turning to space research, neuroscience, and emerging information and computer technology as their hope of escape from the existing world.[13] The 1970s marked the beginnings of what will be referred to in this chapter as the *future factory*, the inroads of futurism into market-based and business-oriented activities of consultancy, paid advice, and a kind of "think outside of the box" in which the radical notions of human imagination of the 1960s somehow merged with an emerging management speak. In the latter, notions such as creativity and human development had new associations. Core to this new futuristic language was, as will be explained, the concept not of *Mankind*, in the sense of the collective subject of a united humanity acting in its future interest discussed in Chapter 8, but *Man*, the individual person carrying, in his or hers consciousness, dormant visions of the future and a presumed infinite potential for his or her own development.

THE LOOK OUT INSTITUTION: THE WORLD FUTURES STUDIES FEDERATION

Origins of the turn from *system* to *self* could be found already in the creation of what was to become the WFSF in 1967. Like many other movements embracing discourses of globality in the 1960s and 1970s, futurism contained a profound rejection of politics. In the case of futurism, this rejection expressed itself in recourse to a notion of expertise as being above or beyond political struggle. Futurists identified politics with the nation state, an outmoded political unity in conflict with their transgressive and transcendental notions of world representation. Politics were oftentimes portrayed as stuck in a historic logic inherited from the age of empire. The notions of world plan, world order, or world society were all supra-political. In this supra-political appeal, they were both radical and profoundly technocratic, in a clear continuity with nineteenth century notions of world order, world consciousness, or "world brain."[14] The previous chapter discussed the belief, circulating among a transnational community of forecasters and modelers, that if only the world in its entirety could be planned and its system logic foreseen, then it could also be remade anew as a more harmonious whole. The World Problem could be fixed, if only the World Goal could be more correctly identified and reset.

[13] Daniel Rodgers, *Age of Fracture* (Cambridge MA: Harvard University Press, 2012); Fred Turner, *From Counter Culture to Cyber Culture. Stewart Woods, the Whole Earth Network and the Rise of Digital Utopianism* (Chicago: The University of Chicago Press, 2010); Patrick McCray, *The Visioneers, How a Group of Elite Scientists Pursued Space Colonies, Natnotechnologies and a Limitless Future* (Princeton NJ: Princeton University Press, 2013).

[14] See Mark Mazower, *Governing the World. The History of an Idea* (London: Penguin Press, 2007) 97.

Technocracy was a rational solution to the failures of political action. Global planners discussed in the previous chapters such as Hasan Ozbekhan and Jan Tinbergen very much embodied this both utopian and arch-rationalist position of active human system design.

In subsequent years, debates on how to reengineer the world system and make it work toward a universal World Goal were increasingly replaced by the idea that humanity itself *was* a system made up of values, communication, information, and feedback in a surrounding environment. Paradoxically, such notions of a human system came out of the same organic systems theories of van Bertalanffy, Simon, and Boulding that we have seen fostered notions of a world system. By the 1970s then, the idea of a general systems theory increasingly applied to the idea of humanity and human beings as the active agent in the world, and hence to the idea that all forms of change had to begin within the human being as the central locus of the system. "World order" was increasingly replaced with the question of "human development."[15] As these fields projected new horizons of transcendence, the world itself, with its problems, inequalities, and imbalances, seemed somehow less important.

The turn in futurism from debates on world order and world structures to questions of human development can be viewed as a gradual outcome of the controversies and quibbles that lay behind the creation of the World Futures Studies Federation. These were in fact highly indicative of inherent tensions both in the specific project of futures studies, and in 1970s visions of globality more generally. The Cold War terrain was full of pitfalls for an organization seeking the "common world future." This terrain did not grow less complicated as the Cold War developed from a bipolar conflict into a quagmire of global geopolitics. Holding the motley crew of world futurists together was also not an easy task. From the mid 1970s on, the World Futures Studies Federation began a process of professionalization and disciplinarization of future research, in which a previous pressing concern with saving the world future as such was gradually replaced with a great emphasis on the importance of future research in its own right. This was of course not at all the same problem, but futures studies were from their inception in a schizophrenic position of both world militancy, and new global expertise.

In addition, futurists were not only distrustful of politics but also of social science, their notion of expertise intended to surpass not only the hopeless field of political struggles but also the boring halls of academia. In the heyday of future research, described in previous chapters, future research and futures studies stood on the margins of social science as a key reflection on the limits of rationality and influence in and on the world. They occupied key intellectuals and personalities precisely as an epistemological adventure and profound reflection on problems of control. Future research was taken very seriously in these decades. We have seen how the American foundations took a profound interest in futures research and forecasting in the 1950s and 1960s, precisely because of the anticipation that these

[15] See Debra Hammond, "Exploring the Genealogy of Systems Thinking," *Systems Research and Behavioral Science*, 2002, 19: 429–39; Manfred Drack, "Ludwig von Bertalanffy's Early Systems Approach," *Systems Research and Behavioral Science*, 2009, 26: 563–72.

activities would open up a new field of mainly applied social science research in areas of strategic interest. This changed markedly in the course of the 1970s and 1980s as future research seemed to leave the arena of social science almost completely, and become dependent on other forms of expertise, including, importantly, consultancy and think tank activity.[16] In this context, the claim to power that underpinned futurists self-presumed positioning as the midwifes and professional conjurers of the future took on a new relevance. At the same time, the integrity of future research within social science began eroding. A reply from the Rockefeller foundation to Jim Dator reads "I cannot honestly encourage you to expect, in the near future, support from this Foundation for a study of 'futuristics'."[17] Dator, along with other American futurists such as John McHale or Hazel Henderson, was indeed indicative for a kind of activity which no longer seemed anchored in mainstream social science but increasingly eclectic and bordering on other areas of interest in the unknowable that flourished in the 1970s: extraterrestrial research, science fiction, radical forms of pedagogy, social invention. In 1986, Alvin Toffler (and his wife Heidi), entirely unoriginal in terms of future thinking but the bestselling author of *The Futurists* and *Third Wave*, was made an honorary member of the Federation. Toffler also delivered the keynote lecture to the highly symbolic world conference in Budapest in 1990, the first conference after the fall of the Iron Curtain.[18]

Such anecdotal evidence marks a more profound change: the composition of the Federation changed markedly in the course of the 1970s and 1980s. In the immediate years of its founding, the WFSF was the theatre for world planners, Marxist revisionist forecasters, dissidents from the East bloc, RAND strategists, and disenchanted Western New Leftists. They had little in common, beside their common sense of urgency about future developments. The WFSF included also a less easily identifiable group of people: psychologists, artists, educators, engineers, urban planners. Over time, this latter population would grow in numbers, while a previous population with roots in social science and planning elites shrank (in fact all but disappeared). Futurists, in the 1970s and 1980s, were no longer systems thinkers, but took a great interest in psychotherapy, social work, pedagogics, as well as information technology, neuroscience, petroleum industries, and business advice. By the mid the 1970s a marked split had occurred between future research as social science and planning, and future research as "futuristics," consultancy, and think tank activity.

In many ways this has to be understood as a result of the way that futures studies parted ways with established forms of social science. Futures studies never turned into a genuine social science enterprise, despite the creation of organizations such as the Futures Research Committee of the International Sociological Association in 1972. While futurists themselves tended to understand this as having to do with the blindfolding of social science against interdisciplinary and non-factual forms of reasoning (and were likely not, as such, wrong) this failure can also be traced to the

16 One of the very few exceptions to this was the professor in Sociology at Yale, Wendell Bell who remained an active futurist throughout his career and attempted to turn future research into an area of advanced study.

17 Letter, Rockefeller Foundation to Dator, August 24, 1971. James Dator papers.

18 Letter from James Dator to Alvin Toffler, Febrary 21, 1991. James Dator papers.

conflicts within futures studies from 1967 on. As discussed in Chapter 7, the World Futures Studies Federation sprung from a 'project' of the international peace movement, Mankind 2000. Mankind 2000 was the peace movement's dream of a world organization, an alternative to the, to them, corrupt UN system. It was an embodiment of the associations of world unity, world federalism, and world parliaments that had been the utopias of the peace movement since the late nineteenth century. As the World Future Studies Federation was eventually created by a decision in Bucharest in 1972, the emphasis was however not on an organization embodying the common future for all Mankind, but on representing the complex world of future research and aiming for the active spreading over the world of futures research in all its facets.[19] The WFSF Charter, signed at the UNESCO headquarters in Paris in 1973, stated that the Federation should be the meeting place for futurists of all ideological and scientific orientations, and work to promote future research in all its different forms.[20] The statutes of the federation, the result of drawn out intellectual labor by the intermediary of stenciled circular letters drafted by Eleonora Masini and the Romanian philosopher, Pavel Apostol, said:

> It is felt around the world that the ideas, hopes, and proposals for futures studies need a new organizational frame, which shall be called the World Future Studies Federation. As a federation it is designed to make cooperative participation in future studies addressed to human and social needs possible and mutually fruitful. The main objective of the federation is to introduce critical future-oriented thinking in all branches of knowledge and action. Studying the future has become a necessity for everyone and is a growing practice in decision-making... The purpose of the WFSF is to promote futures studies and innovative and interdisciplinary critical thinking among all people."[21]

This final vision of a professional organization for futurists differed much from the vision of a planetary federation which would involve ordinary citizens in a gigantic exercise of world future creation, and from the very beginning there were two visions of the "look out institution": Ozbekhan's idea of a kind of democratic world council for problem solving in the name of planetary welfare, and de Jouvenel's much different anti-planning or conjectural clearing house. A professional organization was rejected not only by Galtung but other radical futurists such as John McHale, for whom the very notion of organization itself implied bureaucratic power structures and a lack of creativity not amenable to futurism. Organization was an outdated mode of social organization. To some futurists, this went as far as rejecting everything that resembled organizational structure, such

[19] Memoranda 1, 2, and 3, of the Continuing Committee of the World Future Conferences, Eleonora Masini's records; letters from Arne Sorensen to Robert Jungk, and letters from James Dator to Jungk and Masini, Jungk Nachlass; protocols of the Continuing Committee for Future Research, UNESCO Archives, *Federation Mondiale des Etudes du Futur,* 1972/001 A506(498)71 BRY/ONG/1/boite n. 120.

[20] Charter for the World Future Studies Federation, Unesco Archives, *Federation Mondiale des Etudes du Futur,* 1972/001 A506(498)71; UNESCO Archives, BRY/ONG/1/boite n. 120, Fédération mondiale des études du futur, Bucharest Declaration, September 9, 1972.

[21] "Statutes"; UNESCO Archives, BRY/ONG/1/boite n. 120, Fédération mondiale des études du futur; Pavel Apostol drafts of statutes, James Dator papers.

as, for instance, conferences with prepared papers, and they argued instead for spontaneous self-organization and brainstorming. But in the end, professionalization was a strategic answer to dilemmas posed by the Cold War context. In many countries futures research was a planning activity, and futurists were tied to governmental or professional agencies that were interested in the federation as a professional body of long-term planners. This was the case of Japan, for instance, where future research had originated in technological forecasting institutions in direct proximity to governmental planning (and charged with the creation of the "super technotronic society"). It was also so for the Western futurists from RAND or futuribles who dreamt of turning future research into a new mode of planning, thereby also reasserting an activity that from 1973 on was in profound crisis on the European continent. In the socialist countries, turning future research into a manifest form of planning was, as demonstrated in Chapter 7, an absolute necessity. Socialist futurists were dependent on formal approval by the Academies of Science and to these, future research was part of consolidation and post-industrial economic and social planning. In addition, future research had to be demonstrated to be strictly politically and ideologically neutral.[22] The great emphasis in the Federation on keeping Eastern European futurists within thus gave weight to a notion of political and ideological neutrality, which emphasized professional unity and scientific methodology. The willingness to establish the Federation as a Cold War "bridge" across the blocs led to other concessions with the radicality of the original project of futures studies. The story of the infelicitous 's' in the word 'futures' in the organization's name is important here. Galtung's first proposal for a World Futures Studies Federation contained a plural 's', as the future was a question of many potential world futures and this plurality should be reflected in the name. Another proposal, from the West German sociologist Peter Meinke Gluckert (eventually the first West German minister of the environment) had the Federation labeled with the name World Futures.[23] But the plural 's' hid an issue of huge ideological significance to futurologists of the East bloc, as the idea that the future was open and that tools of future research could be used to open it up for different potential outcomes was not acceptable to the communist regime. It was particularly not so to the Ceausescu regime that hosted the Third World Conference in Bucharest in 1972 (see Chapter 6). Romanian futurists were put under pressure. To Pavel Apostol, charged with writing the statutes of the federation, this pressure was particularly difficult. Apostol was not a mathematician who could hide dissident postulates in models and formulae, nor was he a willing dissident. Apostol was a former labor camp prisoner who was rehabilitated by Ceausescu in 1968. As a philosopher in

[22] See letter from Apostol to McHale on the theme proposal, June 1972, and from Apostol to McHale, May 9, 1972, on the importance of creating a professional organization to protect the scientific status of future research and the independence of futurists. Arne Sorensen, Report on Organizational debates and decisions at the International Future Research Conference Kyoto, May 20, 1970, and Circular letter nr 9 on East European futurists that are not yet authorized to participate in the founding of a world organization, 1972. James Dator papers.

[23] Proposal for Charter from the Continuing Committee for World Future Research Conferences, October 9, 1972, undated Proposal for World Organization, and Bucharest newsletter nr 1, John McHale archives, James Dator papers.

the Academy of Science, Apostol developed a reflection close to the regime idea of nationalist roads to socialism, by arguing that plural futures were in fact possible in the communist system, and that Marxist analyses of the future could have open end points.[24] Meanwhile, the plural 's' was clearly a step too far for Ceausescu, and at the conference in 1973 an apparatchik protested this principle openly, much to Apostol's panic. In 1974, Apostol was stripped of his position and began frantically looking for Western fellowships.[25] Meanwhile, the 's' disappeared from the name of the Federation, only to return by the end of the Cold War in 1990.[26]

The debacle over the plural 's' at the Bucharest conference hid a more profound question concerning the ideological and epistemological plurality of future research, which was such that it in fact threatened the existence of the entire project. As discussed in Chapter 8, the fundamental controversy of future research was the opposition between forms of futurology as scientific prediction, on the one hand, and forms of active futures creation and futures studies, on the other. Early conferences did not only contain Delphi panels and future workshops peacefully side by side, but also shouting matches, tantrums, and accusations of collusion with various establishments—or simply accusations of not being "futuristic" enough. It was in order to resolve such conflicts that the Federation adopted the notion that it should act to promote future research in *all* its forms. The problems created by the fact that the Federation was an odd collection of futurists of different political color and epistemological shape in a heatedly ideological landscape were thus solved by an emphasis on the organization as first of all a professional meeting space. From early on, the Federation also came to the conclusion that if the objective of spreading the methods of future research to the world and thereby "democratize future research" was to be successfully achieved, then work had to be done on futurists themselves so that these really turned into a new form of future experts. Futurists had to be actively educated in future study methods and trained in the canons of future research. As no canon of future research existed in the early 1970s, one of the core activities of the early Federation was to constitute a repertoire of futurism, including collections of future research, addresses, and registers of institutes and futurists, and training in the particular methods of future research. From the early years of the Federation, this appears as one of the central tasks of future research. UNITAR, with its mission of documentation and training in world future problems, was central to this turn to professionalization, and so was the Italian agency IRADES, which housed the Federation secretariat in the early years. In 1973, IRADES convened a Special Future Research Conference devoted to

[24] Apostol, *Omul anului 2000, Junimea* (Bucharest, 1972); Pavel Apostol, "Marxism and the Structure of the Future," in Futures, 1972, 4 (3): 201–10; Pavel Apostol, "Zur Definition und zum Gegenstandsbereich der Methodologie", in *Deutsche Zeitschrift für Philosophie*, 1966, 14(12): 1468–76.

[25] Other Romanian futurists suspected Apostol to be a regime informant. Correspondence between Apostol and Dator, see letter from Apostol to Dator on July 1, 1970, and undated, 1974, James Dator papers. Correspondence between Apostol and Flechtheim, letter PA to OF June 4 1982, Ossip Flechtheim Nachlass. Pavel Apostol CV, Ossip Flechtheim Nachlass. Letter from Agnes Weiss niece of Pavel Apostol to James Dator informing him of Apostol's death, November 8, 1983. James Dator papers.

[26] See WFSF flyers 1973–1995, Eleonora Masini papers.

documentation and training purposes.[27] The 1973 meeting established that the purpose of the Federation was not just to act for the world future as such, but to work for the professionalization of future research as a particular field. This included, the statement said, a turn from previous notions of systems planning, toward the active development of a whole new area of futures studies oriented toward human values and the forecasting of social change.

"Human" or "social forecasting" was a euphemism that came in fact from the collaboration with socialist forecasters through the Future Research Committee of the International Sociological Association, created in Varna in 1970.[28] It stood for prediction of social models and value change, including indicators and scenarios of development that could be put in the hands of world decision makers, and it was compatible with the notion of future research as a form of "social prognostics" which was the acceptable term in the Soviet Union. The term came from the chair of the ISA committee, the Soviet forecaster Igor Bestuzhev Lada, who proposed it as an alternative formulation to a proposal by Robert Jungk that future research should focus on "uses of utopianism."[29] Human forecasting was the scientific invention of utopias. The 1973 conference statement linked social forecasting to the need to develop alternative concepts of human development and new social models. "Man is the fundamental variable of change."[30] This focus on human development required a shift in the composition of future research, indeed a note from Jungk on Memorandum 3 says that pursuing an objective of "man trying to explore himself" should lead to an increased participation in the Federation by psychologists, anthropologists, and educators, instead of the demographers, political scientists, or systems researchers currently present. "We cannot develop human forecasting through them, we should have someone from the human potential movement."[31]

In coming years, exploring human development and working actively for alternative civilizations and models of development became the recurrent theme of the Federation. Its activities overlapped significantly with activities of the UN system and the Club of Rome in the 1970s. The focus on human development included an interest in the potential of new technologies of communication and new emerging forms of cultural identity. By the late 1970s and 1980s, notions of alternative development were further inspired by the introduction of postcolonial theories into the Federation, in particular through the Indian postcolonial theorist, Ashis Nandy (author in 1983 of *The Intimate Enemy*, which included the notion of freeing self and consciousness from the trauma of colonialism through psychoanalysis and radical social work), the Hawaiian anthropologist Maruyama, and two Islamic consultants, the "cofounder of Hawaii's first future research consultancy firm,"

[27] UNITAR meeting, "New perspectives in international cooperation," September 1971. James Dator papers.

[28] Rome Special Future Research Conference 1973, Memorandum 1, 2, 3, 4 January/March 1973, James Dator papers.

[29] Letter from Igor Bestuzhev Lada to Robert Jungk, July 15, 1970. James Dator papers.

[30] Memorandum nr 4, 1973. James Dator papers. For this reason Lewis Mumford was invited to the Rome conference and delivered a paper entitled "Technology and Human Culture."

[31] Robert Jungk reply to Eleonora Masini on the Memorandum 3, undated. "Avoid any DC coloration like the plague and instead find an interest from Marxist anthropologists." James Dator papers.

Sonyi Inayatullah, and Ziauddin Sardar of the Pakistani Future Society.[32] By the late 1970s, the WFSF had organized conferences on intercultural learning and Gandhian thinking for development studies. In 1978 the Federation launched a research project in connection with the UN University and the Mexican presidency of UNESCO on "Alternative Visions of Desirable Societies."[33] It included contributions from Elise Boulding on women's visions of the future, Galtung on the "utopian betrayal" of the international community after Opec, Nandy on emerging visions of non-western societies, and the Marxist ecologist Ivan Illich on language and domination.[34] Preparations for 'Visions of Desirable Societies' went further than the concept of human development and included a reflection on the need for alternative social models that might be found in a development of the human unconscious.

> Is it possible at a deep level, deeper than a consciousness level, to find visions present and maybe even visions common to different cultures? Is it so that structures in the way that we have been discussing them in previous meetings impede the development and even the emergence of such visions? If such structures were overcome in our discussions on desirable societies of which we have little knowledge, could we find them out in our discussions and let them emerge? Maybe we could reach them in some cases at a psychological level where difficulties and psychological possibilities have had some impact from the social and political level, but in other cases the psychological level might be one that is still free from such impact. In Mexico we tried this way and discussed visions by women, by artists...As a consequence we wish to focus on two levels of content and methodology: the conscious level of the presence of the past, and the unconscious level of psychology and visions creation. We might more appropriately speak of visions in the irrational field than in the rational.[35]

This move in the Federation toward unconscious or dormant development models came parallel with a new emphasis on radical social pedagogy and social invention, as well as forms of futuristic field work. In the 1980s, particularly, Eleonora Masini and Elise Boulding created projects aimed at bringing out indigenous and subaltern future visions in rural and poor communities in Africa and Latin America.[36] In India, futures studies split off from its previous proximity to the five-year plan and technology planning office created by Nehru, and became lodged in the Center for the Study of Developing Societies, set up in 1963. In the 1970s and 1980s, the CSDS was directly associated with the WFSF, as a key site for Indian postcolonial thinking focused on community development and social movements in rural India and in direct opposition to the Congress Party. Indian historians such as Chakraborty and Prakash have pinpointed the uses of the trope of the "Indian village" in early postcolonial theory and a use of the notion of tradition

[32] CVs, James Dator papers.

[33] See Eleonora Masini and the World Futures Studies Federation, *Visions of Desirable Societies* (Hawaii, 1983).

[34] Ashis Nandy, "Visions emerging in non Western societies," Elise Boulding, "Women's Visions of the Future," Johan Galtung, "The Utopian Betrayal," Ivan Illich, "Language and Domination." James Dator papers.

[35] Eleonora Masini draft, preparation for "Visions of Desirable Societies" conference, Mexico City 1978. Dator papers.

[36] Eleonora Masini, oral history interview, June 2014.

that was inverted to that proposed by Shils and identified the Western world with an aggressive and technocratic notion of rationality, and the developing world as a site of other futures embodied in forms of tradition.[37] The CSDS was a key site for the development of Indian critical social future theory, including Nandy's theories of reflexive tradition. The utopian notion of a common world future hence localized and fractured into a myriad of different localities and temporalities.[38] It also turned the category of the future from a coming time horizon of humanity to something that could be presently made by people themselves. The minutes from 1982 say that WFSF is a world non-governmental organization that is "*project oriented* and not only utopian," and aims to promote participation among developing countries and be humanistically oriented toward the capacity of men and women to build their own future.[39]

I'M OFF TO PYONGYANG TO SEE SOME FRIENDS. FUTURISM AFTER 1989

By the end of the Cold War, the principle of professionalization and strict ideological neutrality often led future research astray. Futurists remained admirers of the Romanian dictator, Nicolae Ceausescu, who re-emphasized the right to self-development and self-reliance of all developing people in a keynote to a conference in Bucharest in 1985. While professionalization had allowed future research to act as a metaphorical bridge out of the Cold War condition in the late 1960s and early 1970s, the principle of strict neutrality made for an increasingly toothless organization as futurists were confronted with global politics in Egypt, Morocco, China, or India. At this point, "human development" turned out to be the smallest common denominator of radically different world visions. An unsigned document in 1982 warned that the Federation had become two organizations: a first group of individuals "committed to the future" and a new and emerging group for whom the Federation was merely a professional and knowledge resource.[40] A conference in Egypt in 1978 was described as the Federations' first encounter with real cultural differences. The conference, held in connection with a Club of Rome meeting and organized by the Egyptian development economist, Abdel Adel Rahman, had sparked differences between Arabic forecasting officials, and American, and Jewish, futurists.[41] There was a failed attempt to hold a conference in India after a personal intervention by Indira Gandhi directed criticism of the Congress Party professed

[37] Chakraborty 2002; Gyan Prakash, *Another Reason. Science and the Imagination of Modern India* (Princeton: Princeton University Press, 1999); Gyan Prakash, "Writing Post Orientalist Histories of the Third World. Perspectives from Indian Historiography," in *Comparative Studies in Society and History*, 1990, 32 (02): 383–408.

[38] See Ashis Nandy, *The Intimate Enemy. Loss and Recovery of the Self under Colonialism* (Delhi: Oxford University Press, 1991).

[39] Minutes of the WFSF General Assembly, June 7, 1982. James Dator archives.

[40] Unsigned and undated letter, "Reflections on Futures Studies and the WFSF," James Dator papers.

[41] "The Future of Communication and Cultural Identity in an Interdependent World," VIth Conference of Future Studies, 16–19 September, 1978, Cairo (Bucharest: WFSF, 1978).

by the CDS. In 1991, the WFSF newsletter published the Algiers Manifesto, a text calling for international support in respect of the result of the first democratic elections in Algeria, which had resulted in a majority for the Islamic FIS and dethroned the ruling Algerian nationalist party. This raised objections from American and Israeli futurists, who objected to an infringement on the Federation principle of neutrality.[42]

1989 put the Federation to a crucial test. In the mid-1980s, the secretariat, Eleonora Masini and James Dator, started traveling the world looking for signs of a coming peaceful future revolution in countries of Eastern Europe, China, or possibly, North Korea.[43] In particular China with its buddying reformist powers and student movements was identified as a harbinger of the world future, and the Federation thus entered into close contact with the Chinese Society for Futures Studies of the Chinese Academy of Science. The preliminary meeting in 1986 was already a clash of visions. The Chinese were interested in future research as a Marxist planning tool that could engineer a frog leap into the post-industrial society. From a totally different side of the spectrum, the WFSF president (native Hawaiian) Jim Dator gave them a talk on "quantum politics" (see below (quantum as in the elementary particle of Man)). "The future is like a rollercoaster. The future is like a river, and you have no paddle. The future is like an ocean, and you are in a canoe like the ancient Polynesians. The future is like a game of chance, it is entirely unknowable."[44] In 1989 the secretariat of the WFSF was nevertheless set to move to China and be housed by the Bureau of Foreign Experts in the Academy of Science in Beijing.[45] Such plans were dashed by the events in June 1989, at which point the Federation moved instead to Finland.[46] In 1989, Finland created the world's first parliamentary Futures Committee, inspired by the idea that the fall of the curtain changed the country's geopolitical situation and finally put it in charge of its future.

In 1991 there were also direct plans to organize a conference in North Korea, a country in which the social sciences were particularly isolated but in which there was an active interest in future research.[47] Dator wrote eagerly of his plans for an

[42] Magda McHale letter April 17, 1991, and Yezekel Dror letter to Pentti Malaska, March 1, 1991. James Dator papers.

[43] Eleonora Masini letters, June 1988 and to Scientific Council April 5, 1984. In 1986 Toffler wrote to Dator to account for a trip to Moscow during which he met "our old friend" Gorbachev and Betujev Lada and proposed to make Gorbachev an honorary member of the Federation. Alvin Toffler to Dator, November 5, 1986. James Dator papers.

[44] Report on Jim Dator's visit to China on the invitation of Qin Lin Cheng, president of the Chinese society for futures studies. Undated, James Dator papers.

[45] Official invitation, Chinese Academy of Sciences, July 8, 1986. Minutes from the General Assembly December 11, 1984 on the decision to hold conference in China. Letter from Eleonora Masini to council members April 25, 1988, on holding the next conference in China: not many professional groups are able to do this. James Dator papers.

[46] Letter from Qin Licheng (Lin Cheng) to Dator, Academy was a "target." They are from now on unable to partake in international activities. Sept 8, 1989. Jim Dator email December 24, 1990 to Pentti Malaska. Letter from Jim Dator to Sam Cole, June 13, 1989. Letter from Jim Dator to the Scientific Council on the transfer of the secretariat, September 20, 1989. James Dator archives.

[47] Letter from l'Association des Hommes des Sciences Sociales de Coree, Pyongyang, to Dator and Masini, December 17, 1989.

upcoming visit to the dependency theorist Andre Gunder Frank.[48] More importantly, as the Iron Curtain came down in 1989, the Federation became the site for a set of experimental activities in which the countries of Eastern Europe were seen as "future laboratories," test cases for the development of models and future methods that might then be applied to other countries making the democratic transition, such as China or the Soviet Union.[49] The fall of communism gave a new role to the futures research committees in the Academies of Science. As discussed in Chapter 7, these were already, in the communist system, proto-management entities charged with introducing essentially marked-based models of planning into the communist system. After 1989 these committees became central players in the planning of transition and reorganized as forecasting or futures institutes charged with indicators of budding market economies. In Czechoslovakia, the new Dubcek regime set up a parliamentary institute devoted to economic, political, and social prognosis and the production of expert reports on the future.[50] Transition turned Eastern Europe into a new paradise for consultancy, indeed in 1991 RAND opened up an office in Eastern Europe. The World Futures Studies Federation was now one of many international actors who offered its services in the art of liberal future making. "These countries are futurological laboratories because the process has no historical precedence. It starts in the totalitarian state, and it ends in the post-industrial, human, society. Futurists can help guide this process, which could then be put to use in futuristic scenarios for the USSR and China." An invitation from Alexander Dubcek personally to the WFSF presidency reads: "The Federal Assembly is preparing the creation of a parliamentary institute for the future which could work with the WFSF in order to make this country a future-oriented laboratory." The invitation got an enthusiastic response, the Federation offering its "services to any future creating person or body in Czechoslovakia."[51]

MAN: THE FUNDAMENTAL PARTICLE

The consequence of the shift of focus in future research from system to human development was a reformulation of the idea of future research as *method* from an intervention into world order to an intervention into humanity and individuals. With the creation of the World Futures Studies Federation as the professional organization for futurists in 1973, the original project, Mankind 2000, was constituted as an independent entity, registered in Belgium as *Humanité 2000*. The reorganization of Mankind 2000 reflected the fundamental shift from notions of

48 Letter from James Dator to Andre Gunder Frank, December 6, 1989. James Dator papers.

49 See Stuart Umpleby, "Inventory of theories available to guide the reform of socialist societies," prepared for the European society of cybernetics and systems research in Vienna. James Dator papers.

50 Johanna Bockman and Gil Eyal, "Eastern Europe as a Laboratory for Economic Knowledge: The Transnational Roots of Neoliberalism," in *American Journal of Sociology*, 2002, 108(2): 310–52.

51 Letter from Milos Zeman to James Dator, no date, from James Dator to Milos Zeman and Alexander Dubcek, August 16, 1990, and from Dubcek to Dator July 11, 1990. See also Ana Maria Sandi Circular letters about the revolution in Romania and Hungary, January 22, 1990. James Dator papers.

the future as the outcome of a systems logic, to notions of the future as a problem of human development and individual consciousness. The latter seemed indeed to replace what radical futurists in 1967 had referred to within Frankfurt School theory as the "imagination." *Humanité 2000* went back to origins in terms of the Union of International Associations, first created in Mondaneum in 1910 (see Chapter 8). The first declaration of aims of the Mankind 2000 project in 1966 had spoken of the need to promote "a comprehensive, total systems approach to the problems and possibilities of the near future, in the context of future research and planning, having as a time horizon the end of the present century." As Mankind 2000 was refounded in *Humanité 2000*, the focal point was not a systems approach, but the "inner dimension" of human relationships, rather than the "outer horizon" of the system. "The proper study of Mankind is Man, the individual person as the fundamental particle." "We feel that there is considerable danger in considering that all our ills—mental, physical and social—can be combatted by manipulating the outer circumstances of our lives because, apart from tending to reduce the subject to the status of object to be fixed, it also undermines the responsibility for making any effort to change ourselves." An outline document by James Wellesley Wesley states that the ambition was to go back to the original idea of an exhibit of world problems. But at the end of the exhibit, "the visitor would find himself confronted by the most important presentation in the exhibition—the *image of himself* [*sic*] as the central problem and potential of the future."[52] *Humanité 2000* was therefore to part ways with notions of resetting the Goal of the World System, and focus, rather, on the "elementary particle" of change, Man: "the blind spot in the vision of those now engaged in determining what our future goals should be."[53] The challenge was to steer human development toward "the image of what humanity can be."[54] The concern with image was transposed from Polak's and Boulding's preoccupation with the future, as the image of the world, to the image of man himself.

As Mankind 2000 thus parted ways, at least to some extent, with the WFSF, another strand of future thinking came to the fore, which had in fact been present already in 1964. In 1964, the same year that futurists met for the peace conference that also launched the "project," many futurists had also met in London of the Ciba Foundation. The Ciba Foundation was a Swiss foundation devoted to international cooperation in biological, medical, and chemical research, and organized symposia in the 1960s mixing medical and genetic notions of improvement with pedagogical reflections, education, and social work methods. The 1964 meeting was convened in order to examine problems of the future of Man by a range of approaches to Man's psyche and consciousness.[55] From the late 1960s on, *Humanité 2000* needs to be situated in a cloud of organizations that were devoted to the problem of human development and human consciousness. There were *étroit*

[52] "Mankind 2000, Evolution or Revolution?" and "Present Perspectives of Mankind 2000," first by James Wellesley Wesley, 1968, and second by John McHale, 1973, Robert Jungk Nachlass, box 22.

[53] "Present Perspectives of Mankind 2000."

[54] "Present Perspectives of Mankind 2000."

[55] Ciba invitation, Lewis Mumford Archives, box 21.

relationships between *Humanité 2000* and esoteric congregations such as the Teilhard de Chardin Center for the Future of Humanity, the Planetary Citizens Group, The World Society for Ekistics, created by Buckminster Fuller, the World Institute for Social Invention, the Epoch B. Foundation of Jonas Salk, the also transhumanist Prometheus Project,[56] World Watch, the Whole Earth Catalogue of Stewart Brand, or the Better Life Foundation of the Aga Khan and Jimmy Carter.[57] Many of these organizations drew on the idea that the discovery of the atom and the power to manipulate the universe had led Mankind astray, and that the real problem was now to explore and learn how to control the "human elementary particle." The analogy between the colonization of space as a journey into the outer cosmos and the need for a parallel journey into the human atom was not as such new. Hannah Arendt's 1950s remarks on space travel described the colonization of space as a fundamental process of wilderness, and Lewis Mumford's notes on the human condition similarly linked the nuclear revolution with a loss of a human self, and as a fracture that somehow needed to be healed. The idea of a "quantum leap" in the human imagination was a slogan of SANE. However, in the 1970s, the link between the colonization of space and the exploration of human consciousness was no longer unquestionably pessimistic, no longer a question of catching up with a fracture created by technology. Rather, it was both esoteric and escapist, and more importantly, possibilistic in its notion that supporting technologies and virtual networks could now create the concrete underpinnings for a new step in human consciousness. Ekistics, "the science of human settlements" (to which Margaret Mead, the McHales, and Robert Jungk adhered,[58]) placed rational human beings back in the drivers' seat where Kenneth Boulding, the other father of the ecologist Spaceship Earth metaphor, had previously emphasized the inherent destructiveness of the cowboy at the navigation panel. The creation of *Humanité 2000* also saw a feedback loop back to the earlier history of future research as *prospective*, as the organization in 1976 started working directly with the *Société Internationale des Conseillers de Synthèse.* As noted in Chapter 3, the *Conseillers de synthèse* were a kind of management consultants before the name, and emerged from French corporatism and social medicine with strong links to Vichy and eugenic thought. In the 1960s and 1970s, the Conseillers ventured into human resource management. In 1976, funded by King Baudouin of Belgium, Mankind 2000 and the SICS began setting up a social invention databank with the purpose of collecting experiments and information on possible alternative models of development and existence,

[56] Jonas Salk was a virologist credited with being one of the founding fathers of transhumanism and survivalist discourses of bio science and human engineering in the 1970s and 1980s, see Jonas Salk, *Survival of the Wisest*, 1973. The Prometheus project stated that the fate of the human race should be decided by as many people as possible and aimed at survival through future education.

[57] Jungk correspondence with Nicholas Albery, and with Teilhard du Jardin center, Robert Jungk Nachlass, box 18.

[58] World Society of Ekistics, April 29, 1977, letter from Buckminster Fuller to Jungk, August 13, 1977. Robert Jungk Nachlass, box 19. Doxiadis wrote the book *The City of the Future*, and the reference to Mead concerns a set of articles that Mead wrote for the women's magazine *Redwood Magazine* in 1967, "Education for Tomorrow" and "And Children Shall Lead the Way."

"social fictions."[59] Social invention was a curious idea, part citizen participation, part a reflection on new technologies and part a newborn form of social engineering with the futuristic purpose of experimenting with desired societies in the human unconscious. Social invention drew on the notion of the future as a question of active social design. The idea of active social design followed on from the logical structure of the general systems theory discussed in Chapter 8, as it set out the idea that change could be achieved by an intellectual operation which did not predict, but posited an abstract and desired goal and then proceeded to work out the conditions of possibility for its realization. Social invention set out to set an abstract goal, such as happiness, and then dwelled on the model of consciousness or social model that could promote this goal.

These 1970s notions of a new form of social invention emerging from human consciousness drew on the recycling on the complex body of thought which since the 1950s had emerged as part of a general systems theory and by now married the development of information science. In this, von Bertalanffy's organismic theory of general systems mixed with spiritual and metaphysical notions of human existence in a surrounding universe inherited from Paul Otlet, Pierre Teilhard de Chardin, and Emmanuel le Roy.[60] Teilhard de Chardin was a Jesuit priest and paleontologist. Otlet, the forefather of Mankind 2000 as the inventor of Mundaneum and the documentation system in the *bibliographie universel*, was profoundly inspired by the notion of "synthese" (see Chapter 3) in the meaning of a totalizing and universal knowledge of the universe. There were direct links in Otlet's thought between this idea of synthesis and the notion of the *noosphere*, coined by the Russian mathematician Vernadsky during lectures in the College de France in the 1920s and popularized by the French mathematician Le Roy. The noosphere was imagined as a third layer of cosmic existence embedded in the human consciousness. If the first dimension of existence was an outer sphere of the unamenable and unaffectable laws of the universe, and the second dimension consisted of all things within the range of human influence on earth, then the third dimension of the cosmos consisted of the totality of planetary human consciousness, a collective intelligence imagined by Otlet in the drawings for Mundaneum as literally floating around the earth.[61] Ideas of the noosphere had in common, with Bertalanffy's systems theory, the idea of the system as a human microcosmos oriented by a metaphysical or spiritual will to life. The macrocosmos, the universe, had a teleological sense of direction, the completion of the human organism (the image) through the development of collective consciousness.[62] In this sense, the notion of the noosphere was a fundamental

[59] Minutes of the General Assembly of Mankind 2000, September 26, 1976. Robert Jungk Nachlass. Letter from Armaund Braun to Jungk, May 24, 1976, Robert Jungk Nachlass, box 19.

[60] Debra Hammond, *The Science of Synthesis. Exploring General Systems Theory* (Boulder: University of Colorado, 2010); Steffen Ducheyne, "To Treat of the World. Paul Otlet's Ontology and Epistemology and the Circle of Knowledge," *Journal of Documentation*, 2009, 65 (2): 223–44.

[61] See Mondaneum's virtual archive, www.mondaneum.org

[62] Pierre Teilhard de Chardin, *Le Phenomene Humain* (Paris: Editions du Seuil, 1955). Marshall McLuhan, *The Gutenberg Galaxy* (Toronto: University of Toronto Press, 2013). Raphael Josset, "Inconscient collectif et noosphere. Du monde imaginal au village global," *Sociétés*, 2011, 111: 35–48. In 1956 Gunther Anders wrote the essay *Die Antiquierheit des Menschen*, which emphasized that TV

influence on Buckminster Fuller's or Marshall McLuhan's futurism, on James Lovelock's Gaia, and would create also a red thread in the thoughts of American futurists such as Hazel Henderson, Barbara Hubbard, or the couple John and Magda McHale, who from the 1960s on, profiled themselves as a new kind of consciousness coaches and radical future pedagogues in their collaborations with Buckminster Fuller. In 1963, John McHale and Buckminster Fuller collaborated on the Inventory of World Resources at Southern Illinois University. The Inventory included experiments with "mini-earths" and "Dymaxion Worlds" : "man-in-universe" simulations, which took the universe to be the "aggregate of all men's consciously apprehended and communicated experiences". The Inventory was a "great wealth inventory"—a universal stockpile of resources based in human invention. "They do not become used up, they exist in relative abundance". Depletion was a problem of human design.[63] The McHales also created the so-called Center for Integral Study at the Architecture School of the University of Buffalo in 1966, and in 1960 they published *The Future of the Future* on the future of human consciousness.[64] The Center for Integral Study was devoted to advancing science through human wholeness, a wholeness that the McHales believed could be created through futuristic education, interdisciplinarity, and interplay between the arts and para-sciences. CIS worked closely in the coming years not only with Mankind 2000 but also with the so-called Aspen Institute for Humanistic Studies. The latter was created in 1950 by a Chicago businessman, the chairman of the Container Corporation, Walter Paepcke. It developed in the 1970s and 1980s into a leadership think tank, working with corporate and political decision makers.[65] McHale was one of the leading futurists to the original 1967 Mankind 2000 conference, to which he laid out his vision of futures studies as fundamentally devoted to freeing the innate potential of Man:

> A vast range of material means and alternative life conditions, previously unattainable, are now freely available. When the availability of such means lessens survival dependence on the natural cycles, frees man from geographical limits, measurably extends his life expectancy etc., the human condition may be phrased in terms of a multiplicity of both and life choice possibilities.... In considering therefore the design of new forms of social action as no longer constrained by various historical limiting conditions, many alternative modes of individual and group life styles become possible. Our traditional social attitudes and ideologies are inadequate guides to the future. Faced with possible abundance for all, they tend to perpetuate old inequalities and insecurities confronted with freedom, they will assume new forms of slavery.[66]

and radio did not resuture the broken relationship between man and the world, but rather represented a miniaturization of the world, through which the catastrophic consequences of the human condition became merely unreal "phantoms." The English title was *The Obsolescence of Man.*

[63] John McHale and Buckminster Fuller, *Inventory of World Resources, Human Trends and Needs* (Illinois: Southern Illinois University, 1963).

[64] John McHale, *The Future of the Future* (Illinois: Center for Integral Study, 1969); also John McHale, "The Handbook of Futures Research," 1978.

[65] The Institute's executive seminar was intended to provide the space for business and policy leaders to "lift themselves out of themselves" to reflect on critical tasks. In the 1980s the institute seemed to have veered toward strategic management issues and new forms of leadership.

[66] McHale, "Futures research. Integral and communicative aspects," *Mankind 2000.*

Having at his disposal the entirety of the post-industrial technological revolution, Man was now in a position to master the full extent of his environment. Freed from material needs, poverty, and hunger, he could remake himself in his image and reinvent modes of socialization. The cost of this advanced stage of civilization was a particular kind of futures fragmentation that had followed upon the expansion of the physical human world. Such fragmentation, an "atomization of goals," had made it difficult to discern the future and actively grasp "the human condition." "Man cannot be whole if he does not know where the paths that he chooses to follow now lead. He cannot go back towards an animalistic past, but has to develop his evolution in directions that he consciously chooses."[67] Forms of futures learning would have as their purpose to create a new human capacity to master the future and respond to future challenges, solvable through the extension of human capacity. Indeed there was a "race between educational capacity and population growth," the clear implication being that the scenario depicted by the Club of Rome could be solved by the enhancement of human intellectual capacities.[68] In a clear echo of historic eugenic ideas, the "quality of humanity was no longer a God given constant but a self-definition requiring conscious vigilance and affirmation."[69] The quality of humanity, in other words, was a matter of improvement, indeed a matter that could be the object of forms of futuristic rationalization. In the late 1970s and early 1980s, the Center for Integral Studies also worked with the Club of Rome, which in 1979 and 1981 held seminars on alternative social visions.[70]

McHales' contribution to the aims of Mankind 2000 spoke for a new theory of system, a "unified field concept of existence" which aimed to understand the human system in all its facets. If the totality of existence could be grasped, then "prognostic capacity" could be developed, and Man's future rationality restored.

> The continuing development of the person is the central issue for planning for the future and complex future research. We need a unified field concept of human existence—of what is involved in becoming human. Any such fundamental concept would attempt to incorporate in their dynamic interrelationships the biophysical, psychosocial, and essential dimensions of our experience in such a way as to indicate the conditions necessary for our development and optimal interaction in each of these fields, the implications of partial action on the organism as a whole, and the means for upgrading our prognostic ability. This may be seen as an attempt to organize our knowledge, deriving from shared experience, in order to provide an underlying synoptic view and flexible working basis by the aid of which we may, the more effectively, bring into being

[67] John McHale contribution to a context note on Mankind 2000, written by James Wellesley Wesley May 1974, during a meeting with the Société international des conseillers de synthèse in Paris. McHale collection, James Dator papers.

[68] John McHale, "The Future of Education," an overview, 1978, and Draft note on the future of education in the US for the World Future Society, 1980. John McHale papers and Center for Integrative Studies, in James Dator papers, marked box 1.

[69] "The Future of Education," 1978.

[70] John McHale, "Alternative Social Visions," and Magda McHale, "The Neglected Human Resource," to the Club of Rome conference, "Alternatives for Humankind" in Latin America in 1981. John McHale archives, James Dator papers.

> and sustain those conditions best designed to support the continuing development of each person as a human being and founding member of our emerging world society."[71]

The statement was spread by an entire futuristic world in the newsletters and journals *Futuribles*, *The Futurist*, *Futures*, and the Danish journal *Futuriblerne*.

The Center for Integrative Studies also worked closely with the attempts in Hawaii to create a futures university education in so-called futuristics. Jim Dator, who took over the presidency of the World Futures Studies Federation in 1982, struggled to found futuristics as part of the attempt to make Hawaii a metaphorical meeting place for the Western world and Asia in the 1970s.[72] Futuristics built, like integral studies, on the notion of active human design of the system. The point of system change was not the creation of a stable peaceful world order, but the freeing of individual desires, indeed the goal a "society of totally self realizing individualists." This could now be achieved with information and communication technology, computers, and software. "Don't imitate, don't amend. Start with abstract goals, then invent the new structures using new technologies. Computers are a great aid here."[73] Dator was an eclectic personality who flirted both with counterculture ("The counterculture? It's you, baby!") and neoconservatism, particularly as the latter took a both Christian and popular cultural turn with the election of Reagan in 1981.[74] He brought an obsession with new technologies into the Federation. In 1972, Dator made a failed attempt to install a multi-mediashow of the future at the Bucharest conference, oblivious (?) of the fact that computer technology was under tight export control and that cassette tapes were not in free circulation in Romania in 1972. In Hawaii, he launched a virtual future experimentation in connection to the 1973 Hawaiian Governors Commission, *Hawaii 2000*, using cable TV to hook up citizens of the islands to an interactive exercise on the Hawaiian future.[75] Also the McHales worked with cable TV in the form of an interactive television course called *Tune in to the Future*.[76] Cable TV (an "open network") and personal computers led to hopes among futurists that the prized world organization could now be replaced by a virtual planetary future society. If participation could be enabled by satellites, then future world conferences could become true planetary events.[77] More importantly, ICT led to hopes among futurists that technology

[71] "Mankind 2000, Statutes," undated, McHale collection, James Dator papers. A unified field concept of human existence is a term taken from von Bertalanffy's original *A General Theory of Systems*.

[72] As part of this, Dator began building a future archive which today includes the material of the WFSF as well as the McHale collection.

[73] Dator, course outline, "Futuristics," University of Hawaii Department of Political Science, March 1970. James Dator papers.

[74] Dator, Toffler, and a consultant by the name of Clemens Bezold were involved in the creation of an Institute for the Future which was connected to the republican campaigns in the early 1980s. See letters between Dator, Toffler, and Newt Gingrich in James Dator's papers.

[75] *Hawaii 2000. Continuing Experiment in Anticipatory Democracy. The Governor's Conference on Hawaii 2000* (Honolulu: University Press of Hawaii, 1973). 1976 was the 200 year anniversary of the discovery of the Hawaiian islands by Cook. Dator list of request for technological equipment to Pavel Apostol, 1973, James Dator papers.

[76] Letter from Dator to McHales secretary Melanie Taylor. November 5, 1971.

[77] Technology did not really seem to have this effect, when email joined the Federation in the early 1990s, only the secretariat had email (mainly Masini, Dator, and the Finnish Pentti Malaska), certainly not members in the developing world.

could finally be turned from a destructive force, as observed by the first generation of futurists, into a force for the development of consciousness. In 1979, futurists such as Ozbekhan, Cole, Dator, and Toffler contributed to the UN conference on technology in Berlin. The conference's main topic was so-called technology assessment, the evaluation of new technologies in terms of their ability to match human needs and bring out "innate notions of development." This was still based on the idea of technological planning as emancipation.

In American futurism however, such notions of technology as a tool for human realization took a decisively libertarian, anti-collectivist, and anti-planning turn. A good illustration of the links between American futurism and emerging versions of libertarianism was the so-called Committee for the future created by the American billionaire, Barbara Marx Hubbard. Barbara Marx Hubbard was the second wife of the father of scientology, L. Ron Hubbard. Ron Hubbard began his journey into the human universe by writing science fiction novels. Barbara herself began in Washington experimenting with something called Syncon (Figure 9.1). Syncon, *synergetic convergence*, was a terrifically bizarre mix of expectations on the cumulated future effect of transcendental experience, information technology, space colonization, and new management methods. A Syncon process was a "total systems approach for individuals and groups to discover their own next step in the context of needs and resources of others, and evolving capacities for Mankind as a whole."[78] The Los Angeles Syncon Wheel in 1976 was a media event, organized around an actual wheel spinning the individual into the future. The gigantic wheel, which seems modeled on the fortune wheels of American talk shows in the 1950s and 1960s, was built at Samuel Goldwyn Studios. A special management team provided a running summation of needs of individuals and groups placed in the wheel. These needs would be balanced against the whole "evolving system" projected by spinning the wheel. At the rim of the wheel, individuals and groups at the "growing edge in the major areas of human concern will synthesize a picture of the New Man, his physical environment and the directions he can follow to liberate his own potential." Beyond this edge, the arts provided creative stimulus, and beyond the arts, "a satellite of non-verified phenomena will be developed, presenting breakthroughs in paraphysics, parapsychology, states of consciousness, UFO studies, archeological mysteries etc." Within the wheel, the taskforces of different problem areas would compete for the best solution to the most urgent problem facing humanity, and the whole Syncon process would self-replicate on a large scale.[79]

Patrick McCray has described the Committee for the Future as a new, Bay-area-based form of "visioneering" that developed as a form of grass-roots futures movement

[78] Letter to Jim Dator from Barbara Marx Hubbard, September 19, 1972.

[79] The Committee for the Future, The Los Angeles Syncon, 1972. Dator papers. Hubbard herself has a description of the wheels at http://www.digitaluniverse.net/hubbard/topics/view/14482/ (accessed April 24, 2017). See Neale Donald Walsch, *The Mother of Invention. The Legacy of Barbara Marx Hubbard and the Future of YOU* (Hay House, CA, 2011); Barbara Marx Hubbard, 1986, *The Hunger of Eve. One Woman's Odyssey toward the Future* (Stackpole Books, 1986); Barbara Marx Hubbard, *Conscious Evolution. Awakening the Power of our Social Potential* (New World Library, 2015). The first Syncon wheel was held in 1972 at the University of Southern Illinois under the auspices of Buckminster Fuller; Patrick McCray, *The Visioneers*, 73–97.

Figure 9.1 Syncon. Huntsville, Alabama, 1973.
(James Dator Archives.)

in the 1970s.[80] In it, particular American futurist notions of space colonization and explorations of human consciousness merged in decisively escapist fashion. As McCray shows, the concern with expansion of the human universe was a response to *Limits*. Indeed, the purpose of the Los Angeles Syncon process was to "reexamine the Forrester World model taking into account the possibility of developing the extra terrestrial environment for man."[81] Hubbard, who ended up nominated on a Democratic ticket for the vice presidency in 1984, was a key figure in the American pro-space movement that began with the moon landing in 1969. The idea of a positive view of the future instead of the depressing concern with ecocide and planetary boundaries was crucial. The Committee for the Future charter said, "Earth-bound history has ended. Universal history has begun. Mankind has been born into an environment of immeasurable possibilities. We, the Committee for the Future, believe that the long range goal for Mankind should be to seek and settle new worlds. To survive and realize the common aspiration of all people for a future of unlimited opportunity, this generation must begin now to find the means of converting the planets into *life support systems* for the race of Man."[82] The Los Angeles Syncon

80 McCray, *The Visioneers*, 32f.

81 The Committee for the Future, "The Los Angeles Syncon," 1972.

82 Roger Launius and Howard McCurdy, *Robots in Space. Humanity, Evolution, and Interplanetary Travel* (Baltimore: John Hopkins Press, 2008), 62–6, 162, Michael Michaud, *Reaching for the High Frontier. The American Prospace Movement, 1972–1984* (New York: Praeger, 1986), Ch. 3.

process included a leading NASA astronaut, the chief scientific advisor to the space division of American Rockwell, John Michael Smith of Douglas' Delta project, a curator of the Natural History Museum, Willis Harman of the Stanford Research Institute (member of the WFSF and the WFS), Frank Lloyd Wright Junior, and Gene Roddenbery, creator of Star Trek.[83]

FUTURE ARTEFACTS. THE CONSTITUTION OF GLOBAL FUTURE EXPERTISE

The Committee for the Future replicated a structure of planetary society and world organization, organized as a federation of local chapters. It brought together futurists from the networks of the Federation, the Washington World Future Society, and a number of other organizations including consultancies such as the Institute for Alternative Futures, the Institute for the Future, and the Futures Group Inc., all created by futurists in the years 1971–1973.[84] The WFS congratulated itself on its network structure, local chapters, and satellite empowered conferences, and TV broadcasts embodying the "open network" of humanity. Importantly, the consultancy form also seemed to take over previous understandings of futurism as incarnating a world society built on a specific form of world future consciousness. In September 1980, futurists joined forces to again construct a world organization, this time in the shape of the so-called Global Futures Network, a world encompassing (albeit distinctly Western) future consultancy. Market-based advice was now the core *modus operandi*, as was the new economy entrepreneurial language. The brochure publicizing the network came with the selling pitch: "Global futures network. Pioneering the future for you to experience—before it happens!" Network members consisted of a wide range of future organizations, encouraged to all "hold hands in a network for a unified approach to the global future." It promoted yet another epistemological invention, something called "futurontology," the knowledge of how "to transform ideas into action for the global future!" Futurontology was based on *futurience*, the ability to experience the future before it actually happened.

> The Global Futures Network believes that it is possible to build a world where all our dreams really can come true, a world designed to discover and develop the potential greatness that lies within all of us, a world that recognizes that a positive spirit will bring about change in the way that we meet the challenges now facing ourselves and the future. We believe that our greatest days are just ahead… The overriding goal of the Global Futures Network is to invent alternative futures which can be presented to the general public for them to experience and react before the future actually happens. Through such participation and feedback, the network will provide the vehicle whereby the public at large will become themselves the real inventors of the future. In this way, people will again become the policy designers with elected decision makers simply carrying out the public will. Through futurience, self sustaining integrated harmony will be achieved on the global level and people will start to take the positive steps needed

[83] The Committee for the Future, "The Los Angeles Syncon," 1972. James Dator papers.
[84] Flyers and member letters, James Dator papers.

> for positive global change. The future galaxy is the growing number of new global futurists—who are convinced that the so called futures movement is behind the times ![85]

Among the members of the Network were the WFS, Futuribles, Club of Rome, the Committee for the Future, but, perhaps more surprisingly, also the International Federation of Institutes for Advanced Study. Trustees were Robert Jungk, Hazel Henderson, Barbara Hubbard, Willis Harman, Hugues de Jouvenel, Alexander King, and Aurelio Peccei. In fact, the Futures Network was the creation of a feeling spreading among futurists in the 1980s that futurism had become old, that it was now a movement stuck in the past, and that the World Futures Studies Federation, with its UN orientation, had become part of the Establishment. The global consultancy mode was a way of breaking away from this inertia. The global futures galaxy promised by the Global Futures Network was also a "geoglobal theatre," a space for acting out world futures.[86] In 1985 other futurists, part of the Network, the WFSF, and the World Future Society, would realize such a geo-global theatre through the creation of the Millennium Project, a Washington based think tank in the shape of a global network with hubs of futures experts situated in "nodes" all over the world. From 1991 on, the Millennium Project started producing the State of the World index, a collection of indicators of world developments provided by these different nodes.[87] As the chapter has demonstrated, this dream of a planetary society of future experts, producing synthetic or universal knowledge about world developments, had by now a long continuity in futures research. In many ways the Millennium Project was the incarnation of the RAND dream of a D-net of automatized Delphi exercises, as the purpose of the Millennium Institute is to provide a global repertoire of expertise about questions to do with world futures. Meanwhile, the idea of futurism as a world bank of future expertise can be traced right back to the World Palace, Mondaneum. Notions of providing the kind of synthetic or universal knowledge that could create a "prospect of the world" for an international or global mind or World Brain were key elements in the development of forms of intellectual cooperation from the 1920s on.[88] The idea of creating a World Palace of organizations was coupled, through the work of Otlet and the International Institute of Intellectual Cooperation, with a World Institute for Bibliography, a documentation center for the world's knowledge. Otlet's "image" was an exact representation of the world to be constructed through a systematized documentation process based on index cards.[89] Between 1895 and

[85] Global Futures Network, flyer and invitation, September 15, 1980. Robert Jungk Nachlass, box 33. Joined to the letter is also an invitation for the second global future conference in Bombay 1984, under the patronage of Indira Gandhi.

[86] Ibid.

[87] The Millennium Project was created by Jerome Glenn and Theodore Gordon of the Delphi exercises. It acts as a consultancy to the UN, in particular with the Millennium goals. In an interview, Glenn cites the Syncon exercises and the Committee for the Future as the direct inspiration. Jerome Glenn oral history interview, Washington April 2014.

[88] Daniel Lacqua, "Transnational intellectual cooperation, the League of Nations, and the problem of Order, in *Journal of Global History*, 2011, 6: 223–47, 224. Akira Iriye, *Cultural Internationalism and World Order*, 32, 33, 146; Mark Mazower, *Governing the World*, 108.

[89] Ducheyne, "To Treat of the World."

1930, Otlet and la Fontaine designed over 18 million index cards for the "World Book," the Repertoire Bibliographique Universel.[90] In the post-war period, the idea of universal knowledge developed into the future exhibitions, universal repertoires of and depositories of information and statistics, which, quite like the WFSF, embodied the notion first of a metaphorical bridge across the Cold War divide, and second across the fractures of the world. Universal knowledge was a structuring notion in the kind of transversal and interdisciplinary forms of social science research that emerged in the Cold War era, of which future research was very much a product. The International Social Science Council associated with UNESCO promoted interdisciplinary investigations and research that permitted the constitution of the category of world problems—peace and conflict research, futures studies, development studies. In 1971, the new agency, UNITAR, had exactly as its purpose to constitute a repertoire of global information, allowing for forms of synthesis and analysis of the world future.[91] Futurists themselves created many versions of their desired "lookout" institution, the World Future Institute. These varied in shape and form, from Fred Polak's Institute for Technology Assessment and super planning agency, *BeWeTon*, to Flechtheim's *Zentrum Berlin Zukunftsfragen*, de Jouvenel's conjectural clearing house Futuribles, and Jungk's *Bibliothek fur Zukunftsfragen*. When Mankind 2000 was recreated after the constitution of the World Futures Studies Federation, one of its purposes was that of acting as a center for documentation on world futures. Jungk's proposal for Humanite 2000 explicitly mentioned the "Lookout institution," and the need to create a library of the future, a house of the future, and a future research institute. The proposal included a gaming center where individual citizens would be able to go to role play different future images through workshops and computer games.[92] As Humanity 2000 was refounded together with the *Conseillers de synthèse* in 1976, its focus was instead on the notion of world problems, and it began publishing the so-called Encyclopedia of World Problems, which was a clear precursor to the State of the World Index.[93]

In these concerns with universal documentation we see the same inward shift described elsewhere in this chapter, a turn to professionalization and field making of future research itself. The artefacts of future research played a major role in this making. They made up for the fact that future research had no canon, no licence, no university diplomas, and therefore required some other basis of legitimation of its expertise.[94] From an intellectual history perspective, these artefacts are examples of genres that materialized in intellectual history in these decades, and that carried visions of global interconnectedness just as the telegraph or the radio had before. For instance, the mailing list was crucial for 1960s and 1970s forms of international organization, enabling the connection between hundreds and thousands of members,

[90] http://archives.mundaneum.org/fr/le-repertoire-bibliographique-universel, last accessed March 29, 2017. Alex Wright, *Cataloguing the World: Paul Otlet and the Birth of the Information Age* (New York: Oxford University Press, 2014). Lacqua, "Transnational Intellectual Cooperation," 227, 245.

[91] Duhautois, *Etudes sur le futur et conscience globale*.

[92] Jungk, Mankind 2000 activities 1964–1970, dated March 1967. Robert Jungk Nachlass, box 31.

[93] Encyclopedia of World Problems, and outline by Anthony Judge, James Dator papers.

[94] Compare Lisa Stampnitzky, *Disciplining Terror* (New York: Cambridge University Press, 2003), 42–5.

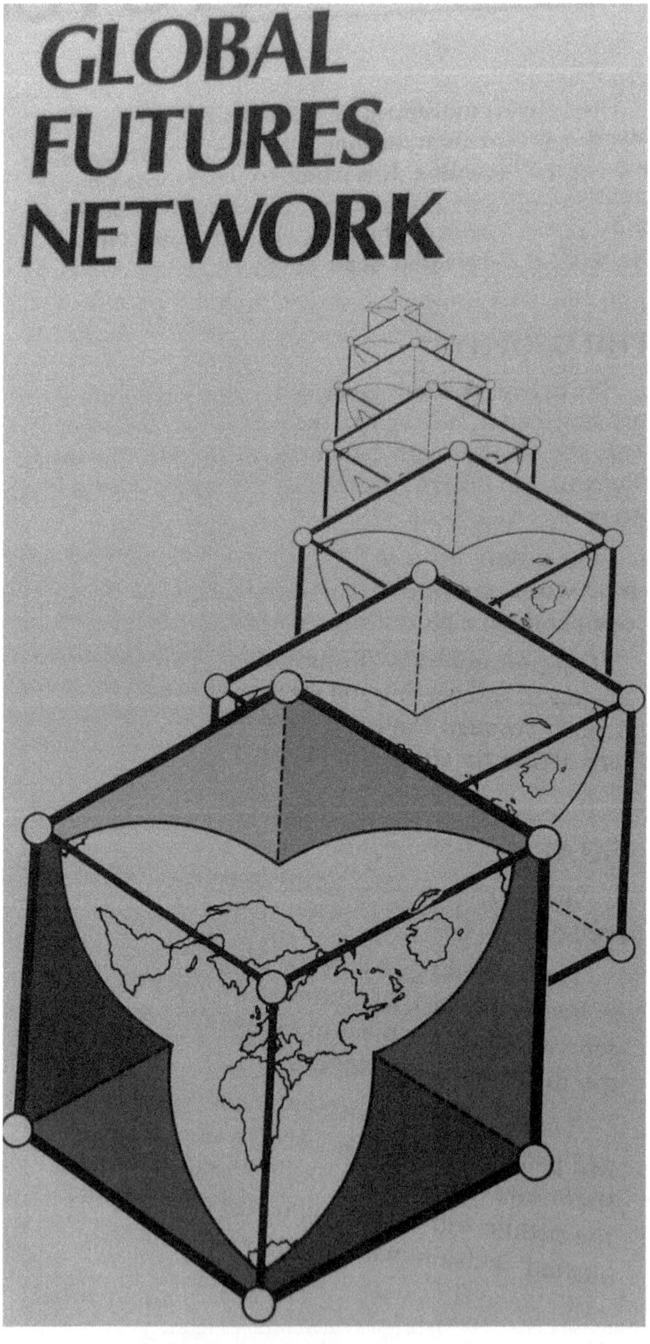

Figure 9.2. The Global Futures Network.
(Flyer, Robert Jungk Nachlass.)

institutes, or chapters in different parts of the world. The mailing list led to the newsletter, the carbon copied letter summarizing news, bits of information, and necessary readings, which was mailed to many hundreds of members usually with the help of someone's children or partner. An essential part of the newsletter was a report on the organization itself, including addresses and registers of members and member institutions. Over time the form of the newsletter developed in sophistication to a collection of various summaries of world and human development. The pages of newsletters and early future journals were complemented with statistical bulletins of indicators, collections of methods of futures research, abstracts, indexations, and bibliographies of published works by futurists, and registers and directories of futurists and their consultancies. In other words the need to create synthetic knowledge of the world was replaced by an emphasis on the need to create knowledge about futurism itself. The meeting at Unitar in 1971 came up with the suggestion of creating a *Bulletin for Social Forecasting*, which in the shape of the journal *Technological Forecasting and Social Change* would monitor the field in East and West and spread citations of future research.[95] The journal *Futures*, from 1969 on, contained regular points of information on the methodological discoveries and new organizations of future research. By the mid 1970s and early 1980s, futurists began publishing the so-called *Futurist Survey* and *Futurist Directory* with the names and addresses of all futurists. The Global Futures Network discussed above included the creation of an electronic knowledge bank on the future, a "global futures digest" to fulfill the needs of the professional futurist, a global futures award to provide status to the field and create an organizational coherence "sorely lacking" and ideas to conduct various global opinion polls on the future. "All of these things will literally invent alternative futures!" (Figure 9.2).

CONCLUDING REMARKS: THE FUTURE FACTORY

The artifacts developed by futurists became collections of expertise with global ambitions, no longer universal in their attempts to project a common future, but *universalising* in their ambition to spread a futurist gospel to the world. The indexes, handbooks, directories, and scenarios created by futurists became a kind of concentration of futuristic forms of expertise, in the words of Eyal, "interventions" into emergent forms of world management.[96] This chapter has shown how the future traveled, in the course of the 1970s, from its radical, potentially world altering connotations as a coming continent of time threatened by humanity (but also offering the sole hope for a reunited Mankind), into a kind of management unit, a category of rationalization and invention. During this process, the scientist notions of prediction as futurology, discussed in Chapters 3 and 4, somehow

[95] Letter from Eleonora Masini to Dator October 29, 1971, from Magda McHale to Dator on February 23, 1971.

[96] Gil Eyal and L. Buchholz, "From the Sociology of Intellectuals to the Sociology of Interventions", *Annual Review of Sociology*, 2010, 36: 117–37.

merged with the radically emancipatory notions of the future as a product of the human imagination discussed in Chapter 7 as informing the project of futures studies. As futurists came together around an overarching interest in professionalization, the future itself seemed to leave through the backdoor. The only future continent left to discover was that set by the "potential of Man." While the notion of consciousness, discussed in Chapters 7 and 8, had emphasized the future as a field of resistance and protest, the idea of exploring human potential led into different territory, that of "consciousness." Consciousness had no links to protest or dissent, it was simply a field of hitherto hidden powers of human beings, an extension of their capacity to control their own future. Futurism in the 1980s and 1990s was inward cosmic travel for a Mankind that had discovered the power of the atom but not its own capacity to conjure a new world, and as such it was no longer a reflection on world making but fundamentally escapist. The normative and radical content embodied in futures studies as they came together between 1967 and 1972 seemed to disappear as the conversation on world futures was increasingly taken over by a new breed of technocrats equipped with big computers and a lot of planetary data. A collateral was that the critique of the "system" and the desire to work out the conditions of possibility for a radical system overhaul disappeared from the 1970s on. This development was not outside of futurism itself, rather futurism was constitutive of it.

10
Conclusion

ONE OR MANY FUTURES

In his article, simply entitled "World Futures," the international relations scholar and literary theorist, R. John Williams describes futurology as the offspring of a counterintuitive meeting between Cold War prediction and what he refers to as "Middle Eastern systems theory." Herman Kahn, the British cybernetician, Stafford Beers, and Buckminster Fuller, Williams proposes, were representatives of a new kind of oracle in world futures. They left a decisive mark on intellectual history by showing that world futures had to be thought in the plural, and not in the singular. Kahn's scenario method is, according to Williams, an example of this meeting between Western mathematical notions of statistical probability on the one hand, and a metaphysical and mystical, indeed oriental, systems theory that depicted potential infinitude and plurality, on the other. What began in a rationalist concern with Cold War security ended up, through this meeting, producing what to Williams is a core element of Cold War culture: religious and avant-gardist notions of futures as hidden in numbers of predictability and stochastical reasoning. In this account, Kahn is not a Cold Warrior. Rather, Kahn is an oracle of the world, a protagonist of a pluralist, and somehow, we infer, peaceful vision of an inherently open and harmonious world future.[1]

Williams demonstrates that the scenario method was brought from Kahn's Hudson Institute into the corporate world and particularly Royal Shell by the enigmatic French engineer, Pierre Wack. At the end of a surprisingly long article (its over seventy pages, where most scholars struggle to fit their argument into a 9,000 word mould), Williams displays a long list of multinational companies involved in future research by the 1970s and 1980s. He uses this list as an illustration of how "futurology" brought a somehow post-modern, mystical, avant garde, and utopian management mentality into post-Cold War global corporations. In William's words: "It was a transformation, in short, as Orientalist and literary as it was computationalist and organizational—the combination of which . . . has come to constitute a pluralist temporality to global capital."[2]

Sexy as William's argument is, it seems unclear what a "pluralist temporality to global capital" is and in what way futurology can be understood as having injected this sense of creativity to world corporations. I think that it would be a mistake to

[1] R. J. Williams, "World Futures." In *Critical Inquiry*, 2016, 42: 473–546.
[2] Williams, "World Futures," 474.

think that the diffusion of the tools of future research, including the scenario method with its purported projections of an "open" and "plural" future, somehow represented an attempt to depict an actual openness to the future, or that scenarios in Kahn's or Shell's sense were genuine attempts to engage with the plurality of world developments.[3] The scenario method might have been surrounded by much talk of openness and plurality (after all, this was its selling point); it is meanwhile somehow not coherent to tell this story without emphasizing that it was a technology for the upholding of a status quo, which in at least Herman Kahn's case was directly related to American hegemony in both international politics and global capitalism. The representation of "oracle" is not a fair description either for Kahn or for Wack, and William's argument understates the powered aspects of prediction and the lines of conflict that traversed future research. Buckminster Fuller's purpose with the Geodesic Dome and the Dymaxion World Map, both cited as precursors to Kahn's scenarios (the Dymaxion World Map represented a cut up globe; according to which the world was a flat set of equally proximate or distant parts), was to project ideas of a whole world and create techniques of consciousness and imagination by which the world might be reconnected and unified in the name of Mankind.[4] This could not be farther from Herman Kahn's purpose, and nor could Fuller's intended audience in architecture students and world publics be any more different from Kahn's target clientele. Kahn was a consultant, who sold his scenarios as a tool both for thinking the future of American politics, and for corporate management. In the late 1960s, not only did Kahn write the scenarios for the Commission for the Year 2000, but he also wrote, at Hudson, "The Future of the Corporation" scenarios that were then sold to corporate clients including some that had been involved in future research since its beginnings: IBM, Kodak, Xerox. Among the clients of Hudson's Corporate Environment Study were in particular Royal Dutch Shell. The Shell Oil Scenarios would become a quintessential tool of market making by monitoring volatility in global carbon markets after the first oil crisis in 1973 and the Iranian revolution in 1979.[5] Pierre Wack, the French engineer who brought the scenario tool to Shell (and from Shell, far into the developing world), might well have been influenced by Indian yogis as Williams shows, but he was also a *prospectiviste*, an engineer and consultant not so different from the French engineers and consultants discussed in Chapter 3, beginning with the transhumanist rationalist and technocrat Jean Coutrot. Coutrot believed that a perfectly rationalized world could be governed by engineers, united by a world encompassing futuristic consciousness.

The list of global corporations making use of scenarios, foresight, Delphi panels, and forecasts in the contemporary world, which impressively figures at the end of William's article, is not an indication of a plurality of world futures. Rather, they

[3] Angela Wilkinson and Roy Kupers, "Living in the Futures." *Harvard Business Review*, 2013, 91 (5): 118–27; Angela Wilkinson and Roy Kupers, *The Essence of Scenarios. Learning from the Shell Experience* (Amsterdam: Amsterdam University Press, 2015).

[4] See Buckminster Fuller Institute, www.bfi.org

[5] Williams, "World Futures"; Timothy Mitchell, *Carbon Democracy. Political Power in the Age of Oil* (London: Verso Books, 2011).

bring out an element that is absent from Williams' argument, having to do with the way that forms of future research emerged from the 1960s and 1970s as core technologies of control and management of the present. My argument about the plurality of world time is different from Williams'. I have proposed that what marks the idea of the future in the post-war period is not, as historians have suggested, a sudden shift from progress to decline after 1973, but rather, a struggle between conceptions of world temporalities as indeed singular or plural. The chapters of this book have shown that the post-war period was marked by heterogeneous and oftentimes directly rivaling conceptions of the world future. These were marked by the opposition between representations of the future as a teleological and foreseeable narrative of a stage-driven logic of modernization, and representations of the future as infinitely plural—because of the variety of human life, politics, and imaginations. The competition between these different conceptions is paralleled by a highly material struggle between the forms of expertise, knowledge, and predictive technologies used to depict, and enact, world futures. The world futures that emanated from the different strands of future research tell an important story of how conceptions of the world, and of human influence on that world, changed during the post-war decades. It also tells a crucial story about the way that forms of prediction enacted conflicts between notions of control over the Cold War world, and what I have referred to as neo-utopian ambitions to find forms of escape, protest, and resistance to that world. The idea of plural futures belongs, to me, in this second category—in notions of the future that attempted to think a radically different present and that used forms of prediction as the basis for conjuring a future that demanded action against the flow of ongoing trends, in other words a change of present structures. As shown in several chapters, the idea of plural futures had a radical connotation to the Cold War era that it would be unfortunate to underestimate: it stood for the idea that only by positing a very different set of objectives for human development could the future of the world, and of humanity, be saved. As it turns out, this was also the difficult, and perhaps too difficult, lesson of future research to the post-Cold War period.

The introduction of this book proposed that focusing on arguments of the singular vs. plural nature of the future permits an established "futures past" historiography to be turned on its head, by pointing out two things. First, there were many genres or modes of future creation across the long period from 1945 to the 1990s, and that these cannot all be referred to as part of one dominant mode of rationalistic or scientist engagement with the future.[6] Futures thinking could draw on a very wide range of repertoires including not least the human imagination and key forms of subjectivity, opinion, and intuitive judgment. Second, these modes or repertoires of future creation were divided by the fundamental conflict line between the future as control and status quo, oftentimes by reference to scientist reasoning, or, on the opposite side of the spectrum, the future as an active human construct and product

[6] Rudiger Graf and Benjamin Herzog, "Von der Geschichte der Zukunftsvorstellungen zur Geschichte ihrer Generierung: Probleme und Herausforderungen des Zukunftsbezugs im 20. Jahrhundert", in *Geschichte und Gesellschaft*, 2015, 42 (3): 497–515.

of the imagination. Arguably, this genealogy of the modern concept of the future gives it a relevance to the contemporary era in which the future would otherwise, as an inherently crisis-ridden concept, seem to have played out its role. I want to refute this idea and turn back to the original Koselleckian notion that the future does not leave the present in times of crisis, it rather returns, because it is crisis that makes the future urgent.[7] As it returns, as is arguably the case at the present moment in which interest in the future is again exploding, the distinction between the future as a problem of scientist reasoning or active imagination, and the future as a problem of control vs. change comes back to the fore of arguments.[8]

Meanwhile, interest in the future as part of reactions to crises do not necessarily proceed to alter and transform the things and trends that are problematic in the present. They might rather serve to perpetuate these, and inscribe them into equilibria and balances of power by which also future-threatening aspects of the present become part of normality. The sociologist Barbara Adam proposes to view the distinction between futures as stabilization and control, on the one hand, and futures as possible embryos of change, on the other, in terms that are different from mine but thought evoking: *present futures* or *futures present*. Present futures are the extrapolated and enclosed futures of the present, the way that it is currently taking place, while futures present are those seeds that might make things different and that might also help us engage with a future that appears in no way as less threatened today than at the height of the Cold War era. To Adams, following in the footsteps of Hans Jonas, acting on and for *futures present* can only take place through an act of love toward future generations, through an extension of the notion of ethical responsibility to encompass the effects of our actions over time, but also, importantly, through forms of knowledge creation, including in the humanities and social sciences, that help us imagine world futures and our place in them.[9]

I would like to think that the historical argument in the pages of this book has some relevance for this act of loving the future, and that this relevance relies in the beginnings of a genealogical argument about contemporary capacities and incapacities in thinking, imagining, and predicting the future. In many ways the narrative of the chapters is more a gloomy account than a hopeful one, because it has more than anything emphasized the enduring role of forms of future knowledge as part of what contemporary sociologists refer to as a "management of expectation," in other words, prediction as a form of power over time. This arguably stands as the central line of continuity in forms of future thinking across the post-war period,

[7] Reinhart Koselleck, "The Temporalization of Utopia," in *The Practice of Conceptual History. Timing History, Spacing Concepts* (Palo Alto: Stanford University Press, 1991), 84–99; Koselleck, "Transformations of Experience," in *The Practice of Conceptual History. Timing History, Spacing Concepts,* 45–83.

[8] See the series of conferences on the theme of anticipation, organized by the UNESCO chair in futures studies in Trento in 2015 and again at Harvard in April 2018; "Brave New World," in Amsterdam 2018; see several large research programs in scenarios and future making including the UK Humanities and Arts Research Council 2015 call "Caring for the Future" and the 2017 call to EU Horizon 2020 with a special title on scenarios.

[9] Barbara Adam and Chris Hargroves, *Future Matters* (Amsterdam: Brill, 2005).

and it might have something to teach us, then, about the reasons why other forms of future thinking, indeed those that emphasized love, imagination, and protest, disappeared.

THE IMAGE OF THE FUTURE

The future has made something of a remarkable return in the humanities and social sciences of recent, and the historical argument made in this book fits with an emerging literature that has proposed that contemporary societies are increasingly involved in a "management of expectation" and in the active creation of "socio technic imaginaries" of the future.[10] According to this literature, tools such as forecasts and scenarios contribute to the shaping of pervasive narratives and images of change that shape patterns of action. A central argument here comes from the sociologist, Jens Beckert, who has argued that expectations of the future are not, as economists believe, a projection of rational preferences along a set of foreknowable and calculable probabilities. Rather, says Beckert in a line of reasoning similar to the early twentieth century Chicago economist Frank Knight, the future is marked by fundamental uncertainty, and in situations of uncertainty, actors resort to beliefs, fictional stories, and images on the future that somehow help to uphold notions of continuity. Beckert's argument crosses the path of the historical narrative of this book in an interesting way here, because Kenneth Boulding, author of the 1956 book, *The Image*, studied with Knight in Chicago. Boulding had in fact begun his studies with John Maynard Keynes in Oxford. Keynes' arguments on the future were different from Knight's.[11] According to Keynes, the speculative activity in capitalism is driven by a set of images on desirable future states, and these images motivate economic actors to creative action in the name of the common good. Frank Knight, meanwhile, was a deeply conservative thinker and Chicago school economist.[12] In Knight's 1922 article, much cited by contemporary risk studies, a difference is made between situations of risk, and situations of uncertainty.[13] Situations of risk can be managed through forms of rationality, and actors attempt, much like the futurists at RAND, to transform situations of uncertainty into situations of predictable risk by making use of probabilistic calculation. Meanwhile, says Knight, there are situations of uncertainty that defy such calculation of risk and demand, in the end, a form of subjective opinion or judgment. It is easy to see that these reflections on uncertainty marked important fields of the social sciences already in the first half of the twentieth century. After 1945, the concern with uncertainty peaked due to the influence of discourses on nuclear war and

[10] Sheila Jasanoff and Sang Yung Kim, *Dreamscapes of Modernity* (Cambridge MA: Harvard University Press, 2015).

[11] Jens Beckert, *Imagined Futures. Fictional Expectations and Capitalist Dynamics* (Cambridge MA: Harvard University Press, 2016) 9, 39, 44–5, 56.

[12] Angus Burgin, "The Radical Conservatism of Frank H. Knight." *Modern Intellectual History* 2009, 6 (3): 513–38.

[13] Frank Knight, *Risk, Uncertainty and Profit*, 1921.

human destruction. Experimentation with gaming at RAND became a core impetus in neoclassical economics and rational choice theory, and, eventually, on the rational expectations theory that Beckert argues against. While these strands became dominant strands in the intellectual history of the Cold War era social sciences, other strands of "Cold War" thinking were deemed less important and partially forgotten.[14] This is arguably the case of Kenneth Boulding's answer to the question of what constituted rationality in situations of omnipresent uncertainty. To Boulding, the only solution to the risks to human survival that he saw as generated by a world economic system driven by military industry was to transform the economics of the armaments struggle into an economics of peace. To Boulding, whose *Image* was a rebuttal of Parsonian systems theory (see Chapter 8), this corresponded to a change from competitive economic exchange relations, into a love-generating system that fostered cooperation and reciprocity and ended up projecting a concept of value that to Boulding was linked to an idea of a universal human value system.[15] The historical process by which such arguments got lost from the mainstream post-war economic canon is a story for another book, but Boulding's argument that the "system" is oriented toward an image that human beings set and can therefore reset is a profound challenge from the less remembered parts of the post-war social sciences to contemporary debates on the future.

As various strands of behavioral research drew the implications of not only Boulding's idea of the image, but many other versions of systems' theoretical thinking in the 1950s and 1960s, images of the future became actual objects of intervention and control. Chapters 4 and 5 have shown how future research was born at RAND as the idea that a general systems theory could generate a general theory of the future, and that the future of human behavior in all fields would then be predictable and subject to human cognition and reach. As the belief in such a general theory began to falter in the course of the 1960s, to no small extent as a result of failures and shortcomings of predictive experimentation itself, prediction left the field of theorizing about human behavior and became, instead, a technology for the active shaping of behavior. As such it emerged as a quintessential Cold War tool for managing an unforeseeable environment, indeed a Knightsean situation of uncertainty, by bearing on the judgments entering into the act of decision making. The focus on decision, or "rational decision," in particular in the context of debates on the future of social and political systems, was directly related to an idea of plurality. But plurality was not in this sense a promising set of open developments, rather, it was a problem of doors to be closed. Indeed plurality posed the problem of how to chose optimal future among a potential diversity of outcomes. The scenario tool hid an ambition that from the development of Delphi in 1964 became central in future research, namely, that of selecting one future from an array of possible futures, on the basis of a judgment on desirability. This problem of sorting among

14 Philip Mirowski, *Machine Dreams. How Economics Became a Cyborg Science* (Cambridge MA: Harvard University Press, 2002), 370–415.

15 Robert Scott, *Kenneth Boulding, a Voice Crying in the Wilderness* (Basingstoke: Palgrave Macmillan, 2015), 76, 91.

the plurality of futures of the present is key to the genealogy of prediction. I have linked this problem to what I argued were technocratic and inherently conservative reflections on a political system driven by the mass, and to an apprehension that this mass might be the source of series of undesirable outcomes. Forms of prediction, in this context, appeared as a necessary and expert-based mechanism of correction to democratic decision making.

Uncertainty, in this context, was not a problem of lack of foreknowledge of future developments, it was inherently a normative problem of the desired forms of continuation of the present. Forms of prediction allowed for treating this problem in a scientific or quasi-scientific way, by making images of consequences part of the process of decision, and by referring to expert judgment. Chapter 5 argued that while the pragmatist philosopher, John Dewey was an influence on liberal conceptions of future research in the 1950 and early 1960s, in fact predictive experimentations such as that performed at RAND went much farther than Dewey's conception of "ends-in-view." By ends-in-view Dewey meant a future-oriented form of pragmatic public deliberation. But actual technologies of prediction did not foremost aim to improve the quality of public deliberation (despite the fact that they were sometimes presented as such, for instance in de Jouvenel's notion of conjecture that I have argued was not a notion of planning but a notion of *anti*-planning); rather, their purpose was to turn the question of the choice of desirable future into a matter of expertise. Indeed, the very concept of rationality had the direct connotation to expert judgment as *the process by which a decision became rational.* This is, it has to be argued, an unconventional notion of expertise, linked not to factual statements or tangible forms of knowledge, but to expectations and judgments on the future.[16]

This leads to an argument by which it might be posited that the history of post-war forms of prediction reasserted values of technocracy, but for an age often understood not only as post-industrial but also as post-positivist or "reflexive," and as marked by inherent forms of uncertainty.[17] If we take the cues from this literature, in such an age, the object of expertise is increasingly uncertainty itself, while expertise is also challenged in a contested public environment. In many ways the history of predictive technologies such as Delphi or scenarios show that they were strategic responses to such a situation of contestation. Prediction as social technology (see Chapter 5) did not in actual fact attempt to bypass the question of values, rather, its purpose was to turn essentially value-laden choices into rational choices through the lever of expertise. It is precisely this that turned prediction into a powerful social or political technology for the post-1968 period. From the second half of the 1960s, future research left its experimental stage and became integrated as a new technology of planning in both Western and socialist planning systems.

[16] See Douglas R. Holmes, *An Economy of Words. Communicative Imperatives in Central Banks* (Chicago: University of Chicago Press, 2014); Martin Giraudeaud, "Remembering the Future. Entrepreneurship Guidebooks in the US, 1945–1975," in *Foucault Studies,* 2012, 13: 40–66.

[17] Bruno Latour, *We Have Never Been Modern* (Cambridge MA: Harvard University Press, 2012); Ulrich Beck, Scott Lash, and Anthony Giddens, *Reflexive Modernization* (London: Polity, 1994); Helga Nowotny, *The Cunning of Uncertainty* (Cambridge MA: Harvard University Press, 2016).

As forecasts, Delphis and scenarios became governmental techniques, they were applied to one predominant problem, which was not as we might think increased economic uncertainty, but the problem of value revolutions and social trends (understood in turn as triggers of economic uncertainty).

In this capacity, forms of prediction were used by national and public planning systems, but also by global corporations, many of them listed in William's appendix, because they seemed to allow for monitoring value change not only in Western publics but also in global imaginations and importantly, in the developing world. As a form of planning which permitted a planners' gaze to be extended both in time (to a new temporal category of twenty-five to thirty years), and space (from the national level to the transnational, interdependent, or global level), predictive technologies could somehow bridge statist and corporate rationalities and bring management methods taken from the large corporation to bear on governmental ways of "seeing the future."[18] Consultancy, the mode of expertise that carried many forms of future research, further enabled the overlap and circulation between public and private forms of planning because as consultants, futurists could act as go-betweens between governmental and corporate logics of decision.

From this viewpoint, it is not at all a paradox that the real interest in futurology took off at the very same moment that historians have depicted as marking the turn *from* the future. From the oil crises on, what had in the corporate world begun in experiments with decision games, forecasts, and scenarios as ways of improving decision making became techniques for envisioning new and turbulent world market relationships that set a premium on the active management of expectations. Scenarios, in this context, allowed companies such as Shell to set out normative, guiding images of price movements and thereby contribute to a much desired stabilization of world commodity markets. At the same time, forecasting also became a preferred tool of transnational organizations. The Geneva historian, Michel Christian, shows how the socialist bloc began systematic use of forecasts in international trade from the early 1970s on, as a way of coordinating long-term relationships with the developing countries over commodities.[19] The integrated or "total" forecasts discussed in Chapter 6 thus left the realm of the socialist national economy, and became the means for oversight of world relations. As futurists engaged in this attempt to transpose predictive methods from representations of nuclear strategy and domestic sociocultural revolutions in the Western world, to a reflection on global temporalities, they contributed actively to reinventing predictive technologies as tools of control for global developments, and political technologies of a high modernist process of globalization. In 1975, the OECD, bringing in Daniel Bell as a consultant, introduced scenarios as a planning tool for trade relationships between the Western world and the developing countries in its so-called Interfuturs project. Interfuturs used scenarios as the strategic response to

[18] James C. Scott, *Seeing Like a State.*

[19] Michael Christian, "UNCTAD and Trade Negotiations 1965–1976," forthcoming in Sandrine Kott et al. *Planning in Cold War Europe.*

the post-OPEC context, by using the scenario method as a tool to set out new and "harmonious" images of an emerging world market in which a new set of world economic actors might share a stake.[20]

Inside the Western world, economic and social forecasting became a response to the critique of planning that was part of the value revolutions of the late 1960s. As Matthias Schmelzer has shown, Western governments were deeply troubled by the rejection of growth and affluence that seemed to have taken place in the social sphere after 1968 and that seemed to mark a turn around on post-war mentalities. Growth did not, said the OECD's Interfuturs report, have "physical limits"; it had "socio-psychological limits" in the form of growing reactions to change.[21] Somehow, these reactions had to be managed. It was in this context that Western governments, inspired by the uses of forecasting in the corporate field, identified future research, forecasting, and prospective as new techniques and "savoir gouvernemental," which somehow permitted them to create a measure of oversight over the many futures of the present, depicted in diagrams and charts of the period as the futures stretching out from a tree.

These arguments can be read as part of a much needed historicization of the notion of uncertainty, which the contemporary social sciences treat as an endemic and omnipresent phenomenon. It was as part of a management of values and images surrounding change that prediction had importance, because it allowed for the active management of future images in global populations by shaping shared expectations about the future. As such futurology embodied a radically different take on planning from that which had dominated the first half of the twentieth century—not that of setting down quantitative and mainly economic objectives, but that of creating normative, desirable, and persuasive images of change.

This gave a tremendous and powerful role to the activity of prediction. Importantly, in some countries, that have not been dealt with within the pages of the book, this very point led to thorough debates on how future research could be taken from planning circles into the public sphere as a genuine means of deliberation. This happened for instance in Sweden in the mid 1970s as future research was set up as an alternative to planning and as a form of public debate of the question of energy futures. The argument here, put forward by the peace activist and Nobel prize laureate Alva Myrdal, was that future research was not any empirical social science, but one of a particular power and importance, as it concerned a choice of future that could not be relegated to experts. This rejection is interesting in the light of the fact that in most places, it was precisely as expert-led planning that future research found its role.[22]

[20] Jenny Andersson, "Shaping the Future of World Markets," forthcoming in Sandrine Kott et al., *Planning in Cold War Europe.*

[21] *Interfutures. Facing the Future, Mastering the Probable and Managing the Unpredictable* (Paris: OECD, 1979).

[22] Jenny Andersson, "Choosing Future. Alva Myrdal and the Construction of Swedish Future Studies," *International Review of Social History*, 2006, 51 (02): 277–95.

THE PROBLEM OF FORECLOSURE

William's argument is part of a number of works that in recent years have emphasized the links between Cold War science and forms of avant-garde, counterculture, or dissent. These arguments have also brought out the cultural, utopian dimension, and images and literary representations of forms of future thinking untreated by historians of Cold War science. The productive contribution of this literature has been to debunk a representation of Cold War science as built on a hegemonic idea of mechanistic rationality, and to point instead to the plurality of forms of knowledge production that include, for instance, science fiction, or, as Williams suggests, Middle Eastern mystique. Williams' argument is not so different here from Fred Turner's description of countercultural hippie communities in the San Francisco Bay area and their creation of the so-called Whole Earth Catalogue. These countercultural communities, Turner argues, were central in the development of a Silicon Valley futurism, which evolved over time into a kind of cyber culture entirely compatible with the post-modern language of the new economy.[23] The process that Turner describes is similar to the process in which futurists left their previous positions of dissent against Cold War culture, and seemed to embrace pro-market stances of consultancy and human creativity. While futurists of the 1980s and 1990s retained a language of creativity and imagination, of "thinking outside of the box!" they merged this language with a kind of new economy jargon. The notion of alternative futures, which had stood in the 1960s for plural world developments and alternative world orders, became associated with the plurality of consciousness, social models, and market innovations. Whether this was, as Williams argued an opening, or a form of closure, is debatable. Arguably, it changed the nature of future research from a concern with the world to a concern with the human self. Futurists' belief in the power of imagination relied on the idea that only by imagining different, and better worlds, would humanity be able to see the absurdity of the world it had actually created and hence be spurred to seek action. As the call to the radical imagination turned into a much less radical notion of consciousness, much of the systemic and critical qualities of future research seemed to disappear. Consciousness was not a matter of a critical stance against a certain world order or political project, it was, rather, a reflection on the future exploitation of human potential. As such, consciousness also lacked the relationship to the idea of resistance or responsibility that early futurists had identified in the imagination. Consciousness was no longer about saving the future by implanting forms of future responsibility in the minds of human beings, it was rather about the unleashing of an unlimited stream of possible human futures. As world was replaced by notions of self-fulfillment and self-development, somehow, the category of the future disappeared from the field of futurism. What remained, as futurists turned to a process of professionalization and consultancy, were debates about future research and futurists themselves.

[23] Fred Turner, *From Counter Culture to Cyberculture. Stewart Brand, the Whole Earth Network, and the Rise of Digital Utopianism* (Chicago: University of Chicago Press, 2012), 175 f.

This corresponded to a process by which future research also seemed to break with established social science. The first pages of this book made the suggestion that future research is indicative of a core post-war debate about the limits of human perception and influence, and the ability to shape the fate of individuals and societies. Future research was, at a particular moment from the mid 1960s to the mid 1970s, a frontier of the social sciences. It seems important to understand why it fell from the forefront of the social sciences, and the effects that this change had on its conception and practice. A tendency in historical research has, as argued, been to understand the demise of future research as part of a "crisis of predictability" following the end of the long post-war era. This can be dated either to 1973 or to 1989 as the gateposts of the present.[24] For sure, the end of the Cold War changed the raison d'etre of future research, which became somehow less concerned with imminent disaster and the potential collapse of the future, and in many ways more concerned with present developments of transition, consumer preferences, the quality of democracy. The spirit of militancy that was triggered by the Cold War, in what Samuel Moyn has referred to as the Last Utopia—the conversion of utopian energy toward the struggle for human rights—also ran out of steam as history came to an end and democracy and liberal markets seemed to have won the battle.[25] Meanwhile, the argument in the previous pages has rather pointed to developments in the nature of future research itself. Such developments colluded, arguably, with epistemic developments in the social sciences to undo the future as an object of social science interrogation. As Peter Wagner has shown, from the 1970s on, social science was divided into subfields in which ideas of traceable structures were increasingly replaced with questions of meaning and cultural relevance.[26] Social science increasingly lost its privileged relationship with nation states and also began doubting its problem-solving role among many other forms of knowledge production including, indeed, consultancy. There is a nostalgic dimension to this argument that it seems important to avoid, meanwhile, as the German historian, Ariane Leendertz, suggests, as notions of risk, reflexivity, and complexity made it into the social sciences, the immediate purpose of these epistemic approaches was no longer to solve social problems.[27] The erosion of forms of systems thinking might well be considered in this context. The idea of the "system," an aggregate and of course in many ways problematic epistemic construct, had enabled views of the future, as a tangible question of the temporality of a system consisting of manifold man–nature relationships, in which all forms of action had aggregate consequences over time. Depictions of a system with a predictable logic allowed for conceptions of intervention on a totally unprecedented level by the late 1960s

[24] Matthias Schmelzer, "The Crisis Before the Crisis: The Problems of Modern Society and the OECD 1968–1974," in *European Review of History* 2012, 19 (6): 999–1020.

[25] Samuel Moyn, *The Last Utopia. The Struggle for Human Rights in History* (Cambridge MA: Harvard University Press, 2011).

[26] Peter Wagner, *Sozialwissenschaften und Staat. Frankreich, Italien, Deutschland 1945–1985* (Frankfurt: Campus Verlag, 1991); Peter Wagner et al., *Social Sciences and the Modern State. National Experiences and Theoretical Crossroads* (New York: Cambridge University Press, 1991).

[27] Leendertz, "Losing Control." Unpublished.

and early 1970s, as demonstrated most notably by the Club of Rome report.[28] As systems theory migrated into computer and information science, complexity theory, and even chaos theory, somehow the legitimacy of examining the future both as a question of structure, and as a question of human agency within the system, lost in importance. At the same time, the critical strand in futures thinking seemed to leave the field of future thinking and be substituted by forms of predictive expertise focused on processes of market making, innovation, or business management. The corollary was that the future seemed to disappear as a category for moral or political reflection on the world.

This did not as such mean that futurology died. Rather, it meant that futures research migrated from the halls of mainstream social science into much more marginal fields and activities with a different set of purposes. Forms of future research lived on in fields such as management studies or risk research, innovation studies, or, more recently, in an eclectic and quite disconcerting area of neuroscience and transhumanism. Above all, the militancy and utopianism of future research changed character, as future research increasingly became a kind of global technocracy or world expertise. Importantly, in some of these areas, not only did the notion of alternative futures change meaning, but so did the reflexivity and critical epistemological stance of 1960s futures studies. Futurists' awareness of the powered role in the self-fulfilling prophesy looked much different when such arguments were no longer linked to a critique of dominant rationality assumptions, but to notions of performance and effectiveness in "thinking outside of the box."

The argument can be contrasted here with another strand of the social sciences, which, mainly influenced by critical theory, and in disciplines such as geography, anthropology, and international studies, has been concerned with the problem of foreclosure and particularly with the problem of foreclosure of contemporary governmentalities such as "liberal" or "neoliberal." To these scholars, contemporary forms of dealing with the future are marked not by openings, not by understandings of the future as a territory for possible change and alternative, but quintessentially, for a kind of perpetual present embodied in and created by the activity of prediction. As argued by Gregoire Mallard and Andrew Lakoff, the purpose of predictive technologies is to make claims on the future that serve to control the present, and as proposed by the geographer Ben Anderson and the international relations theorist Claudia Aradau, prediction serves to close down future horizons by focusing on immanent threats to existence which effectively turns the future into an empty sphere.[29] The arguments made in the previous pages both reaffirm and challenge these narratives. Several chapters of the book have indeed been concerned with tracing the history of prediction as a core political technology of the present, and

[28] Clifford Siskin, *System. The Shaping of Modern Knowledge* (Cambridge MA: MIT Press, 2016) 7; Paul Edwards, *A Vast Machine. Computer Models, Climate Data and the Politics of Global Warming* (Cambridge MA: MIT Press, 2010), 2–5, 139.

[29] Ben Anderson, "Preemption, Precaution, Preparedness. Anticipatory Action and Future Geographies," in *Progress in Human Geography*, 2010, 34 (06): 277–98; Gregoire Mallard and Andrew Lakoff, "How Claims to Know the Future are Used to Influence the Present"; Claudia Aradau and Rens van Munster, *Politics of Catastrophe. Geneaologies of the Unknown* (London: Routledge, 2011).

as an inherently powered technology of future making. Other chapters, however, have sought to bring out that such forms of future making were contested in important ways, and that prediction can therefore not be described as caught up in a linear trajectory from Cold War concerns of security to present day neoliberal arguments. As new actors such as the peace movement and environmentalist movement, or, indeed, important Third World actors, began making use of forms of prediction by the mid 1960s, they did so in order to challenge the dominant visions of the future that Cold War prediction had produced, and the geopolitical structures that it reflected. In so doing they challenged future-oriented modes of knowledge creation such as Delphi. The future workshop conceived by Robert Jungk is an example of this, as are the manifold models, planetariums, and exhibits, that were designed to trigger visions of a future that could not even be imagined so far was it from actual developments. These unimagined futures were not catastrophes, they were utopias, dreams of a radically better world. What might be understood as the entry of forms of neoliberal imaginaries into the field of future research was perhaps the cumulative result of the failures of these forms of utopian imaginaries. As a universalist concern with shared and common world futures broke down in the aftermath of the collision between the Third World and the industrialized nations after NIEO and OPEC, what was left was a vision of the future of world markets. As the notion of humanity seemed somehow disqualified, people, in the sense of individuals, became viewed as the primary future-makers. It is in this context and through the rise of futuristic consultancy after 1989 that future research can be understood as a carrier of neoliberal imaginaries. The Ngram views used by Williams that show the peak of the notion of plural or alternative futures from the 1970s on must be seen in the light of this argument of the disintegration of the notion of one world with a common and shared future.[30]

*

Prediction was not just a matter for an avant garde policy scientist or rationalist expertise: prediction was a fundamentally heterogeneous enterprise, in which highly morally charged notions of humanity and the world met. Prediction could be both radical pedagogy and expertise, both scientist and utopian. Against a post-war notion of the future as the "long term" stood a distinctly different idea of the future as a field of resistance, love, and imagination. According to the latter, the future was not a logical and foreseeable construct, but a domain of active human consciousness, transcendence, and being. As futures studies somehow married futurology by the mid-1970s on and the different strands of future research came together in a dominant idea of expertise, it was this radical content that was lost.

[30] See Sibylle Duhautois, *Etudes sur le futur et conscience globale* (Ph.D. Diss, Paris, Centre d'Histoire de Sciences Po, 2017).

Bibliography

PRIMARY SOURCES

Archives

Daniel Bell papers, Pusey Library, Harvard University Archives.

Kenneth Boulding Archives, the Bentley Historical Library, Ann Arbor.

Archives of the Carnegie Corporation, Butler Library, Columbia University, New York.

Commission for the Year 2000 papers, American Academy for the Arts and Sciences (AAAS), Cambridge, MA.

Records of the Committee for Nuclear Disarmament and Peace, International Institute for Social History, Amsterdam.

Records of the Congress for Cultural Freedom, University Library of Chicago Special Collections Research Center.

James Dator papers, University of Hawaii, Manoa, Honolulu.

Bertrand de Jouvenel papers, Bibliothèque nationale de France, Département des manuscrits (NAF 28143).

Fédération mondiale des études du futur (World Futures Studies Federation), UNESCO Archives, Paris.

Ossip Flechtheim Nachlass, Deutsches Exilarkiv, Deutsches Nationalbibliotek, Frankfurt am Main.

Ford Foundation Archives (at the time consulted in New York, now in Rockefeller Archives Center).

Olaf Helmer papers, RAND Archives and Library, Santa Monica.

Archives of Research Committee 07 of the International Sociological Association, possession of Markus Schulz, New York University.

Robert Jungk Nachlass, Literaturarchiv, Salzburg University, Salzburg.

Eleonora Masini, records of the World Futures Studies Federation. Private possession, Rome.

John McHale's archives in the Dator collection, University of Hawaii Manoa, Honolulu.

Lewis Mumford Collection, Rare Books and Manuscript Section, University of Pennsylvania Libraries.

Documents pertaining to the creation of the Sixième section, Maison des Sciences de l'homme, Paris.

Rockefeller Archives Center (RAC), New York.

Alvin Toffler papers, Butler Library, Columbia University, New York.

Interviews

Interview with Wendell Bell, Yale University, April 24, 2013.

Interview with Jim Dator, June 16, 2010, Paris.

Interviews with Hugues de Jouvenel, December 5, 2011, April 22, 2012, June 15, 2013.

Interview with Jerome Glenn Washington, March 12, 2014.

Interview with Ted Gordon, April 24, 2013.

Interview with Stephen Graubard, New York, March 20, 2013.

Interview with Lars Ingelstam and Göran Bäckstrand, Stockholm, May 3, 2012.

Interview with Eleonora Masini, June 24, 2010, Rome, and January 18, 2012, Rome.

Interview with Bart van Stenbergen, February 16, 2012.

Newspapers and Magazines

Cahiers de la Fondation française pour l'étude des problemes humains 1941–1945, Fondation française pour l'étude des problemes humains.

Chroniques D'Actualite De La SEDEIS, 1955–1959. Appeared under the name of *Faits et Conjonctures*, 1953–1954.

Futures, 1969–.

Futuribles, 1959–.

The Futurist, newsletter published by the World Future Society, 1972–.

Futurum. Zeitschrift fur zukunftsforschung, herausgegeben von Ossip K. Flechtheim, Berlin, 1968–1970.

Life Magazine, December 6, 1968, 119–123.

New York Times Magazine, devoted to futures research, April 19, 1964.

Prospective, 1958–1960, Centre Internationale de Prospective.

Revue Internationale des Sciences Sociales, 21, 4, 1969, UNESCO, "Social Science Courier."

Science Journal, "The Future of Future Research," Special Issue, 3, 10, 1967.

Technological Forecasting and Social Change, 1970–.

To-day and To-Morrow, 1923–1924.

PRINTED SOURCES

Agar, Herbert et al. *The City of Man. A Declaration on World Democracy*. New York, Viking, 1941.

Al Hacq, Muhtad. *The Poverty Curtain*. New York, UNITAR, 1976.

Anders, Gunther. *Die Antiquiertheit des Menschen*. Munchen, 1956.

Apostol, Pavel. "Zur Definition und zum Gegenstandsbereich der Methodologie." *Deutsche Zeitschrift für Philosophie*, 14, 12, 1966: 1468–76.

Apostol, Pavel. "Marxism and the Structure of the Future," in *Futures*, 4, 3, 1972: 201–10.

Apostol, Pavel. *Omul Anului 2000, Junimea*. Bucharest, 1972.

Arendt, Hannah. *Between Past and Future. Eight Exercises in Political Thought*. New York, Penguin Classics, 1954.

Arendt, Hannah. *The Human Condition*. Chicago, The University of Chicago Press, (1958) 1998.

Aron, Raymond. *L'opium des intellectuels*. Paris, Calmann Levy, 1955.

Arrow, Kenneth. *Social Choice and Individual Values*. New York, John Wiley, 1971.

Bell, Daniel. "The Power Elite Reconsidered." *American Journal of Sociology*, 64, 3, 1958: 238–50.

Bell, Daniel. "Ten Theories in Search of Reality: The Prediction of Soviet Behavior in the Social Sciences". *World Politics*, 10, 3, 1958: 327–65.

Bell, Daniel. *The End of Ideology. On the Exhaustion of Political Ideas in the 1950s*. Chicago, The Free Press of Glencoe, 1960.

Bell, Daniel. *The End of Ideology*. Cambridge MA, Harvard University Press, 1962 (Second edition).

Bell, Daniel. "Twelve Modes of Prediction. A Preliminary Sorting of Approaches in the Social Sciences." In *Daedalus*, 3, 1964: 845–80.

Bell, Daniel. "Government by Commission," *The Public Interest*, 5, 1966: 3–10.

Bell, Daniel. "The Study of the Future." *The Public Interest*, 1, 1966: 119–131.

Bell, Daniel. "Foreword," to Harvey Perloff. *The Future of US Government. Toward the Year 2000*. New Jersey, 1971.

Bell, Daniel. "Preliminary Memorandum, October 22, 1965," in Daniel Bell and Stephen Graubard, eds. *Toward the Year 2000. Work in Progress*. Cambridge MA, MIT Press, 1997 (1967), 17–20.

Bell, Daniel. "The Year 2000. The Trajectory of an Idea," in Daniel Bell and Stephen Graubard, eds. *Toward the Year 2000. Work in Progress*. Cambridge MA, MIT Press, 1997 (1967), 1–17.

Bell, Daniel. *The Coming of Post-Industrial Society: A Venture in Social Forecasting*. New York, Basic Books, 1999 (1973).

Bell, Daniel and Graubard, Stephen, eds. *Toward the Year 2000: Work in Progress*. Cambridge MA, MIT Press, 1997 (1967).

Bell, Daniel and the American Academy for the Arts and Sciences. *Report of the Commission for the Year 2000*. Cambridge, MA, 1974.

Benjamin, Walter. *Theses on the Philosophy of History*, 1940, IX.

Berger, Gaston. "Husserl et Hume." *Revue internationale de philosophie*, 1939: 342–53.

Berger, Gaston. *Caractère et personnalité*. Paris, Presses universitaires de France, 1955.

Berger, Gaston. *Phénoménologie du temps et de prospective*. Paris, Presses universitaires de France, 1964.

Berger, Gaston and Febvre, Lucien. *L'encyclopedie francaise. Tome XX: Le monde en devenir*. Paris, 1959.

Bestoujev Lada, Igor. "Les recherches sur la prevision sociale en URSS." *Cahier du centre d'etudes et de recherches Marxistes*, Paris, 3, 1968.

Bestoujev Lada, Igor. "Forecasting: An Approach to the Problems of the Future." *International Social Science Journal*, 21, 4, 1969: 526–34.

Bestoujev Lada, Igor. "La prevision, une des methodes de l'exploration de l'avenir." *Revue International des Sciences Sociales*, 21, 4, 1969: 563–74.

Bestoujev Lada, Igor. "Utopias of Bourgeois Futurology." *The Futurist. Newsletter of the World Future Society*, December 1970.

Bestoujev Lada, Igor. "Bourgeois 'Futurology' and the Future of Mankind" Reprinted in Alvin Toffler. *The Futurists*. New York, Random House, 1972, 194–210.

Bestoujev Lada, Igor. "Futures Research in the Soviet Union." *Futures*, 8, 2, 1976: 181–5.

Bestoujev Lada, Igor. *Essai de futurologie*. Moscow, Editions du progress, 1985.

Bestoujev Lada, Igor. "Futures Research in the USSR, Part II: 1981–1985." *Futures*, 4, 1986: 628–37.

Bestoujev Lada, Igor. "Why I Did not Write the History of the Institute of Sociology." *Sociological Research*, 36, 4, 1997: 89–95.

Bloch, Ernst. *Dass Prinzip Hoffnung*. Berlin, Suhrkamp Verlag, 1954.

Bloch, Ernst. "Man and Citizen According to Marx." In Erich Fromm, ed. *Socialist Humanism*. London, Penguin, 1967, 200–06.

Bloch, Ernst. *The Principle of Hope*. Cambridge MA, MIT Press, 1986.

Bloch, Ernst. *The Spirit of Utopia*. Palo Alto, Stanford University Press, 2000.

Botez, Mihai. *Introducere in prospectiva*. Bucharest 1971.

Botez, Mihai. "Cooperative Management of Force Induced International Situations. An Exercise in Formal Modeling." *Policy Sciences*, 8, 1977: 455–68.

Botez, Mihai. "A View from Eastern Europe." *Technological Forecasting and Social Change*, 26, 1984: 121–26.

Botez, Mihai. "East European Intellectuals and the National Communist State." *Praxis International*, 3, 1988: 350–9.

Botez, Mihai and Celac, Marina. "Undesirable vs. Desirable Societies." UN University, 1983.

Boulding, Elise and Boulding, Kenneth. *The Future. Images and Processes*. New York, London, Sage, 1995.

Boulding, Kenneth. "General Systems Theory—The Skeleton of Science." *Management Science*, 2, 3, 1956: 197–208.

Boulding, Kenneth. *The Image. Knowledge in Life and Society*, University of Michigan Press, Ann Arbor, 1956.

Boulding, Kenneth. "National Images and International Systems." *Journal of Conflict Resolution*, 3, 2, 1959: 120–31.

Braudel, Fernand. "Histoire et sciences sociales: La longue duree." *Annales*, 4, 1958: 725–53.

Brzezinski, Zbigniew, Samuel Huntington, Michel Crozier, and Jojo Watanuki. *The Crisis of Democracy. Report on the Ungovernability of Democracy to the Trilateral Commission*. New York, New York University Press, 1973.

Bundy, William P. "A Look Further Ahead." In *Goals for Americans. The Report of the President's Commission on National Goals*. New York, 1960, 360–72.

Chichilnisky, Graciela, et al. *The Bariloche Report*. Spectrum, Utrecht University Press, 1978.

Cole, Sam. *Global Models and the International Economic Order*. Unitar, Pergamon Press, 1979.

Cole, Sam et al. "Scenarios of World Development." *Futures*, 10, 1, 1978: 3–20.

Commissariat General au Plan. *La France face au choc du futur*. Paris, 1972.

Cornish, Edward. "The World Future Society's First Conference." *The Futurist*, 1, 3, 2007: 43.

da Sola Pool, Ithiel. "The International System in the Next Half Century." In Daniel Bell and Stephen Graubard, eds. *Toward the Year 2000: Work in Progress*. Cambridge MA, MIT Press, 1997 (1967), 319–22.

de Jouvenel, Bertrand. *L'economie dirigee. Le programme de la nouvelle generation*. Paris. Libraire Valois, 1928.

de Jouvenel, Bertrand. *Du pouvoir*. Geneva, Editions du cheval aile, 1945.

de Jouvenel, Bertrand. *De la souveraineté*. Paris: Editions Marie Therèse Génin, 1955.

de Jouvenel, Bertrand. *L'art de la conjecture*. Monaco, Editions du rocher, 1962.

de Jouvenel, Bertrand. "Du principat," *Revue Française de la Science Politique* 14, 6, 1964: 1053–86.

de Jouvenel, Bertrand. "Political Science and Prevision." *American Political Science Review* 59, 1, 1965: 29–38.

Deutsch, Karl. "Towards an Inventory of Basic Trends and Patterns in Comparative and International Politics." *American Political Science Review*, 54, 1, 1960: 34–57.

Dewey, John. "Liberating the Social Scientist." *Commentary*, 4, October 1947, 378.

Flechtheim, Ossip K. "History: Theodicy or Odyssey." *Phylon, the Atlanta University Review of Race and Culture*, 4, 1, 1941: 78–88.

Flechtheim, Ossip K. "Toynbee and the Webers." *Phylon, the Atlanta University Review of Race and Culture*, 4, 3, 1943: 248–64.

Flechtheim, Ossip K. "Teaching the Future: A Contribution to the Intellectual and Moral Growth of the Participants." *Journal of Higher Education*, 16, 9, 1945: 460–5.

Flechtheim, Ossip K. "Futurology: The New Science." *Forum*, 3, 1949: 206–9.

Flechtheim, Ossip K. "Zur Kritik der Marxschen Geschichtskonzeption" [1939], Cahiers Vilfredo Pareto, 3, 5, 1965: 141–58.

Flechtheim, Ossip K. *History and Futurology*. Meisenham, A. Glein, 1966.

Flechtheim, Ossip K. *Futurologie. Moglichkeiten und Grenzen*. Frankfurt, Edition Voltaire, 1968.

Flechtheim, Ossip K. "Warum Futurologie?" *Futurum*, 1, 1968: 3–23.

Flechtheim, Ossip K. *Futurologie: Der Kampf um die Zukunft*. Berlin, Verlag Wissenschaft und Politik, 1971.

Fromm, Erich. "Introduction." In Erich Fromm, ed. *Socialist Humanism, an International Symposium*. London, Penguin Press, 1967, 9–19.

Fromm, Erich, ed. *Socialist Humanism, an International Symposium*. London, Penguin Press, 1967.

Fuller, Buckminster. R. *Operating Manual for Spaceship Earth*. Carbondale, Southern Illinois University, 1968.

Gabor, Dennis. *Inventing the Future*. London, Secker and Warburg, 1963.

Gaither, et al. *Report of the Study for the Ford Foundation on Policy and Program*. Detroit, Ford Foundation, 1949.

Galtung, Johan. "A Structural Theory of Violence." *Journal of Peace Research* 1, 2, 1964: 95–119.

Galtung, Johan. "On the Future of the International System." In Robert Jungk and Johan Galtung, eds. *Mankind 2000*. Oslo, PRIO, 1968, 12–41.

Galtung, Johan. "Violence, Peace, and Peace Research." *Journal of Peace Research*, 6, 3, 1969: 167–91.

Galtung, Johan. "On Future Research and its Role in the World." In Japan Society for Futurology. *Proceedings of the International Future Research Conference,* Kyoto, 1970: 103–17.

Galtung, Johan and Robert Jungk. "The Near Future of Mankind, 1970–2000." In Robert Jungk and Johan Galtung eds. *Mankind 2000*, Oslo, 1968: 367–78.

Galtung, Johan and Jan Stoetzel, eds. *Images of the World in the Year 2000*. Vienna, European Coordination Center, 1970.

Goals for Americans. The Report of the President's Commission on National Goals. New York, 1960.

Gordon, Theodore J. *The Future*. New York, Basic Books, 1965.

Gordon, Theodore J. "Cross-Impact Matrices: An Illustration of their Use for Policy Analysis." *Futures*, 1, 6, 1969: 527–31.

Gordon, Theodore J. and Olaf Helmer. *Report on a Long-Range Forecasting Study*. Santa Monica, RAND, 1964.

Gvishiani, Dhermen. *Trajectories of the Future*. Springfield VA, 1972.

Hawaii 2000. Continuing Experiment in Anticipatory Democracy. The Governor's Conference on Hawaii 2000. Honolulu, University Press of Hawaii, 1973.

Heidegger, Martin. *Sein und Zeit*. Halle, Niemayer, 1927.

Helmer, Olaf. *The Prospects of a Unified Theory of Organizations*. RAND discussion paper, Santa Monica, RAND, 1957.

Helmer, Olaf. "The Prospects of a Unified Theory of Organisations." *Management Science*, 4, 2, 1958: 172–76.

Helmer, Olaf. *Social Technology*. New York, Basic Books, 1966.

Helmer, Olaf. *Analysis of the Future: The Delphi Method*. Santa Monica, RAND, 1967.

Helmer, Olaf. *The Future of Science*. Santa Monica, RAND, 1967.

Helmer, Olaf. "Science." *Science Journal* (London). Special issue, "The Future of Future Research," 3, 10, 1967: 49–51.

Helmer, Olaf. *Systematic Use of Expert Opinion*. Santa Monica, RAND, 1967.

Helmer, Olaf and Bernice Brown. *Improving the Reliability of Estimates Obtained from a Consensus of Experts*. Santa Monica, RAND, 1964.

Helmer, Olaf and Norman Dalkey. *The Use of Experts for the Estimation of Bombing Requirements: A Project Delphi Experiment*. Santa Monica, RAND, 1951.

Helmer, Olaf and Nicolas Rescher. *On the Epistemology of the Inexact Sciences*. Santa Monica, RAND, 1958.

Hempel, Carl. "The Function of General Laws in History," *The Journal of Philosophy*, 39, 2, 1942: 35–48.

Hempel, Carl. "The Nature of Mathematical Truth," *The American Mathematical Monthly*, 52, 10, 1945: 543–56.

Hempel, Carl. "Studies in the Logics of Explanation." *Philosophy of Science*, 15, 2, 1948: 135–75.

Hoffman, Stanley. "An American Social Science, International Relations." *Daedalus*, 106, 3, 1977: 41–60.

Huntington, Samuel. "Political Development and the Decline of the American System of World Order," in Daniel Bell and Stephen Graubard, eds. *Toward the Year 2000: Work in Progress*. Cambridge MA, MIT Press, 1997 (1967), 315–17.

Huxley, Aldous. *Ape and Essence*. Chicago, Dee, 1948.

Ikle, Fred, C. "Social Forecasting and the Problem of Changing Values, with Special Reference to Soviet and East European Writings." *Futures*, 3, 2, 1971: 142–50.

Ikle, Fred, C. "Social Forecasting and the Problem of Changing Values, with Special Reference to Soviet and East European Writings." National Technical Information Service, Springfield, Virginia, 1971.

International Sociological Association, Transactions of the 7th World Congress in Sociology, Varna, September 8–14, 1970, "Contemporary and Future Societies: Prediction and Social Planning."

Jantsch, Eric. *Technological Forecasting in Perspective*. Paris, OECD, 1967.

Jantsch, Eric. *Perspectives on Planning*. Paris, OECD, 1970.

Jantsch, Eric. "Technological Forecasting at National Level in Japan. Notes From a Brief Visit." *Technological Forecasting and Social Change*, 2, 1970: 325–7.

Jantsch, Eric. "The New Testament." *Futures*, 3, 1, 1971: 68–72.

Japan Society for Futurology. *Challenges from the Future. Proceedings from the Kyoto conference on future research*. Kyoto, 1970.

Jaspers, Karl. *The Future of Mankind*. Chicago, The University of Chicago Press, 1961.

Jonas, Hans. *Dass Prinzip Verantwortung*. Frankfurt am Main, Insel Verlag, 1979.

Jonas, Hans. "The Concept of God after Auschwitz." *The Journal of Religion*, 67, 1, 1987: 1–13.

Jungk, Robert. *Tomorrow Is Already Here*. New York, Harcourt Brace, 1954.

Jungk, Robert. *Brighter than a Thousand Suns*. New York, Houghton Mifflin Harcourt, 1958.

Jungk, Robert. "A Plea for Social Imagination." *Our Generation Against Nuclear War. An International Quarterly Journal*, 2, 3, 1964: 9–14.

Jungk, Robert. "The Future of Future Research." *Science Journal* 3, 10, 1967: 1–3.

Jungk, Robert. "The Role of the Imagination in Future Research." *Proceedings of the international future research conference*, Kyoto, 1970, 1–7.

Jungk, Robert and Johan Galtung. *Mankind 2000*. Oslo, PRIO, 1968.

Jungk, Robert and Norbert Müllert. *Future Workshops: How to Create Desirable Futures*, London, 1987.

Jungk, Robert and Hans Josef Mundt. *Deutschland ohne Konzeption? Am Beginn einer neuen Epoche*, Munich, 1964.

Kahn, Herman. *On Thermo Nuclear War*. Princeton, NJ, Princeton University Press, 1960.

Kahn, Herman and Anthony J. Wiener. *The Year 2000: A Framework for Speculation on the Next Thirty-Three Years*. New York, Hudson Institute, 1967.

Kaplan, A., A. L. Skogstad, and M. A. Gishik, "The Prediction of Social and Technological Events." In *Public Opinion Quarterly*, 1950, 14, 93–110.

Kolakowski, Leszek. *Towards a Marxist Humanism*. New York, Grove Press, 1969.

Kolakowski, Leszek. *Main Currents of Marxism*. Volume 3, *The Breakdown*. Oxford, Clarendon Press, 1978.

Kristol, Irving. "American Conservatism 1945–1995." *The Public Interest*, 121, 1995: 80–5.

Khrushchev, Nikita. *Report of the Central Committee of the Communist Party of the Soviet Union of the 20th Party Congress*. Moscow, Foreign Languages Publishing House, 1956.
Kumar, Kristian. "Futurology, the View from Eastern Europe." *Futures*, 4, 1, 1972: 90–5.
Lasswell, Harold. *Power and Personality*. London, W.W. Norton and Company, 1948.
Laszlo, Erwin. Goals for Mankind: A Report to the Club of Rome on the New Horizons of Global Community. New York, Club of Rme, 1977.
Lee, Kenneth. "Non Alignment as Applied to Peace Organisations." In *Our Generation Against Nuclear War*, London, 1964: 73–4.
Lem, Stanislav. *The Futurological Congress*. New York, Houghton Mifflin Harcourt, 1985 (1971, 1974).
Lipset, Seymour Martin and Paul Lazarsfeld, "The Psychology of Voting," in *Handbook of Social Psychology*, 2, 1954: 1124–75.
Livingston, D. "The Study of Science Fiction as Forecasting Methodology." *Proceedings of the international conference in future research*, Kyoto, 1970, 71–9.
Malitsa, Mircea. *Contemporanul cronica anului 2000*, Bucharest, Editura Politica 1969.
Malita, Mircea, Mehdi Elmandjra, and the Club of Rome. *The Learning Report of the Club of Rome. Learning to Bridge the Human Gap*. Bucharest, Club of Rome, 1978.
Malitsa, Mircea. *Contemporanul cronica anului 2000*, Bucharest, Editura Politica 1969.
Marcuse, Herbert. *One Dimensional Man. Studies in the Ideology of Advanced Industrial Society*. Beacon Press, New York, 1964.
Marcuse, Herbert. "Socialist Humanism." In Erich Fromm, ed. *Socialist Humanism, an International Symposium*. London, Penguin Press, 1967, 97–106.
Marshall, Alfred. *Industry and Trade*. London, Macmillan, 1920.
Marx Hubbard, Barbara. *The Hunger of Eve. One Woman's Odyssey Toward the Future*. Stackpole Books, 1986.
Marx Hubbard, Barbara. *Conscious Evolution. Awakening the Power of our Social Potential*. New World Library, 2015.
Masini, Eleonora. "Memories of the World Futures Studies Federation." Unpublished manuscript, July 2002.
Masini, Eleonora and the World Futures Studies Federation, *Visions of Desirable Societies*. Honolulu, University of Hawaii Press, 1983.
McHale, John, "Futures Research. Integral and communicative aspects." In Robert Jungk and Johan Galtung, eds. *Mankind 2000*. Oslo, 1968.
McHale, John. *The Future of the Future*. Illinois, Center for Integral Study, 1969.
McHale, John. "Problems in Social and Cultural Forecasting." In Japanese Society for Futurology. *Proceedings of the International Future Research Conference*. Kyoto, 1970, 9–17.
McHale, John. *The Handbook of Futures Research*, 1978.
McLuhan, Marshall. *The Gutenberg Galaxy. Toronto,* University of Toronto Press, 2013.
Mead, Margaret. *Culture and Commitment. A Study of the Generation Gap*. London, 1970.
Mead, Margaret. "A Note on the Contribution of Anthropology to the Science of the Future." to the American Anthropological Association Symposium on Cultural Futurology." 1971.
Mead, Margaret. "The Life Cycle and its Variations. The Division of Roles," in Daniel Bell and Stephen Graubard, eds. *Toward the Year 2000: Work in Progress*. Cambridge MA, MIT Press, 1997 (1967), 239–44.
Meadows, Donella et al., *The Limits to Growth: A Report for the Club of Rome's Project on the Predicament of Mankind*. New York, the Club of Rome, 1972.
Moynihan, Daniel. *The Negro Family, the Case for National Action*. Washington, US Department of Labor, 1965.

Moynihan, Daniel. "The Professionalization of Reform." *The Public Interest* 1, 1965: 6–14.
Mumford, Lewis. *The Story of Utopias*. London, Boni and Liveright, 1922.
Mumford, Lewis. *Technics and Civilization*. London, Harcourt Brace, 1934.
Mumford, Lewis. *The Condition of Man*. London, Harcourt Brace, 1944.
Mumford, Lewis. "Gentlemen, you are mad." *Saturday Review of Literature*, March 2, 1946: 5–6.
Mumford, Lewis. *Man: A Programme for Survival*. Abingdon, Abbey Press, 1946.
Mumford, Lewis. *Values for Survival*. Oxford, Abingdon Press, 1946.
Mumford, Lewis. "An Apology to Henry Adams." *The Virginia Quarterly Review*, 38, 2, 1962: 196.
Mumford Lewis. *The Myth of the Machine. The Pentagon of Power*. New York, Harcourt Brace, 1970.
Neumann, John von and Oskar Morgenstern, *A Theory of Games and Economic Behaviour*. Princeton, NJ, Princeton University Press, 1944.
Ogden, W. F. "Prospecting for the Future." *Social Frontiers*, 1, 1935: 20–2.
Otlet, Paul. *The Annual of International Life*. Brussels, Mondaneum, 1909.
Ozbekhan, Hazan. "The Role of Goals and Planning in the Solution of the World Food Problem," in Robert Jungk and Johan Galtung, eds. *Mankind 2000*. Oslo, 1968, 117–50.
Ozbekhan, Hasan. *The Predicament of Mankind. Quest for Structured Responses to Growing World Wide Complexities and Uncertainties. A Proposal*. New York, Club of Rome, 1970.
Ozebekhan, Hasan. "Toward a General Theory of Planning." In Eric Jantsch, ed., *Perspectives on Planning*. Paris, OECD, 1970: 47–155.
Polak, Fred. *The Image of the Future*. Amsterdam, Elsevier, 1954.
Polak, Fred, "Towards the Goal of Goals." In Johan Galtung and Robert Jungk, eds., *Mankind 2000*, Oslo, Institute for Peace Research, 1969: 307–31.
Polak, Fred. "Mankind 2000 International." In Japanese Society for Futurology. *Challenges from the Future: Proceedings of the International Future Research Conference*. Kyoto, 1970, 70–7.
Polak, Fred. *Prognostics: A Science in the Making Surveys of the Future*. Amsterdam, Elsevier, 1971.
Polanyi, Michael. *The Logic of Liberty*. London, Keegan Paul, 1951.
RAND. *A Problem in Logistics: the Jeep Problem*. Santa Monica, 1946.
RAND. *An Experiment in Estimation*. Santa Monica, 1947.
RAND. *Strategic Gaming*. Santa Monica, 1960.
RAND. *A Use of Simulation for the Study of Future Values*. Santa Monica, 1966.
Randolph, Robert. "Social and Technological Forecasting in the Soviet Union." *Futures*, 8, 6, 1976: 485–95.
Recent Social Trends. Report of the President's Research Committee. New York, McGraw Hill Books, 1933.
Richta, Radovan. "Die wissenschaftlich technischen Revolution und die Alternativen der modernen Zivilisation." *Futurum*, 1, 1968: 205–28.
Richta, Radovan, ed. *Civilisation at the Crossroads: Social and Human implications of the Scientific Revolution*. Prague, International Arts and Sciences Press, 1969.
Richta, Radovan and Ota Šulc. "The Perspective of the Scientific and Technological Revolution". In Galtung and Jungk, eds., *Mankind 2000*. Oslo, Institute for Peace Research, 1969, 199–244.
Richta, Radovan et al. *Civilizace na Rozcesti. Společenské a lidské souvislosti vědeckotechnické revoluce*. Prague, Svoboda, 1966.

Riesman, David. *The Lonely Crowd. A Study of the Changing American Character.* New York, Doubleday, 1952.

Rostow, Eugene. "Thinking about the Future of International Society." In Daniel Bell and Stephen Graubard, eds., *Toward the Year 2000: Work in Progress.* Cambridge MA, MIT Press, 1997 (1967), 310–14.

Rostow, W. W. "Histoire et sciences sociales, la longue duree," in *Annales*, 4, 1959: 710–18.

Rostow, W. W. *The Stages of Economic Growth: A Non-Communist Manifesto.* Cambridge, MA, Harvard University Press, 1960.

Roszak, Theodore. *The Making of a Counterculture.* New York, Basic Books, 1969.

Sackmann, Harold. *Delphi Assessment.* Santa Monica, RAND, 1974.

Sackmann, Harold. "A Sceptic at the Oracle." *Futures*, 8, 5, 1976: 444–6.

Sauvy, Alfred. *Le tiers monde.* Paris, Presses Universitaires de France, 1952.

Shils, Edward. *The Intellectual Between Tradition and Modernity, the Indian Situation.* The Hague: Mouton and Company, 1961.

Sicinski, Andrej. "Surveys of Media of Mass Communication Public Opinion Research Center. *Polish Sociological Bulletin*, 1–2, 1961.

Sicinski, Andrej. "Public Opinion Surveys in Poland." *International Social Science Journal*, 15, 1963: 91–110.

Sicinski, Andrej. "Surveys as Media of Mass Communication of the Polish Public Opinion Research Center." *International Communication Gazette*, 9, 3, 1963: 237–41.

Sicinski, Andrej. "Peace and War in Polish Public Opinion," *Polish Sociological Bulletin*, 1967, 2: 25–40 (abstracted in English).

Sicinski, Andrej. "The future: A Dimension being Discovered". In Johan Galtung and Robert Jungk, eds. *Images of the World in the Year 2000*, Oslo, Peace Research Institute, 1968, 121–59.

Sicinski, Andrej. "Dallas and Warsaw: The Impact of a Major National Political Event on Public Opinion Abroad." *The Public Opinion Quarterly*, 33, 2, 1969: 190–6.

Sicinski, Andrej. "Les etudes prospectives en Pologne." *Analyse et Prevision*, 16, 1–3, 1973: 197.

Sicinski, Andrej. "Recent transformations in the role of writers." *Diogenes*, 21, 81, 1973: 70–87.

Sicinski, Andrej. "The Concepts of 'Need' and 'Value' in the Light of the Systems Approach." *International Social Science Council Information*, 17, 1, 1978: 71–91.

Sicinski, Andrej. "Theoretical Assumptions of Empirical Research of Specific Ways of Everyday Life (styles of life)." *Greek Review of Social Research*, 35, 1979: 67–74.

Sicinski, Andrej. (1983). How is a Vision of a Desirable Society Possible Today? In Eleonora Masini, ed., *Visions of Desirable Societies.* Oxford, Pergamon Press, 1983, 101–8.

Siciński, Andrej. *Dominant and Alternative Life Styles in Poland: An Outline.* United Nations University, 1985.

Steenbergen, Bart van. "Critical and Establishment Futurology." In *Challenges from the Future. Proceedings from the International Future Research Conference.* Kyoto, Japan Society of Futurology, 1970, 93–103.

Šulc, Ota. "A Methodological Approach to the Integration of Technological and Social Forecasts." *Technological Forecasting and Social Change*, 1, 1969: 105–8.

Šulc, Ota. "Futures Research in Czechoslovakia." *Futures*, 5, 6, 1973: 573–9.

Šulc, Ota. "Integration of Scientific Forecasts. Methodology of Integration of Scientific Forecasts in the Process of National Science Policy Making." *Technological Forecasting and Social Change*, 30, 1986: 251–60.

Teilhard de Chardin, Pierre. *Le Phenomene Humain*. Paris, Editions du Seuil, 1955.
Tinbergen, Jan. *Towards a Better International Economic Order*. UNITAR 1970.
Tinbergen, Jan, ed. *Reshaping the International Economic Order*. New York, Club of Rome and Unitar, 1976.
Toffler, Alvin. *Future Shock*. New York, Bantham Books, 1971.
Toffler, Alvin. *The Futurists*. New York, Random House, 1972.
Umpleby, Stuart. "The Illinois Delphi Exploration of Possible Futures." *The Journal of Aesthetic Education*, 4, 1, 1970: 129–132.
Umpleby, Stuart and Charles Osgood. "A Computer Based System for Exploration of Possible Futures for Mankind 2000," Mankind 2000.
von Karman, Theodore. "Towards New Horizons," 1947.
von Neumann, John and Oskar Morgenstern. *A Theory of Games and Economic Behaviour.* New Jersey, 1944.
World Futures Studies Federation. "World Alternative Systems." Dubrovnik, 1976.
World Futures Studies Federation. "The Future of Communication and Cultural Identity in an Interdependent World, VIth Conference of Future Studies, 16–19 September, 1978, Cairo." Bucharest, WFSF, 1978.
World Futures Studies Federation. "Alternative Visions of Desirable Societies" Mexico City, 1981.
World Futures Studies Federation. "The Future of Development." Beijing, 1988.
Yefremov, Ivan. *Andromeda—A Space Age Tale*. Moscow, Progress Publishers, 1959.

SECONDARY SOURCES

Abdelal, Ravi. *Capital Rules. The Construction of Global Finance*. Cambridge MA, Harvard University Press, 2007.
Abela, Alex. *Soldiers of Reason. The RAND Corporation and the Rise of American Empire*. New York, Houghton Mifflin Harcourt, 2009.
Abraham, Itty. *The Making of the Indian Atomic Bomb. Science, Secrecy and the Post Colonial State*. London, Verso, 1998.
Abromeit and Cobb, *Herbert Marcuse. A Critical Reader*. Abingdon, Routledge, 2004.
Adam, Barbara and Chris Groves. *Future Matters: Action, Knowledge, Ethics*. Amsterdam, Brill, 2007.
Allison, Graham T. *Essence of Decision. Explaining the Cuban Missile Crisis*. Boston, Little Brown and Company, 1971.
Amadae, Sonja M. *Rationalizing Capitalist Democracy. The Cold War Origins of Rational Choice Liberalism*. Chicago, University of Chicago Press, 2003.
Amadae, Sonja M. *Prisoners of Reason. Game Theory and Neoliberal Political Economy*. Cambridge MA, MIT Press, 2016.
Anderson, Ben. "Preemption, Precaution, Preparedness. Anticipatory Action and Future Geographies." *Progress in Human Geography*, 34, 6, 2010: 277–98.
Andersson, Jenny. "Choosing Futures: Alva Myrdal and the Construction of Swedish Futures Studies, 1967–1972." *International Review of Social History* 51, 2, 2006: 277–95.
Andersson, Jenny. "The Great Future Debate and the Struggle for the World." *American Historical Review*, 117, 5, 2012: 1411–31.
Andersson, Jenny. "Midwives of the Future. Futurism, Futures Studies and the Shaping of the Global Imagination". In Jenny Andersson and Egle Rindzeviciute, eds. *Transnational Perspectives on the Long Term in Science and Politics in the Cold War: Forging the Future*. Routledge, New York, 2015, 16–38.

Andersson, Jenny and Sibylle Duhautois. "The future of Mankind." In van Munster, Rens and Casper Sylvest, eds. *Assembling the Planet. Politics of Globality After 1945*. New York, Routledge, 2016, 106–26.

Andersson, Jenny and Anne Greet Keizer. "Governing the Future: Science, Policy and Public Participation in the Construction of the Long Term in the Netherlands and Sweden." *History and Technology*, 30, 1–2, 2014: 104–22.

Andersson, Jenny and Pauline Prat. "Gouverner le long terme. La production bureaucratique des futurs en France." *Gouvernement et Action Publique*, 3, 3, 2015: 9–29.

Andersson, Jenny and Egle Rindzeviciute, eds. *Transnational Perspectives on the Long Term in Science and Politics in the Cold War: Forging the Future*. New York, Routledge, 2015.

Anker, Paul. "Buckminster Fuller as Captain of Spaceship Earth." *Minerva*, 45, 4, 2007: 417–34.

Appadurai, Arjun. *The Future as Cultural Fact*. London, Verso, 2013.

Aradau, Claudia and Rens van Munster. *Politics of Catastrophe. Geneaologies of the Unknown*. New York, Routledge, 2011.

Armitage, David "What's the Big Idea? Intellectual History and the Longue Durée." *History of European Ideas*, 38, 4, 2012: 493–507.

Armitage, David and Jo Guldi. *The History Manifesto*. New York, Cambridge University Press, 2014.

Aronova, Elena. "The Congress for Cultural Freedom, Minerva, and the Quest for Instituting Science Studies." *Minerva*, 50, 2012: 307–37.

Audier, Serge. *Neoliberalisme, une archeologie intellectuelle*. Paris, Grasset, 2012.

Ayson, Robert. *Thomas Schelling and the Nuclear Age*. New York, Routledge, 2004.

Baker, Kevin. "Virtually Nigeria. USAID, the Future, and Post Colonial Expertise." In Jenny Andersson and Egle Rindzeviciute, eds. *The Struggle for the Long Term in Transnational Science and Politics. Forging the Future*. London, Routledge, 2016, 185–205.

Bartelson, Jens. *Visions of World Community*. New York, Cambridge University Press, 2009.

Bartelson, Jens. "The Social Construction of Globality." *International Political Sociology*, 4, 3, 2010: 219–35.

Bayly, Christopher, Sven Beckert, Matthew Connelly, et al. "AHR Conversation: on Transnational History." *The American Historical Review*, 111, 5, 2006: 1441–64.

Becht, Lukas. "From Euphoria to Frustration. Institutionalising a System of Prognostic Research in the People's Republic of Poland." Unpublished.

Beckert, Jens. *Imagined Futures. Fictional Expectations and Capitalist Dynamics*. Cambridge MA, Harvard University Press, 2016.

Bell, Duncan, ed. *Victorian Visions of Global Order. Empire and International Relations in 19th Century Political Thought*. Cambridge, Cambridge University Press, 2007.

Bell, Duncan. "Writing the World: Disciplinary History and Beyond." *International Affairs*, 85, 1, 2009: 3–22.

Bell, Duncan. "Making and Taking Worlds." In Samuel Moyn and Andrew Sartori, eds. *Global Intellectual History*. New York, Columbia University Press, 2013, 254–79.

Bell, Wendell. *Foundations of Futures Studies. Human Science for a New Era*. Transaction Publishers, New Brunswick, 1998. Volume 1 and 2.

Berghahn, Volker R. *America and the Intellectual Cold Wars in Europe*. New York, Berghahn, 2002.

Beroud, Samuel and Matthieu Leimgruber. "A Pilot Fish Ahead of the Sharks? The Changing Fortunes of the OECD During the Long 1970s," unpublished, 2014.

Bevernage, Bernard and Lorentz, Chris, eds. *Breaking up Time: Negotiating the Borders Between Present, Past and Future*. Amsterdam, Vandenhoeck and Ruprecht, 2013.
Blum, Alain and Martine Mespoulet. *L'Anarchie bureaucratique. Statistique et pouvoir sous Staline*. Paris, La Découverte, 2003.
Bockman, Johanna. *Markets in the Name of Socialism: The Left-Wing Origins of Neoliberalism*. Palo Alto, Stanford University Press, 2011.
Boudia, Soraya. "La genèse d'un gouvernement par le risqué". In Pierre Benoit Joly et al., eds. *Du risque a la menace. Penser la catastrophe*. Paris, La Decouverte, 2013, 69–88.
Brenner, N., J. Peck, and N. Theodore. "After Neoliberalization?" *Globalizations*, 7, 3, 2010: 327–45.
Brick, Harold. *Daniel Bell and the Decline of Intellectual Radicalism. Social Theory and Political Reconciliation in the 1940s*. Madison, Wisconsin University Press, 1986.
Brick, Howard. "Optimism of the Mind. Imagining Post Industrial Society in the 1960s and the 1970s." *American Quarterly*, 44, 3, 1992: 349–80.
Brick, Howard. *The Age of Contradiction. American Thought and Culture in the 1960s*. Ithaca, Cornell University Press, 2000.
Brinkley, Alan. "The Problem of American Conservatism." *The American Historical Review*, 99, 2 1994: 409–29.
Brown, Timothy. *Weimar Radicals. Nazis and Communists Between Performance and Authenticity*. New York, Berghahn, 2009.
Burchell, Graham, et al. *The Foucault Effect. Studies in Governmentality*. Chicago: University of Chicago Press, 2012.
Burgin, Angus. "The Radical Conservatism of Frank Knight." *Modern Intellectual History*, 6, 3, 2009: 513–38.
Burgin, Angus. *The Great Persuasion. Reinventing Free Markets Since the Depression*. Cambridge MA, Harvard University Press, 2012.
Butler, Andrew. "Futurology." In *Oxford Handbook of Science Fiction*. Oxford, Oxford University Press, 2011.
Catanus, Ana-Maria. "Breaking the Barriers of Romanian Conformism. Dissent and the Scientific Critique of Communism in Mathematician Mihai Botez thinking." *History of Communism in Europe*, "Avatars of Intellectuals," 2, 2011: 345–68.
Catanus Ana Maria. "Official and Unofficial Futures of the Communist System." In Jenny Andersson and Egle Rindzeviciute, *The Struggle for the Long Term in Transnational Science and Politics. Forging The Future*. London, Routledge, 2015, 169–89.
Cazes, Bernard. *Histoire des futurs. Les figures de l'avenir de saint Augustin au 21eme siecle*. Paris, Editions Seghers, 1986.
Chakraborty, Deepek. *Provincialising Europe. Post-Colonial Thought and Historical Difference*. Princeton NJ, Princeton University Press, 2004.
Clavin, Patricia. "Defining Transnationalism." *Contemporary European History*, 14, 4, 2005: 421–39.
Clavin, Patricia. "Time, Manner, Place: Writing Modern European History in Global, Transnational and International Contexts." *European History Quarterly*, 40, 4, 2010: 624–40.
Collier, Stephen and Andrew Lakoff. "Distributed Preparedness: The Spatial Logic of Domestic Security in the United States." *Environment and Planning D: Society and Space*, 26, 1, 2008: 7–28.
Connelly, Matthew. *Fatal Misconception. The Attempt to Control World Population*. Cambridge MA, Harvard University Press, 2009.

Connelly, Matthew. "Future Shock. The End of the World as They Knew It." In Niall Ferguson et al. eds. *The Shock of the Global: The 1970s in Perspective.* Cambridge MA, Harvard University Press, 2011, 337–51.

Conrad, Sebastian. "What Time is Japan? Problems of Comparative (intercultural) Historiography." *History and Theory*, 38, 1, 1999: 67–83.

Conrad, Sebastian. *What is Global History?* Princeton NJ, Princeton University Press, 2016.

Conrad, Sebastian and Dieter Sachsenmaier. *Competing Visions of World Order. Global Moments and Movements, 1880s–1930s.* Basingstoke, Palgrave Macmillan, 2007.

Coser, Lewis A. *Refugee Scholars. Their Impact and Experiences.* New Haven, Yale University Press, 1984.

Cosgrove, Denis. *Apollo's Eye: a Cartographic Genealogy of the Earth in the Western Imagination.* Washington, John Hopkins University Press, 2001.

Cywar, Alan. "John Dewey. Towards Domestic Reconstruction." *Journal of the History of Ideas*, 30, 3, 1969: 385–400.

Dahan Dalmedico, Amy, et al. eds. *Les modeles du future.* Paris, La Decouverte, 2006.

Dard, Olivier. *Jean Coutrot, de l'ingenieur au prophete.* Presses Universitaires franc comtoises, 1999.

Dard, Olivier. *Bertrand de Jouvenel.* Paris, Seuil, 2008.

Dean, Mitchell. "Liberal Government and Authoritarianism." *Economy and Society*, 31, 1, 2002: 37–61.

Denord, Francois. *Neoliberalisme version francaise. Histoire d'une ideologie politique.* Paris, Demopolis, 2007.

Denord, François. "French Neoliberalism and Its Divisions: From the Colloque Walter Lippmann to the Fifth Republic." In Phillip Mirowski and Dieter Plehwe, eds. *The Road From Mt. Pèlerin: The Making of the Neoliberal Thought Collective,* 45–67. Cambridge MA, Harvard University Press, 2010.

Denord, Francois and Odile Henry, "La modernisation avant la lettre. Le patronat français et la rationalisation (1925–1940)." *Sociétés Sontemporaines*, 4, 68, 2007: 83–104.

Desrosières, Alain. *La politique des grands nombres: Histoire de la raison statistique.* Paris, La Decouverte, 1993.

Djelic, Marie-Laure and Sigrid Quack, eds. *Transnational Communities. Shaping Global Economic Governance.* New York, Cambridge University Press, 2010.

Doering-Manteuffel, Anselm and Lutz Raphael, *Nach dem Boom. Perspektiven auf die Zeitgeschichte seit 1970.* Bonn, Vandenhoeck and Ruprecht, 2012.

Drack, Manfred. "Ludwig von Bertalanffy's Early Systems Approach." *Systems Research and Behavioral Science*, 26, 2009: 563–72.

Drouard, Alain. *Une inconnue des sciences sociales. La fondation Alexis Carrel sur letudes des problems humains.* Paris, INED, 1992.

Ducheyne, Steffen. "To Treat of the World. Paul Otlet's Ontology and Epistemology and the Circle of Knowledge." *Journal of Documentation*, 65, 2, 2009: 223–44.

Duhautois, Sibylle. "Etudes sur le futur et conscience globale dans les organisations internationales." Ph.D. Diss., Centre d'histoire de Sciences Po, Paris, 2017.

Edwards, Paul. *The Closed World: Computers and the Politics of Discourse in Cold War America.* Cambridge MA, MIT Press, 1997.

Edwards, Paul. *A Vast Machine: Computer Models, Climate Data, and the Politics of Global Warming.* Cambridge MA, MIT Press, 2010.

Ekbladh, David. *The Great American Mission: Modernization and the Construction of an American World Order.* Princeton NJ, Princeton University Press, 2010.

Elias, Norbert. *Uber die Zeit.* Merkur, Stuttgart, 1982.

Engel, Amin. *Gershem Scholem*. Chicago, The University of Chicago Press, 2017.
Engerman, David. "American Knowledge and Global Power." *Diplomatic History* 31, 4, 2007: 599–622.
Engerman, David. *Know Your Enemy. The Rise and Fall of America's Soviet Experts*. New York, Oxford University Press, 2009.
Engerman, David. "Social Science in the Cold War." *Isis*, 2, 2010: 393–400.
Engerman, David and Corinna Unger. "Introduction: Towards a Global History of Modernization." *Diplomatic History*, 33, 3, 2009: 375–85.
Engerman, David, Nils Gilman, Michele Haffele, Michael and Latham. eds. *Staging Growth. Modernisation, Development and the Global Cold War*. Amherst and Boston, University of Massachusetts Press, 2003.
Erickson, Paul. "Mathematical Models, Rational Choice, and the Search for Cold War Culture." *Isis*, 10, 1, 2010: 386–92.
Erickson, Paul. *The World the Game Theorists Made*. Chicago, The University of Chicago Press, 2015.
Erickson, Paul, Jennifer Klein, Lauren Daston, Rebecca Lemov, Timothy Sturm, and Michael Gordin, eds. *How Reason Almost Lost its Mind: The Strange Career of Cold War Rationality*. Chicago, The University of Chicago Press, 2013.
Escudier, Alexandre. "Temporalisation et modernité politique: penser avec Reinhart Koselleck." *Annales*, 6, 2009: 1269–301.
Evangelista, Matthew. *Unarmed Forces. The Transnational Movement to End the Cold War*. Ithaca, Cornell University Press, 2002.
Eyal, Gil and Larissa Buchholz. "From the Sociology of Intellectuals to the Sociology of Interventions." *Annual Review of Sociology*, 36, 2010: 117–37.
Eyal, Gil, Ivan Szelényi, and Eleanor Townsley. *Making Capitalism Without Capitalists: Class Formation and Elite Struggles in Post-Communist Central Europe*. London, Verso, 1998.
Fabian, Johannes. *Time and the Other: How Anthropology Makes its Object*. New York, Columbia University Press, 2014 (1983).
Fair Schulz, Axel and Mario Kessler, eds. *German Scholars in Exile*. Plymouth, Lexington Books, 2011.
Fetzer, James, "Carl Hempel's Challenge to Logical Positivism." *The Stanford Encyclopedia of Science* (Fall 2017 Edition), Edward N. Zalta (ed.), URL = <https://plato.stanford.edu/archives/fall2017/entries/hempel/>.
Ferguson, Niall, Charles Maier, Eres Manela, and Daniel Sargent, eds. *The Shock of the Global: The 1970s in Perspective*. Cambridge MA, Harvard University Press, 2011.
Fischer, Frank. *Technocracy and the Politics of Expertise*. New York, SAGE, 1990.
Fischer, Frank. "Beyond Empiricism. Policy Inquiry in Post Positivist Perspective." *Policy Studies Journal*, 26, 1, 1998: 129–46.
Fischer, Frank, ed. *Handbook of Critical Policy Studies*. Edward Elgar, 2015.
Fligstein, Neil and Douglas MacAdam. *A Theory of Fields*. New York, Oxford University Press, 2012.
Fontaine, Philippe. "Stabilizing American Society: Kenneth Boulding and the Integration of the Social Sciences, 1943–1980." *Science in Context*, 23, 2, 2010: 221–65.
Fortescue, Stephen. *The Communist Party and Soviet Science*. Basingstoke, Palgrave MacMillan, 1986.
Fortescue, Stephen. *Science Policy in the Soviet Union*. London, Routledge, 1990.
Freire, Pauolo. *Pedagogy of the Oppressed*. New York, Heder, 1968.
Fressoz, Jean Baptiste. *L'apocalypse joyeuse*. Paris, Seuil, 2013.

Friedman, Walter. *Fortune Tellers: the Story of America's First Economic Forecasters*. Princeton NJ, Princeton University Press, 2013.

Frietsche, Peter. *Stranded in the Present. Modern Time and the Melancholy of History*. Palo Alto, Stanford University Press, 2004.

Fritzche, Sonja. "East Germany's 'Werkstatt Zukunft': Futurology and the Science Fiction Films of 'defa-futurum'." *German Studies Review*, 29, 2, 2006: 367–86.

Galison, Peter. "Aufbau/Bauhaus: Logical Positivism and Architectural Modernism." *Critical Inquiry*, 16, 4, 1990: 709–52.

Galison, Peter. *Einstein's Clocks and Poincaré's Maps: Empires of Time*. Boston, WW Norton & Company, 2004.

Galison, Peter and Barton Bernstein. "In Any Light: Scientists and the Decision to Build the Superbomb, 1952–1954." *Historical Studies in the Physical and Biological Sciences*, 19, 2, 1989: 267–347.

Galison, Peter and Lorraine Daston. "Fear and Loathing of the Imagination in Science." *Daedalus*, 127, 1, 1998: 73–98.

Galison, Peter and Lorraine Daston. *Objectivity*. New York, Zone Books, 2007.

Garsten, Christina and Adrienne Sorbom. "Risk, Resilience and Alternative Future. Scenario Building at the World Economic Forum," 2017. Unpublished.

Gary, Brett. "Dueling Deweys. Moralism, Scientism and American Social Science History." *Reviews in American History*, 23, 4, 1995: 623–60.

Gemelli, Giuliana, "Communaute intellectuelle et strategies institutionelles. Henri Berr et la fondation du Centre international de synthese." *Revue de Synthese*, 108, 2, 1987: 225–59.

Gemelli, Giuliana. *Fernand Braudel*. Paris, Odile Jacob, 1995.

Gemelli, Giuliana, ed. *The Ford Foundation and Europe, 1950's–1970's: Cross-Fertilization of Learning in Social Science and Management*. European Interuniversity Press, Brussels, 1998.

Gerovitch, Slava. "'Mathematical Machines' of the Cold War: Soviet Computing, American Cybernetics and Ideological Disputes in the Early 1950s." *Social Studies of Science* 31, 2, 2001: 253–87.

Gerwitch, Julian. "The Futurists of Beijing. Alvin Toffler, Zhao Ziyang, and China's New Technological Revolution, 1979–1991." Unpublished.

Ghamari Tabrizi, Sharon. "Simulating the Unthinkable. Gaming Future War in the 1950s and 1960s." *Social Studies of Science*, 30, 2, 2002: 163–223.

Ghamari Tabrizi, Sharon. *The Worlds of Herman Kahn. The Intuitive Science of Thermo Nuclear War*. Cambridge MA, Harvard University Press, 2005.

Gilcher-Holtey, Isobel., H. G. Haupt, and Willibald Steinmetz, eds. *Writing Political History Today*. Munchen, Campus Verlag, 2013.

Gilman, Nils. *Mandarins of the Future. Modernisation Theory in Cold War America*. Baltimore, John Hopkins Press, 2003.

Gilman, Nils. "The New Economic Order. A Reintroduction." *Humanity*, 6, 2015: 1–17.

Gordin, Michael. *Red Cloud at Dawn*. New York, Faber, Strauss and Giroux, 2009.

Gordin, Michael, Helen Tilley, and Gyan Prakash. "Introduction. Utopia and Dystopia Beyond Space and Time." In Michael Gordin, Helen Tilley, and Gyan Prakash eds. *Utopia, Dystopia. Conditions of Historical Possibility*. Princeton University Press, Princeton, 2010, 1–21.

Graf, Rudiger and Benjamin Herzog. "Von der Geschichte der Zukunftsvorstellungen zur Geschichte ihrer Generierung: Probleme und Herausforderungen der Zukunftsbezugs im 20. Jahrhundert". *Geschichte und Gesellschaft*, 42, 3, 2015: 497–515.

Graham, Otis. *Toward a Planned Society. From Roosevelt to Nixon*. Palo Alto, 1976.

Greif, Mark. *The Age of the Crisis of Man. Thought and Fiction in America, 1933–1973*. Princeton, NJ, Princeton University Press, 2015.

Grémion, Pierre. *Intelligence de l'anticommunisme: Le congrès pour la liberté de la culture à Paris, 1950–1975*. Paris, Seuil, 1995.

Grémion, Pierre. "The Role of the Social Sciences in East–West Relations." *Technology in Society*, 23, 3, 2001: 427–39.

Guiader, Vincent. "Socio-histoire de la prospective." Ph.D. Diss, Université de Paris Dauphine, Paris, 2008.

Guilhot, Nicolas. *The Democracy Makers. Human Rights and the Politics of Global Order*. New York, Columbia University Press, 2008.

Guilhot, Nicolas. "The Realist Gambit. Post War American Political Science and the Birth of IR Theory." *International Political Sociology*, 2, 4, 2008: 281–304.

Hacking, Ian. *The Taming of Chance*. Cambridge, Cambridge University Press, 1990.

Hacking, Ian. *The Emergence of Probability: A Philosophical Study of Early Ideas About Probability, Induction and Statistical Inference*. Cambridge, Cambridge University Press, 2006.

Hall, John. *Apocalypse: From Antiquity to the Empire of Modernity*. New York, John Wiley & Sons, 2013.

Halton, Eugene. *From the Axial Age to the Moral Revolution. Karl Jaspers and Lewis Mumford*. London, Palgrave Macmillan, 2012.

Hammond, Debra. "Exploring the Genealogy of Systems Thinking." *Systems Research and Behavioral Science*, 2002, 19: 429–39.

Hammond, Debra. *The Science of Synthesis. Exploring General Systems Theory*. Boulder, University of Colorado, 2010.

Harrington, Michael. *The Other America*. New York, 1964.

Hartmann, Heinrich and Jacob Vogel, eds. *Zukunftswissen. Prognosen in Wirtschaft, Politik und Gesellschaft seit 1900*. Campus Verlag, Frankfurt, 2011.

Hartog, Francois. "The Modern Régime of Historicity in the Face of Two World Wars." In Bernard Bevernage and Chris Lorenz, eds. *Breaking Up Time: Negotiating the Borders Between Present, Past and Future*. Amsterdam, Vandenhoeck and Ruprecht, 2013, 124–33.

Hartog, Francois. *Régimes d'historicité. Présentisme et expériences du temps*. Paris, Seuil, 2014.

Harvey, David. *The Condition of Postmodernity. An Enquiry into the Origins of Cultural Change*. London, Verso, 1989.

Hecht, Gabrielle. "Planning a Technological Nation." In Thomas Hughes and Agatha Hughes, eds. *Systems, Experts and Computers. The Systems Approach in Management and Engineering, World War II and After*. Cambridge MA, MIT Press, 2003, 133–61.

Hecht, Gabrielle. *Being Nuclear: Africans and the Global Uranium Trade*. Cambridge MA, MIT Press, 2012.

Heyck, Hunter. "Producing Reason." In Mark Solovey and Hunter Cravens, eds. *Cold War Social Science*, Toronto, Toronto University Press, 2013, 99–117.

Heyck, Hunter. *Age of System. Explaining the Development of the Social Sciences*. Baltimore, John Hopkins University Press, 2016.

Holmes, Douglas R. *An Economy of Words. Communicative Imperatives in Central Banks*. Chicago, University of Chicago Press, 2014.

Hölscher, Lucien. *Die Entdeckung der Zukunft*. Frankfurt, Fischer, 1999.

Hölscher, Lucien. "The History of the Future. The Emergence and Decline of a Temporal Concept in European history." In *Conceptual History Newsletter*, 5, 2002: 10–15.

Hölscher, Lucien. "Mysteries of Historical Order: Ruptures, Simultaneity and the Relationship of the Past, the Present." In Bernard Bernanke and Chris Lorenz, eds. *Breaking up Time.* Amsterdam, Vandenhoeck and Ruprect, 2013, 134–52.

Horowitz, Daniel. *The Anxieties of Affluence. Critiques of American Consumer Culture 1939–1979.* Amherst, University of Massachusetts Press, 2004.

Horton, Carol. *Race and the Making of American Liberalism.* Oxford, Oxford University Press, 2008.

Hounshell, David. "The Cold War, RAND, and the Generation of Knowledge 1946–1962." Santa Monica, RAND History Project, 1998.

Hughes, Thomas and Agatha Hughes. *Lewis Mumford, Public Intellectual.* Oxford, Oxford University Press, 1990.

Hughes, Thomas and Agatha Hughes. *Systems, Experts and Computers. The Systems Approach in Management and Engineering, World War II and After.* Cambridge MA, MIT Press, 2003.

Hunt, Lynn. *Measuring Time, Making History.* Budapest, Central European University Press, 2008.

Iriye, Akira. *Cultural Internationalism and World Order.* Baltimore, John Hopkins Press, 1997.

Iriye, Akira. *Global Community. The Role of International Organizations in the Making of the Contemporary World.* Berkeley, University of California Press, 2002.

Iriye, Akira, and Pierre-Yves Saunier, eds. *The Palgrave Dictionary of Transnational History.* New York, Palgrave, 2009.

Isaac, Joel. "The Human Sciences in Cold War America." *Historical Journal* 50, 3, 2007, 725–46.

Isaac, Joel and Duncan Bell. *Uncertain Empire. American History and the Idea of the Cold War.* Oxford, Oxford University Press, 2012.

Isserman, Maurice and Michael Kazin. *America Divided. The Civil War of the 1960s.* New York, Oxford University Press, 2000.

Jacoby, Russell. *Picture Imperfect.* New York, Columbia University Press, 2005.

Jameson, Frederick. *Postmodernism, or, the Cultural Logic of Late Capitalism.* New Orleans, Duke University Press, 1991.

Jardini, David. *Out of Blue Yonder. The Transfer of Systems Thinking from the Pentagon to the Great Society.* Washington, Carnegie Mellon University, 1996.

Jasanoff, Sheila. "Future Imperfect. Science, Technology and the Imaginaries of Modernity." In Sheila Jasanoff and Sang-Yun Kim, eds. *Dreamscapes of Modernity. Sociotechnical Imaginaries and the Fabrication of Power.* Cambridge MA, Harvard University Press, 2015.

Jay, Martin. *The Dialectical Imagination. A History of the Frankfurt School and the Institute for Social Research.* Berkeley, University of California Press, 1996.

Jordan, John M. *Machine Age Ideology. Social Engineering and American Liberalism 1911–1939,* Chapel Hill, University of North Carolina Press, 2010.

Jordheim, Helge. "Against Periodisation. Koselleck's Theory of Multiple Temporalities." *History and Theory,* 51, 2012: 151–71.

Judt, Tony. *Reappraisals. Reflections from the Twentieth Century.* New York, Random House, 2008.

Kaplan, Fred. *The Wizards of Armageddon.* Palo Alto, Stanford University Press, 1983.

Katz, Michael. *The Undeserving Poor. From the War on Poverty to the War on Welfare.* New York, Pantheon Books, 1990.

Kellner, Douglas. "One Dimensional Man. Introduction to the Second Edition." In Herbert Marcuse, *One Dimensional Man.* Abingdon, Routledge, 1991, 11–13.

Kern, Stephen. *The Culture of Time and Space. 1880–1918*. Cambridge MA, Harvard University Press, 2003.

Kessler, Mario K. *Ossip K. Flechtheim. Politischer Wissenschaftler und Zukunftsdenker, 1909–1998*. Koln, Bohlau Verlag, 2007.

Kopeček, Michal. "The Rise and Fall of Czech Post-Dissident Liberalism after 1989." *East European Politics and Societies*, 25, 2, 2011: 244–71.

Koselleck, Reinhart. "Modernity and the Planes of Historicity." *Economy and Society*, 10, 2, 1981: 166–83.

Koselleck, Reinhart. *Futures Past. On the Semantics of Historical Time*. Cambridge MA, MIT Press, 1985.

Koselleck, Reinhart. *Zeitschichten: Studien zur Historik*. Frankfurt, Suhrkamp Verlag, 2000.

Koselleck, Reinhart. *The Practice of Conceptual History: Timing History, Spacing Concepts*. Palo Alto, Stanford University Press, 2002.

Krementsov, Nikolai. *Stalinist Science*, Princeton NJ, Princeton University Press, 1996.

Kumar, Kristian. *From Post-Industrial to Post-Modern Society: New Theories of the Contemporary World*. New York, John Wiley & Sons, 2009.

Laqua, Daniel. "Transnational Intellectual Cooperation, the League of Nations, and the Problem of Order." *Journal of Global History*, 6, 2011: 223–47.

Latham, Michael. *Modernization as Ideology: American Social Science and "Nation Building" in the Kennedy Era*. Chapel Hill, NC, 2000.

Latour, Bruno. *We Have Never Been Modern*. Cambridge MA, Harvard University Press, 2012.

Launius, Roger and Howard McCurdy, *Robots in Space. Humanity, Evolution, and Interplanetary Travel*. Baltimore, John Hopkins Press, 2008.

Leehman, Hartmut and James Sheehan, eds. *Interrupted Pasts. German Speaking Refugee Historians in the United States after 1933*. Cambridge, Cambridge University Press and German Historical Institute, 1991.

Leendertz, Ariane. "Losing Control. Complexity Theory, Public Policy, and The Exhaustion of Solutionism." 2016. Unpublished.

Lemov, Rebecca. "Hypothetical Machines. The Science Fiction Dreams of Cold War Science." *Isis*, 101, 2, 2010: 401–11.

Leonard, Robert. *Von Neumann, Morgenstern, and the Creation of Game Theory. From Chess to Social Science*. Cambridge, Cambridge University Press, 2010.

Levitas, Ruth. "Educated Hope. Ernst Bloch on Abstract and Concrete Utopia." *Utopia Studies*, 1, 2, 1990: 13–26.

Light, Jennifer. *From Warfare to Welfare. Defense Intellectuals and Urban Problems in Cold War America*. Baltimore, The John Hopkins Press, 2003.

Light, Jennifer. "Taking Games Seriously." *Technology and Culture*, 49, 2, 2008: 345–75.

Lightcap Meek, Esther. *Comfort With Reality. Michael Polanyi's Realism and Why It Matters*. Eugene Oregon, Concorde Books, 2017.

MacKenzie, Donald. *An Engine, Not a Camera. How Financial Models Shape Markets*. Cambridge MA, MIT Press, 2008.

Mahrane, Y., M. Fenzi, C. Pessis, E. Vieille Blanchard, A. Korczak, and C. Bonneuil, "De la nature à la biosphère: la construction de l'environnement comme problème politique mondial, 1945–1972." *Vingtième Siècle-Revue d'histoire*, 113, 2012: 127–41.

Mallard, Gregoire and Andrew Lakoff. "How Claims to Know the Future Are Used to Understand the Present." In Michelle Lamont et al., eds. *Social Knowledge in the Making*. Harvard University Press, 2012, 339–79.

Mandler, Peter. *Return from the Natives. How Margaret Mead Won the Second World War and Lost the Cold War*. New Haven, Yale University Press, 2013.

Manjoo, F. "The Future Toffler Saw is Already Upon Us," *New York Times*, July 6, 2016.
Masurek, Malgorzata. "Between Sociology and Ideology. Perception of Work and Sociologists Advisors in Communist Poland, 1956–1970." *Edition Sciences Humaines*, 1, 16, 2007: 11–31.
Mazlish, Bruce. *The New Global History*. New York, Routledge, 2006.
Mazon, Brigitte. *Aux origins de l'Ecole des hautes etudes en sciences sociales. Le role du mecenat americain, 1920–1960*. Paris, La Decouverte, 1988.
Mazower, Mark. *Governing the World. The History of an Idea*. London, Penguin Press, 2007.
McCray, Patrick. *The Visioneers: How a Group of Elite Scientists Pursued Space Colonies, Nanotechnologies, and a Limitless Future*. Princeton NJ, Princeton University Press, 2012.
Medina, Eden. *Cybernetic Revolutionaries. Technology and Politics in Allende's Chile*. Cambridge MA, MIT Press, 2011.
Medvetz, Tom. *Thinktanks in America*. Chicago, The Chicago University Press, 2012.
Mervart, Jan. "Czechoslovak Marxist Humanism and the Revolution," *Studies in East European Thought*, published online March 2017.
Mespoulet, Martine. "La 'renaissance' de la sociologie en URSS (1958–1972): Une voie étroite entre matérialisme historique et recherches sociologiques concrètes." *Revue d'histoire des sciences humaines*, 15, 1, 2007: 57–86.
Mespoulet, Martine. *Construire le socialisme par les chiffres. Enquete et recensement en URSS de 1917 a 1991*. Paris, Institut National d'Etudes Demographiques, 2008.
Michaud, Michael. *Reaching for the High Frontier. The American Prospace Movement, 1972–1984*. New York, Praeger, 1986.
Miller, Craig, Daniel Deudney and Paul Edwards. *Changing the Atmosphere: Expert Knowledge and Environmental Governance*. Cambridge MA, MIT Press, 2001.
Mindell, David. *Between Human and Machine. Feedback, Control and Computing Before Cybernetics*. Baltimore, John Hopkins University Press, 2002.
Mirowski, Phillip. *More Heat than Light: Economics as Social Physics, Physics as Nature's Economics*. Cambridge, Cambridge University Press, 1991.
Mirowski, Phillip. *Machine Dreams. How Economics Became a Cyborg Science*. Cambridge, Cambridge University Press, 2002.
Mirowski, Phillip and Dieter Plehwe, eds. *The Road from Mt Pelerin. The Making of the Neoliberal Thought Collective*. Cambridge MA, Harvard University Press, 2009.
Mitchell, Timothy. *The Rule of Experts. Egypt, Technopolitics, Modernity*. Berkeley, University of California Press, 2002.
Mitchell, Timothy. *Carbon Democracy. Political Power in the Age of Oil*. London, Verso Books, 2011.
Moll, Peter. *From Scarcity to Sustainability. Futures Studies and the Environment, the Role of the Club of Rome*. Peter Lang, Brussels, 1991.
Moyn, Samuel. *The Last Utopia: Human Rights in History*. Cambridge, MA, Harvard University Press, 2010.
Moyn, Samuel. "Introduction." In Samuel Moyn and Andrew Sartori, eds. *Global Intellectual History*. New York, Columbia University Press, 2013.
Muller, Tim B. *Krieger und Gelehrte. Herbert Marcuse und die Denkssysteme Im Kalten Krieg*. Hamburg, Hamburger Edition, 1991.
Munster, Arno. *Principe esperance ou principe responsabilite*. Paris, Le Bord de l'eau, 2010.
Nandy, Ashis. *The Intimate Enemy. Loss and Recovery of the Self under Colonialism*. Delhi, Oxford University Press, 1991.
Naumann, Katia. "East Central European Experts in International Scientific Institutions: Research Planning in the International Social Science Council and the European

Coordination Center for Research and Documentation in Social Sciences (Vienna Centre)." forthcoming in Sandrine Kott et al. *Planning in Cold War Europe*. Munchen, de Gruyter, 2018.

Nehring, Holger. "National Internationalists: British and West German Protests against Nuclear Weapons, the Politics of Transnational Communications and the Social History of the Cold War, 1957–1964." *Contemporary European History*, 14, 4, 2005: 559–82.

Nehring, Holger. "Genealogies of the Ecological Movement: Planning, Complexity and the Emergence of 'the Environment' as Politics in West Germany, 1949–1982." In Sverker Sörlin and Paul Warde, eds. *Nature's End*. Houndmills, Palgrave, 2009, 115–38.

Nehring, Holger. *Politics of Security. British and West German Protest Movements and the Early Cold War*. Oxford, Oxford University Press, 2013.

Nowotny, Helga. *The Cunning of Uncertainty*. Cambridge MA, Harvard University Press, 2016.

Nye, Mary Ann. *Michael Polanyi and his Generation. Origins of the Social Construction of Science*. Chicago, The University of Chicago Press, 2011.

O'Connor, Alice. *Poverty Knowledge. Social Science, Social Policy and the Poor in Twentieth Century US History*. Princeton NJ, Princeton University Press, 2009.

Ogle, Vanessa. *The Global Transformation of Time: 1870–1950*. Cambridge MA, Harvard University Press, 2015.

Olsen, Niklas. *History in the Plural. An Introduction to the Work of Reinhart Koselleck*. New York, Berghahn, 2012.

Oreskes, Nancy and John Kriege, *Science and Technology in the Cold War*. Cambridge MA, MIT Press, 2014.

Osbourne, Peter. *The Politics of Time. Modernity and Avant Garde*. London, Verso, 1995.

Panchasi, Roxana. *Future Tense: The Culture of Anticipation in France Between the Wars*. Ithaca, Cornell University Press, 2009.

Pestre, Dominique and Amy Dahan. *Les sciences pour la guerre, 1940–1960*. Paris, EHESS, 2004.

Platt, Jennifer. *Fifty Years of the International Social Science Council*. Paris, UNESCO, 2002.

Popp, Raphael. "An Application of Modernisation Theory During the Cold War. The Case of Pahlavi Iran," *The International History Review*, 30, 1, 2008 76–98.

Porter, Theodore M. *Trust in Numbers: The Pursuit of Objectivity in Science and Public Life*. Princeton NJ, Princeton University Press, 1995.

Rabinbach, Aaron. *In the Shadow of the Catastrophe. German Intellectuals between Apocalypse and Enlightenment*. Berkeley, California University Press, 2001.

Radkau, Joakim. *Geschicte der Zukunft. Prognosen, Visionen, Irrungen in Deutschland von 1945 bis Heute*. Munchen, Carl Hansen Verlag, 2017.

Rayward, Raymond. *International Organization and the Dissemination of Knowledge. Essays of Paul Otlet*. Amsterdam, Elsevier, 1990.

Reggiani, Alexi. *God's Eugenicist. Alexis Carrel and the Sociobiology of Decline*. New York, Berghahn Books, 2007.

Rescher, Nicolas. *Predicting the Future. An Introduction to the Theory of Forecasting*. New York, State University of New York Press, 1998.

Reynaud, Terence. *Restarting Socialism. The New Beginning Group and the Problem of Renewal of the German Left, 1930–1970*. Ph.D. Diss. University of California, Berkeley, 2015.

Richardson, A., *Carnap's Construction of the World. The Aufbau and the Emergence of Logical Empiricism*. Cambridge, Cambridge University Press, 1998.

Rindzeviciute, Egle. "Purification and Hybridisation of Soviet Cybernetics: The Politics of Scientific Governance in an Authoritarian Regime." *Archiv für Sozialgeschichte*, 50, 2010: 289–309.

Rindzeviciute, Egle. "Toward a Joint Future beyond the Iron Curtain: East–West Politics of Global Modelling," in Jenny Andersson and Egle Rindzeviciute, eds. *The Struggle for the Long Term in Transnational Science and Politics: Forging the Future*. New York, Routledge, 2015, 115–43.

Rindzeviciute, Egle. *Power of System. How the Policy Sciences Opened up the Cold War World*. Ithaca, Cornell University Press, 2016.

Rindzeviciute, Egle, "A Struggle for the Soviet Future: The Birth of Scientific Forecasting in the Soviet Union," *Slavic Review*, 75, 1, 2016: 52–76.

Riska-Campbell, Leena. *Bridging East and West: The Establishment of the International Institute for Applied Systems Analysis (IIASA) in the United States Foreign Policy of Bridge Building, 1964–1972*. Helsinki, Helsinki University Press, 2011.

Robertson, Tim, "Total War and the Total Environment: Fairfield Osborn, William Vogt and the Birth of Global Ecology." *Environmental History*, 17, 2012: 336–64.

Robin, R. *The Making of the Cold War Enemy. Culture and Politics in the Military Industrial Complex*. Princeton NJ, Princeton University Press, 2009.

Rocca, Gordon L. "'A Second Party in Our Midst': The History of the Soviet Scientific Forecasting Association." *Social Studies of Science* 11, 2, 1981: 199–247.

Rodgers, Daniel. *Age of Fracture*. Cambridge MA, Harvard University Press, 2013.

Rohde, Joy. *Armed with Expertise. The Militarization of American Social Research During the Cold War*. Ithaca, Cornell University Press, 2013.

Rosa, Hartmut. *Alienation and Acceleration. Toward a Critical Theory of Late Modern Temporality*. London, Verso, 2010.

Rosenberg, Daniel. and Anthony Grafton. *Cartographies of Time: A History of the Timeline*. Princeton NJ, Princeton Architectural Press, 2013.

Rosenboim, Or. *The Emergence of Globalism. Visions of World Order in Britain and the United States*. Princeton NJ, Princeton University Press, 2017.

Rosental, Paul-André. *La santé au travail, 1880–1986*. Paris, La Decouverte, 2006.

Rosental, Paul-Andre. *Destins de l'eugenisme*. Paris, Seuil, 2016.

Ross, Dorothy. *Origins of American Social Science*. Cambridge MA, Harvard University Press, 1991.

Ross, Dorothy. "The Changing Contours of the Social Science Disciplines," in Theodore M. Porter and Dorothy Ross eds. *The Cambridge History of Science*. Vol. 7: *The Modern Social Sciences*. Cambridge, Cambridge University Press, 2008, 205–37.

Satterwhite, James H. *Varieties of Marxist Humanism. Philosophical Revision in Post War Eastern Europe*. Pittsburg, University of Pittsburg, 1992.

Saunier, Pierre Yves. "Circulations, connexions et espaces transnationaux." *Geneses*, 4, 2004: 110–26.

Schmelzer, Matthias. "The Crisis Before the Crisis: the Problems of Modern Society and the OECD, 1968–1974." *European Review of History*, 19, 6, 2012: 999–1020.

Schmelzer, Matthias. *The Hegemony of Growth. The OECD and the Making of the Economic Growth Paradigm*. Cambridge, Cambridge University Press, 2016.

Schmelzer, Matthias. "Born in the Corridors of the OECD. The Forgotten Origins of the Club of Rome. Transnational Networks and the 1970s in Global History." *Journal of Global History*, 12, 2017: 26–48.

Schulz-Forberg, Hagen, ed. *Zero Hours. Conceptual Insecurities and New Beginnings in the Interwar Period*. Brussels, Peter Lang, 2016.

Scott, James C. *Seeing like a State. How Certain Schemes to Improve the Human Condition Failed*. New Haven, Yale University Press, 1998.

Scott, Robert. *Kenneth Boulding, a Voice Crying in the Wilderness*. Basingstoke, Palgrave Macmillan, 2015.

Scott Smith, Giles. "The Congress for Cultural Freedom, the End of Ideology and the Milan Seminar of 1955." *Journal of Contemporary History*, 37, 3, 2002: 437–55.

Seefried, Elke. "Towards *The Limits to Growth*? The Book and Its Reception in West Germany and Britain, 1972–73." *Bulletin of the German Historical Institute London* 33, 1, 2011: 3–37.

Seefried, Elke. "Steering the Future. The Emergence of 'Western' Futures Research and its Production of Expertise, 1950s to early 1970s." *European Journal of Futures Research*, 2, 1, 2014: 1–12.

Seefried, Elke. "Reconfiguring the Future. Politics and Time from the 1960s to the 1980s." *Journal of European History*, 13, 3, 2015: 306–16.

Seefried, Elke. "Rethinking Progress. On the Origin of the Modern Sustainability Discourse, 1970–2000." *Journal of Modern European History*, 13, 3, 2015: 377–400.

Seefried, Elke. *Zukunfte. Aufstieg und Krise der Zukunftsforschung 1945–1980*. Berlin, Walter de Gruyter, 2015.

Sheller, M. *Aluminum Dreams: the Making of Light Modernity*. Cambridge MA, MIT Press, 2014.

Shlapentokh, Vladimir. *The Politics of Sociology in the Soviet Union*. New York, Westview Press, 1987.

Siskin, Clifford. *System. The Shaping of Modern Knowledge*. Cambridge MA, MIT Press, 2016.

Smith, Mark. *Social Science in the Crucible. The American Debate over Objectivity and Purpose, 1918–1941*. Durham, Duke University Press, 1994.

Solovey, Mark. "Project Camelot and the 1960s Epistemological Revolution Rethinking the Politics-Patronage-Social Science Nexus." *Social Studies of Science*, 31, 2, 2001: 171–206.

Solovey, Mark. "Cold War Social Science: Specter, Reality or Useful Concept," in Mark Solovey and Hunter Cravens, eds. *Cold War Social Science. Knowledge Production, Liberal Democracy and Human Nature*, Toronto, Toronto University Press, 2012, 1–25.

Solovey, Mark. *Shaky Foundations: The Politics-Patronage-Social Science Nexus in Cold War America*. New Brunswick, Rutgers University Press, 2013.

Solovey, Mark and Hunter Cravens, eds. *Cold War Social Science. Knowledge Production, Liberal Democracy and Human Nature*, Toronto, Toronto University Press, 2012.

Sommer, Viteszlav. "Forecasting the Post Socialist Future. From Futurology to Prognostika." In Jenny Andersson and Egle Rindzeviciute, eds. *The Struggle for the Long Term. Transnational Perspectives on the Future in Politics and Social Science. Forging the Future*. Routledge, London, 2015, 144–69.

Sommer, Viteszlav. "Scientists of the World Unite! Radovan Richta's theory of revolution," in Elena Aronova and Simone Turchetti, eds. *Science Studies During the Cold War and Beyond. Paradigms Detected*. Abingdon, Routledge, 2016, 200–15.

Sommer, Viteszlav. "Are We Still Revolutionaries." *Studies in East European Thought*, published online, Spring 2017.

Sörlin, Sverker and Paul Warde. "Making the Environment Historical—An Introduction," in Sverker Sorlin and Paul Warde, eds. *Nature's End: History and the Environment* Houndmills, Palgrave, 2009, 1–23.

Sörlin, Sverker, and Paul Warde. "Expertise for the Future. The Environment and the Emergence of Modern Prediction, 1920–1970". In Jenny Andersson and Egle Rindzeviciute, eds. *The Struggle for the Long Term in Transnational Science and Politics. Forging the Future*. London, Routledge, 2015, 38–63.

Stampnitzky, Lisa. *Disciplining Terror: How Experts Invented Terrorism*. New York, Cambridge University Press, 2013.

Steinmetz Jenkins, Daniel. "Inverse Marxism. Friedrich Hayek, Raymond Aron, and the Congress for cultural freedom seminar in Milan, 1955." Unpublished.

Sternhell, Zeev. *Ni droite ni gauche. L'ideologie fasciste en France*. Paris, Seuil, 2013.

Stonor Saunders, Francis. *Who Paid the Piper? The CIA and the Cultural Cold War*. London, Granta, 1999.

Sutela, Pekka. *Economic Thought and Economic Reform in the Soviet Union*. Cambridge, Cambridge University Press, 1991.

Sylvest, Casper and Rens van Munster, *Nuclear Realism. Global Political Thought During the Thermo-Nuclear Revolution*. Abingdon, Routledge, 2016.

Tolon, Kaya. *The American Futures Studies Movement. Its Roots, Motivations, and Influences*. Ph.D. Diss., Iowa State University Digital Repository, 2011.

Tolon, Kaya. "Futures Studies: A New Science Rooted in Cold War Strategic Thinking." In Mark Solovey and Hunter Cravens, eds. *Cold War Social Science, Knowledge Production, Liberal Democracy and Human Nature*. Toronto, Toronto University Press, 2012, 45–63.

Tournès, Ludovic, ed. *L'argent de l'influence: Les fondations américaines et leurs réseaux européens*. Paris, Seuil, 2010.

Turner, Fred. *From Counterculture to Cyberculture. Stewart Brand, the Whole Earth Network, and the Rise of Digital Utopianism*. Chicago, The University of Chicago Press, 2006.

Unger, Corinna. "Histories of Development and Modernization: Findings, Reflections, Future Research." *H-Soz-u-Kult*, 9, 2010.

Unger, Corinna. "Towards Global Equilibrium: American Foundations and Indian Modernization, 1950s–1970s." *Journal of Global History*, 6, 2011: 121–42.

Vaïsse, Justin. *Neoconservatism: The Biography of a Movement*. Cambridge MA, Harvard University Press, 2010.

Van Lente, Harro. "Navigating Foresight in a Sea of Expectations, Lessons from the Sociology of Expectations." *Technology Analysis and Strategic Management*, 24, 8, 2012: 789–802.

van Munster, Rens and Casper Sylvest. *Politics of Globality. Assembling the Planet*. London, Routledge, 2016.

Vauchez, Antoine and Stephanie Lee Mudge. "Building Europe on a Weak Field. Law, Economics and Scholarly Avatars in Transnational Politics." *American Journal of Sociology*, 118, 2, 2012: 449–92.

Vielle Blanchard, Elodie. *Les limites a la croissance dans un ordre global*. Ph.D. Diss., Paris, EHESS, 2011.

Vieille Blanchard, Elodie. "Technocornucopian Futures Versus Doomsday Futures." In Jenny Andersson and Egle Rindzeviciute, eds. *Transnational Perspectives on the Long Term in Science and Politics in the Cold War: Forging the Future*. London, Routledge, 2015, 16–38.

Wagar, Warren. *HG Wells and the World State*. New Haven, Yale University Press, 1969.

Wagner, Peter. "Social Science and Planning During the Twentieth Century." In Dorothy Ross and Michael Porter, *The Cambridge History of Science*, Vol. 7. *The Modern Social Sciences*. Cambridge, Cambridge University Press, 2007, 591–606.

Walsch, Donald Neale. *The Mother of Invention. The Legacy of Barbara Marx Hubbard and the Future of YOU*. Hay House, CA, 2011.

Waters, Malcolm. *Daniel Bell*. London, Routledge, 1996.

Weber, T., "Gandhi, Peace Research and Buddhist Economy." *Journal of Peace Research*, 36, 3, 1999: 349–61.

Weissman, Susan. "The Role of Purges and Terror in the Formation of the USSR." *Critique*, 27, 1, 1999: 145–57.

Westad, Odd Arne. *The Global Cold War: Third World Interventions and the Making of Our Times*. Cambridge MA, Harvard University Press, 2005.

Westbrook, Richard D. *John Dewey and American Democracy*. Ithaca, Cornell University Press, 1993.

Wiese, Christian. "Zionism, the Holocaust, and Judaism in a Secular World," in Tirosh-Samuelson and Wiese, eds. *Order from Disorder. The Legacy of Hans Jonas. Judaism and the Phenomenon of Life*. Amsterdam, Brill, 2007, 159–93.

Wilkinson, Angela and Roy Kupers. "Living in the Futures." *Harvard Business Review*, 91, 5, 2013: 118–27.

Wilkinson, Angela and Roy Kupers. *The Essence of Scenarios. Learning From the Shell Experience*. Amsterdam, Amsterdam University Press, 2015.

Williams, John R. "The Future." *Critical Inquiry*, 42, 2016: 473–546.

Wittner, Lawrence. *The Struggle against the Bomb*. Volume 1. *One World or None. The History of the World Nuclear Disarmament Movement Through 1953*. Palo Alto, Stanford University Press, 1993.

Wittner, Lawrence. *The Struggle against the Bomb, Volume II, Resisting the Bomb, 1954–1970*. Palo Alto, Stanford University Press, 1997.

Wittner, Lawrence and P. van den Dungen. "Peace History. An Introduction.' *Journal of Peace Research*, 46, 4, 2003: 363–75.

Wolin, Richard. *The Politics of Being. The Political Thought of Martin Heidegger*. New York, Columbia University Press, 1982.

Wolin, Richard. *The Frankfurt School Revisited*, Routledge, New York, 2006.

Wolin, Richard. *Heidegger's Children. Hannah Arendt, Hans Jonas, Hans Kollwitz, Herbert Marcuse*. Princeton, Princeton University Press, 2007.

Young-Bruehl, Elisabeth. *Hannah Arendt: For Love of the World*. New Haven, Yale University Press, 2004.

Index

Note: Page numbers with italic *f* affixed denote Figures